ARGUMENTATION:
Inquiry and Advocacy
Second Edition

George Ziegelmueller
Wayne State University

Jack Kay
University of Nebraska

Charles Dause
University of Detroit

Prentice Hall, Englewood Cliffs, New Jersey 07632

This text is dedicated to

Bill and Ruth

In memory of Elenore

Library of Congress Cataloging-in-Publication Data
Ziegelmueller, George W.
    Argumentation : inquiry and advocacy / George Ziegelmueller, Jack
Kay, Charles Dause.
        p.   cm.
    Includes bibliographical references.
    ISBN 0-13-046038-9
    1. Debates and debating.   I. Kay, Jack.   II. Dause, Charles A.,
            III. Title.
    PN4181.Z5   1990
    808.53—dc20   89-36241
                                                                      CIP

Editorial/production supervision: Karen Winget
Cover design: Wanda Lubelska
Manufacturing buyer: Ed O'Dougherty

© 1990, 1975 by Prentice-Hall, Inc.
A Division of Simon & Schuster
Englewood Cliffs, New Jersey 07632

Printed in the United States of America
10   9   8   7   6   5   4   3   2   1

ISBN 0-13-046038-9

PRENTICE-HALL INTERNATIONAL (UK) LIMITED, *London*
PRENTICE-HALL OF AUSTRALIA PTY. LIMITED, *Sydney*
PRENTICE-HALL CANADA INC., *Toronto*
PRENTICE-HALL HISPANOAMERICANA, S.A., *Mexico*
PRENTICE-HALL OF INDIA PRIVATE LIMITED, *New Delhi*
PRENTICE-HALL OF JAPAN, INC., *Tokyo*
SIMON & SCHUSTER ASIA PTE. LTD., *Singapore*
EDITORA PRENTICE-HALL DO BRASIL, LTDA., *Rio de Janeiro*

Contents

Preface

This second edition of *Argumentation: Inquiry and Advocacy* maintains the basic philosophical perspective of the earlier edition, but at the same time, it is a completely new formulation of that perspective. The past twenty years have witnessed an unusually abundant and rich series of writings dealing with both argumentation theory and the practices of academic debate. These writings have inevitably influenced our thinking in ways both great and small. We have, however, consciously avoided the temptation to include a little something about each of these new views. Instead, we have tried to provide a coherent theory of the *fundamental* concepts of argumentation for *beginning* students.

Four general beliefs have guided our efforts. First, as the title of this text suggests, we believe that it is essential to emphasize the role of argumentation in both the *inquiry* into problems and in the *advocacy* of solutions and beliefs. It is ironic that over the past ten years as various educational reports and commissions have called for more systematic training in the processes of critical thinking and logical problem solving, some writers in philosophy and rhetoric have deemphasized the inquiry aspects of argumentation and focused almost exclusively on argument as persuasion. We believe strongly in the dialectical function of argumentation, and we also believe that instruction in argumentation is an excellent means of teaching critical thinking. At the same time we recognize the necessity of teaching students how to present their critically explored positions in ways that will be acceptable to specific audiences, in specific fields, and in accordance with the rules of specific forums.

Second, this book is premised on the belief that the field-invariant standards of argumentation and informal logic are useful and historically valid. The tests of data and reasoning, the fallacies, and the special methods of refutation were derived from experience and have been repeatedly used and tested in philosophical, religious, legal, and academic forums for centuries. The necessity for group cooperation requires the acceptance of some standards of validity beyond personal perceptions. Moreover, the recognition of nonrational variables or field-variant criteria may warrant consideration of additional standards, but it does not justify rejection of the empirically useful field-invariant standard of argument and informal logic.

Third, we believe that reasoned advocacy requires an understanding of the constraints and opportunities that exist in specific fields, forums, and formats. Ethical advocates adapt to these unique situations, not by abandoning their carefully researched and analyzed positions, but by adapting strategies and tactics appropriate to the occasions and by developing advocacy skills that will allow them to focus on critical ideas as they communicate their positions.

Finally, this book has been guided by the belief that academic debate is an excellent vehicle for teaching students how to use the concepts of argumentative inquiry and advocacy. Argumentation can, of course, be taught apart from debate, and this textbook provides exercises and practicums for those who cannot, or do not wish to, use debate as a teaching method. However, whenever possible, we encourage teachers to include debate activities in the teaching of argument, since debate requires the most thorough integration of the inquiry and advocacy phases of argumentation. Oral advocacy, in any of the debate formats, provides the incentive for thorough investigation and uses procedures that require critical evaluation, selectivity, and focusing of argument.

In addition to these general principles which have guided our writing, three additional features of this text are, perhaps, worthy of note. First, over the past decade, interest in nonpolicy debate has grown rapidly. Although the first edition of *Argumentation: Inquiry and Advocacy* provided some discussion of major aspects of nonpolicy debate, the treatment in this edition is both expanded and updated. Second, we recognize that many of the concepts in this text are not necessarily easy for students to understand or apply. We have, therefore, tried to make the material as accessible as possible. To this end we have provided summaries at the ends of chapters, practicums with answers, and cartoons to illustrate concepts. Third, several new and expanded topics of discussion are presented in this second edition. A new section on briefing has been added to the chapter on logical outlining. The formal fallacies are identified at appropriate places throughout the textbook, and cost-benefits analysis is included in the chapter on the analysis of policy controversies. An entirely new chapter on advocacy skills is also provided; this chapter focuses on those presentational factors that are most specific to argument.

ACKNOWLEDGMENTS

A number of individuals have assisted us with this project, and we wish to acknowledge their help. Foremost among those whom we wish to thank is Charles Dause of the University of Detroit. Charles was the coauthor of the first edition of *Argumentation: Inquiry and Advocacy*. Because he has been a university administrator for a number of years, he did not feel that he could assist with this edition. Nevertheless, Charles's ideas and understanding as expressed in the first edition have enlightened and influenced us in our task.

Two people who have contributed directly to this volume are Bernard Slanec and Ruth Kay. Bern is an old college friend who agreed to help us enliven the textbook material with his personable and animated sketches. We are delighted with his work and thank him for making his talents available to us. In addition to being the wife of one of the authors, Ruth Kay is a secondary school teacher and a national leader in high school forensics. She is responsible for many of the exercises and practicums that appear throughout the text. We thank her for sharing her teaching skills with us.

A number of other individuals have helped us in less obvious, but nevertheless, important ways. For their assistance in gathering resource materials, checking footnotes, and serving as sounding boards for ideas, we thank Matthew Sobnosky, Larry Dawson, Sydne Kasle, Dean Groulx, and Scott Warrow. For their help in the preparation of the final manuscript we thank Julie Lee, Bill Ziegelmueller, and Louise Saad.

There are three other groups of people who made substantial contributions to this book. We are very appreciative of the constructive suggestions for revision, which we received from colleagues who used the earlier edition of *Argumentation: Inquiry and Advocacy* in their classes. Many of their suggestions have been incorporated in this edition. The comments of the reviewers of this edition, Diane Casagrande, Dale Herbeck, John Morello, and Halford Ryan, were unusually helpful. Several of their suggestions resulted in changes in our final manuscript. Finally, we wish to acknowledge the encouragement, support, and direction of Stephen Dalphin and his staff at Prentice-Hall. We have appreciated their confidence in our work and the great freedom that they gave to us to write the kind of book we wanted.

CHAPTER ONE
A PERSPECTIVE ON ARGUMENTATION

The president of the United States sits across the table from the premier of the Soviet Union. The two world leaders discuss how to go about reducing the number of nuclear weapons. While the leaders talk about achieving a nuclear arms treaty, their armies face each other in a distant part of the world, fully prepared to violently confront one another on the battlefield.

A high school senior is seated in the living room, talking to her parents. She tells them she wants to attend a college in another state. The parents tell her she should go to the local college. The discussion soon becomes heated. The young woman thinks to herself, Should I continue to put up with this or should I tell them I'm going to do what I want and storm out of the room?

Two six-year-olds stand inches apart on the playground at recess. The taller child says: "You better stop teasing my cousin." The other child responds, "What's it to you?" The taller child thinks for a moment, Should I tell the kid what's wrong with teasing or should I just punch the kid to make my point?

The people in these scenes are quite different, ranging from world leaders to small children. The situations differ dramatically in importance, from the future of the world to a playground spat. Yet, the scenes depict an activity in which we engage every day—the act of disagreeing. The scenes also reveal a choice which

we as human beings must make—whether to use language or force to resolve disagreements.

Civilized societies believe that argument is an appropriate and useful means by which to resolve disagreements. Through the study of argument we move away from "the law of the playground" where bullies rule. We move away from "the law of the sword" where physical might rules. We move closer to "the law of reason," a world in which the power of language and reasoning is cherished.

ARGUMENTATION DEFINED

Philosophers, rhetoricians, and communication scholars have devoted considerable attention to defining argument and argumentation. Many scholars distinguish between *making* an argument and *having* an argument; that is, between argument as a product and argument as a process. Some scholars view argumentation as an interpersonal or psychological activity; other scholars approach argumentation as a logical or philosophical activity.[1] Whatever definition is used, however, most scholars agree that the study of argumentation must be concerned with the claims made by human beings.

Specifically, we view *argumentation as the study of the principles by which beliefs and actions are evaluated and related to one another.* In its broadest sense, *argumentation is a language-based social phenomenon that enables us to discover what beliefs and actions are reasonable in any social context and that is concerned with the selection and organization of ideas to justify particular positions.*

Consider, for example, the situation in which Karen feels that Professor Erickson unfairly graded her term paper. Karen's feeling that the evaluation is unfair constitutes a belief. Karen thinks about the situation, carefully analyzing what action she should take. Karen reviews the criteria that Erickson specified for the assignment. She looks at grades received by others on their term papers. As Karen does this she is engaging in the inquiry dimension of argumentation, seeking to discover the appropriate claims. Karen then decides on a particular course of action. She schedules an appointment with Professor Erickson during which she presents her claims and requests a higher grade on her term paper. During this meeting Karen engages in the advocacy dimension of argumentation, presenting her claims to Erickson.

As this example demonstrates, argumentation is a process involving two important dimensions: *inquiry and advocacy.*

Argumentation as Inquiry

The *inquiry* dimension of argumentation *involves discovering appropriate beliefs and actions.* Argumentation is concerned with the ways in which we evaluate and relate ideas. We engage in argumentation not only when we critically examine the ideas of others, as Karen did when she decided that Professor Erickson's evaluation was unfair. We also engage in argumentation when we organize concepts into arguments of our own, as Karen did when she sorted through the claims she would make in her meeting with Professor Erickson.

Whether we are evaluating ideas or relating ideas to one another, we are making claims as to what is true or reasonable to believe in a particular social context. The process we use to determine what is true or reasonable is partly linguistic, partly grammatical, partly logical, and party psychological. The process is guided by such tools as analysis, the discovery and testing of evidence and premises, the tests of argument, and the principles of organization. Each of these tools is informed by standards of truth and reasonability, which have evolved and been found useful over many generations and across cultures. A central focus of argumentation, thus, is on discovering and applying the general standards for determining what is true or reasonable.

Argumentation as Advocacy

The *advocacy* dimension of argumentation *involves using language strategies to justify our beliefs and actions to others.* Whenever we make a judgment or support a particular course of action, we can expect others to ask us to justify our position. Sometimes the aim of our justification will be merely to help others understand the basis of our belief or action. At other times we will offer reasons in the hope of persuading others to accept our belief or to act the way we wish them to, as Karen did when she met with Professor Erickson. Argumentation as a means of advocacy requires an understanding of the fields, forums, and formats for advocacy, the strategies for argument, refutation, cross-examination, and presentational skills.

Although we have presented the inquiry and advocacy dimensions of argumentation as two distinct stages, it is important to realize that the stages are interdependent. Whenever we advocate a particular position we discover areas of our argument that need additional support, taking us back to the inquiry stage. Whenever we go through the investigative process of inquiry, we test the arguments we will use, taking us forward to the advocacy stage.

THE RELEVANCE OF ARGUMENTATION

The relevance of skill in argumentation seems self-evident to anyone living in a democratic society. The notion of full and free public debate on the vital issues facing society is deeply rooted in the documents and ideas comprising the American conscience. Yet, as we look at the events of the past decade we are forced to ask if reasoned inquiry and advocacy truly dominate our sociopolitical arena.

Anti-abortion groups have forcefully shut down abortion clinics. Animal rights groups have exploded bombs at research centers conducting experiments on animals. The superpower nations of the world continue to rely on the might of nuclear weapons to maintain peace. Strikes, protests, and the reliance on physical threats testify to a lack of faith in the effectiveness of reasoned inquiry and advocacy.

Our nation's political campaigns have tended to highlight image above issues, making a candidate's slick, televised image more important than careful, reasoned discussion and debate of the issues for which the candidate stands. Special interest pleadings often appear to be more effective in gathering public support than do public debates or carefully researched study reports.

How relevant, then, is argumentation to decision-making and persuasion in our everyday lives?

Confrontation and Coercion

We learn at a very early age that confrontation and force is one method by which we may secure something we desire. Whether the situation involves a young child using a temper tantrum to secure parental attention, the nation attempting to advance its political agenda by using aggression, or the terrorist hijacking a plane to advance a political cause, confrontation and force is a reality in our world. Protests and mass marches have become commonplace in our society. Farmers, unionists, abolitionists, segregationists, women, and gays have all, at times, used public demonstrations as a means of seeking support for their causes. To the extent that confrontation strategies are intended to *coerce* or *force* people or institutions to change, they are philosophically unacceptable. Coercion assumes, rather than tests, the rightness of a position, and as a result, it suppresses opposition and denies the freedom and integrity of all who oppose the position. Fortunately, in American society, change has almost never come about through the use of force alone.

To the extent that demonstrations and marches seek to bring about change by dramatically calling attention to a problem, they depend ultimately on reasoned advocacy. The civil rights marches and demonstrations of the late 1950s and early 1960s were effective in drawing attention to the social plight of black people and in creating public sentiment in their behalf. But the resulting civil rights legislation, which attempted to respond to these grievances, was the culmination of years of careful study, analysis, and debate. The use of protest, physical threat, and coercion do not deny the value of argumentation skills. Rather, such assertions of force serve to make more urgent the need for thorough and fair inquiry and for skillful and creative advocacy.

Emotion and Special Pleading

Inquiry and advocacy rarely, if ever, take place in a purely rational atmosphere. Emotion, self-interest, ignorance, and group pressures impose considerable limitations on argumentation. The decision of whether or not to marry a particular man or woman will not be a wholly rational decision—nor, perhaps, should it be. How you *feel* about a prospective mate is important. The depth of your feelings, the circumstances of your feeling, and the intensity of the feelings are all relevant factors in your decision to marry or not to marry. But love and sexual desire can be confused, and feelings can and do change. A wise couple will not only explore their immediate feelings toward each other but will also consider whether or not they share similar values and goals in life, whether they enjoy the same friends and activities, and whether their life-styles are compatible. Thus, reasoned scrutiny of the relevant facts, values, *and* emotions are more likely to lead to a happy, fulfilling, and long-lasting marriage than is a purely emotional response.

Just as emotions affect our personal decision-making, self-interest and group pressure may sometimes complicate and confuse our group and societal decision-making. Intellectually, most Americans have come to accept the equality of all races and sexes, but self-concerns about social status and employment opportunities have repeatedly slowed the progress of equal rights activities. In spite of increases in violent crimes, the assassination of public figures, and many examples of successful firearms control in other nations, powerful lobbies have limited gun control legislation in this country. Although we may not always agree with particular pressure groups, they are not necessarily irrational. Pressure groups represent the legitimate concerns of special classes of citizens, and these concerns should be considered along with other facts and values. If certain powerful groups sometimes seem to have disproportionate influence, it must be remembered that changes, nevertheless, do occur. Solutions are worked out. Skilled advocates learn how to construct arguments based on self-interest, to relate self-interest to a higher motive, or to refute the assumption that a special interest will be endangered. Ignorance or lack of understanding by an audience may require less complex argumentation as well as greater education through a variety of different media, but human beings are capable of learning and changing. Thus, self-interest may be *a* factor in public policy-making, but it need not be—and usually is not—*the* deciding factor. Ignorance may make rational advocacy more difficult, but it does not preclude it.

THE CERTAINTY OF ARGUMENTATION

Whether we are concerned with finding answers to personal problems, business problems, or societal problems, we can never be absolutely certain that we have made the correct choice. The study of argumentation provides a variety of tests that are helpful in evaluating the methods and materials used in arriving at conclusions. As helpful as these tests are, however, they cannot provide *absolute* assurance of the effectiveness or wisdom of our conclusions. What these standards can do is help us in gauging the *probable* correctness of our positions.

Limitations on the Ability to Know

To the extent that natural scientists deal in controlled, measurable phenomena, they can provide answers that appear to be certain. Even these answers, however, are subject to limitations imposed by measurement devices, formulas, and theoretical perspectives. For centuries, scientists proclaimed the atom to be the irreducible unit of matter, but in the early twentieth century new theoretical perspectives provided by Einstein and others proved the falseness of this scientific "fact." When we move out of the realm of the physical sciences into the fields of human relations, politics, and ethics, our ability to be certain of the accuracy of a position becomes even more restricted. There are several reasons why we can never be absolutely certain about the correctness of our conclusions.

First, our knowledge is limited. Because we are human beings and not gods, we can never know all there is to know about anything, even ourselves. Biographers have been studying the life of Abraham Lincoln for decades, and yet there remain many uncertain and unexplained aspects of his life history. After centuries of study, historians are still not certain about the real causes behind the decline and fall of the Roman Empire or the factors that produced the American Revolution.

But even if we could have all of the pertinent facts regarding any situation, we would still be limited by our perceptions. Inevitably, human beings tend to perceive events from the perspective of their own previous experiences and values. Thus, even given a complete body of data, a white American historian and a black American historian might come to considerably different conclusions concerning the motivations behind, and effects of, the Emancipation Proclamation.

When we consider contemporary problems, the third limitation, that of time, becomes of major importance. The world and relationships among phenomena are constantly changing so that it becomes impossible for anyone to keep completely up-to-date on any current situation. It may take decades and even centuries to discover enough of the facts concerning the impact of colonial rule in Africa before a proper understanding of that issue can be achieved. Such an understanding is denied to a contemporary citizen, politician, or historian. Thus, while we are obliged to seek to discover what is correct, the limitations of knowledge, perspective, and time prevent us from ever being certain that we have achieved that goal.

If we can never be certain that we are right in our beliefs or actions, why should we be concerned with attempting to discover what is "true"? To say that we cannot know with *certainty* the correctness of our answer to a particular problem or situation *is not to deny the exixtence* of true facts or proper perspectives. Clearly, Lee Harvey Oswald either killed President John F. Kennedy or he did not. In spite of months of extensive investigation by the Warren Commission, we cannot be *asolutely certain* that Oswald fired the shots that killed Kennedy. Our lack of certainty, however, does not mean that there is no objective reality in the specific situation. Indefinite worldwide increases in acid rain pollution will either destroy our lakes and forests or they will not. Our present inability to be completely certain of our environmental predictions does not mean that the adequacy of our answer is unimportant. There is an objective reality, even if, as human beings, we are incapable of knowing it with certainty.

Implications of Probability of Perception

The fact that even the most conscientious application of argumentation cannot lead to certainty of knowledge has important implications. First, it implies that human beings can and must operate in society on the basis of less-than-certain conclusions. To refuse to make judgment or to avoid taking a stand until we are certain of our conclusions is to cease to function in any meaningful way. We are not free to avoid making decisions because we cannot make them with absolute certainty. We must act on probabilities.

It is helpful to think of our ability to know truth as though it exists on a continuum. At one end is complete uncertainty and at the other complete certainty. As we investigate a question, the degree of our commitment to a given answer may progress from uncertainty, to possibility, to probability, to high probability. Since we can never achieve certainty, we must be satisfied to act on the basis of high probability. The degree of certainty depends to a large extent on the arena in which the decision occurs. For example, in a court of law, considerable proof is required to convict—proof beyond a reasonable doubt. Such a high degree of proof may not be required in many of the personal decisions we make, for example, in deciding whether to buy a brand name or a generic product. The arena in which the argument occurs largely determines the level of certainty to which we must strive.

A second implication of our inability to be absolutely certain of our answers concerns our degree of emotional commitment to those answers. If we know our answers are only probably correct, then dogmatic adherence to them must be considered inappropriate. It is possible for a person to have deep convictions without becoming dogmatically committed to them. Intelligent advocacy requires that we be willing to set forth and defend our commitments, but it also requires us to be willing to listen to, and to learn, from others. Dogmatic advocacy, on the other hand, assumes such certainty of truth that it precludes the possibility of new knowledge or additional insights. In short, intelligent persons should never let the advocacy of their beliefs override the search for more greater certainty.

The third implication of our limited ability to be certain of our beliefs concerns our attitudes toward those who differ with us. Once we understand that limitations exist on our ability to know, it becomes more difficult for us to view our opponents as liars and distorters of truth. The public sometimes finds it difficult to understand how political leaders can oppose each other in so many controversies and still have warm and genuine respect for one another. The explanation is that such leaders, like all intelligent advocates, have come to look on their opponents as partners in a joint search for wise decisions. Thus, our opponents in committee meetings, parliamentary assemblies, or public debates ought not be viewed as barriers to wise action but as testers of our own wisdom.

PRACTICUM: LIMITATIONS ON THE ABILITY TO KNOW

John is a fifty-three-year-old assembly line worker who has been married to Jane for thirty years. John has smoked two packs of cigarettes a day since he was sixteen. For many years his coworkers and his wife have urged John to quit smoking. They argue that even if he is not concerned for his own health, John should be concerned for the health of Jane because secondary smoke causes cancer. John's response to this argument is that he has lived in the same house with Jane for thirty years and that despite breathing side-stream smoke, Jane has not developed cancer.

What three limitations on the ability to know should cause us to question John's response to the claim that secondary smoke is dangerous?

THE ETHICS OF ARGUMENTATION

A fundamental assumption we make is that language is powerful. Language can be used to accomplish good, as in the case of a consumer advocate who successfully argues to have a dangerous product removed from the market. Language can also be used to accomplish evil, as in the case of a person who convinces a friend to participate in a bank robbery. It is the power of language that requires us to consider the ethical and moral dimensions of argumentation.

Argumentation inherently involves ethical and moral choices. How thorough must we be in investigating a problem? Should we conceal opposing evidence from our opponents? Is telling a lie appropriate if we are accomplishing some higher purpose? Should we ever mislead our audience? These questions involve ethical and moral choices, which an advocate must inevitably confront.

Throughout this book we emphasize tools and procedures that lead to *responsible* inquiry and advocacy. These tools, however, must be guided by a fundamental respect for the power of language. Such a respect leads advocates to discover that moral and ethical inquiry and advocacy is *responsible* inquiry and advocacy.

Virtually every arena in which argumentation occurs has a written or unwritten code for moral and ethical behavior.[2] Such codes frequently identify specific acts that are considered unethical and prescribe penalties for unethical behavior. For example, the code of ethics of the American Forensic Association specifies that fabrication and distortion of evidence is unethical. Debaters engaging in fabrication of evidence can be excluded from participation in the National Debate Tournament. The Cross Examination Debate Association and the National Forensic League subscribe to similar codes. Similarly, state bar associations all have codes of ethical conduct. Attorneys who violate these codes can be dismissed from the bar and lose their right to practice law.

Apart from specified codes, there are ethical standards inherent to the process of argumentation. As we have learned, the inquiry stage of argumentation involves a truth-seeking function. Anything we do that distorts the search for what is true interferes with the fundamental purpose of inquiry. Hence, approaching inquiry as a means of justifying our preconceived notions or distorting the evidence used to support ideas must be regarded as unethical behavior. Inherent to the advocacy stage of argumentation is free expression. The advocacy stage of argument recognizes that the chance for truth to emerge is much greater when we subject ideas to full and free debate. We must not deny our opponents the opportunity for equal expression of their ideas. Argument forums, as we will discuss later, go to great lengths in order to ensure that advocates are provided with equal opportunity to express and test ideas.

The inherent nature of inquiry and advocacy, as well as the ethical and moral codes which govern our argumentation arenas, are important guides to responsible argumentation. The responsible student of argumentation uses these guides to develop a high degree of respect for the power of language and the importance of responsible debate.

SUMMARY

Argumentation is the study of the principles by which beliefs and actions are evaluated and related to one another. In its broadest sense, argumentation is a language-based social phenomenon that enables us to discover what beliefs and actions are reasonable in any social context and that is concerned with the selection and organization of ideas to justify particular positions. Argumentation thus involves both inquiry—discovering appropriate beliefs and actions—and advocacy—using language strategies to justify our beliefs and actions to others. In the inquiry stage we are guided by such tools as analysis, the discovery and testing of evidence and premises, the tests of argument, and the principles of organization. In the advocacy stage we are guided by an understanding of the fields, forums, and formats for advocacy, the strategies for argument, refutation, cross-examination, and presentational skills.

In spite of personal emotions and special interest appeals, argumentation is a relevant aspect of both personal and societal decision-making. When making personal decisions, strong emotions cannot be ignored, but they should be examined and evaluated along with other pertinent data. When making societal decisions, the appeals of special interest groups will be a factor to be considered, but they will not usually be *the* deciding factor. Efforts to bring about change through forceful demonstration are unacceptable in a democratic society, but the use of peaceful demonstrations to dramatize a problem may accelerate the processes of public inquiry, advocacy, and political action.

Although we can never be absolutely certain of the correctness of our choices, the principles and methods of argumentation can help us judge the probable truth of our beliefs. Our ability to be certain is constrained by our limited knowledge, our limited perspectives, and our time-bound nature. Because we cannot be certain, we must act on the basis of probabilities; we should avoid dogmatism, and we should welcome opposition.

The power of language requires us to consider the ethical and moral dimensions of argumentation. Argumentation inherently involves ethical and moral choices. The tools of inquiry and advocacy, as well as the ethical and moral codes which govern our argumentation arenas, are important guides to responsible inquiry and advocacy. Responsible students of argumentation use these guides to develop a high degree of respect for the power of language and the importance of responsible debate.

NOTES

[1]Three excellent sources that review various definitions of argument and argumentation are Cox and Willard, Rowland, and O'Keefe.

[2]A detailed discussion of establishing a code of ethics for intercollegiate forensics is presented in Parson (13–22).

SELECTED BIBLIOGRAPHY

COX, ROBERT J., and CHARLES A. WILLARD, eds. *Advances in Argumentation Theory and Research.* Carbondale: Southern Illinois University Press, 1982.

COX, ROBERT J., MALCOLM SILLARS, and GREGG WALKER, eds. *Argument and Social Practice: Proceedings of the Fourth SCA/AFA Conference on Argumentation.* Annandale, VA: Speech Communication Asociation, 1985.

O'KEEFE, DANIEL. J. "Two Concepts of Argument." *Journal of the American Forensic Association* 13 (1977): 121–28.

PARSON, DONN, ed. *American Forensics in Perspective: Papers from the Second National Conference on Forensics.* Annandale, VA: Speech Communication Association, 1984.

PERELMAN, CHAIM. *The Realm of Rhetoric.* Notre Dame, IN: University of Notre Dame Press, 1982.

RHODES, JACK, and SARA NEWELL, eds. *Proceedings of the Summer Conference on Argumentation.* Annandale, VA: Speech Communication Association, 1980

ROWLAND, ROBERT C. "On Defining Argument." *Philosophy and Rhetoric* 20 (1987): 140–59.

TOULMIN, STEPHEN. *Uses of Argument.* Cambridge, MA: Cambridge University Press, 1958.

TOULMIN, STEPHEN, RICHARD RIEKE, and ALLAN JANIK. *An Introduction to Reasoning.* New York: Macmillan, 1984.

VAN EEMEREN, F. H., R. GROOTENDORST, and T. KRUIGER. *The Study of Argumentation.* New York: Irvington, 1984.

WENZEL, JOSEPH W., ed. *Argument and Critical Practices: Proceedings of the Fifth SCA/AFA Conference on Argumentation.* Annandale, VA: Speech Communication Association, 1987.

WILLARD, CHARLES A. *Argumentation and the Social Grounds of Knowledge.* Tuscaloosa: Univeristy of Alabama Press, 1983.

ZAREFSKY, DAVID, MALCOLM O. SILLARS, and JACK RHODES, eds. *Argument in Transition: Proceedings of the Third Summer Conference on Argumentation.* Annandale, VA: Speech Communication Association, 1983.

ZIEGELMUELLER, GEORGE, and JACK RHODES, eds. *Dimensions of Argument: Proceedings of the Second Summer Conference on Argumentation.* Annandale, VA: Speech Communication Association, 1981.

STUDY QUESTIONS

1. Do the activities of special interest organizations such as anti-abortion groups or gun control lobbies in any way compromise the principles on which the study of argumentation is based?
2. Can the concept of *probability* be applied to the religious beliefs of an individual or group?
3. Does the concept of unnegotiable demands clash with the perspective of argumentation described in this chapter?
4. What ethical concerns are raised when special interest groups use coercive or confrontational strategies, or both?

EXERCISES

1. Obtain a copy of your school's Code of Conduct for Students or some other document that specifies penalties for academic dishonesty at your institution. What standards for ethical behavior are established in the document? How are these standards justified in the document?
2. Find a letter to the editor in a newspaper that supports or opposes a particular action by government. Identify the factors that may limit the author's ability to know. Identify the perceptual factors that affect the certainty of the author's argument.
3. Discuss the following statement with your friends: "There is no such thing as truth. Truth is always in the eye of the beholder."

ANSWERS TO PRACTICUM

1. John's knowledge is limited. He is basing the conclusion on his limited personal experience, ignoring the many scientific studies on this issue.
2. Personal perceptions limit John's conclusion. John is a lifelong smoker who does not want to quit smoking. He does not want to discover that smoking may be harmful to his wife.
3. The limitation of time should cause us to question John's conclusion. Just because Jane has not yet developed cancer does not mean that she will not in a few years.

CHAPTER TWO
BASIC CONCEPTS

All of us, at one time or another, have had the experience of participating in informal "rap sessions." Such sessions may involve heated disputes concerning one or more controversial topics. Although we may enjoy the free give-and-take of such exchanges, they seldom enlighten us or resolve the question at issue. Why is it that such discussions, involving intelligent people freely expressing their views, so often end in confusion and misunderstanding? The answer, in part, is that these sessions operate without any basic ground rules and that the participants function with little or no awareness of their responsibilities as investigators or advocates. Rap sessions may serve important social and emotional purposes, but when enlightened understanding and decision-making are the goals, conformity to certain fundamental principles of argumentation is essential.

To understand the importance of these principles, we need only look to our legislative and legal systems. When an individual is accused of a crime, we demand a clear statement of the indictment against him or her; we prescribe that the individual is not guilty until proven otherwise; and we carefully outline what the prosecution must prove to establish guilt. In our legislative bodies, governing boards, and social and professional organizations we have established rules of conduct, which recognize similar obligations. According to the rules of parliamentary procedure, one, and only one, motion may be debated at a time; only arguments relevant to the specific motion are allowed; and we require different sized majorities to pass a motion depending on its importance. Few of us would approve of a legal or policy-making body that operated without fundamental guidelines. In short, in situations where decisions important to our personal, professional, and public lives are being considered, we demand adherence to concepts that will help ensure orderly and responsible inquiry and advocacy.

This chapter discusses certain basic concepts that operate, either formally or informally, in all serious investigations and debates. Propositions function to ensure well-focused inquiry and advocacy, and concepts such as presumption, burden of proof, issues, and prima facie case establish basic standards for reasonable decision-making.

PROPOSITIONS

In order to ensure that a topic may be investigated and discussed in a systematic and efficient manner, it is necessary that the problem area be carefully defined. Clear phrasing of a question can provide a meaningful basis for argument, whereas vague phrasing or no phrasing at all will inevitably lead to misunderstandings and to superficial analysis. A student forum concerned with local real estate practices may never reach the action stage if it does not stop to state its objectives. A debate over U.S. foreign policy can wander off on tangents if the direction and nature of the change being proposed are not clearly defined by the advocates. In short, the prerequisite for adequate analysis of any question is the careful phrasing of a statement expressing the basis of the controversy. In argumentation we call such a statement a *proposition*.

Proposition is a general concept that applies to a variety of different forms of expression. In business meetings propositions are phrased as motions: "I move that eight thousand dollars be appropriated for the repair of the air conditioning system." In legislative assemblies they are usually phrased as bills: "Be it enacted by the state of Michigan that casino gambling be made lawful." Boards of inquiry are charged with the responsibility of answering a specific question: "What were the causes of the failure of flight 299?" In academic debate the proposition is phrased as a resolution: "Resolved: That television is detrimental to children." Regardless of its specific form, a proposition's primary function remains the same: to make clear what is being proposed or examined—to isolate the essence of the controversy.

Some preliminary investigation often must occur before a final statement of a proposition evolves. In legal cases, the prosecuting attorney or plaintiff's lawyer will carefully study the facts of the situation and the nature of the relevant laws before deciding on a formal statement of charges. In legislative assemblies, proposed bills are usually sent to committees for consideration, appraisal, and rewriting, if necessary. Only after a proposal has gone through this process is it brought before the entire assembly for debate. In parliamentary debate a resolution may be reworded by amendments or by general consensus several times during the course of its consideration. Even in committee meetings considerable discussion may have to occur before the group can decide on the exact nature of its problem area. In interscholastic debate the final wording of the proposition is arrived at after months of investigation, discussion, and deliberation. Inexperienced advocates sometimes become frustrated by the processes involved in the phrasing of bills, resolutions, and other forms of propositions, but the effort expended in working out an acceptable phrasing is necessary if a clear clash of issues and a thorough analysis are to follow.

Types of Propositions

All propositions—questions, resolutions, motions, bills, and so forth—may be classified as either propositions of fact/value or propositions of policy. It is important to identify these two types of propositions because (as you will discover in the next chapter) the methods for analyzing issues vary according to the nature of the propositions. Although it is, of course, possible to distinguish further between statements of fact and statements of value, this is unnecessary because the methods of analyzing issues are the same for both.

Propositions of fact/value *Propositions of fact/value are descriptive, predictive, or evaluative statements that assert the existence or worth of something.* Courts of law, boards of inquiry, and study commissions are agencies concerned with descriptive judgments. They attempt to determine the existence of past or present events or relationships. "Sue Smith killed her husband"; "Atmospheric ozone causes permanent damage to the lungs"; "Atlantis University athletes accepted payoffs for throwing the championship basketball game"—these are examples of propositions of fact/value that describe existence.

Propositions of fact/value may also assert claims regarding future events or relationships. Economic analysts, sports commentators, and even fortune tellers offer predictions of future events that they must justify. The following are examples of propositions of fact/value that predict future existence: "Southern California will win the Rose Bowl this year"; "The cost of the new domed stadium will exceed five hundred million dollars"; "John Lennon will return to earth as a dove with olive branches in its teeth."

Finally, propositions of fact/value may go beyond the assertion of past, present, or future existence and declare the worth of something. TV and music critics, philosophers, and comparative shoppers make evaluative judgments such as "Chrysler products are the best engineered automobiles"; "Blasphemy is the greatest sin"; "The Star Wars movies were the most original series in movie history." Propositions of fact/value that assert the worth of something are characterized by evaluative terms that suggest goodness, badness, desirability, undesirability, and so on.

Propositions of policy *A proposition of policy is a statement that asserts that a course of action should be taken.* Every time an editorial urges you to vote for a particular candidate, every time a member of Congress calls for the passage of a pending bill, and every time a member of a social club proposes sponsorship of a dance, a question of policy is under consideration. Propositions of policy may propose either general or specific courses of action, but they always go beyond simply describing or evaluating a situation to advocating that something be done. The analyses of propositions of policy inevitably require the consideration of subordinate fact/value questions, but because propositions of policy involve the added dimension of future action, a broader framework for analysis is necessary (see Chapter 4). The following are examples of propositions of policy: "The federal government should establish a system of free respite and nursing home care for all infirm U.S. citizens"; "Shellie should marry Bill"; "College tuition should be raised by 10 percent"; "Space exploration should become a higher national priority." A term such as "should" or "ought to" appears in most propositions of policy.

Phrasing Propositions

In order for a proposition to serve its intended purpose of isolating the essence of the controversy, its statement must be phrased very carefully. Four standards should be followed in phrasing propositions.

Change from existing beliefs or policies   *The proposition should be phrased to indicate a change from present beliefs or policies.* Propositions are phrased in terms of change in order to provide a general idea of the "felt difficulty." There is no reason for inquiry or advocacy if everyone is content with existing beliefs and policies. Moreover, by always phrasing propositions in favor of change, other related concepts have a fixed point. In criminal courts, for instance, the statement of the indictment is always phrased in terms of the alleged guilt: "Betty Bronski is guilty of mail fraud." This phrasing never varies since part of its function is to clearly identify the prosecution and the defense and to indicate their respective responsibilities. Similarly, in academic debates, a properly worded proposition identifies the affirmative as the side supporting the change proposed by the resolution and the negative as the side opposed to that change. Since the obligations of advocates of change are different from those of defenders of the status quo, it is important to define these positions in a consistent and fixed manner.

Nature and direction of the change   *The statement of the proposition should indicate both the nature and direction of the change desired.* A proposition should identify the kind of change in belief or action being proposed, and it should indicate the philosophical or political movement away from the present belief or policy. Notice how the proposition "Resolved: That the U.S. government should terminate all military aid to the governments and people of Africa" provides precise focus and facilitates direct clash of arguments. On the other hand, the proposition "Resolved: That U.S. foreign policy to one or more African nations should be changed" indicates neither the nature nor the direction of change being proposed. The term "changed" is bidirectional, so it is not clear whether U.S. foreign policy commitments to Africa should be increased or decreased. Moreover, the specific kind of foreign policy change desired—economic, military, humanitarian—is not indicated. Such open-ended wording provides an extremely broad focus and makes it difficult to anticipate where the clash of arguments will occur. The proposition "Resolved: That First Amendment rights should be increased" indicates a clear direction of change but fails to suggest the nature of the increase. Because this proposition leaves the affirmative free to pick and choose among First Amendment rights, the specific areas of clash are unpredictable. The assertion that "history has inaccurately judged the literary worth of Mark Twain's writings" suggests the nature of the change in belief desired (a more accurate judgment), but fails to reveal the new direction in judgment desired. The topic does not indicate whether Mark Twain's literary worth has been overvalued or underrated.

The broad wording of propositions allows for greater latitude in the development of advocates' cases, but in doing so, it places the opposition to the proposition at a real disadvantage. When the defense cannot anticipate the nature or direction of the attack, the task of providing a thorough response becomes extremely difficult. Obviously, prosecuting attorneys would find it easier to charge defendants simply with "wrongdoing," but our legal system requires that the specific nature of the crime be spelled out so that the defendant can respond more adequately. The more specifically a proposition prescribes both the nature and the direction of the change being advocated, the more clearly drawn will be the line between the defender and the advocate of change, and the less likely we are to have definitional arguments and confusion.

One central idea   *The statement of the proposition should contain one central idea.* Inquiry and advocacy are easier and clearer when a single topic is considered at a time. Inclusion of more than one primary idea in a resolution encourages confused, contradictory, and superficial analysis. To argue, for instance, that "the University of Kansas should expand its student union recreational facilities and grant greater student representation in its governing councils" invites analytical difficulties. Although both aspects of this proposition relate to student life at the University of Kansas, different kinds of issues are raised in each half of the topic. The question of financial feasibility is relevant to the first half of the topic but not to the second, and concerns about representative constituencies and fairness are important to the second but not the first. A further difficulty with dually worded propositions is that one might favor one-half of the proposition but not the other. The statement that "the University of North Carolina is the best and most prestigious university in the South" involves two different judgments. Even if you agreed that North Carolina is the best university in the South, you could disagree with the judgment that it is the most prestigious.

In legislative and business sessions our rules of parliamentary procedure encourage working propositions as single ideas. If someone proposes a motion with a dual idea, parliamentary procedure permits the division of the motion so that separate and distinct ideas can be considered independently. When an amendment to a motion is proposed, parliamentary procedure prescribes that the amendment must be considered and acted on first before moving to the main motion. Such rules are certainly not arbitrary. They simply recognize that we can debate profitably only one idea at a time.

Neutral terminology   *The proposition should be phrased in neutral terminology.*
This final guideline suggests that the phrasing of the proposition should not be
biased. The judgment that "the writings of foul-mouthed, sex-crazed authors are
an unhealthy influence on American youth" may be colorful, but such language
is loaded in favor of the proposition. Phraseology such as "authors who use sexually explicit language are an unhealthy influence on American youth" is more
neutral and encourages a fairer appraisal. The proposition "Resolved: That our
antiquated and psychologically destructive grading system should be abolished"
begs the question. The framers of this resolution have incorporated their value
judgments into the statement. Such phrasing makes objective consideration of
the problem more difficult. Every attempt should be made, then, to phrase debate
propositions so that the phrasing itself gives no advantage to either side.

PRESUMPTION

A second fundamental construct of argumentation is the concept of presumption.
Presumption describes the inherent advantage in opposing change. This concept recognizes
that in every argumentative situation the person who is advocating change will
lose if nothing is done. Presumption makes no judgment concerning the wisdom
of present beliefs or policies. Although presumption may have the effect of causing present beliefs or policies to continue, this occurs by default—because what
already exists continues to exist—and not because present beliefs or policies have
necessarily been justified. Presumption exists in all fields of experience, although
its formal manifestations differ and the weight assigned to it may vary.

Institutionalized Concept

In our courts of criminal law the "presumption of innocence" is institutionalized. In the United States, if you are arrested and accused of a crime, the
court system will assume that you are not guilty until the police and prosecution
prove otherwise. This presumption ensures your acquittal unless guilt is proven
beyond a reasonable doubt. If the prosecution fails to present a sufficient case
against you, the presumption of innocence requires that you be set free regardless
of the adequacy of your own defense. Presumption in the legal system attempts
to return you to your prior status in society—a status of innocence. Your return
to innocence may occur, not because of an overwhelming weight of evidence supporting the judgment of innocence, but rather because of insufficient evidence
to justify changing your status to guilty.

Presumption also exists in all of our policy-making bodies. Although the
procedures and bylaws of most policy agencies do not use the term "presumption," their voting procedures, in effect, establish such a concept. Failure to achieve
a majority vote in favor of any proposed change maintains the status quo. When
a state legislator proposes a bill to replace the existing state sales tax with a
graduated income tax, presumption is against the proposed income tax. If more
than 50 percent of the legislators are not persuaded that an adequate case has

The advantage of preoccupation of ground.

been built in favor of the graduated income tax, presumption means that it will not come into being, and by default, the sales tax continues. Often, policy bodies are aware of serious problems with the status quo, but the present system continues because of the inability to agree on an acceptable alternative. The present policy is maintained simply because of its preoccupation of the ground; it is already there.

The scientific community also recognizes the advantage of existing beliefs. When a new theory is proposed, presumption is against its acceptance. That theory must be tested against all other possible explanations before it will be accepted. Before a new medicine can be marketed, rigorous standards must be met and repeated tests must have been conducted. Inadequately controlled tests or isolated successes are not sufficient to overcome belief in present theories, medications, or procedures. Laypersons often hear about new theories or new cures for diseases months or even years before the new theories or cures are finally accepted by the scientific community. As long as there is inadequate or insufficient data, approval is withheld, and present theories and cures are maintained.

Even in our private lives presumption operates. You may wish to get married and may enjoy the company of the person you are currently dating. You may, nevertheless, remain unmarried because you are not convinced that this is the person with whom you want to spend the rest of your life.

Although presumption in some form exists in all fields, the standards necessary for overcoming presumption and the point at which presumption operates vary with the situation. Parliamentary bodies, for example, typically establish two-thirds or even three-fourths votes as necessary in order to change certain procedural rules or to amend constitutions and bylaws. In these situations, the group has decided to establish a particularly strong presumption against change. In an effort to guard against the institutionalization of unnecessary administrative agencies, some state legislatures have passed "sunset laws." These laws establish a yearly termination date for agencies and programs in order to prevent their automatic continuation. Sunset laws, thus, seek to allow for temporary changes while maintaining a presumption against the continuation of those changes.

Purpose of Presumption

Presumption's description of how the world operates is useful in argumentation situations because it provides us with a fundamental decision rule. Presumption identifies the existence of a kind of mental and physical inertia. Basically, it recognizes that the failure to make a positive decision is a decision, nonetheless. The use of presumption as a decision rule does not give an advantage to existing policies and beliefs. It merely recognizes an advantage inherent in any decision-making situation. If new beliefs are not accepted, old beliefs remain. If new policies are not implemented, old practices continue. A family's failure to decide to buy a new car results in their continued use of existing means of transportation. A local country club's inability to agree on a new membership fee structure means that existing fees continue to be charged. Because of presumption there cannot be a tie in an argumentation situation. There is no policy or belief vacuum. Until change is justified, the present system continues.

BURDEN OF PROOF

The concept of burden of proof is the logical opposite of presumption. *The burden of proof is the inherent obligation of those advocating change to provide sufficient evidence and arguments to overcome the presumption of existing beliefs or policies.* The concept of burden of proof requires that changes be based on something more than whim. It asks the advocate of change to provide reasonable justification for the proposed change. What constitutes a reasonable justification depends on the particular rules or practices of the argumentative community or forum and varies with the advocacy situation. For example, a university judicial board will typically require only substantial evidence in order to discipline a student. In our criminal justice system, however, the prosecution must establish the truth of its claim by the more rigorous standard of preponderance of the evidence. Only by meeting the burden of proof, as defined by the particular argumentative community, can presumption be overcome.

The obligation of the burden of proof provides an important safeguard. By requiring those who attack existing beliefs, policies, reputations, or institutions to be prepared to support their attacks, we help to prevent irresponsible charges and thoughtless actions. If we removed books from our school libraries every time certain citizen groups objected to particular authors, we would be acting irresponsibly. At the very least, such groups ought to be required to demonstrate the harmful effects of the attacked authors' ideas and to establish that banning their works

1. Phyllis feels that the grade of "C" she received from Professor Kay was unfair and should be changed to an "A." She presents her case to Professor Kay. In this situation who has the burden of proof? Where does presumption reside?

2. The president of the United States appears on national television and presents a new proposal for national health insurance. Does the president's new proposal have presumption?

3. Jeff, a student at Wayne State University, is participating in a public debate on the proposition that the university should build a new engineering building. Jeff is opposed to the proposition because he feels the existing building is adequate. Jeff's opponent is Jane Carter, a professor of engineering. Jane argues that Jeff has the burden of proof because he is merely a student and she is a full professor. Is Professor Carter correct?

4. Ron argues that Erma Bombeck is a great humorist. Juanita argues that Erma Bombeck is a poor humorist. Who has the burden of proof? Where does presumption reside?

would prevent students from acting undesirably. The knowledge that our accusations and assertions must be supported and defended provides for responsible behavior and better decisions.

The burden of proof always resides with the advocate of change; it never shifts during the controversy. The burden of proof is the specific obligation of the advocate as determined by the statement of the proposition. As long as the advocate's position towards the proposition continues unchanged, his or her burden of proof remains the same. All advocates share a responsibility to support any arguments that they advance. Even though this general obligation to prove what is asserted constitutes *a* burden of proof common to both advocates and defenders of change, *the* burden of proving the proposition rests only with the initial supporters of change.

The term *burden of rebuttal* is frequently used to refer to the obligation that all parties in a controversy have to respond to arguments once they are advanced and supported. When the advocates of change have met their burden of proof, the opponents are faced with an obligation to respond. The burden of rebuttal should normally shift back and forth between proponents and opponents throughout a controversy.

ISSUES

One of the most important basic concepts of argument is that of issues. The term *issue* has a variety of meanings in everyday usage. It can mean anything from a controversial question to an isolated argument. In argumentation, however, this word has a very specific meaning. In argument, *issues are inherent questions vital to the advocate's cause.* The concept can be better understood by dissecting the definition.

First, issues are *inherent* in the proposition for inquiry or advocacy. This means that issues are not created by the participants in the dispute, but rather exist within the statement and historic context of the resolution. In our legal system you can discover the issues by analyzing the specific indictment in light of the written law and legal precedents. Similarly, in other fields of argument, you must analyze in depth the statements and context of the proposition in order to discover these crucial potential areas of clash.

Second, issues are *vital to the advocate's cause.* Issues are absolutely essential to the proof of the proposition. Advocates of change must win every issue in order to establish the truth of the proposition. Failure to win an issue means that a critical part of the analysis is unproven. An illustration may help explain this point. Let us suppose that you have been charged with the first degree murder of your next-door neighbor. In the course of the trial, the prosecution is able to establish (1) that the victim was strangled to death while in a drunken stupor; (2) that you were seen in the vicinity of the crime at the approximate time of the victim's death; (3) that you and he had had a number of heated arguments over his failure to pay you money he owed you, his frequent loud parties, and his repeated sexual advances toward your younger sister; (4) that you had publicly threatened to "blow his head off"; and (5) that on the night of his murder your neighbor had had a raucous party to which he attempted to lure your sister. In short, the prosecution has established the existence of a violent crime, opportunity, motive, and premeditation—all issues. However, if in your defense, you could prove that you were physically incapable of committing the crime—because of a partially paralyzed hand, for example—the prosecution would lose. Because the question of ability to commit the crime is vital to this case, the prosecution could not afford to ignore this issue.

That an issue is essential to the proof of the proposition distinguishes issues from arguments. Arguments are used to support issues. Therefore, advocates of change can lose any number of arguments and still win the issue. Even if two or three supporting arguments are lost, the remaining argument(s) may still be sufficient to carry the issue. In the above case, three arguments were offered to prove the issue of motive: money owed, loud parties, and sexual advances. Even if the prosecution lost two of these arguments (perhaps the borrowed money was repaid, and you are hard of hearing and were not really affected by the loud parties), the remaining argument (sexual advances) would be sufficient to establish a motive and carry the issue. Thus, issues are absolutely essential to the proof of the proposition and are distinguished by this from ordinary arguments.

Finally, issues are expressed in the form of *questions.* This formal consideration is contained within the definition for the sake of clarity. Issues should be phrased in question form so that the advocate of change must answer yes and the defender of existing beliefs or policies may answer no. In our sample murder case, an appropriate formal phrasing of the capability issue would be, Was the accused physically capable of strangling the victim?

A distinction is sometimes made between real and potential issues. *Potential issues* are all of the issues that exist within a given proposition, and *real issues* are the vital inherent points that actually become a basis of clash. The process of analysis is concerned with the identification of potential issues. Persuasive and strategic considerations determine which of the potential issues will, in fact, become real issues. The ability to anticipate the potential and real issues is what distinguishes the successful lawyer from the hack, what causes one member of a committee to seem more insightful than the others, and what allows one person to make important personal decisions confidently while others hesitate over even small decisions. To be able to isolate the vital considerations in a proposition is essential to the process of argument.

PRIMA FACIE CASE

A final fundamental concept of argumentation is the prima facie case. In order to overcome the presumption of the present belief or policy, an advocate of change is obligated to present a prima facie case in behalf of the new belief or policy. The term *prima facie,* literally defined, means "at first sight" or "on the face of it" or "before further examination." In legal terms, a prima facie case is that which will suffice until contradicted and overcome by other evidence. For our purpose, a *prima facie case can be defined as a case that is initially adequate to overcome the presumption of the present system and to force its defenders to respond.*

The concept of a prima facie case allows us to relate the ideas of presumption, burden of proof, and issues. Because of the presumption of existing beliefs or policies, advocates of change must assume the burden of proving a prima facie case. Whether or not the case presented is logically sufficient to meet the burden of proof depends on whether or not it provides positive answers to each of the issues inherent in the proposition.

SUMMARY

There are two basic types of propositions: propositions of fact/value and propositions of policy. These types are distinguished because each requires different analytical procedures. Propositions of fact/value are descriptive, predictive, or evaluative statements that assert the existence or worth of something. Propositions of policy are statements that assert a course of action should be taken.

Careful phrasing of propositions facilitates the analysis process. Four guidelines should be followed in phrasing topics for inquiry and advocacy: (1) The proposition should be phrased to indicate the change from existing beliefs or policies. (2) The statement of the proposition should indicate both the nature and direction of change desired. (3) The statement of the proposition should contain one central idea. (4) The proposition should be phrased in neutral terminology.

Presumption describes the inherent advantage in opposing change. Presumption makes no judgment regarding the wisdom of present beliefs or policies; it simply recognizes that, absent change, what already exists continues to exist in all fields, although its formal manifestations and the weight assigned to it may vary. Presumption functions in argument as a fundamental decision rule.

The burden of proof is the inherent obligation of those advocating change to provide sufficient evidence and arguments to overcome the presumption of existing beliefs or policies. The burden of proving the proposition always resides with the advocates of change, but all advocates share *a* burden of proving any arguments they set forth. Burden of rebuttal refers to the obligation to respond to arguments once they are advanced and supported.

Issues are inherent questions vital to the advocate's cause. Issues exist within the statement and historic context of the resolution. Issues are distinguished from arguments in that issues are essential to the proof of a proposition. Advocates of change must win every issue; they do not have to win every argument.

A prima facie case is one that initially overcomes the presumption, fulfills the burden of proof, and provides a positive response to each of the issues.

SELECTED BIBLIOGRAPHY

EHNINGER, DOUGLAS, and WAYNE BROCKRIEDE. Pp. 81-87 in *Decision by Debate.* New York: Dodd, Mead, 1963.

WHATELY, RICHARD. *Elements of Rhetoric,* edited by Douglas Ehninger. Carbondale: Southern Illinois University Press, 1963.

ZAREFSKY, DAVID. "Argument as Hypothesis Testing." Pp. 205–15 in *Advanced Debate: Readings in Practice and Teaching,* edited by David A. Thomas and Jack Hart. Lincolnwood, IL: National Textbook, 1987.

ZAREFSKY, DAVID. "A Reformulation of the Concept of Presumption." Paper presented at Central States Speech Association, Chicago, April, 7, 1972.

STUDY QUESTIONS

1. What is the rationale behind the statement, "In case of a tie, the defender of existing beliefs and policies wins"?
2. What happens when the parties in an argumentative setting cannot agree on the statement of a proposition?
3. Are there any unique problems in determining presumption in propositions of fact/value, particularly evaluative propositions?

EXERCISES

1. Select from a newspaper or newsmagazine an editorial that advocates a new policy. After reading the editorial, phrase a specific proposition that articulates the proposed policy. Identify the "issues" raised in the editorial and distinguish the "issues" from the "arguments." Does the editorial succeed in presenting a prima facie case?
2. Identify each of the propositions below as either a proposition of fact/value or a proposition of policy.

    a. Resolved: That it is more important for colleges to teach students how to think than to prepare them for specific jobs.

    b. Resolved: That the United States should withdraw all of its military troops from foreign countries.

    c. Resolved: That the single-automobile family will be nonexistent by the twenty-first century.

    d. Resolved: That the University of Nebraska has a better graduate program in history than the program at Wayne State University.

    e. Resolved: That tuition will have to be increased next fall.

    f. Resolved: That the tuition increase planned for next fall is unjustified.

    g. Resolved: That the planned tuition increase should be repealed.

3. Each of the propositions below has some weakness in its phrasing. Identify the weaknesses and rephrase each proposition so that it correctly isolates the essence of the controversy.

    a. Resolved: That our laws concerning abortion should be changed significantly.

    b. Resolved: That domestic automobile producers should be subject to federal safety and pollution standards.

    c. Resolved: That the United States should reduce its military expenditures and use the money to revitalize urban areas.

    d. Resolved: That the Supreme Court has unjustifiably relaxed controls against abusive and unnecessary police practices.

    e. Resolved: That our system of funding public elementary and secondary education should be overhauled.

4. Identify where presumption resides and which side has the burden of proof in each of the propositions listed under Exercise 2 above.

ANSWERS TO PRACTICUM

1. Phyllis has the burden of proof because she is requesting a change from present conditions. Presumption resides with the grade remaining as "C."

2. No, presumption still remains with the existing system of insurance. Even though the president is a respected leader, presumption always resides with the present system. The president in this situation has the burden to prove the desirability of the new policy.

3. Professor Carter is incorrect. Even though she is a full professor, she still has the burden of proof when advocating a new action. Jeff is defending the existing system, which has presumption.

4. This question can be answered in two ways. First, we could claim that the information presented in the example is insufficient to determine who has the burden of proof and where presumption resides. The concept of presumption requires us to have knowledge of existing beliefs. Therefore, we would need to know whether or not the audience felt that Bombeck was a great humorist. Second, we could claim that Juanita has the burden of proof since she is challenging the presumptive evidence that Erma Bombeck is a great humorist. Bombeck has a syndicated column and frequently appears on talk shows.

CHAPTER THREE
ANALYSIS OF
FACT/VALUE
CONTROVERSIES

In Chapter 2 we identified the importance of issues in proving a proposition. Discovering the issues requires in-depth investigation. Two general approaches are helpful in the discovery of issues. These are (1) analysis of the background of the controversy and (2) application of analytical formulas to the controversy. These two methods complement one another. The study of the background of the controversy aids in understanding the *substance* of the issues, and the application of analytical formulas provides specific perspectives that identify the general *nature* of issues. Both of these general approaches are applicable to each of the two types of propositions, although different analytical formulas are used for propositions of fact/value and for propositions of policy. In this chapter we discuss examination of the background of the controversy and the analytical formula of stasis analysis as they relate to fact/value propositions.

ANALYSIS OF THE BACKGROUND
OF THE CONTROVERSY

No controversy involving fact/value exists in a vacuum. Instead, such controversy occurs within a context. Frequently the controversy or a subset of the controversy has been vigorously debated in the past. Before you can begin to apply analytical formulas, you must have a thorough knowledge of the context in which the controversy exists. A study of the background of the controversy can provide the definitional, historical, and value perspectives that are necessary starting points for the discovery of issues. The study of the background of a controversy is a five-step process, which includes understanding the terminology of the controversy, consideration of the immediate cause for discussion, examination of the nature and history of the present belief, examination of the nature and history of the proposed belief, and discovery of common ground.

Understanding the Terminology of the Controversy

Scholars of speech communication have increasingly recognized the importance of language in understanding conflict. Careful analysis of the language strategies used by the participants in a controversy helps us to understand the precise focus of the controversy. Such analysis may also be helpful in discovering the perceptual and value positions of the various advocates in a given controversy.

The definition of terms affects every step of the argumentation process—from initial research to final judgment. Your understanding of the critical terms of the proposition will be central to your overall analysis. It will determine what materials are researched and what arguments are selected. If you are committed to a particular advocacy position, you may be tempted to select a particular definition that gives your side of the controversy a perceived advantage. Although the selection of such a self-serving definition may sometimes be justified, it is wise to remember that all definitions are subject to argument and must be defended.

In general, the appropriateness of competing definitions is determined by comparing definitions to see which is better. A variety of standards may be used to determine the better definition. Four standards are most frequently applied.

1. The *field context* standard suggests that a word or phrase is best defined by discovering how experts in a particular field of study use the word or phrase. For example, the word "bar" may be defined in many ways. However, if the term appears in a statement concerning the practice of law, the field context standard would justify defining "bar" as "the members of the legal profession who have been certified to practice law."

2. The standard of *grammatical syntax* indicates that debate propositions are phrased in such a way as to correspond to the rules of grammar and syntax. Consider the following proposition: "Resolved: That all U.S. military intervention in Central America is immoral." An advocate choosing to ignore grammar might argue that this proposition calls only for demonstrating the immorality of action that is "all U.S." or exclusively by the United States (as in the term "all-American") and for ignoring actions that involve cooperation between U.S. and Salvadoran soldiers. Such an interpretation violates the rules of grammar in that "all" in the proposition modifies "U.S. military intervention" and not just "U.S." A hyphen would have been used between "all" and "U.S." if the first interpretation were intended.

3. The standard that *each word must be meaningful* implies that each and every word in a proposition is purposeful. We assume that defining the words and phrases of a proposition should not result in contradictions and should not render meaningless other words or phrases in the proposition. The standard that each word must be meaningful became an important issue in an academic debate on the proposition "Resolved: That a unilateral freeze by the United States on the production and

development of nuclear weapons would be desirable." The team defending the proposition argued that the United States already had nuclear superiority over the Soviet Union. The opposing team argued that the affirmative team was defending only half the proposition, limiting analysis to "production" and ignoring "development." The affirmative team countered by claiming that "production" and "development" are synonymous terms. The negative team was able to convince the judge that this interpretation rendered the term "development" meaningless. Advocates must be sure to account for *all* the words in the proposition.

4. The standard that *words must establish limits* stems from the belief that just as the purpose of a proposition is to limit debate, so, too, must words limit the proposition. Advocates who define words and phrases so broadly as to encompass virtually everything make it difficult for their opponents to prepare adequately. For example, advocates debating a proposition on labor unions would be guilty of violating this standard if they defined labor unions as "any collaboration by two or more citizens." Such an interpretation unreasonably broadens the meaning of the term "labor unions." Just as advocates should not define terms too broadly, they should not be overly restrictive in their definitions. Defining "labor unions" as "only organizations of unskilled workers" would likely represent too restrictive a definition.

Dictionaries are, of course, a good place to begin to study the meaning of terms. Advocates often start with such general dictionaries as *Webster's* and *Random House.* These dictionaries define terms in order of usage, with most common definitions listed first and more obscure definitions listed last. Field-specific dictionaries are of even greater value in defining terms used in such fields as law, politics, economics, and science. Virtually every discipline has its own specialized dictionaries. A variety of guides to reference books that will help in locating specialized dictionaries can be found in most libraries. Advocates debating a proposition involving legal issues should examine *Black's Law Dictionary, Corpus Juris Secundum, Words and Phrases,* and *Dictionary of Economic and Statistical Terms.* Each of these dictionaries provides numerous definitions for terms frequently used in the field and provides the various contexts for each definition. Advocates should attempt to obtain the most recent edition available because terms may rapidly change meaning.

Dictionaries provide generalized definitions which may or may not be consistent with the way in which the term is used in a particular dispute. Therefore the language of the controversy itself should be considered. Examine state and federal laws that use the term, court cases on the issue, and debates on the controversy contained in government documents and journals. When examining such material ask: What meanings are assigned to the various terms in the controversy? Do all sides use the same terms to convey the same meanings? What value judgments are revealed in the language used to define the controversy? Answers to these questions will help the advocate focus on the center of the controversy as well as discover the points of clash in the debate.

Consideration of the Immediate Causes for Discussion

After understanding the definition of terms, the next question to ask is: Why has this particular controversy become important at this point in time? An answer to this question provides the advocate with an initial view of the contemporary events and values that have raised a specific controversy to a level of social significance. It is not at all uncommon for a single event or series of events to raise a controversy from obscurity to the forefront of our thoughts. A disaster in the U.S. space program leads us to ask if the benefits of human exploration of space outweigh the risk to human lives. An airplane hijacking sparks international debate on the effectiveness of measures to combat terrorism. A political scandal rekindles debate on public morality. An unwanted pregnancy of a friend or relative leads us to reconsider our personal position on abortion. Although the analysis of any controversy must go much deeper than consideration of the immediate causes for discussion, such a consideration will lead the advocate to discover the events that are of immediate concern.

Examination of the Nature and History of the Present Belief

One of the most dangerous temptations involved in analyzing any controversy is to consider *only* the contemporary circumstances that give rise to proposals for change. Every controversy, no matter how contemporary, is rooted in the past. In order to gain insight into the nature of an existing belief, the advocate must place the controversy in perspective by considering its origins and historical development. An analysis of the contemporary problems in the Middle East, for instance, is misguided without an understanding of the historical events leading up to the creation of the state of Israel and the significant events from that time until the present. Understanding the specific rationale for an existing belief at different points in time helps us understand how the controversy developed and thus provides valuable insight into contemporary circumstances.

People often have a generalized sense that a problem exists. Environmental enthusiasts who decry the danger of nuclear power plants without an awareness or understanding of existing nuclear regulation serve neither the environmental cause nor themselves well. Before we can seriously demonstrate that nuclear power is unsafe, we must first examine the nature and effects of the current regulations imposed by the Nuclear Regulatory Commission and the Environmental Protection Agency. These agencies were established to protect our environment. Where have they succeeded? Where have they failed? Why have they failed? These are questions that must be answered before any reasonable analysis of the current situation can be developed.

Examination of the Nature and History of the Proposed Belief

Analysis of the nature and historical development is important not only when examining *existing* beliefs but also when examining *proposed* beliefs. Few proposed changes in belief are entirely new. Most have been considered in one form or another in the past. Examination of past controversies can provide insight into the potential strengths and weaknesses of such proposed beliefs. The notion that the Mafia was involved in the assassination of President John F. Kennedy is a belief that has been repeatedly advanced by some authors. The morality of premarital sexual relations is a controversy that has been the subject of extensive debate on and off during the past fifty years. Examination of these past controversies is a vital part of the analysis of any contemporary debate concerning these issues.

Discovery of Common Ground

A final element of the study of the background of the controversy is the discovery of common ground. Common ground is composed of those facts or values on which both sides in the controversy agree. Large areas of common ground may be discovered in every fact/value controversy. In a fact/value debate over the seriousness of the AIDS epidemic, both sides might agree on the present extent of the problem, but disagree on its likely future spread. The identification of common ground in any controversy serves to narrow the potential issues and to spare wasting time researching and analyzing areas that will not become important clashes in the controversy.

STASIS FORMULA FOR FACT/VALUE PROPOSITIONS

We frequently debate propositions involving questions of fact/value. Argument in a court of law normally centers on the determination of fact—for example, is the defendant guilty? Argument in a political campaign often focuses on questions of value—for example, is a particular political philosophy good? The analytical formula useful in analyzing questions of fact/value is known as *stasis analysis*.[1] This approach is a codified scheme for investigating the background of a controversy involving fact/value. Stasis analysis provides four frames of reference that are useful in hunting for arguments in controversies involving fact/value. These four reference points are the frames of jurisdiction, definition, existence of fact, and quality.

The Frame of Jurisdiction

The frame of jurisdiction asks the question: Is the advocate of change topical? In order for argument to take place in an orderly manner, advocates must know precisely what ground is available to them. The frame of jurisdiction becomes a hunting ground for arguments that suggest what ground belongs to the affirmative and what ground belongs to the negative. The proposition identifies the judgments available to the advocates of change, the affirmative, and thus proscribes their ground. All judgments outside of the proposition are available to those opposed to the change.

The advocate of change must carefully consider the terms of the proposition and may select only those judgments that derive from legitimate interpretations of the words and phrases contained in the proposition. The use of illegitimate interpretations results in the advocate's proposal being considered not germane or not topical. Parallels for the frame of jurisdiction or topicality are found in

our courts and legislative bodies. The various courts in the United States have limits placed on their jurisdiction. Grossman and Wells (147) write that the "Court should consider first in every case whether or not it has jurisdiction. If it does not, then it has no power to decide the case on its merits."[2] For example, a case filed in a criminal court seeking damages under civil law would be dismissed because the criminal court does not have jurisdiction in the matter. Even though the case may have merit, it would not be considered by the criminal court. Similarly, a piece of legislation calling for the state of Nebraska to institute a mandatory seat belt law would not be considered by the U.S. Congress because that body lacks jurisdiction to adopt a law for a particular state. The issue of jurisdiction or topicality thus becomes a preconsideration issue, one that must be resolved before the merits of a particular case may be considered.

Advocates considering the issue of jurisdiction must look to the rules for debate in the particular arena in which they are operating in order to determine the standard for jurisdiction. Jurisdiction in the U.S. Congress is determined by looking at such documents as the Constitution of the United States and the procedural rules for debate in the Senate and the House. College debaters participating in the National Debate Tournament, sponsored by the American Forensic Association, operate under a guideline that indicates that the "better definition" among advocates, determined on the basis of the weight of analysis and evidence drawn from experts in the field of the proposition, is used to determine jurisdiction or topicality.[3] Collegiate debaters participating in tournaments sponsored by the Cross Examination Debate Association are instructed to use definitions consistent with the intent of the debate proposition.[4] Individuals engaged in public debate often find that they are limited to definitions judged reasonable by the audience to whom they are speaking. Advocates must look to the arena in which they are debating to discover the appropriate standards for determining jurisdiction.

The frame of jurisdiction was an important consideration at a meeting of a university's Board of Regents. The meeting's agenda indicated that a motion would be offered calling for a small state college to become part of the university system. After the motion was made and a speaker was presenting arguments in favor of the action, a regent interrupted with a point of order. "Board members," she said, "I object to consideration of this question because only the State Legislature has the authority and jurisdiction to determine what units are to be included in the university system." After consulting the bylaws of the Board of Regents, the board president ruled the motion out of order and all debate on the issue ceased.

The Frame of Definition

After determining that the advocate of change is operating within the jurisdiction of the proposition, the next step is to consider the frame of definition. Before the existence of a fact or the validity of a value judgment can be established, the nature of that fact or value must be identified. Let us suppose we are serving on the jury at a federal trial involving sedition. Before we can determine whether or not the defendant is guilty of sedition, we must understand what sedition means according to federal criminal statutes. If we claim that a particular academic major leads to greater career success, we will have to define what is meant by career success. If we are arguing that our favorite college football player deserves to win the Heisman trophy, we must look to the criteria used for selecting Heisman winners. Whatever the context of the controversy—be it law, selection of college majors, or sports—it is impossible to establish a fact or value without first determining the nature of the fact or value.

The criteria or definitions used as a basis for further analysis are generally derived from the specific subject matter of the controversy and from the arena in which the controversy occurs. Many controversies occur within arenas governed by a precise body of standards for determining the selection of definitions and criteria. In U.S. criminal courts, judges, lawyers, and jurors use extremely precise definitions of such actions as murder, assault, and rape. Definitions, along with a history of the legislation and case law establishing the definitions, can be found in *Black's Law Dictionary* and *Corpus Juris Secundum*. Rigorous definitions and criteria typify courts, legislative bodies, regulatory agencies, and the sciences. In each of these arenas the act of inquiry requires the advocate to discover the criteria and definitions judged acceptable by the professional community in which the controversy occurs.

Definition was critical in a court case involving a doctor who was seeking the court's permission to remove a terminally ill patient from the respirator that was sustaining her life. Witness after witness, including the woman's parents, testified that the patient was being condemned to a life without quality—that for all intents and purposes, the patient was already dead. The judge's decision was that despite the hopelessness of the situation and despite that the patient was doomed to a vegetative existence, the court must render a decision based on fact, not on emotion or compassion. The judge pointed out that the law clearly and precisely defines life, and that according to all legal definitions of life, removing the patient from the respirator constitutes murder.

Controversies also occur in arenas that do not have codified definitions or criteria. Consider, for example, debate in a local community that was selected as a potential site for a radioactive waste disposal facility. Many residents argued that the facility would not be safe. The debate seemed unresolvable until one resident suggested that the town needed to agree on what constitutes a safe or acceptable risk. To deal with this issue the residents called in nuclear waste experts who convinced them that a safe facility was one in which the chances of accidental release of radioactivity was less than one in one million. Having agreed on a definition of safety used by a number of federal regulatory agencies, the residents then went ahead with the debate.

Advocates have an important responsibility to select appropriate standards and definitions on which to base their judgments. When arguing in an arena with carefully established standards and criteria, the advocate must be aware of the sources for such information. Lawyers and legislators rely on previous court decisions and legislative acts. Scientists rely on previous experimentation. When arguing in an arena that lacks established standards and criteria, the advocate should rely on the general principles of argumentation, the criteria and standards used in analogous situations, as well as on the personal values of the advocate and audience. For example, public arguments regarding euthanasia or abortion require the advocate to turn to philosophers, religious scholars, noted jurists, and community standards in an effort to define murder.

The frame of definition suggests that we must know what it is we are looking for before we can find it. Critical terms in the statement of fact/value must be defined.

The Frame of Existence of Fact

Many people believe that a fact is something uncontroversial—something self-evident. Although it is true that some facts are self-evident, it is important to note that a fact is established not by determining widespread acceptance but by applying relevant criteria or definitions. A prosecutor, in attempting to determine whether or not to charge someone with murder, must determine if the available evidence is sufficient to meet the legal definition of murder. A mother, trying to decide if her son is mature enough to use the family car on a date, will examine the boy's attitudes and behavior in past situations to see if they reveal the characteristics of maturity. A doctor, in determining if a patient is dead or alive, will examine her patient's heartbeat, respiration, and brain activity to see if they conform to the medical criteria for determining the existence of life.

As in the frame of definition, the nature of the subject matter and the arena in which the controversy occurs guide the advocate in discovering appropriate arguments. In a court of law to establish that a defendant is guilty of sedition requires the prosecution to demonstrate that the defendant's actions conform to the legal definition of sedition. To demonstrate this the prosecutor would present witnesses who could testify about the defendant's motives—that the defendant intended to overthrow the government of the United States. The prosecutor would also present physical evidence that the defendant had acquired the means by which to assault the government—automatic weapons, armed forces, and the like. Finally, the prosecutor would present witnesses who observed the defendant engage in various acts of sedition—assassination of federal officials, destruction of federal property, disruption of federal activity. By addressing the criteria of motives, means, and actions, the prosecutor demonstrates that sedition has in fact occurred.

It is important to note that the issues relevant to the frame of existence of fact are not concerned simply with the existence of random facts; rather, the issues center around the conformity of the facts to the established criteria. Thus, the frame of existence of fact directs the advocate to look for those conditions, circumstances, or facts that are relevant to the criteria or definition. When the available facts conform to the criteria, the advocate can usually be said to have established a case.

The Frame of Quality

The frame of quality alerts the advocate that there may be special criteria or unusual facts that need to be considered before a conclusion can be reached. Conclusions must sometimes be tempered by an examination of the situation from a different perspective.

Courts of law recognize the frame of quality by permitting the plea of innocent because of insanity. When the plea is entered, the prosecution must be prepared to establish all the usual issues in a case for that crime and, in addition, must address itself to the special quality of insanity. This special consideration may change the perspective of the jury and its ultimate judgment. The jury may determine that a murder occurred and that the defendant committed the murder. Despite this finding of fact, the jury may decide the defendant to be innocent by reason of insanity.

Consider, for example, a very unusual case heard by a university judicial board. The board was convened to hear a case in which a professor charged a student with cheating on a test. Under university regulations, cheating could result in the student's being expelled. The board heard evidence from the professor that established the student had indeed cheated. The student admitted that he had cheated. Yet, the judicial board, after considering some very special circumstances in the case, declared the student innocent. The decision was based on testimony that the professor had encouraged his students to cheat, telling them that no one passed his tests unless they did cheat and that cheating was fine provided that one was clever enough not to get caught.

In effect, the frame of quality directs the advocate to look beyond the normal frames of reference to consider unusual circumstances and concepts. Valid judgments must be based on appropriate perspectives.

Each of the following examples emphasizes a particular frame of stasis analysis. For each example identify whether the issue involves jurisdiction, definition, existence of fact, or quality.

1. The movie *Friday the 13th Part 42* deserves to win the Academy Award for best picture. The movie's box office sales are the highest of any movie of the year. Movie critics as well as the public have claimed that the movie is the best picture of the year. The film has won numerous awards in foreign and domestic film competitions.

2. Mrs. Clark is an electrician working on the construction of an office building. She is told by the construction supervisor that she must assist the bricklayers before she can begin work on the electrical wiring. Mrs. Clark decided to complain to the president of the bricklayer union, claiming she was being asked to perform duties that are outside her job description. The president of the bricklayer union refused to help Mrs. Clark, telling her to take the complaint to the electrical workers union.

3. Susie studied very hard for her final exam in History 101. She needs an "A" on the final in order to earn an "A" for the class. On the morning of the exam Susie feels terribly ill. She visits the Student Health Center where the doctor tells her she has the flu and needs bed rest. Susie returns to her dorm room and calls the history professor. "Professor Reynolds, I know you have a policy that does not allow make-up exams. However, I just returned from the health center and the doctor told me to rest in bed. Is there any way you will allow me to take the exam at another time?" Professor Reynolds replies: "Given the special circumstances, I will change my policy on make-up tests. Stop by my office when you're feeling better. Be sure to bring me a note from the health center."

4. "Plagiarism is the act of passing off the words and ideas of someone else as if they are your own," Professor Herbert tells Sandy. "You have admitted to me that you know the speech belongs to a student who took a speech class last year. Since you admit that you committed plagiarism, I have no alternative but to fail you in my class."

The stasis system, then, provides four frames of reference from which to view propositions of fact/value. The frames of jurisdiction, definition, existence of fact, and quality can help an advocate know where to begin the search for issues and may suggest the general substance of those issues.

SUMMARY

There are two general approaches to the discovery of issues: the investigation of the background of a controversy and the application of analytical formulas.

Examination of the background of a controversy requires the advocate to understand the terminology of the controversy, consider the immediate causes of the controversy, examine the nature and history of the present belief, examine the nature and history of the proposed belief, and discover common ground.

The stasis formula is an analytical method that is specifically applicable to propositions involving fact/value judgments. The formula provides four frames of reference from which statements of fact and value may be examined. These four reference points are the frames of jurisdiction, definition, existence of fact, and quality.

NOTES

[1]The concept of stasis or status dates back to classical Greece and Rome in the writings of such rhetoricians as Quintilian, Hermagoras, and Cicero. Two particularly informative essays on the subject are by Hultzen and Dieter.

[2]There are a few exceptions in which a court may postpone considering jurisdiction or actively alter jurisdiction (Grossman and Wells, 150-52).

[3]Charter of the National Debate Tournament, Rule 4, Section E, Subsection 3, Part b, 1985.

[4]See, for example, Tomlinson (99).

SELECTED BIBLIOGRAPHY

DEATHERAGE, LORAL, and MICHAEL PFAU. *Arguing Topicality: Perspectives and Techniques.* Kansas City, MO: National Federation of State High School Associations, 1985.

DIETER, OTTO A. L. "Stasis." *Speech Monographs* 17 (1950): 345-69.

FLANINGAM, CARL D. "Value-Centered Argument and the Development of Decision Rules." *Journal of the American Forensic Association* 19 (1982): 107-14.

GROSSMAN, JOEL B., and RICHARD S. WELLS. *Constitutional Law and Judicial Policy Making.* New York: Wiley, 1971.

HERBECK, DALE, and JOHN KATSULAS. "The Affirmative Topicality Burden: Any Reasonable Example of the Resolution." *Journal of the American Forensic Association* 22 (1985): 133-45.

HULTZEN, LEE S. "Status in Deliberative Analysis." In *The Rhetorical Idiom: Essays in Rhetoric, Oratory, Language, and Drama,* edited by Donald C. Bryant. Ithaca, NY: Cornell University Press, 1958.

McDONALD, DANIEL. *The Language of Argument.* 3d ed. New York: Harper & Row, 1980.

MATLON, RONALD J. "Debating Propositions of Value." *Journal of the American Forensic Association* 14 (1978): 194-204.

PRENTICE, DIANA, and JACK KAY. *The Role of Values in Policy Debate.* Kansas City, MO: National Federation of State High School Associations, 1986.

TOMLINSON, JAMES E. "Current Issues in the Cross Examination Debate Association." *National Forensic Journal* 4 (1986): 91-103.

WENZEL, JOSEPH W. "Toward a Rationale for Value-Centered Argument." *Journal of the American Forensic Association* 12 (Winter 1977): 150-58.

ZAREFSKY, DAVID. "Criteria for Evaluating Non-Policy Argument." In *Perspective on Non-Policy Arguments,* edited by Don Brownlee, 9-16. Long Beach, CA: (Cross Examination Debate Association), 1980.

STUDY QUESTIONS

1. Why is it important to precisely define the terms used in a controversy?

2. Several standards are available for determining the better definition. Which of these standards seem most appropriate in arguments in the scientific community? In the law? When arguing with friends? In public policy-making?

3. Two ways of analyzing a controversy are analysis of the controversy's background and the application of the stasis formula. Why should the advocate use *both* of these methods?

EXERCISES

1. Using the current Cross Examination Debate Association proposition or any proposition of fact/value, discuss the five elements of background analysis.
   a. The terminology of the proposition.
   b. The immediate causes for discussion.
   c. The nature and history of the present belief.
   d. The nature and history of the proposed belief.
   e. The possible sources of common ground.
2. Phrase a proposition of fact/value for which the stasis formula frame of quality would be particularly relevant. Briefly discuss the ways in which the quality frame of analysis modifies the definitional and existence of fact frames.
3. The word "fact" is used in many fields. Scientists talk about facts. Religious scholars use the term. The field of law requires that facts be discovered. How would you go about discovering the meaning of the word "fact" in each of these fields?
4. Find an article written by someone who argues that abortion is immoral. What stasis frame is emphasized in the article?

ANSWERS TO PRACTICUM

1. The frame of definition.
2. The frame of jurisdiction.
3. The frame of quality.
4. The frame of existence of fact.

CHAPTER FOUR
ANALYSIS OF POLICY CONTROVERSIES

Policy propositions require us to examine facts and values as they relate to a particular course of action. In this chapter we present a number of tools that help the advocate discover issues in propositions of policy. As is the case with fact/value propositions, discovering issues in policy propositions involves two approaches. These are (1) analysis of the background of the controversy and (2) application of analytical formulas to the controversy.

As we approach policy propositions we must remember the relationship of fact/value judgments to policy considerations. Each issue of a policy proposition is in effect a fact/value proposition. The policy proposition ''Resolved: That condoms should be freely distributed in all public schools in the United States'' involves a series of fact/value judgments. We would use stasis analysis to discover the proof requirements for such issues as the harms of unwanted pregnancies and sexually transmitted diseases, the ability of condoms to prevent pregnancy and disease, and the value judgments involved in the public schools' distributing condoms. Stasis analysis is thus essential to policy propositions as well as to fact/value propositions.

ANALYSIS OF THE BACKGROUND OF THE CONTROVERSY

The process for analyzing the background of a policy controversy is identical to the process described in Chapter 3 for analyzing the background of a fact/value proposition. The advocate uses the same five-step process, which includes understanding the terminology of the controversy, consideration of the immediate causes for discussion, examination of the nature and history of the present policy (or belief), examination of the nature and history of the proposed policy (or belief), and discovery of common ground.

Students debating the intercollegiate debate topic that called for the federal government of the United States to significantly expand its exploration and/or development of the space beyond the earth's mesosphere began their investigation at the definitional level. The students used science dictionaries and documents from the National Aeronautics and Space Administration (NASA) to discover the meaning of such terms as "exploration and development," "space," and "earth's mesosphere." After understanding the terminology of the controversy, the students explored current newspapers and newsmagazines to discover the immediate causes for discussion. They read about how events such as the *Challenger* disaster, in which a U.S. space shuttle exploded, tragically killing all seven crew members, had slowed the NASA space program. Students next spent time reading about the formation of NASA, enabling them to examine the nature and history of the present policy of space exploration and development. Students then turned to the proposed policy, looking at past congressional debates on unsuccessful attempts to increase space exploration and development. They also found articles written by scientists and government decision-makers who proposed that the government should expand the space program with such efforts as colonizing space and doing more deep-space exploration. The debates and articles allowed students to examine the nature and history of the proposed policy. Finally, the students noted that there was considerable agreement on the need to increase exploration, but that most disagreement involved the need to expand development. Students thus discovered common ground.

APPLICATION OF ANALYTICAL FORMULAS

The in-depth study of the background of a controversy should provide needed insight into the substance of a proposition. The application of analytical formulas to propositions of policy helps to carry the analysis process a step further by relating that substance to the specific requirements of the arena of argument. The formulas provide a means of categorizing arguments and of viewing the crucial relationships within a controversy.

The two formulas described below respond to the unique characteristics of different policy situations. The *stock issues formula* provides a systematic approach to questions of policy which can then be focused into a clear statement of the specific course of action being advocated. The *cost-benefit systems analysis formula* is adapted to controversies involving specific comparison of a multitude of policy options.

Stock Issues Analysis for Propositions of Policy

Although the five-step process suggested for the study of the background of a controversy provides vital insights into the nature of the policy proposition under examination, it does not really constitute a systematic methodology for breaking the proposition down into its vital component parts. In searching for such a methodology it is imperative that we examine more closely the obligations of those who advocate change in policy. Any methodology for breaking down propositions of policy must grow out of the nature of policy propositions in order to be universally applicable. A more careful examination of the nature of policy propositions reveals that certain specific obligations exist in the advocacy of any specific change of policy. The identification of these specific obligations provides a methodology for approaching the analysis of propositions of policy called the "stock issues."

Stock issues, very simply, *are hunting grounds for arguments. They provide general phrasing of potential issues that correspond to the inherent obligations of the advocate of change.* Since each of the stock issue categories corresponds to an obligation of the advocate of policy change, each of these categories constitutes a vital area of concern—an area in which the advocate of change may lose his or her case. Although there are several ways of structuring these obligations into an analytical scheme, the fivefold classification of jurisdiction, ill, blame, cure, and cost seems to be the clearest. The *stock issue of jurisdiction* derives from the obligation of advocates of change to provide proposals consistent with the terminology (scope) of the proposition. The *stock issue of ill* grows out of the obligation of advocates to show a significant past, present, or future problem or harm. The *stock issue of blame* grows out of the obligation to relate that ill causally to the basic structure or philosophy of present policy. The *stock issue of cure* grows out of the obligation of advocates to outline a specific plan of action and demonstrate how it will solve the problem of the ill. The *stock issue of cost* grows out of the obligation to respond to disadvantages. In developing these stock issues concepts, the proposal to substitute a guaranteed annual cash income for the present welfare system will be used as an illustrative case study. The case study uses the proposition "Resolved: That the federal government should replace the existing welfare system with a guaranteed annual cash income for all U.S. citizens."

The stock issue of jurisdiction   The stock issue of jurisdiction asks the question, Is the affirmative proposal topical? The process for answering this question uses the same concepts we presented in Chapter 3 in our discussion of the *frame of jurisdiction* in the stasis formula for fact/value propositions. In policy propositions we look to the specific plan offered by the affirmative in our effort to determine jurisdiction. If the specific plan is outside the jurisdiction of the proposition, it is said to be nontopical. Jurisdiction is determined by careful definition of the terms of the proposition. As indicated in Chapter 3 in our discussion of the terminology of a controversy, the standards useful in determining appropriate definitions include *field context, grammatical syntax, each word must be meaningful,* and *words must establish limits.*

In the guaranteed annual cash income proposition, advocates must start by examining the terms of the proposition in order to determine what ground belongs to the affirmative and what ground belongs to the negative. The academic fields of political science and economics offer rather precise definitions of all the terms

identified in the proposition. For example, political science defines the federal government as a union of states, represented by the U.S. Congress, the president, and the Supreme Court. Thus the advocate must propose a solution at the federal level. A plan that called for the five states with the largest percentage of poverty to guarantee an income to their citizens is not within the jurisdiction of the affirmative.

The stock issue of ill   The stock issue of ill asks the question, Are there significant harms or ills or needs within the present system? There must be a *felt difficulty* with the present policy. For the advocate of change, ill becomes a hunting ground for arguments that suggest the existing way of doing things results in serious internal problems or fails to achieve certain important goals. The advocate must demonstrate that the ill is a significant problem. Significance can be established *qualitatively* by showing the *impact* of the ill as well as *quantitatively* by showing the *extent* of the ill. For the defender of the present system, the ill issue becomes a place to look for arguments to deny the existence of harms or to minimize their significance.

Advocates of a guaranteed annual cash income as a replacement for the welfare system argue a variety of *felt difficulties* with the existing system. Many argue, for instance, that the existing welfare system fails to provide a subsistence income for a large proportion of its recipients. The number of people affected establishes quantitative significance by showing the extent of the problem. Qualitative significance is established by showing that living below subsistence levels has impacts such as starvation and malnutrition. If the failure to provide

subsistence income can be proven to be widespread and to result in significant harms, the advocate has met the obligation to establish the ill issue.

A decision to make a change in a course of action may be motivated not only by internal problems within the existing system but also by the present system's failure to satisfy certain external goals. Many advocates of a guaranteed annual cash income believe that government aid should be administered so as to protect the dignity and self-respect of the poor. They argue that the present system demeans the poor by requiring inspections of their expenditures and by providing direct goods and services. If the goal of avoiding practices which degrade can be established as a significant consideration in analyzing the welfare structure, the advocate may have found a ground for establishing the system's failure to meet a desirable objective.

The stock issue of ill, then, identifies a vital area of analysis because no change in policy will be made unless it can be demonstrated that the existing system fails to achieve its own primary goals or unless it can be demonstrated that the system does not achieve other desirable objectives.

The stock issue of blame   The stock issue of blame asks the question, Is the present system inherently responsible for the existence of the ills? The existence of certain problems or the failure to achieve certain goals does not necessarily mean that present policies have failed or that a new course of action is required. A totally new policy approach is warranted only if it can be shown that *by its very nature* the present system *cannot* (structure), *will not* (attitude), or *should not* (philosophy) overcome the problems or achieve the goals. In other words, the advocate of change has the obligation to prove that the harms in the present system are inherent—that the solution of harms or achievement of goals is precluded by the present system's structure, deep-seated attitudes, or philosophy.

The advocate attempting to establish the blame or inherency issue must be prepared to demonstrate one or more of the following conditions. First, the advocate may identify *structural inherency*. In this form of inherency, the advocate offers proof that the structure of the present system perpetuates certain ills or prevents the attainment of certain goals, thus demonstrating that the present system *cannot* solve the ills or attain the goals. Second, the advocate may identify *attitudinal inherency*. This form of inherency admits that the present system has the capability to solve the ills, but claims that the system *will not* do so because of a deeply rooted attitude. Simple opposition to an idea is not necessarily attitudinal inherency— the attitude must be one that is not easily subject to change. Often deep-rooted attitudes result from a perverse motive such as bias or self-interest. For example, advocates calling for the nationalization of the health care industry may argue that the reason the poor are denied medical care is because doctors are guided by the perverse motive of greed. Third, the advocate may identify *philosophical inherency*. This form of inherency requires the advocate to identify the overriding orientation of the existing system. Very often the philosophical commitment of the present system admits that the ills could be solved, but claims that the ills *should not* be solved because greater ills would result.

The identification of the inherent structural, philosophical, or attitudinal characteristics of a policy cannot be completely accomplished without establishing some reference point and that reference point is an opposing policy system. In other words, to determine the inherent nature of an existing system it is necessary to examine the basic values (philosophy or attitudes) and major components (structure) of that system in relation to the basic values and major components of an opposing policy.

By comparing the values and structural components of public assistance with those of a guaranteed annual income, three inherent differences in the nature of the two systems may be identified. Structurally, the existing system of public assistance provides the poor with in-kind services (medical care and public housing) and controlled spending (food stamps and clothing allowances). The structure of a guaranteed income involves the provision of unsupervised cash payments. Attitudinally, the system of public assistance is influenced by the prevalent public attitude that a person who does not work is not as worthy as a person who does work. The attitude underlying the guaranteed annual income is that all citizens are equally worthy. Philosophically, the public assistance system operates with the paternalistic belief that many of the poor are incapable of choosing what is best and, therefore, it is the responsibility of government to establish restrictions on payments. The guaranteed annual income imposes only a financial criterion for assistance, adopting the philosophy that government paternalism is wrong.

The identification of the inherent characteristics of the present system is only part of the analytical responsibility imposed by the blame issue. To complete the blame analysis, the inherent characteristics of the present system must be causally linked to the continued existence of the ills. An affirmative might argue, for example, that the inherent feature of public assistance is the public's attitude that those who do not work are less worthy than those who do work. The affirmative claims that it is this public attitude that is responsible for (causes) inadequate benefit levels. Welfare's philosophical commitment to assist only the deserving poor could be identified as the reason why large numbers of poor families receive no assistance at all. The present system's philosophical and structural preference for services and vendor payments could be said to cause the poor to feel demeaned.

Within the stock issue of blame, then, the advocate of change is obligated to identify characteristics of the present policy that are inherent to its structure, attitude, or philosophy and to demonstrate the ways in which these characteristics are causally related to the ills of that policy. The opponent of change may seek to deny that the alleged inherent characteristics are, in fact, fundamental to the present system and suggest minor, nonstructural repairs or may accept the characteristics as inherent and deny the causal link to the ill. This area of analysis is crucial to the advocate because it is generally less costly to repair an existing system than it is to junk it for a completely new one.

The stock issue of cure The stock issue of cure asks the question, Will the affirmative proposal remove the ills of the present system? The cure issue shifts the focus of the analysis from a consideration of the existing policy to a consideration of the action proposed in the statement of the proposition. This stock issue identifies a hunting ground for arguments growing out of the advocate's obligation to outline a specific plan of action and to demonstrate how the plan will solve the specific ills and deal with the specific causal factors under consideration. Even if it can be demonstrated that a significant ill exists and is causally

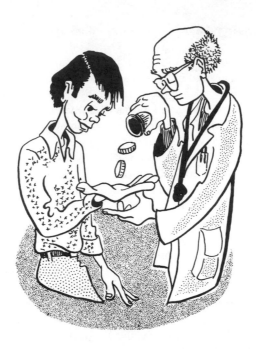

related to inherent features of the existing policies, a course of action that fails to guarantee a solution to the problem is not likely to be adopted.

The specific form and the degree of specificity of the cure will depend on the forum in which the proposition is being debated. In a legislative body, the cure may be quite detailed and take the form of a bill or law. In academic debate, the plan, generally outlined in a minute or so, includes a statement of specific mandates for change—an administrative agency, a method of funding, and enforcement provisions. In a public forum, the cure may be presented with even fewer details, although advocates may refer to specific pieces of legislation.

Advocates of a guaranteed annual income generally outline proposals that involve total federal financing and administration of a guarantee to all U.S. citizens of a minimum yearly cash payment. The proposals generally stipulate a specific minimum income level based on family size and geographic location, a procedure for determining income levels and for distributing funds, and a mechanism for raising the necessary money to finance the program. Advocates argue that by substituting a totally federal program for a program committed to state and local administration, racial discrimination can be eliminated. They further argue that a program of total federal financing will equalize the financial burden among the states and allow even the residents of less affluent states to receive subsistence benefits. By guaranteeing this level of subsistence to all citizens, the program is said to eliminate the problem of poor families who receive no welfare assistance at all. Finally, by providing the assistance in cash, it is argued, the program eliminates the ''demeaning'' control over spending, which characterizes the present welfare system.

Within the cure issue, opponents of a guaranteed annual income seek to demonstrate that the adoption of such a program will not alleviate the alleged

ills. They may argue, for example, that the affirmative proposal will not be sufficient to eliminate the ills and that other intervening factors, such as poor spending habits, will cause the ills to continue.

The stock issue of cure, therefore, provides a hunting ground for arguments
that suggest the change in policy will or will not achieve its stated or implied objectives. Such considerations are crucial to the advocate of change since a course
of action that fails to solve the problems of existing policies provides no solution
at all.

The stock issue of cost   The stock issue of cost asks the question, Do the
advantages of the affirmative proposal outweigh the disadvantages? Any change
in policy will incur some cost, some disruption, some social or material burden.
The advocate of change is obligated to be prepared to demonstrate that the disadvantages of the proposed change are not so great as to outweigh any benefits.
Frequently a course of action clearly cures a problem inherent in the present
system, but must be rejected because of its excessive social or material cost. Just
as the advocate of change must demonstrate the significance of an ill through extent and impact, so too must the opponent of change prove the negative impact
and extent of a disadvantage.

Opponents of a guaranteed annual income forward a variety of cost
arguments. First, they argue that the plan creates a work disincentive, providing
evidence that many people will simply not work if a comfortable standard of living is guaranteed by the government. A second cost argument is the claim that
such a guarantee will perpetuate poverty by reducing retraining incentives and
eliminating the mechanism by which many poor people work their way off the
welfare roles.

Each of the following statements emphasizes a particular stock issue. For each statement, identify whether the issue involves jurisdiction, ill, blame, cure, or cost.

1. Federal funding and management of nursing homes would improve the quality of life for institutionalized elderly citizens.

2. Private nursing homes are profit motivated. The profit motivation leads them to cut corners and to get by with minimum care, supplies, and personnel.

3. The care the elderly receive in nursing homes is substandard. Many elderly people suffer and die because of the horrible conditions found in many privately owned nursing homes.

4. If the federal government were to take over nursing homes, there would need to be cuts in other federal programs. The federal government just does not have the money to run nursing homes in addition to maintaining a strong national defense. Increased federal funding of nursing homes will endanger the defense of the United States.

5. Nursing homes are defined as "institutions that provide, on a long-term basis, specialized medical and custodial care to individuals unable to provide for their own needs."

The advocate of change is obligated to respond to negative cost arguments by denying their existence, minimizing their importance, or demonstrating that they are outweighed by the benefits of the affirmative proposal. The case for a proposed course of action can be lost if the cost of that action is as significant, or more significant, than the ill it is designed to cure.

The stock issues of jurisdiction, ill, blame, cure, and cost, therefore, constitute a systematic approach for breaking a proposition of policy into its component parts. The stock issues identify the inherent responsibilities of the advocate and thus suggest the general areas that must be addressed in a substantive way by the real issues. The real issues may be more specifically worded and differently structured, but the stock issues concepts will be contained within them.

Cost-Benefit Systems Analysis for Propositions of Policy

In recent years there has been a growing sophistication of analysis in public policy decision-making. Today's governmental and business decision-making often reflects the merger of two analytical schemes: cost-benefit analysis and systems analysis.[1]

Cost-benefit analysis reflects an attempt to tighten up decision-making by requiring a rigorous method for determining the precise costs and benefits of competing policy solutions to problems. Viewed from the framework of stock issues analysis, cost-benefit analysis focuses on the cure and cost issues. Insofar as possible, the cost-benefit analyst quantifies the costs and benefits of various policy alternatives and seeks to devise the optimum solution.

Cost-benefit analysis has been called "the cornerstone of regulatory reform efforts" of three U.S. presidents: Ronald Reagan, Jimmy Carter, and Gerald

Ford (Meier, 287). The use of cost-benefit analysis in government was formally enacted in 1981, when the Office of Management and Budget adopted a policy for assessing the effects of proposed regulations on business. The policy requires a cost-benefit analysis for any regulation that would cost industry over one hundred million dollars. For an agency to propose a regulation, it must be able to show that the benefits exceed costs. For example, a regulation that cost industry five hundred million dollars would be assumed worthwhile if it, in some way, returned to society more than five hundred million dollars.

Cost-benefit analysis requires that costs and benefits be translated into quantifiable terms. This includes quantifying the value of items that previously have been viewed as unquantifiable. Government agencies charged with health and safety regulation are now required to set a monetary value on human life. For example, a human life may be assigned a value of two hundred fifty thousand dollars. A government regulation that cost industry twenty-five million dollars would have to save more than one hundred lives in order to be judged cost-beneficial. Economic reality places limits on how much government and industry can spend. For example, deaths and injuries caused by automobile accidents could be reduced by requiring car manufacturers to install air bags in cars. Automobile manufacturers have successfully prevented the National Highway Traffic Safety Administrtion from requiring air bags by claiming that the costs outweigh the benefits (Meier, 98).

Cost-benefit analysis often occurs within the systems analysis approach to decision-making, a method of analysis borrowed from the fields of economics and behavioral science. The pioneers of systems theory in academic debate, Brock, Chesebro, Cragan, and Klumpp (27), define a system as ''an assembly of objects

all of which are related to one another by some form of regular interaction or interdependence so that the assembly can be viewed as an organic organized whole.'' A *system* can be defined as *a whole that functions as a whole by virtue of the interdependence of its parts. Systems analysis,* in its simplest form, *is an attempt to study interacting components as a whole.*

A simple illustration may help to clarify these concepts. The U.S. federal government can be considered a system that functions as a whole by virtue of the interdependence of its parts (the executive, legislative, and judicial branches). A systems analysis of the federal government would be an analysis of these interacting components as they relate to each other to comprise what we call the federal government. Although systems analysis does involve breaking a whole down into its parts or components, those components are not analyzed independently, but rather as they interact within the framework of the whole system.

Systems analysis is especially appropriate when controversies are not sufficiently focused to permit the statement of a proposition in terms of a single proposed course of action. Such controversies typically center around relatively open-ended questions, and the participants are initially uncommitted to a specific policy. An excellent example of this type of controversy involves the educational system of the United States. Participants in this controversy raised numerous concerns regarding the quality of public education in the United States. This led to the question: What can be done to improve the quality of public education in the United States? Everyone involved in the controversy concerned themselves with the functioning of an existing system, but they did not focus on a comparison of two specific policies. Instead, they recognized that policy alternatives are multidimensional. Participants in the controversy applied systems analysis by debating the accepted and proposed goals of the public education system and by comparing, quantifying, and weighing the various costs and benefits associated with multiple policies that sought to improve the quality of education.

A variety of models and formulas exist that can be used in conducting a cost-benefit systems analysis of policy controversies. Regardless of the model or formula used, four questions are critical: (1) What components and relationships comprise the system? (2) What goals are and should be fulfilled by the system? (3) Whats costs and benefits are associated with alternative policies? (4) What is the optimum policy that emerges from a comparison of the costs and benefits of policy alternatives?

System components and relationships   The starting question for cost-benefit systems analysis is: *What components and relationships comprise the system?* Answering this question requires the investigator to identify precisely the system and its components and relationships. Identifying the system in which a controversy occurs is often self-evident. For example, in the controversy involving how to improve public education in the United States, the system involved is obviously the public schools.

After identifying the appropriate system or systems, cost-benefit systems analysis requires the identification of the major components that make up the system. Although every system contains an infinite number of potential components, the investigator must thoroughly research the system to discover the components that are essential to the system. In such analysis, components are not important so much for what *they are* as for what *they do*. In the example of the analysis involved in improving the public education system, one might identify such components as academic standards for students, certification standards for teachers, federal aid to education, local school boards, curriculum content, and compulsory education laws.

In addition to identifying components, cost-benefit systems analysis requires the investigator to understand the functional relationships that exist between the various components of the system. In the example of the analysis of improving public education, the components of academic standards for students, certification standards for schools, and so forth, are not important for what they *are* but for *how they relate to each other* in the total system. For example, it is important to understand the relationship between certification standards for teachers and academic achievement of students.

Goals of the system A second question that must be asked when engaging in cost-benefit systems analysis is: *What goals are and should be fulfilled by the system?* This question highlights the assumption of cost-benefit systems analysis that every system is purpose-oriented, that every system functions to achieve certain goals. For an evaluation of a system to take place, the goals of the system must be determined and placed in some priority order. Nothing is more difficult in the process than to make the value judgments that underlie goal determination and priority setting. Insofar as possible the value judgments must be quantified. The process of determining system goals has two aspects: (1) the discovery of the stated or implied goals of the existing system and (2) the determination of optimum system goals.

The discovery of the goals of the existing system involves an in-depth investigation into the stated goals of those who designed the system and of those who operate the system. Frequently, stated goals and actual goals may differ, so the process of assessing existing objectives may involve exhaustive research. If a system is to be evaluated fairly, however, it must first be evaluated in terms of its own goals.

The determination of optimum system goals involves evaluation rather than description. It may well be that a problem within a system is the result of inappropriate goals. The dropout rate from public schools, for instance, may increase because the public education system does not place enough emphasis on developing a curriculum that students see as relevant to their employment potential. Often the search for optimum system goals may lead to an examination of the larger systems of which the system under examination is only a part. Optimum system goals for the public education system, for example, may have to be found in an examination of the total educational and economic system.

Costs and benefits of alternative policies A third question fundamental to cost-benefit systems analysis is: *What costs and benefits are associated with alternative policies?* After identifying optimum goals of a system, the investigator generates a list of policy alternatives that potentially enable a system to better achieve its optimum goals.

Each of the policy alternatives is viewed as a new input into the system. The new inputs, in turn, must be assessed in terms of their effects on the various component relationships within the system and in terms of their ability to achieve system goals. It is at this stage the investigator must attempt to quantify precisely the costs and benefits associated with system change. For example, one of the possible methods for improving the quality of public education is to implement more rigorous academic standards in the areas of mathematics and science. Studies may be undertaken to demonstrate that such a proposal could enhance the future earning potential of 30 percent of students. However, this effect would have to be compared with the potential result that more students would drop out of school, thus negatively impacting on the system goal that all students receive an education.

Optimum policy   The fourth question involved in cost-benefit systems analysis is the most difficult: *What is the optimum policy that emerges from a comparison of the costs and benefits of policy alternatives?* At this stage the investigator shifts attention away from analysis and moves toward synthesis, attempting to pull together the previous assessment of system goals, policy costs, and policy benefits in an effort to propose the best policy for achieving the goals of the system.

Fundamental to this fourth stage is determining a *decision rule*—the cost-benefit ratio minimally sufficient for changing the system. For example, the decision rule of the Federal Aviation Administration, an agency dedicated to promoting airline safety, sets the cost-benefit ratio at one life (benefit) to $650,083 (cost). That is, to be viewed as worthwhile, an additional safety regulation that would save at least one human life must not cost more than $650,083. The decision rule is the starting point for determining optimum policy. After deciding on this rule, the investigator attempts to determine which combination of policies yields the greatest benefits with the least costs.

In sum, the combination of cost-benefit analysis and systems analysis provides an inductive model that is optimally useful for the analysis of controversies that have not yet been focused on a specific course of action. As a tool for the analysis of policy controversies it should be thought of as complementing the stock issues formula rather than as an alternative to stock issues. It is possible, and frequently desirable, to use the two formulas together. Although the stock issues approach has its primary usefulness in policy controversies that are clearly focused on a specific course of action, stock issues concepts are also useful in systems analysis. Likewise, cost-benefit and systems analysis, with their emphasis on precisely identifying costs and benefits and on the relationships of interdependent components within a system, can provide useful insights into the nature of an existing system even within the framework of a stock issues analysis.

SUMMARY

The analysis of issues is facilitated by the investigation of the background of the controversy and the application of analytical formulas. Examining the background of the controversy requires the advocate to understand the terminology of the controversy, consider the immediate causes of the controversy, examine the nature and history of present policy, examine the nature and history of the proposed policy, and discover common ground. The two analytical formulas for policy propositions are stock issues and cost-benefit systems analysis.

The stock issues provide an analytical formula for policy propositions that are clearly focused. The five stock issues are jursidiction, ill, blame, cure, and cost. Each of these categories corresponds to an inherent obligation of the advocate of policy change.

The cost-benefit systems analysis formula is adapted to policy controversies that are not yet focused on a specific policy proposal. Four considerations are essential in applying cost-benefit systems analysis: (1) identifying the components and relationships that comprise the system, (2) identifying the goals that are and should be fulfilled by the system, (3) identifying the costs and benefits associated with alternative policies, and (4) determining the optimum policy that emerges from comparing the costs and benefits of policy alternatives.

NOTES

[1]Cost-benefit analysis is used throughout public policy decision-making. Important works on cost-benefit analysis include those by Stokey and Zeckhauser, F. Thompson and Jones, M. Thompson, and Green. A key scholar in the development of systems theory is Ludwig von Bertalanffy. One of the best applications of systems analysis to academic debate is by Brock, Chesebro, Cragan, and Klumpp.

SELECTED BIBLIOGRAPHY

BROCK, BERNARD L., JAMES W. CHESEBRO, JOHN F. CRAGAN, and JAMES F. KLUMPP. *Public Policy Decision-Making: Systems Analysis and Comparative Advantages Debate.* New York: Harper & Row, 1973.

CHERWITZ, RICHARD A., and JAMES W. HIKINS. "Inherency as a Multidimensional Construct: A Rhetorical Approach to the Proof of Causation." *Journal of the American Forensic Association* 14 (Fall 1977): 82–90.

DEATHERAGE, LORAL., and MICHAEL PFAU. *Arguing Topicality: Perspectives and Techniques.* Kansas City, MO: National Federation of State High School Associations, 1985.

DIETER, OTTO A. L. "Stasis." *Speech Monographs* 17 (1950): 345–69.

GREEN, MARK J. "Cost-Benefit Analysis as a Mirage." In *Reforming Regulation,* edited by Timothy B. Clark, Marvin H. Kosters, and James C. Miller, 113–16. Washington: American Enterprise Institute.

HERBECK, DALE, and JOHN KATSULAS. *Paradigms of Debate.* Kansas City, MO: National Federation of State High School Associations, 1988.

HULTZEN, LEE S. "Status in Deliberative Analysis." In *The Rhetorical Idiom: Essays in Rhetoric, Oratory, Language, and Drama,* edited by Donald C. Bryant. Ithaca, NY: Cornell University Press, 1958.

LICHTMAN, ALLAN J., and DANIEL M. ROHRER. "The Logic of Policy Dispute." *Journal of the American Forensic Association* 16 (Spring 1980): 236–47.

MEIER, KENNETH J. *Regulation: Politics, Bureaucracy, and Economics.* New York: St. Martin's, 1985.

PRENTICE, DIANA, and JACK KAY. *The Role of Values in Policy Debate.* Kansas City, MO: National Federation of State High School Associations, 1985.

STOKEY, EDITH, and RICHARD ZECKHAUSER. *A Primer for Policy Analysis.* New York: Norton, 1978.

THOMAS, DAVID A., ed. "A Forum on Policy Systems Analysis." *Journal of the American Forensic Association* 22 (Winter 1986): 123–66.

THOMPSON, FRED, and L. R. JONES. *Regulatory Policy and Practices.* New York: Praeger, 1982.

THOMPSON, MARK S. *Benefit-Cost Analysis for Program Evaluation.* Beverly Hills: Sage, 1980.

VON BERTALANFFY, LUDWIG. *General System Theory: Foundations, Development, Applications.* New York: Braziller, 1968.

STUDY QUESTIONS

1. What are the differences between the concept of "issues" and the concept of "stock issues"?

2. Under what conditions would one prefer the cost-benefit systems analysis over stock issues analysis?

3. Critics of stock issues analysis claim that this method is inferior to cost-benefit systems analysis because it encourages a "static" view of reality as compared with the emphasis on "process" reality encouraged by cost-benefit systems analysis. Do you agree with this criticism? Why or why not?

4. Critics of cost-benefit systems analysis claim that this method is flawed because of the inability to quantify the value of human life and human suffering. Do you agree with this criticism? Why or why not?

5. Why is it important for individuals who are analyzing propositions of policy to be able to analyze propositions of judgment?

EXERCISES

1. Using the current National Debate Tournament proposition or any proposition of policy, discuss the five elements of background analysis.
   a. The terminology of the proposition.
   b. The immediate causes for discussion.
   c. The nature and history of the present belief.
   d. The nature and history of the proposed belief.
   e. The possible sources of common ground.

2. Using the current National Debate Tournament proposition or any proposition of policy, prepare an analysis of the existing system using the first two steps of the cost-benefit systems analysis method. Include in your analysis a diagram of the components, relationships, and goals of the system.

3. Obtain a copy of the June 8, 1988, *Congressional Record,* pages H4030–38. These pages contain a debate on the Pepper–Royal bill for long-term home health care. Which stock issues are emphasized by speakers in favor of the bill? Which stock issues are emphasized by speakers opposed to the bill?

4. Phrase a negative cost argument on the current National Debate Tournament proposition or on any policy proposition of your choosing and analyze it using the frames of stasis analysis.

ANSWERS TO PRACTICUM

1. Cure.
2. Blame.
3. Ill.
4. Cost.
5. Jurisdiction.

CHAPTER FIVE
THE NATURE OF
ARGUMENT

Even before babies begin to talk there are indications that they can make simple associations between the satisfaction of certain physical wants and the external environment. As babies grow into childhood and then adulthood this process of making associations continues. To become aware of associations among things, events, or concepts is to think. For a baby or young child most thinking occurs at a fairly concrete level. Babies' associations tend to be among things they can see and touch. Once babies develop the ability to use language, however, they can begin to deal with the world indirectly through symbols. Babies, thus, enormously increase their range of potential associations and their abilities to think.

Unfortunately, not all of the associations we make during our lifetimes are valid. If you interpret the friendly smile of a member of the opposite sex as a sign that he or she wants affection, you may be reasoning incorrectly and as a result suffer some momentary embarrassment. In this instance, no serious harm will have occurred. On the other hand, if a child reasons that an orange-flavored aspirin tastes good and that several more aspirins would be better, the health and life of that child could be endangered. And if, during an economic recession, national policymakers wrongly interpret certain economic conditions as indication of an upturn and fail to enact appropriate measures to deal with the recession, months of additional lost production and personal hardship may result.

Not all errors in reasoning can be avoided, but the more we understand how relationships are drawn, the better equipped we are to guard against mistakes. To help you develop such an understanding, this chapter explains the nature of argument. More specifically, our purposes are (1) to define argument, (2) to consider the assumption of uniformity, which underlies the reasoning process, and (3) to examine each of the three major elements of a complete argument.

ARGUMENT DEFINED

An argument may be thought of as a *complete unit of proof*. As such, an argument consists of three basic elements. *These elements are the data, the reasoning process, and the conclusion.* Each of these elements is essential for the rigorous analysis of an argument. In the actual presentation of arguments, certain of these elements are sometimes omitted on the assumption that they are so obvious or self-evident that the listener or reader does not require their expression. Because of the brevity and clarity necessary for good communication, such omissions are usually warranted. Nevertheless, it is important for you to know what constitutes a complete unit of proof and to be aware of the unstated element(s). As you inquire into your own beliefs and as you critically receive messages from others, you should attempt to identify unexpressed elements and to subject them to the same scrutiny as the stated parts of the argument.

The data provide the raw material for an argument. The reasoning process is the means of interpreting the data, and the conclusion expresses the specific interpretation. The following model illustrates the process involved in creating a simple argument.

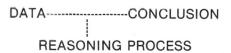

DATA-------------------CONCLUSION

REASONING PROCESS

Suppose you read the claim that the United States should not engage in military intervention in Latin America because such action will lead to a devastating and prolonged war such as Vietnam. In this example, the statement that Vietnam led to a devastating and prolonged war is the data; that the United States should not intervene in Latin America is the conclusion; and that Latin America is like Vietnam is assumed by the reasoning process.

ASSUMPTION OF UNIFORMITY

Our ability to relate data and reach conclusions through the reasoning process rests on an important, fundamental assumption. That assumption is referred to as the assumption of uniformity. This concept simply expresses the belief that there is order and predictability in the universe.

The acceptance of the idea of regularity is both necessary and reasonable. If there were not uniformity, we simply could not build on experiences, under-

stand the past, or predict the future. The assumption of uniformity is absolutely essential for learning to occur. To relate ideas, events, or experiences in a meaningful way, there must be order and regularity. Fortunately, our attempts to discover order in the universe have met with widespread success so that the assumptions of uniformity appears to be reasonable, as well as necessary. Biologists have successfully classified plants and animals into species and genus. The universe's unvarying characteristics have made it possible for physicists to predict physical behavior based on laws of energy and motion. And the consistency of the world provides the basis for mathematicians' tools of statistical analysis. Because uniformity does exist, we can expect to find similarities among phenomena and to discover that experiences recur. It is these similarities and this repetition that permit the associations we make when we reason and allow us to project our knowledge beyond the immediate situation.

An awareness of the assumption of uniformity is helpful not only because it offers fundamental understanding but also because it provides a standard for evaluating the adequacy of arguments. Many of the tests of data and reasoning may require consistency, uniformity, and regularity. The legitimacy of these requirements rests on the assumption of uniformity.

DATA

Simply defined, *data are the starting points of argument, the substance from which we reason.* Data are to argument what foundations are to buildings. To be structurally adequate, a building must be built on a solid foundation. To be analytically sound, arguments must be built on satisfactory data.

Two general kinds of data are used as starting points for investigation and argument—premises and evidence. *Premises are the fundamental assumptions or beliefs that we bring to a situation and that we accept without external support. Evidence consists of source materials that are external to us and that are used to lend support or proof to a conclusion.*

Types of Premises

Two types of premises may be used as data—perceptual premises and value premises. It is important to identify the perceptual and value premises operative in a given controversy in order to know the ground on which arguments can be safely built and in order to protect against the thoughtless acceptance of unwarranted assumptions and values.

Perceptual premises *Perceptual premises are assumptions about the nature of things.* These assumptions are based on our own personal views of the world. Many centuries ago, people assumed the earth was flat. This assumption grew out of the experiences of the people at the time. To the extent that this belief influenced their thinking on related matters, it functioned as a perceptual premise. Even today, many of our personal conclusions about what we should do or think are based on perceptual premises. Differences among the American public regarding policies toward communist nations, for example, are, to a considerable extent, based on different perceptions of the nature of communism.

Perceptual premises function as data because they are accepted without serious question. They have a certain face validity of their own, and confidence in them becomes ingrained and unchallenged. At some point, our perceptual premises may have been based on the past experiences of ourselves or others, but, over time, the original bases for them have been forgotten—or at least have become unimportant. The authority of perceptual premises is derived from their self-evident nature.

Value premises *Values are judgments concerning the worth of something.* Value premises put into statement form our concepts of good and evil, right and wrong, and important and trivial. Different perceptions of what we consider to be worthwhile underlie such perennial societal controversies as abortion and the death penalty. Advocates of abortion place a higher premium on the rights of the mother than on the rights of the unborn fetus, and advocates of capital punishment value the protection of society over the life of a single individual. Our value premises are derived from our parents and communities, from our religions and our friends. Regardless of how they are obtained, value premises provide the basis for many of our arguments.

It is important for us to be willing to explore value premises. One reason for irrelevant and unproductive argument is that competing advocates sometimes assume the correctness of their value premises and ignore the existence of a competing value system. When this occurs, the opponents inevitably "talk past" each other without clashing on fundamental issues.

Types of Evidence

There are two general types of evidence: factual evidence and expert opinion evidence. As evidence, both facts and expert opinions are external to the investigator or advocate.

Factual evidence *Factual evidence consists of potentially verifiable statements that describe real objects and events.* If a statement has no potential for verification, it is not factual. Factual evidence is potentially verifiable because it seeks only to describe events and objects. The report of a scientific experiment is factual evidence because it has the potential for verification by another scientist performing the same experiment. The description of an automobile accident is factual evidence because it has the potential for verification by other witnesses. *Actual* verification is necessary to establish the *validity* of a factual statement, but the *potential* for verification is all that is required in order to determine that the kind of claim being made is factual.

Descriptions of objects and events (factual evidence) can appear in a variety of forms. One form is that of *verbal examples,* which are detailed descriptions of specific cases, instances, or situations. The detailed description of the scene after a tornado, for instance, would be a verbal example. *Newsweek* magazine used the following verbal example as partial proof for a claim that neither private nor government medical care adequately meets the needs of all U.S. citizens.

> Gary Myers of Southfield, MO, still owes $200 for the treatment that his nine-year-old son, Jason, received last year for a heart-valve problem, and another $400 for the surgery his 11-year-old daughter, Erica, underwent for ingrown toenails that threatened to turn gangrenous. Then there's another $800 for the therapy his wife, Renee, required for a back injury she suffered in an automobile accident last fall. To avoid further financial trouble, she is postponing the hysterectomy her doctor says she needs. But that isn't going to help. Because of her back, Renee can't resume her job in a sewing factory. And Gary can't qualify for coverage under the Medicaid program for the poor. Why? The $509 minimum wage he earns each month as a security guard puts him exactly $4 above the eligibility limit. The couple has filed for bankruptcy. ("Forgotten Patients," 52)

Another form that factual evidence can take is that of *statistics.* Although there is a tendency to think of them as something more than numerical representations of examples, statistics are merely that. Statistics may appear in a variety of forms—raw numbers, percentages, ratios, averages, and the like—but they are essentially convenient ways of expressing large numbers of examples. If a public opinion poll indicates that a particular political candidate is supported by only 35 percent of the electorate, the statistic is a projection based on a limited number of examples. Statistics give the impression of being more representative than isolated examples, and they usually are. But the ways the statistics were derived need to be examined before reaching a conclusion.

A final form of factual evidence is *descriptive historical statements.* Such statements merely report that something happened at a certain time and place. Descriptive historic statements are closely related to verbal examples, but generally appear in less detail. When a party store owner testifies in a courtroom that at 4:30 in the morning of July 23 two men entered his store with guns in hand and demanded all of the money in his cash register, he is making a descriptive historic statement.

Expert opinion evidence   *Expert opinion evidence consists of authoritative statements that explain factual evidence.* Factual evidence simply describes objects and events, but expert opinion evidence *interprets the meaning* of those objects or events. Expert opinion evidence's claim to our belief rests on the special knowledge or experience of the individual offering the judgment. The opinions of ordinary, nonexpert individuals do not constitute evidence because they have no claim to special authority. Ordinary citizens in courts of law are known as lay witnesses, and they are not permitted to make judgments or interpret situations. Lay witnesses may only provide factual evidence; only experts are permitted to offer expert opinion evidence. We give special credence and status only to judgments made by those with specialized credentials. When a ballistics expert examines a bullet and a gun and concludes that the bullet was fired from that gun, we are willing to accept the judgment because of his or her specialized knowledge.

REASONING PROCESSES

Identification of the various forms of data can help direct you to the information necessary to construct an argument, but it does not help you understand the specific ways in which relationships among data can be established. Basically, phenomena may be associated in one of two manners, either inductively or deductively.

Inductive Reasoning

Inductive reasoning is sometimes defined as reasoning from the specific to the general. This definition is inadequate on two counts. First, it fails to identify the nature of the process involved in moving from the data to the conclusion. This movement from data to conclusion involves a process essentially different from that of deductive reasoning.

Second, the definition does not accurately describe the nature of all inductive conclusions. Although it is true that inductive reasoning may involve the examination of numerous particular instances in order to arrive at a general (or class-inclusive) statement, it is also true that it may involve a comparison among particulars to arrive at a conclusion specific to only one instance. For example, if we examined fifty cows and discovered that all of them gave milk, we might arrive at the generalization that all cows give milk. But if we examined road and weather conditions in two neighboring states and determined that they were similar and if we discovered that studded snow tires had reduced accidents in one of the states, we might arrive at the specific conclusion that studded snow tires would reduce accidents in the second state. In both examples the reasoning process began with specific data, but in the latter instance the reasoning led to a specific conclusion rather than to a class conclusion. Thus, while it is proper to say that inductive reasoning proceeds from specifics, it is misleading to indicate that induction always results in generalized conclusions.

Properly conceived, *inductive reasoning may be thought of as the synthetic process used in moving from particulars to probable conclusions.*

Synthetic process   The process of synthesis involves the bringing together of elements into a whole. Inductive reasoning is synthetic in nature because it is concerned with bringing data together into a meaningful pattern or whole. Raw data are not self-explanatory. Any effort to establish relationships requires some extension beyond the data. This extension beyond the data is known as the *inferential leap.* In the illustration with the cows, the conclusion that all cows give milk was possible only because we were willing to move beyond fifty cows to state a general conclusion about all cows. In the studded snow tire example, the similarities between the two neighboring states with regard to road and weather conditions encouraged the extension of the comparison to the third condition, the success of studded snow tires. Inductive reasoning, then, is synthetic in that it reaches beyond the data through an inferential leap to identify a uniform pattern.

Begins with the particulars   Induction begins with particulars, which may be specific cases, instances, or situations. Sometimes the particulars are drawn from our own experiences, but more often they are based on other people's descriptions of real experiences. When a number of examples are required, statistical summaries are helpful. Our illustration with the cows was presumably based on direct personal experience, but note how that experience was expressed in a statistical summary (fifty cows). Statistical measurements may also be useful in making specific detailed comparisons. The comparison of road and weather conditions in our other example would require detailed statistical descriptions of the two states with regard to the number of miles of paved roads, the amount of snowfall, the variations in temperature, and so forth. Although statistics are helpful in capsulizing and presenting particulars, it should be remembered that it is the real instances or situations, and not the numbers, that are the ultimate basis of the reasoning process.

Probable conclusions   The conclusions arrived at through induction are only probably true. Since induction requires a movement beyond the raw data, inductive conclusions are always less certain than the original data. If we had actually observed fifty cows giving milk, we could be reasonably certain of our initial data, but because we have not had direct experience with all cows, we cannot be as certain of our conclusion. Thus, even if the absolute validity of the initial data can be established, the form of inductive reasoning does not allow for certain conclusions.

Inductive reasoning, then, interprets data by creating a synthesis; this synthesis reaches beyond the data through an inferential leap to identify a probable uniform pattern.

Deductive Reasoning

Deductive reasoning is often defined as reasoning from the general to the specific. This definition, like its counterpart definition of induction, is inadequate on two counts. First, it too fails to describe the nature of the process involved in moving from the data to the conclusion. We must distinguish between the synthetic process of induction and the analytic process of deduction.

Second, the definition does not accurately describe the nature of all deductive conclusions. Although it is true that all deductive reasoning moves from the more general to the less general, deductive conclusions are not necessarily specific. For example, if we begin with the general statement that all medical doctors have college degrees and then identify Mr. Smith as a medical doctor, we arrive at the specific conclusion that Mr. Smith has a college degree. On the other hand, if we begin with the general statement that all buildings should be built on solid foundations and then include houses in the category of buildings, we arrive at the less general—but not specific—conclusion that all houses should be built on solid foundations. Thus, deductive reasoning proceeds from general statements and arrives at specific applications or less general class conclusions. Properly conceived, *deductive reasoning may be thought of as the analytic process used in moving from generalities to structurally certain conclusions.*

Analytic process   The process of deduction is analytical in nature because it is concerned with the breaking down of a whole into its parts. The synthesis of induction seeks to arrive at new insights by bringing concepts together through an inferential leap, whereas the analysis of deduction attempts to apply established insights to new or different situations by including or excluding the parts of a whole. In the medical doctor illustration, the assertion that all medical doctors have college degrees was the established insight. By including Mr. Smith in the category of medical doctors, we were able to apply our established insight to a part (Mr. Smith) of the whole class (all medical doctors). In the other illustration, the need of all buildings for solid foundations was the established insight. By including houses in the category of buildings, we were able to apply our established insight to a part (houses) of a whole class (buildings). Deductive reasoning, then, is analytical in that it relates parts to the whole through inclusion in, or exclusion from, a class.

Begins with the generalities   Deductive reasoning begins with general statements that may be descriptive or evaluative in nature. But whether descriptive or evaluative, these initial generalizations must establish class categories. In order for analysis to occur, there must first be a whole. Statements concerning general classes of things provide that whole. In the medical doctor illustration, the statement that all medical doctors have college degrees was the initial generality, which provided the whole for analysis. In everyday discourse, the initial general statement of a deductive argument is often not explicitly stated, but whether expressed or not, generalities are the starting point for, and the basis of, all deductive arguments.

Structurally certain conclusions   The form of deductive reasoning provides for a conclusion that is structurally certain. The conclusion of a deductive argument does not extend beyond the original data, but rather is contained within the initial generalization. So long as none of the rules of deduction is violated, the form of inclusion in, or exclusion from, the terms of the original statement provides for a certain conclusion to follow. In our examples, once we included Mr. Smith in the category of medical doctors and once we included houses in the category of buildings, the conclusions followed inevitably. In deductive reasoning, then, it is possible to be as certain of the truth of our conclusions as we are of the truth of the first statements. If the content of the initial generalization is incorrect, the content of the conclusion will probably be incorrect, but the structure of the deductive process assures that conclusions will follow consistently.

CONCLUSIONS

Data provide the substance out of which an argument may be constructed, and the reasoning process offers the means for interpreting that substance. *The conclusion expresses the specific condition, relationship, or judgment identified by the reasoning process's interpretation of the data.* All conclusions are aimed at providing answers to one of three fundamental questions: Is it? (question of existence); What is it? (question of essence); or Why is it? (question of explanation).

Conclusions of Existence

Conclusions of existence assert that something is real or manifest or in a state of being. When you walk into your house or apartment and hear the shower running and the television blaring, you may conclude that someone else is home. When an archaeologist digs in the desert and discovers the foundations of many large buildings, bronze and iron utensils, and pieces of intricately designed pottery, he or she concludes that an advanced society once existed on that spot. When economists note sharply reduced employment, declining investment, and lower production, they declare that we are in a state of recession. Conclusions that express existence are specific to a particular situation, case, or limited group.

Conclusions of Essence

Conclusions of essence identify an essential feature or basic attribute or characteristic property of something. When you tell your friends that college professors are hard-hearted because every time you have gone to one with a hard luck story they have failed to respond, you are identifying the essence (hard-heartedness) of college professors. When economists cite high unemployment during the recessions of 1961, 1970, and 1980 and conclude that during recessions unemployment is at a high level, they are concerned with establishing an essential characteristic (high unemployment) of recessions. Conclusions that prove essence are universal in that they include all members of a class. Existence may

Identify each of the following statements as either inductive or deductive argument.

1. All persons are mortal. Plato is a person. Therefore, Plato is mortal.

2. Minnesota has operated with a public education system that allows parents to choose the school that their children attend. The competition among schools in Minnesota to attract students has resulted in a better educational system. Essentially, the state of Nebraska is similar to Minnesota. Therefore, it seems reasonable to believe that a free choice educational system like the one in Minnesota would improve education in Nebraska.

3. I hear you are going to get an Old English sheepdog as a pet. That's great. I've seen a lot of sheepdogs and each one was very gentle. Sheepdogs are a great choice for people with children.

4. We all know that cheaters never prosper. Last week I learned that Beverly cheated on an exam. I'm willing to bet that Beverly won't prosper in school.

5. Scientific studies have overwhelmingly established that all narcotic drugs are physically and mentally addictive. Recently the surgeon general of the United States indicated that the nicotine contained in cigarettes is a narcotic drug. Clearly, since cigarettes contain a narcotic, they result in physical and mental addiction.

be specific and individual, but essences are inseparable from the class and are therefore universal to the class.

Conclusions of Explanation

Conclusions of explanation relate phenomena so as to account for their existence or to make their existence intelligible. We are interested not only in knowing what exists and what kinds of things they are but also in knowing *why* things exist and *why* they are as they are. When you become aware that each summer you gain extra pounds and that you also eat lots of ice cream and conclude that the ice cream is the cause of your extra weight, you have drawn a conclusion of explanation. Social scientists who have observed that population growth declines as societies become more prosperous have concluded that the two situations are functionally related. Their conclusion of explanation is that economic growth causes a decline in the birth rate. Conclusions of explanation may be specific or universal depending on the data and the reasoning process used.

SUMMARY

An argument is a complete unit of proof. It consists of three elements: data, reasoning process, and conclusion. Our ability to relate data and draw conclusions by means of the reasoning process rests on the assumption of uniformity. This concept simply expresses the belief that there is order and predictability in the universe. Our past successes in identifying regularity contribute to our confidence in accepting this assumption.

Data are the starting points of argument, the substance from which we reason. The two general kinds of data are premises and evidence. Premises are fundamental assumptions that we accept without external support. Evidence is source material that is external to us and that is used to prove a conclusion. Premises and evidence are discovered rather than created. Both perceptual premises and value premises may be used as data. Perceptual premises are assumptions about the nature of things; value premises are judgments concerning the worth of things. The two forms of evidence are factual evidence and expert opinion evidence. Factual evidence consists of potentially verifiable statements that describe real objects and events. Expert opinion evidence consists of authoritative statements that explain factual evidence.

The reasoning process establishes associations among data by means of induction or deduction. Inductive reasoning is a synthetic process that begins with particulars and arrives at probable conclusions. Deductive reasoning is an analytic process that begins with generalities and arrives at structurally certain conclusions.

Conclusions express the specific condition, relationship, or judgment identified by the reasoning process's interpretation of data. All conclusions are aimed at providing answers to one of three fundamental questions: Is it? (question of existence); What is it? (question of essence); or Why is it? (question of explanation).

NOTES

[1]Although this model of argument is similar to one proposed by Stephen Toulmin, it differs from it in significant ways. We do not use the term "warrant" because we believe it to be less precise than "reasoning process." Indeed, Professor Toulmin intends "warrant" to encompass more than the reasoning process and to include psychological means of associating ideas. Our model also omits reference to the concepts of backing, rebuttal, and reservations. It does not seem to us that these elements are necessary to explain the fundamental nature of an argument; they indicate instead the interrelationship among arguments. This interrelationship is discussed in a more functional way in Chapter 10 under logical outlining. (See Toulmin, 94–145.)

SELECTED BIBLIOGRAPHY

BARKER, STEPHEN F. *The Elements of Logic.* New York: McGraw-Hill, 1965.

"Deduction." *The New Encyclopedia Britannica.* Vol. 3. Chicago: Encyclopedia Britannica, Inc. 1985, p. 954

"Forgotten Patients." *Newsweek,* August 22, 1988, 52.

HOUDE, R. "Deduction." *The New Catholic Encyclopedia.* Vol. 4. New York: McGraw-Hill, 1967, p. 715.

HOUDE, R. "Induction." *The New Catholic Encyclopedia.* Vol. 7. New York: McGraw-Hill, 1967, p. 481–2.

PERELMAN, CHAIM, and L. OLBRECHTS—TYTECA. *The New Rhetoric: A Treatise on Argumentation.* Translated by John Wilkinson and Purcell Weaver, 185–459. Notre Dame, IN: University of Notre Dame Press, 1969.

ROY, JACK, and HARRY ZAVOS. "Reasoning and Argument: Some Special Problems and Types." In *Perspectives on Argumentation,* edited by Gerald R. Miller and Thomas R. Nilsen, 80–109. Chicago: Scott, Foresman, 1966.

SALMON, WESLEY C. *Logic.* Englewood Cliffs, NJ: Prentice-Hall, 1984.
TOULMIN, STEPHEN. *The Uses of Argument.* Cambridge: Cambridge University Press, 1958.

STUDY QUESTIONS

1. What is the difference between the term "argument," as defined in this chapter, and the term "issue," as defined in Chapter 2?
2. Why is inductive reasoning commonly linked to the "scientific" method and deductive reasoning linked to the "philosophical" method?
3. How do analysis and synthesis differ?
4. Could argument occur if we did not subscribe to the assumption of uniformity?
5. What are the similarities and differences between premises and evidence?
6. What is gained by distinguishing between the three types of conclusions (existence, essence, and explanation)?

EXERCISES

1. Select ten sample arguments from speeches, editorials, or articles:
   a. In each sample try to identify the three elements of the argument (data, reasoning process, and conclusion). Where an element is missing, try to supply it.
   b. Do the conclusions in the sample arguments assert existence, essence, or causation?
   c. Identify the reasoning used in the argument samples as either inductive or deductive.
2. Examine textbooks in mathematics, natural science, and social science to see what evidence you can discover to support the assumption of uniformity. To what extent do the principles of these fields describe uniform conditions?
3. Prepare a brief report in which you explain the differences between the processes of synthesis and analysis. Examine unabridged dictionaries, encyclopedias, and science textbooks in preparing your report.
4. It has been said that science is concerned only with factual evidence. Discuss this statement with a professor of biology, chemistry, or physics. Ask the professor if her or his study is based on any perceptual or value premises.

ANSWERS TO PRACTICUM

1. Deductive.
2. Inductive.
3. Inductive.
4. Deductive.
5. Deductive.

CHAPTER SIX
DISCOVERING DATA

In Chapter 5 we discussed the nature of argument and identified the data, reasoning process, and conclusion as the essential components of any argument. We learned that data consist of premises and evidence. In Chapters 3 and 4 we outlined several methods by which you can begin the process of analyzing controversies. Consideration of the background of the controversy and application of the analytical formulas, however, provide only a general framework for beginning to discover the arguments and the issues involved in any controversy. To discover the real substance of arguments and issues, you must immerse yourself in the subject matter of the controversy. In this chapter we discuss how you can discover and use data.

Discovering premises is a mental process in which the advocate rigorously examines discourse and community norms to find relevant perceptions and values. Discovering evidence is a physical process in which the advocate systematically conducts library or field research, or both, to obtain relevant facts and opinions.

IDENTIFYING PREMISES

Deeply held perceptions and values are difficult to discover because, by their very nature, they have become so much a part of us that we accept them almost unconsciously. To discover premises requires us to consider three methods by which premises are revealed. These methods are conscious expression, symbolic revelation, and community inference.

Consciously Expressed Premises

Advocates who recognize the importance of premises often clearly state the perceptual or value assumption on which their argument is based. Consider, for example, Angie's opening statement in a classroom debate on abortion.

> I realize that many of you have deep feelings on the subject of abortion. Some of you are pro-life, some of you are pro-choice. Regardless of your particular belief, I hope you will share with me one fundamental assumption—human life is sacred. The belief that life is sacred is the key to the arguments I will be presenting.

In this introduction Angie clearly identifies the value assumption that human life is sacred as the starting point of her arguments.

As you examine the arguments raised by others, be sure to look for verbal clues to the premises being used. Words and phrases such as "fundamentally I believe," "a basic precept," or "the basis for my belief" are signposts that may be followed by the perceptual or value premise used by the advocate.

Premises are also frequently expressed in extended narratives used by an advocate to contrast opposing views. Consider, for example, a growing controversy in the fields of mathematics and physics. A new science is emerging in these fields—the science of chaos. The new science attacks the very foundation or perceptual premise of traditional science—the bias toward studying the orderly. James Gleick (5) presents a narrative contrasting chaos and traditional science:

> Chaos breaks across the lines that separate scientific disciplines. Because it is a science of the global nature of systems, it has brought together thinkers from fields that had been widely separated. . . . Chaos poses problems that defy accepted ways of working in science. It makes strong claims about the universal behavior of complexity. The first chaos theorists. . .shared certain sensibilities. They had an eye for pattern, especially pattern that appeared on different scales at the same time. They had a taste for randomness and complexity, for jagged edges and sudden leaps. Believers in chaos—and they sometimes call themselves believers, or converts, or evangelists—speculate about determinism and free will, about evolution, about the nature of conscious intelligence. They feel that they are turning back a trend in science toward reductionism, the analysis of systems in terms of their constituent parts: quarks, chromosones, or neurons. They believe that they are looking for the whole.

Notice how this narrative reveals the perceptual premises of both traditional science and the science of chaos. The new science emphasizes the study of "disorder," whereas traditional science focuses on "order." The new science places a premium on examining the "whole," the old science highlights "reductionism" or an emphasis on parts.

Symbolically Revealed Premises

Given that we often do not think consciously about premises, we should not always count on advocates to explicitly state the perceptual and value assumptions that underlie their arguments. In instances where premises are not consciously stated, we must rigorously examine the advocate's use of symbols. Perceptions and values are expressed symbolically through language. By carefully analyzing language, we can begin to sense the premises that shape a controversy.

A careful examination of the language used in argument is vital to discovering perceptual premises. As you read or listen to arguments, you should attempt to determine what assumptions about reality are being made. The language used by the arguers will often be quite revealing. Consider, for example, the case of a high school counselor who tried to convince a twelfth grade student that he should consider the field of medicine. The aptitude and interest tests the student had taken clearly revealed tremendous potential for success in medicine. Yet, the student told the counselor: "My father is a minister, my father's father was a minister, I'm going to be a minister. That's the way it has always been and always will be. It is so destined." The perceptual premises from which the student operated, clearly revealed in his language choices, was that of destiny and determinism. The student believed that the world was a place in which divine destiny ruled. The counselor, on the other hand, operated from the perceptual premise of free will—that human beings could and should choose what they want to do.

The examination of language is also important in discovering the role that values play in our arguments. Philosophers who have studied values offer a number of schemes for categorizing values. Generally, values are said to fit into one of four classes: artistic or aesthetic, moral or ethical, political, and utilitarian. Artistic or aesthetic values include terms like "beauty," "symmetry," "good taste," and their opposites. Moral or ethical values involve terms like "right" or "wrong," "just" and "unjust," and "good" and "bad." Political values focus on concepts such as democracy, rights, law and order, and freedom. Utilitarian values are described by terms like "effectiveness," "practicality," and "solvency."

By carefully examining the advocate's language choices, we can gain a sense as to the values being emphasized. Notice the emphasis on political values in a statement by Mrs. William Kent at a March 13, 1912, hearing before the House Committee on the Judiciary—a hearing devoted to the question of allowing women the right to vote:

> Mr. Chairman, the United States is committed to a democratic form of government, government by the people. Those who do not believe in the ideals of democracy are the only ones who consistently oppose woman's suffrage.
>
> I heard a man arguing against woman's suffrage by saying he believed in a division of labor, the men to vote and women to have other duties, equally useful. You cannot make such a division in a democracy, if you believe in self-government, any more than you can give all the eating and sleeping to half the community while the other half does something else equally useful. (Miller, 376)

Milton Rokeach presents another system for classifying values. Rokeach categorizes values as either terminal or instrumental. Terminal values refer to those associated with particular goals or desired states of existence. Terminal values include such concepts as equality, freedom, family, national security, a world at peace, and self-respect. Instrumental values, in contrast, provide the means for attainment of a terminal value or describe a desired mode of behavior. Ambition, honesty, independence, responsibility, and broadmindedness are examples of instrumental values.

Rokeach's system suggests one important characteristic of values. Values do not exist independently of one another. Individuals and communities hold multiple values, and those values are related in two ways. Values may be categorized as core and subordinate. Freedom is a core value, and the various types of freedom—speech, religion, or choice—are subordinate values. Even though a person may value all forms of freedom, it may not be possible to exercise all forms on an equal basis. In making value and policy decisions, one form of freedom may need to take precedence over another to better guarantee the core value.

An important concept in understanding the interrelationship of values is the value hierarchy. A value hierarchy is built by arranging competing core or subordinate values in order of importance. For example, as Americans, we value both freedom and national security. There are times when the government argues that certain types of freedom—for instance, freedom of the press—must be subordinated to national security in order to ultimately protect the country and thereby all forms of freedom.

The only real clue we have as to the value hierarchy being used by an advocate is through careful study of the language used to make the argument. What terms are emphasized? Which examples are used? Which examples are ignored?

A careful reading of the language used by a high school principal and the language of a member of the American Civil Liberties Union during a debate on censorship of high school newspapers revealed two distinct value hierarchies in conflict. The principal started with the core value of "freedom." To achieve freedom, the principal argued that students must have the right to obtain an education in an environment "free of disruption." Uncensored newspapers resulted in disruption, the principal claimed. The rights of the individual were clearly subordinated to the protection of the school. The value hierarchy demonstrated in the principal's language was (1) freedom; (2) protection of society; (3) individual responsibility. The civil libertarian agreed with the core value of freedom, but shifted the order of two and three, and replaced the language of "individual responsibility" with "individual liberties and rights." The hierarchy thus changed to (1) freedom; (2) individual liberties and rights; (3) protection of society.

Virtually no controversy is devoid of perceptual and value assumptions. Politicians, members of the media, and private citizens often emphasize value issues to the exclusion of more quantifiable issues such as dollars and cents or numbers of lives lost. In the cause of freedom, millions of human beings have perished in wars. Values are fundamental to our way of thinking, to our way of arguing, and to our way of legislating. By understanding and critically examining the language of perceptions and values, we are in a better position to see how these concepts are used as data.

Community Inferred Premises

We frequently face situations in which we do not have access to previous verbal statements by the people involved in the controversy. Supose that on the first day of argumentation class your teacher required you to debate another student on the issue of surrogate mothers. You would be confronted with a situation in which you did not have a verbal text from which to discover premises. In such situations we are forced to infer the premises held by our opponents and audience. We make inferences about community premises by examining our personal premises and by analyzing our audience.

Examining personal premises The starting point for making inferences about community premises is the examination of our own beliefs and assumptions. A careful, critical examination will usually reveal some previously accepted values or perceptions, which would be difficult to justify to others or even to oneself. One student preparing for an intercollegiate debate topic on consumer product safety faced just such a problem. Amy believed that *all* business owners were willing to seriously endanger the lives of their customers in order to turn a profit. In her first debate on the topic, Amy discovered that her position was extreme and not self-evident to others. Had Amy subjected her own belief to critical examination, she likely would have rejected it as a starting point for argument or inquiry.

To separate self-evident premises from less fundamental beliefs we should ask ourselves three questions: What do I believe? Why do I believe it? and Can the basis of my belief be reasonably denied? The ancient belief that the world was flat was based on personal perceptions of the world and was consistent with the limited knowledge of the physical universe. Thus, for many generations the flatness of the earth could not reasonably be denied.

In America today, certain members of political extremist groups vigorously oppose government programs that promote affirmative action. This belief is based on certain other beliefs. These beliefs include the assumptions that the government of the United States has been taken over by Zionists and that the Holocaust in which six million Jews were murdered by the Nazis never occurred.[1] No matter how deeply members of a political extremist group believe in these last two assumptions, they can not call them self-evident since so many other "reasonable" people reject them.

The process of discovering fundamental, self-evident assumptions requires us to strip away first-level and second-level assumptions and to move toward the assumption that is *essential* to our belief. Suppose we believe firmly that the United States should cease all economic and political contact with Communist nations. This premise is based on certain other beliefs: the assumption that Communist countries are an evil empire that seeks world domination, and the assumption that economic and political ties promote communism. Just as the first-order assumption is not self-evident to most reasonable people, neither are these two second-order assumptions. We must press further to discover a universally self-evident premise. A premise basic to both of these second-order assumptions is that the free world should not be taken over by communism. This premise would appear to be self-evident, although still not universally acceptable. Contained within this third-order premise is the idea that personal and political freedom are desirable. Because this concept is universally consistent with Western experience, it may be said to be self-evident, and it can be accepted as a starting point for inquiry and advocacy.

By forcing one's analysis of beliefs to increasingly more fundamental and self-evident beliefs, it is possible to identify those personal perceptions and personal values that can serve as data. The test of "universally self-evident" is, of course, an arbitrary one, but it does provide a useful guideline as to the depth of premise analysis required.

Conducting audience analysis   The second way in which we can discover community premises is by performing audience analysis. Although audience analysis fails to guarantee the discovery of universally self-evident premises, it does allow us to discover premises that are acceptable to a particular community or audience. When these premises coincide with our own, they may be used as starting points for argument before that particular audience, even though they lack universal self-evidence.

Skillful advocates recognize that knowledge of their audience's premises can be enormously helpful in determining the starting point for argument. Successful politicians rely on information about specific audiences which they receive from staff aides and local sources. Intercollegiate debaters spend considerable time studying the judging philosophy statements written by judges in an effort to understand the criteria that are applied. Ethical advocates will not adjust their overall conclusions to conform to the beliefs of their audience, but whenever possible they will attempt to build arguments on the perceptual premises and values that they share with their audience.

In order to use your audience's premises effectively, you need to gather considerable information about the attitudes of the specific audience. There are three primary methods of conducting audience analysis to discover commonly shared perceptual premises and values: audience-published reports, interviews, and demographically based inference.

Documents or statements of principles published by groups provide a first major source of audience information. Service clubs, political organizations, and community and religious groups all exist to promote certain principles, and these principles are generally set down in some code, creed, or constitution. In addition, many groups also publish organizational magazines or newsletters, which may furnish additional insights into the common premises of the group.

Interviews and discussions with group members can provide a second important source of audience information. Whenever possible we should meet with members of the audiences we will be addressing. Such meetings provide us the opportunity to discuss the attitudes of the audience. Lawyers, for example, interview prospective jurors in an effort to determine whether or not particular perceptions or values will prevent a juror from rendering a fair decision.

A third source of information about audience premises involves demographically based inference. Demography studies the various groups that comprise a population. Such study assumes that individuals who share particular demographic characteristics—for example, age, gender, race, and socioeconomic status—are likely to share similar attitudes. By knowing the demographic composition of an audience, you can reasonably infer key beliefs and attitudes held by the audience. For example, in speaking to an audience composed of college graduates between the ages of forty-five and sixty-four, you can reasonably expect them to value political participation. Demographic information collected by political scientists clearly demonstrates that people in this demographic group tend to vote (Bibby, 252).

In general, our goal in audience analysis should be to gain as comprehensive a knowledge of our audience's premises as possible. We must strive to know *why* our audience believes as it does—not simply *what* it believes. Only when we understand the basis of our audience's beliefs can we hope to identify and build on *commonly shared* premises.

The discovery of premises alerts you to where there is disagreement between your arguments and those of your opponent and audience. To address this disagreement you must turn to data external to your audience: evidence. In the next section we discuss how to find evidence.

RESEARCHING FOR EVIDENCE

Research involves the systematic collection of evidence. Research skills stand at the very heart of the inquiry phase of argumentation. Researching for evidence is as important in argumentation as it is in solving perplexing medical problems. No new vaccine or treatment for presently incurable diseases will be found without months and even years of thorough research. Likewise, we will not find the answers to our important personal problems or to the problems facing society until we first engage in systematic research. Skill in research, then, is vital to any student of argumentation.

It is helpful to think of the process of researching for evidence as one that will be challenging and adventuresome. If we begin research with the assumption that the probable *truth* of our question is *out there to be found,* we will begin to view research as an exciting process of discovery, and we will begin to experience the same joy of exploration as do pioneers in any field. Moreover, if we view research as a means of finding truth, we will be more likely to use evidence responsibly and with respect.

We should recognize that researching for evidence involves a systematic process. In the field of medicine a substantial amount of time is devoted to searching out cures for diseases. Billions of dollars are spent in the hope of finding cures to diseases such as cancer, Alzheimer's, and even the common cold. These billions of dollars are not given away randomly. Instead, the money is placed into those research programs that are well designed and work systematically to discover the causes of disease and the effectiveness of various solutions. A systematic approach to research similar to that used in medicine is helpful in dealing with any problem.

When faced with the task of researching for evidence, the most common question is, Where do I begin? The purpose of this section is to provide assistance in finding a systematic approach to research. Specifically, we seek to answer four questions: (1) Where do I begin? (2) Where do I find evidence? (3) How do I read for evidence? (4) How do I record evidence for future use?

Developing a Research Plan

Effective research plans do not start with running to the library and pulling books from the shelves in the hope of finding something relevant. Instead, the effective advocate begins by outlining a research plan. In this section we describe two types of research plans: general issues research and specific argument research.

General issues research is used when the advocate first learns of the proposition to be debated. Using the techniques of analysis identified in Chapter 3, the advocate begins by determining what he or she already knows about the controversy. We suggest asking the following questions:

1. What do I already know about the proposition?
2. Why is it important to debate this proposition?
3. What have I read recently in newspapers and newsmagazines that may guide my research?
4. Do the terms of the proposition have clearly defined, obvious meanings?
5. Do I know any groups or individuals who favor the proposition? Who oppose the proposition?
6. Will specialized sources of information be needed to understand the proposition?
7. Will very recent information be important in dealing with the proposition?
8. What issues will be important in the topic?

The purpose of these questions is to help you decide on particular research strategies. For example, if you discover that you know very little about the proposition, you should begin library research by selecting a few articles that provide a general overview of the topic. Determining which groups or individuals support or oppose the proposition will help you find specific references in the library. Thinking about the words used in newspaper and newsmagazine articles will help you discover key terms to look up in library indexes.

Specific argument research is used after you have developed a basic familiarity with the key issues within the proposition. Here you look for very specific evidence to support the arguments that comprise an issue. Suppose that you are debating the proposition "Resolved: That nuclear power plants are usafe." Your general issues research has led you to discover that nuclear power plants routinely release small quantities of radiation into the environment. Specific argument research is then used to find evidence that even small levels of radiation cause damage to human beings.

Compiling the Bibliography

The next step in the research process involves finding the best sources of evidence on the general issues and specific arguments. The thoroughness of your research and the completeness of your analysis depend upon finding the best sources of information.

Before beginning your search for evidence, you must learn how to use your library facilities efficiently. Many university libraries offer tours led by a reference librarian. Most libraries also publish guides to assist students in learning how to use the library resources. As you learn to use your library be sure to discover where the reference section is located, where government documents are shelved, how to use microform readers, what computer search facilities are available, what type of interlibrary loan system is offered, and the availability of reference librarians to answer particular questions. Spending a few hours familiarizing yourself with the library will save countless hours of frustration in finding sources.

Searching indexes manually After becoming generally familiar with the library, you should learn how to use a variety of reference guides. This section describes some of the most frequently used guides and how to manually search these guides. These guides will help you in developing a bibliography of sources from which to find evidence. Our discussion is divided into seven categories of sources (books, periodicals, newspapers, almanacs and fact books, government documents, essays, and bibliographies). If you are interested in more detailed and complete reference source listings consult Eugene P. Sheehy's *Guide to Reference Books* or *Reference Books: How to Select and Use Them* by Saul Galin and Peter Spielberg.

Most indexes to books, references, and other sources are arranged alphabetically by subject and by author. Looking up references by subject matter can be tricky and requires the researcher to experiment with a number of search terms. For example, in doing research on radical extremist groups, we found that some indexes categorized such information under the heading "subversive groups, domestic," other indexes featured the information under the heading "domestic terrorism," still other indexes placed the information under the headings "right-wing extremist groups" and "left-wing extremist groups." The best advice is to think of the alternate ways in which the idea you are researching can be expressed. In addition, there are a number of books to which you may turn that list various headings and synonyms that may be found in indexes. Two such guides are *The Library of Congress Subject Heading List* and *Sears List of Subject Headings*. Reference librarians also have access to a variety of sources that may help in deciding which descriptors to use when using particular indexes.

Books: Researchers usually begin their search for sources of evidence by looking for books on the topic. Books are useful because they generally provide a thorough treatment of a topic and because they are more likely to place the specific controversy in its historical context. You should keep in mind, however, that it often takes a year or longer for a book to be published, and, therefore, it may not contain the most recent information available on a subject. The typical starting point in the search for books on a given topic is the card catalog of the campus or public library. A detailed explanation of how to use the card catalog is available in your library. In general, the card catalog allows you to look up books by subject matter, author, and title. The card catalog is a logical starting point because it lists books readily available to the researcher. The weakness of any card catalog, of course, is that it is limited to the books contained in a given library. If that library happens to be weak in the area of your research, the card catalog will be of limited usefulness in preparing a meaningful book bibliography.

If you need to move beyond the resources of your campus or public library, the most useful source is the *Cumulative Book Index* (prior to 1928, the *United States Catalog*). This work can be found in the reference section of most libraries and contains the most comprehensive record of books printed in the United States since 1928 (since 1899 if the *United States Catalog* is used). In addition, you may wish to consult *Books in Print* and *Paperback Books in Print*. All of these reference sources are organized alphabetically by author, by title, and by subject.

Periodicals: To find current information and perspective on a topic, you should turn to periodical articles. The most frequently used index to journals and magazines is the *Reader's Guide to Periodical Literature*. The *Reader's Guide* indexes the most widely read general magazines published in the United States. It is organized alphabetically by author and subject. The weakness of the *Reader's Guide* is that it lists few of the more specialized periodicals.

Virtually every subject area has one or more indexes specializing in journals relevant to that field. Many of these specialized indexes are noted in Galin and Spielberg's *Reference Books*. Your reference librarian is also a valuable source of information for finding the latest field-specific indexes. Specialized periodical indexes, which you are likely to find useful, are the *Social Sciences Index* (listing journals in such fields as psychology, sociology, and political science), the *Humanities Index* (listing journals in such fields as literature, music, and the arts), *Public Affairs Information Service* (*PAIS*) (listing journals and books relevant to public policy decision-making), the *Guide to Legal Periodicals, Magazine Index* (providing citations for more than 370 popular magazines), *Index Medicus* (listing journals relevant to medical issues), *Business Periodicals Index,* and the *Social Sciences Citation Index* (particularly useful in specialized research because it lists not only all articles written by a particular author but also the articles in which the author is cited). Most of the indexes are arranged alphabetically by subject and by author. The first several pages of the indexes usually provide details for using the source effectively.

Newspapers: Many propositions require very recent information or detailed contemporary commentary. An excellent source for such information is newspapers. Many university libraries offer an extensive collection of newspapers on microfilm. Comprehensive newspaper indexes include *Times* (London) *Index, National Newspaper Index* (indexes the *Christian Science Monitor, Los Angeles Times, New York Times, Wall Street Journal,* and the *Washington Post*), *New York Times Index* (provides extensive abstracts of articles contained in the newspaper), *Bell & Howell Newspaper Indexes* (indexing the *Chicago Tribune, Chicago Sun-Times, Denver Post, Detroit News, Houston Post, Los Angeles Times, New Orleans Times-Picayune, San Francisco Chronicle,* and the *Washington Post*), and the *Official Washington Post Index* (provides abstracts of most news articles in the *Washington Post*). Another useful source, especially when seeking to discover how others argue on a particular issue, is

EXCERPT FROM THE NEW YORK TIMES QUARTERLY INDEX

FREEDOM AND HUMAN RIGHTS. See also
Blacks (in US)
Botswana, Jl 31
Brazil, Jl 4
Burma, Jl 27,28,31
Chile, Ag 2,26
Cuba, Jl 11,25,26, Ag 4
Education and Schools, Jl 27
Freedom of Religion
Freedom of Speech
Freedom of the Press
Haiti, S 23,30
India, Ag 12
Japan, S 20
Kenya, Ag 4, S 24
Latin America, Jl 27
Minorities (Ethnic, Racial, Religious)
Music, Jl 5, S 1,8
Nicaragua, Jl 9, Ag 14
Nigeria, Ag 11
Political Prisoners
Refugees and Expatriates, Ag 21
Salvador, El, Ag 5
Search and Seizure
Sri Lanka, Republic of, S 25
Tibet, Jl 31
Turkey, S 22
Union of Soviet Socialist Republics (USSR), Jl 4, Ag 14,17, 25, S 29,30
　Soviet Union shows increased support for human rights during Geneva meeting of United Nations Human Rights Subcommission on Prevention of Discrimination and Protection of Minorities; change of attitude allows sub-commission to approve three measures dealing with death penalty, judicial indepedence and rights of the mentally ill; subcommission also votes to take Rumania to World Court for refusing to allow Rumanian expert to attend meeting (M), S 3,1,3:5

Subject heading

Other subject headings
and dates to check

Relevant articles,
with date, section,
page number, and column
(M) = medium length
article of 1-3 columns
(L) = long article of over 3
columns
(S) = short article of
under 1 column

Source: *The New York Times Quarterly Index,* July-September 1988, 139-40. Copyright©1988 by the New York Times Company. Reprinted by permission.

Editorials on File, containing selected editorials on a variety of subjects appearing in newspapers from across the United States.

Almanacs and fact books: Frequently the researcher needs to find a fact or a date or a specific statistic. Although these may be found in books or periodical articles, the use of almanacs and fact books can save a considerable amount of time. Four such sources are particularly valuable: *The Statistical Abstract of the United States,* the *World Almanac, Facts on File,* and the *American Statistics Index.*

The Statistical Abstract of the United States is probably the best source of statistics about all aspects of the United States. Statistics are compiled on literally every important aspect of American life, and these statistics usually cover a period of fifteen to twenty years before the publication date to assist in putting current statistical information into perspective. An additional feature of the *Statistical Abstract* is that sources are given for most statistics. This makes cross-references possible when more detailed information is needed. Each volume contains an extensive subject index. It is one of the best organized sources of statistical data.

The *World Almanac* is similar to the *Statistical Abstract,* although not quite as well organized. The *Almanac* probably contains a larger amount of data about the United States than does the *Statistical Abstract* and also contains sections on the history and present conditions of every country in the world. The book is organized alphabetically by subject, profession, and occupation.

Facts on File is a weekly (made cumulative monthly, quarterly, and yearly) summary of the most important facts from news events gathered from the major metropolitan newspapers. It is an encyclopedia of current events and is the place to look for brief summaries of the most important events of the week. Its subject indexes are precise and easy to use. The major limitation of *Facts on File* is that sources of information are not provided.

The *American Statistics Index,* although not a fact book in itself, provides citations to statistical studies by the government. The index is the most comprehensive listing of quantitative studies exploring all aspects of business, economics, and public policy decision-making.

Government documents: The U.S. government is a prolific publisher of books, hearings, pamphlets, bulletins, and the proceedings of Congress. On any question of public policy, the researcher will find government documents, especially congressional hearings, to be an excellent source of expert testimony on all sides of the controversy. Unfortunately, there is no central, easy-to-use index for government publications. The *only* index which provides a comprehensive listing of all publications of all federal government agencies and departments is the *Monthly Catalog of United States Government Publications.* Although other indexes of government publications exist for the years preceding 1940, the *Monthly Catalog* is the only comprehensive compilation of government publications since that date. The organizational system of the *Monthly Catalog* is a bit complex, and some practice is necessary to learn to use it efficiently. The best method is to ask a reference librarian to show you how to use it and then to spend some time practicing with it.

Two other indispensable indexes to government documents are the *Congressional Record Index* and the *CIS Index.* The *Congressional Record Index* provides a guide to speeches delivered on the floor of Congress. The *CIS Index,* published by the

Step one: Look up subject in the *index* volume and obtain the CIS abstract number (usually a number preceded by an "H," "S", or "PL")

Discrimination in education

Discrimination by federally assisted instns and programs, Fed prohibitions clarification, S543-5

Discrimination by federally assisted instns and programs, impact of *Grove City Coll* decision on discrimination cases, H521-68

Educ aid programs background info, H342-3

Educ aid programs, FY87-FY93 authorization, H343-5

Educ aid programs, FY89-FY93 authorization, S543-22

Educ aid to schools with low-income and disadvantaged students, programs oversight, H341-33.3

Educ antidiscrimination laws enforcement at colls and univs, Educ Dept response to court orders, H401-57, H403-24

Educ Dept civil rights compliance programs, FY87 approp, S181-5.2

Educ Dept civil rights compliance programs, FY88 approp, H181-59.14

Educ Dept magnet school assistance programs, FY88 approp, H181-59.3

Nomination of Legree S Daniels to be Asst Sec, Civil Rights, Educ Dept, S541-30.2

Racism effects on minority youth, H961-40

School dists consolidation to achieve desegregation, restrictions on Fed courts authority, H521-48

Student loan indebtedness economic impact, J842-7

Step two: Look up the abstract number in the *abstract* volume

H961-40 RACE RELATIONS AND ADOLESCENTS: COPING WITH NEW REALITIES.
Mar. 27, 1987. 100-1.
iii+102 p. GPO $3.00
S/N 052-070-06350-5.
CIS/MF/4
•Item 1009-B-10; 1009-C-10.
•Y4.C43/2:R22.
MC 87-18820. LC 87-602289.

Hearing before the Select Committee on Children, Youth, and Families to examine the impact of racial prejudice and discrimination in education on minority youth.

H961-40.1: Mar. 27, 1987. p. 3-26, 37-56.
Witnesses: ORFIELD, Gary, prof, political science, public policy, and educ; dir, natl school desegregation research project, Univ of Chicago.

KELLEY, Bruce, program dir, Calif Tomorrow.

COMER, James P. (Dr.), child psychiatry prof, Child Study Center, Yale Univ.

Statements and Discussion: Problems of continuing racial segregation in northern urban area housing and schools (related tables, p. 12-15 passim); overview of relations involving immigrant minorities in California schools, focusing on racial tension and violence; background and history of the black experience in U.S. society; adverse effects of racial discrimination on minority youth.

Source: *CIS Annual: Index to Congressional Publications and Legislative Hearings,* 1987, 202.
CIS Annual: Abstracts of Congressional Publications, 1987, 506.

Congressional Information Service, is vital in researching government hearings. This index covers all Congressional publications except for the *Congressional Record.*

Essays: Much of the valuable material for the scholar in any field exists not in book or periodical article form, but rather as essays in edited collections. The typical reference sources are not much help in locating such essays. Book sources will tend to list only the title of the total collection rather than the titles of individual essays, and periodical sources tend not to include essays in their listings. The work that fills this void is the *Essay and General Literature Index*. Published annually since 1900, this work is a guide to essays and short articles contained in collections. The works indexed are from most major fields, and the organization is alphabetical by author, subject, and, occasionally, by title.

Bibliographies. The wise researcher recognizes that she or he is not the first person to research most topics. Bibliographies on a wide variety of subjects are routinely compiled and stored in libraries. One excellent source of bibliographies is the *Bibliography Index*. Your reference librarian will also be able to direct you to specialized bibliographies. The major drawbacks of relying on bibliographies prepared by others are that you have no idea as to how exhaustive they are, and the bibliographies will not contain the most recent information.

Searching indexes with a computer   The large number of indexes available may make the research process appear extremely time-consuming and tedious. In fact, compiling a comprehensive bibliography on a subject used to be a task that required the researcher to spend days in the library, carefully looking through fine print indexes to a variety of sources, then running to the shelves to discover if the article titles were indeed relevant to the research question. Fortunately, com-

PRACTICUM: SELECTING INDEXES

You are researching a topic dealing with relations between the United States and the Soviet Union. Each of the following statements describes a research problem that you might encounter. Identify the index or indexes you would select to solve each problem.

1. You are looking for a book by C. L. Johnson about U.S.-Soviet relations. You are unsure of the book's title. Your college library does not have a very strong international policy section, so it is not surprising you cannot find the book listed in the card catalog.

2. Several weeks ago the president of the United States and the premier of the Soviet Union had a summit meeting. Both leaders made statements that you feel will help you support the argument that relations between the two countries are improving.

3. You need specialized information on the impact of the U.S.-Soviet summit meeting held several years ago. In particular, you are looking for analysis by a noted political scientist.

4. You need to find statistics providing a comparison of the economy of the Soviet Union and that of the United States.

5. A professor tells you that the U.S. Congress held a series of hearings on U.S.-Soviet relations, but she cannot remember the exact date on which the hearings took place or the name of the committee that conducted them.

6. In building your affirmative case, you rely extensively on the work of J. McDonald, a professor of international relations. You want to find out how other political scientists evaluate McDonald's work.

puter technology has advanced to the point where bibliographies can be compiled quickly and efficiently.

Many research libraries have access to on-line electronic data bases. More than 300 on-line data bases are currently available in such fields as current events, law, medicine, religion, the humanities, the arts, science, business, and the social sciences. These data bases often allow researchers not only to compile subject bibliographies, but even to view article abstracts and full articles on the computer screen.

Most research libraries require that computer searches be conducted by specially trained librarians. The researcher discusses the search with the reference librarian, and together they determine the indexes to be searched, the key words or descriptors to be used, and the time span of the search. The librarian then uses a computer and modem to access the data base. Suppose we are researching the subject of abortion. We might start out using the key word descriptor "abortion," and time span of the last five years, and the following indexes: *Reader's Guide, PAIS, CIS, Index Medicus, Magazine Index,* and *Religion Index.* In a matter of seconds the computer indicates that more than 30,000 citations exist (that is, the word "abortion" is contained in the titles of more than 30,000 articles). Recognizing that we cannot possibly search out 30,000 articles, we narrow our search with the help of the librarian. By adding such limiting words as "therapeutic," "legalized or legal," and "moral aspects of" we generate a more manageable list of ninety-five articles. We then have several options. The most expensive option is to have the complete text of the articles listed on the computer screen. This could cost several hundred dollars. A less costly option is to have the article abstracts displayed on screen. Depending on the source, this option could cost between twenty and one hundred dollars. An even less expensive option is to have only the article citations listed on screen. The ninety-five citations on abortion cost only twelve dollars using this option. The least expensive option is to have the citations printed off-line and mailed. Often the cost is only a few dollars for such a search.

As technology increases and electronic data bases are used more frequently, the costs are likely to decrease, and more people will have access to the services. Several electronic data bases are already available for home use. Many people who own a personal computer and telephone modem subscribe to electronic bulletin boards such as CompuServe, The Source, and BRS after Dark. Subscription information and starter kits are available at most computer software stores. The bulletin boards offer access to a number of bibliographic information retrieval systems. CompuServe, for example, enables users to conduct daily searches of the Associated Press Wire Service, the *Washington Post,* and the *St. Louis Post-Dispatch.* Users are able to create their own electronic clipping files. After specifying a series of key words, the information service scans the wire service stories and files all stories in which the key words appear. Users are able to read those stories on-line shortly after they come across the wire service. As with computer searches conducted in the library, you must be careful to limit your searches or the costs can become quite high.

Reading for Evidence

Gathering the necesary sources of evidence is only the first step in research. Finding the right sources of evidence does not automatically guarantee that you will discover the necessary evidence. You must now read the gathered sources to make decisions on what evidence to record.

The most important thing to remember when reading for evidence is that such reading is *purposeful*. In other words, you are reading with a limited purpose in mind and cannot afford to waste time reading tangential information. The first question you must ask before beginning reading for evidence, then, is, What am I looking for? The clearer the purpose of your reading, the more profitable the reading will be.

The purpose of reading for evidence will vary depending on the stage of research. In the early stages, you are frequently reading merely to discover whether or not the sources of evidence are relevant to the proposition under consideration. Book and article titles are often misleading, so you must discover and quickly eliminate those sources that are tangential to your research purpose. At this point, the reading technique of skimming is desirable. By quickly checking chapter titles, prefaces, subheadings, and summaries, you can make a relatively rapid determination as to the potential usefulness of a source. Instead of wasting valuable time in careful reading of an irrelevant source, skimming allows you to dispose of such sources quickly.

In the first stages of research and analysis, you should be reading for *ideas* as well as for *evidence*. At this point, your reading should be most careful and thorough to make sure that you fully understand the context of the ideas and evidence discovered. Because analysis is just beginning, it is difficult to determine what evidence will be useful. Much of the evidence recorded at this point in research will end up being of little use in the ultimate analysis of the proposition. This does not mean, however, that you should not record evidence during this stage. It is much easier to discard unneeded evidence than to retrieve relevant evidence that had been read earlier but not recorded. You should, therefore, record any potentially useful evidence during the early stages of research. The purpose of reading at this stage is to gather as many relevant ideas and as much evidence to support those ideas as possible.

In the later stages of research and analysis, the purpose of reading for evidence changes. With the analysis nearly complete and a considerable amount of evidence already recorded, the purpose of your reading becomes much more specific. The *quantity* of evidence becomes less important and the *quality* of the evidence becomes the controlling factor. You should be looking for relatively few items of evidence to support specific arguments. You are no longer engaged in general research on the topic. Rather than consulting general books or articles on the proposition, you are more likely to be working with much more specialized sources. Since the research purpose is specific, the technique of skimming again becomes useful. Sources are now skimmed, not for their general relevance to the proposition, but rather for their likelihood of containing a specific item of evidence. The early stages of reading for evidence may produce much recorded material, but in the later stages it is not uncommon to spend hours searching for one specific item.

Reading for evidence, then, is purposeful. If you always have a clear concept of the purpose of your reading, you are much less likely to waste time on sources that are irrelevant to your specific needs. Since the reason for reading evidence varies with the stage of research, you must adapt your reading methods to the purpose of the reading.

Recording Evidence

Since few of us have photographic memories, it is necessary to record the evidence we discover. Whether we are preparing a term paper or gathering material for a debate, evidence must be recorded for future reference. This section addresses the problems involved in recording evidence. These problems center around two questions: What should be recorded? (the evidence itself) and How should it be recorded? (documentation form).

Recording the evidence itself   No single method will guarantee that the researcher will record all of the right evidence needed on a specific research project. The choice of what evidence to record is ultimately a subjective judgment of the individual researcher and is dependent on the nature of the specific research project, the nature of the subject matter, and the type of evidence that the researcher is looking for at any particular time. Specific content rules cannot be generalized here, but four formal guidelines for the recording of evidence may be helpful: (1) record single ideas, (2) record reasons rather than conclusions, (3) record evidence consistent with its context, and (4) record evidence in a length appropriate to its anticipated use.

First, the suggestion that single ideas should be recorded makes the process of information retrieval possible. Evidence is recorded in order to be used in the future. As we will suggest later, evidence should be recorded on index cards and filed under subject headings. If a particular piece of evidence contains more than a single idea, it becomes impossible to file the evidence accurately without duplicating it. When a quotation contains multiple ideas of use to the researcher, the ideas should be separated and recorded individually.

Second, the evidence recorded should consist of conclusions accompanied by reasons rather than just conclusions. It is important to remember that data are the starting points of argument. If we record only conclusions, we have recorded only authoritative restatements of the arguments we seek to support. Evidence that gives the reasons for these conclusions provides a more specific and acceptable basis for our own arguments.

Third, the evidence recorded should be consistent with the context within which it exists. The researcher is faced with an ethical decision here. Frequently, by taking evidence out of its context one can change substantially the meaning and impact intended by the source. As a general rule, you should record evidence in the *exact form* in which it is found, noting any inconsistencies in context. If editing or paraphrasing is necessary, this should be done only after the accurate, complete recording of evidence is accomplished.

Finally, the evidence should be recorded in a length appropriate to its anticipated use. If the research is in preparation for a term paper or other forms of scholarly writing, then it may be appropriate to record rather lengthy quotations on occasion to ensure completeness of context. If the evidence is to be used orally in support of an argument, on the other hand, the demands of the oral communication situation require that shorter quotations be used. In recording evidence for possible oral presentation, it may be wise to break up a longer quotation into several shorter, more specific ones.

Documenting the source of evidence   Accurate and complete documentation of all evidence recorded is vital no matter what the purpose of the research. In any research project there are always occasions when the researcher will wish to go back to a previously read and recorded source for one reason or another. Adequate documentation the first time around makes this process faster and more efficient. Thorough documentation is also helpful in evaluating the comparative worth of evidence when making decisions on which items of evidence to use in a paper or speech. In addition, careful documentation is essential so that others may be able to examine the accuracy of your research. There are, unfortunately, too many verified instances of falsification and misrepresentation of evidence to ignore the importance of this safeguard.

A suggested form for documentation is contained in the accompanying illustration of a sample evidence card. First, evidence should be recorded on index

SAMPLE EVIDENCE CARD

Aff.—Blame Limits of Collective Bargaining in Promoting Safety	Index topic
Kenneth J. Meier (Political Science Professor, U. of Oklahoma) *Regulation: Politics, Bureaucracy, and Economics,* 1985, p. 290.	Author Qualification Source, Date, Page
"Collective bargaining approaches, however, have some major limitations. Because safety benefits are long-term in nature, unions have a greater incentive to stress short-term benefits such as wages rather than use scarce bargaining capital on safety issues (Bacow, 1982: 206). Effective collective bargaining also assumes that unions possess accurate information about job hazards; in cases such as exposure to hazardous substances, this may not be true. Finally, collective bargaining offers no protection to the 72 percent of the workers who do not work in unionized facilities (Bacow, 1982: 218)."	Exact quotation
[Note: Meier cites Lawrence S. Bacow in *Social Regulation,* 1982].	Brackets to indicate inserted material

cards to facilitate organized filing. Including an index topic further assists the process of filing the evidence for systematic retrieval. Adding the qualifications of the author assists in evaluating the comparative credibility of the evidence. The details on the source of the evidence make checking and further reference possible. The footnote form used for most term papers and theses and the *Debate Program and Tournament Standards* of the American Forensic Association both require the researcher to be able to supply the following source information: the name of the book, magazine, or other publication; the date of publication; and the specific page of the quotation.

Filing Evidence

After you have gathered a large number of evidence cards, you will need to organize the evidence so that you can retrieve specific pieces of evidence efficiently. Whether you are writing a term paper or preparing for a public debate, being able to quickly retrieve necessary information is important to successful advocacy.

One popular scheme for organizing evidence is to divide the evidence into three categories: (1) evidence supporting the proposition (affirmative), (2) evidence opposing the proposition (negative), and (3) general descriptive evidence (evidence that may be used on either the affirmative or the negative side).

The affirmative and negative categories should next be further divided according to major issues. The general descriptive category could be arranged topically. If you are filing evidence for a policy debate proposition, the five stock issues

SAMPLE EVIDENCE CARD FILING SYSTEM

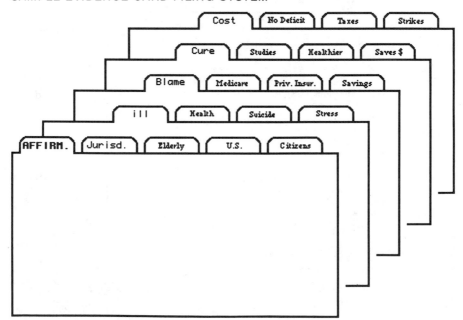

of jurisdiction, ill, blame, cure, and cost could serve as your major subdivisions of both the affirmative and the negative evidence. Each one of these subdivisions could then be further divided according to specific arguments. Similarly, if you are debating a fact/value proposition, the four stasis frames of jurisdiction, definition, existence of fact, and quality could be used. Each of these subdivisions could then be further divided according to specific arguments.

ETHICAL USE OF DATA

Throughout this chapter numerous references have been made to the importance of fairness and accuracy in recording and using evidence and premises. Inaccuracy and unfairness in the use of data may result from many circumstances—from deliberate deception, from hurried and careless recording of evidence, or from the use of evidence inaccurately recorded by someone else. The misuse and distortion of premises and evidence have repeatedly been documented in many areas of inquiry and advocacy. Championship college debaters, medical researchers, lawyers, government researchers, politicians, and even college presidents have been discovered misusing and fabricating evidence.

Fortunately, the very nature of our processes of inquiry and advocacy makes it unlikely that distorted data will go undetected for very long. Because other investigators often conduct parallel or related research and because opposing advocates usually check each other's sources, fabricated or inaccurately used data are likely to be revealed sooner or later.

Even short-term distortions can, however, have serious consequences. All argument and analysis are based on data, so errors in evidence and premises can lead to faulty conclusions and to inappropriate solutions. Years of an individual's life may be wasted in prison or millions of dollars may be wasted on unwise programs before false data are discovered.

Not only may the specific consequences of the misuse of data be undesirable, but the possible impact of numerous distortions is equally serious. The result of the repeated unethical use of data may be to undermine overall confidence in the reliability of the methods of argumentation. Once loss of faith in reasoned inquiry and advocacy occurs, then only intuition and propaganda will be left as our guides.

Adherence to a few simple guidelines can help the advocate avoid even unintentional distortions of data: (1) do as much of your own research as possible; (2) record all evidence carefully and accurately; (3) use data in ways consistent with its context; and (4) never use evidence collected by inexperienced or unreliable persons or groups.

SUMMARY

Discovering premises is a mental process in which the advocate rigorously examines discourse and community norms to find relevant perceptions and values. Premises may be consciously expressed by an advocate, symbolically revealed in the language of the controversy, or inferred within a particular community. Discovering premises requires us to analyze language, to examine our own premises, and to conduct audience analysis.

Research involves the systematic collection of evidence. The research process begins with the development of a clear research plan. Different plans are needed for general issue research and for specific argument research.

There are a number of excellent guides available to assist researchers in the discovery of both factual and expert opinion evidence. Key sources for evidence include books, periodicals, newspapers, fact books, government documents, essays, and bibliographies. Frequently used indexes include the card catalog, *Reader's Guide to Periodical Literature, Social Sciences Index, Public Affairs Information Service (PAIS), Newspaper Index, Monthly Guide to Government Publications, CIS Index, Essay and General Literature Index,* and the *Bibliography Index.* An important time-saving device in developing bibliographies is on-line computer searches. Searches must be carefully planned to avoid excessive costs.

Reading for evidence should be purposeful. Four guidelines should be followed in recording evidence: (1) record single ideas; (2) record reasons rather than conclusions; (3) record evidence consistent with its context; and (4) record evidence in a length appropriate to its anticipated use. Accurate and complete documentation of all evidence recorded is essential. Retrieving evidence efficiently and quickly requires that the evidence be systematically filed.

The ethical use of data requires that you do as much of your own research as possible, record all evidence carefully and accurately, use evidence in ways consistent with its context, and never use evidence collected by inexperienced or unreliable persons or groups.

NOTES

[1]The claim that the Holocaust never occurred is made by some members of a group known as the Institute for Historical Review based in Costa Mesa, California.

SELECTED BIBLIOGRAPHY

BIBBY, JOHN F. *Politics, Parties, and Elections in America.* Chicago: Nelson-Hall, 1987.

GLEICK, JAMES. *Chaos: Making a New Science.* New York: Penguin, 1987.

HAMPLE, DALE. "Testing a Model of Value Argument and Evidence." *Communication Monographs* 44 (1977): 106–20.

MILLER, MARION MILLS. *Great Debates in American History.* Vol. 8. New York: Current Literature, 1913.

PRENTICE, DIANA, and JACK KAY. *The Role of Values in Policy Debate.* Kansas City, MO: National Federation of State High School Associations, 1985.

RHODES, JACK, and GLENDA RHODES. "Guidelines for Library Service to College and High School Debaters." *Reference Quarterly* (Fall 1987): 87–94.

RIVERS, WILLIAM L. *Finding Facts: Interviewing, Observing, Using Reference Sources.* Englewood Cliffs, NJ: Prentice-Hall, 1975.

ROKEACH, MILTON. *The Nature of Values.* New York: Free Press, 1973.

STEELE, EDWARD D., and CHARLES W. REDDING. "The American Value System: Premises for Persuasion." *Western Speech Journal* 26 (Spring 1962): 85–90.
STEWART, CHARLES J., and WILLIAM B. CASH, Jr. *Interviewing: Principles and Practices.* 5th ed. Dubuque: Wm. C. Brown, 1988.
VERCH, STEPHEN L., and BRENDA J. LOGUE. "Increasing Value Clash: A Propositional and Structural Approach." In *CEDA Yearbook 1982,* edited by Don Brownlee. Wingate, NC: CEDA (Cross Examination Debate Association), 1982.

STUDY QUESTIONS

1. Why is it important to discover the premises used by our audience and our opponents?
2. Discovering symbolically revealed premises requires careful examination of the language used in argument. How can we examine language use in a systematic manner?
3. What questions would be useful in examining your own personal premises? What questions would be useful in conducting an audience analysis?
4. Why is it important to develop a research plan before beginning research on a controversy?
5. Why is it important to record evidence precisely?
6. What ethical responsibilities does the researcher have in recording and using evidence?

EXERCISES

1. Using the transcript of a contemporary public speech, identify all of the data used by the speaker. For each item of data indicate whether it is a perceptual premise, a value premise, factual evidence, or expert opinion evidence.
2. Build a preliminary bibliography on an argumentative proposition that you are currently working on by finding and recording three sources from each of the following bibliographic guides:
   a. The card catalog of your campus or public library.
   b. The *Reader's Guide to Periodical Literature.*
   c. The *Public Affairs Information Service.*
   d. The *New York Times Index.*
   e. The *Monthly Guide of United States Government Publications.*
   f. The *CIS Index.*
   g. The *Essay and General Literature Index.*
   h. The *Cumulative Book Index.*
3. Prepare fifteen evidence cards to be turned in to your instructor. In recording this evidence you should follow the guidelines for recording evidence and the documentation form suggested in this chapter.
4. Visit your campus or local library and ask about the availability of on-line computer searching. Be sure to ask about the costs involved.

5. Using the *Bibliography Index,* locate a bibliography on the debate topic used in class. Ask the reference librarian about finding specialized bibliographies relevant to your topic.

ANSWERS TO PRACTICUM

1. *Cumulative Book Index.*
2. The various indexes to newspapers would provide the most help, particularly the *National Newspaper Index,* the *New York Times Index,* and the *Times* (London) *Index.*
3. *Social Sciences Index.*
4. The various almanacs would be most useful, particularly the *World Almanac* and the *American Statistical Index.*
5. The best source is the *CIS Index.* The *Monthly Guide of U.S. Government Publications* could also be used.
6. *Social Sciences Citation Index.*

CHAPTER SEVEN
TESTING DATA

Each day we are bombarded with a multitude of facts, opinions, and premises concerning the important questions of our society. Whether we are listening to a newscast, talking with friends, or reading a newspaper, we are confronted with various types of data that are frequently in conflict with each other. Unfortunately, many people become the mental slaves of what they read or listen to because they do not have criteria by which to measure the accuracy or acceptability of the data offered.

How do we determine whether or not a given piece of data is sufficient to serve as the starting point for argument? This chapter identifies a series of tests to which data may be subjected. The tests serve not only as an aid to selecting premises and evidence during the research process, but also as a way of examining and refuting data offered by others. We begin by offering the general tests of data. Next, we present specific tests for premises and for evidence.

GENERAL TESTS OF DATA

Three general tests are available for all forms of data. These tests are the tests of internal consistency, external consistency, and relevancy.

The Test of Internal Consistency

The test of internal consistency asks the question, Is the data consistent with other data from the *same source*? This test suggests that we must look carefully at the premises, facts, and opinions expressed by a source to determine whether or not they are consistent with each other. Inconsistencies between or among premises, facts, and opinions expressed by a single source raise serious questions concerning the credibility of the source of the data. Unexplained inconsistencies at any level of data suggest that the source of the data may be guilty of careless thinking and superficial analysis. Such data are always an inadequate basis for argument and are easily and persuasively refuted by anyone familiar with the consistency problems of the source.

Courtroom attorneys pay particular attention to the problem of internal consistency as they listen to witnesses. In one trial a defense attorney successfully attacked the testimony of a key prosecution witness by exposing internal inconsistency. The attorney reminded the jury that the witness, in testimony given at the preliminary hearing, claimed that the assailant had a scar on his left cheek. During the trial the witness said that the assailant did not have a scar. By exposing the inconsistency, the attorney successfully undermined the credibility of the witness.

The Test of External Consistency

The test of external consistency asks the question, Is the data consistent with other data from *unrelated sources*? This test suggests that each piece of data must be examined in the light of other known data from other sources.

Consider, for example, a statement made by *New York Times* columnist Tom Wicker in an article appearing in the December 21, 1988, *Omaha World-Herald* (53): "The facts are, however, that for all the doom-shouting and breast-beating, the deficit is not much out of line, and deficit reduction is not by any means the highest national priority" (Copyright©1988 by the New York Times Company. Reprinted by permission). Wicker's statement is inconsistent with a wide variety of sources in which the federal deficit is regarded as the major problem facing the United States. During the 1988 presidential election campaign the Democratic and Republican candidates both claimed the federal deficit to be a key problem that demanded immediate action. Many economists agreed with the assessment by the candidates. Public opinion polls revealed that most Americans were concerned with the growing deficit. Applying the test of external consistency to Wicker's statement helps us realize that we should not use the statement as data without having additional support.

The discovery of inconsistencies between unrelated sources does not automatically invalidate the credibility of the data, but it does require that further examination be conducted to determine which of the sources is more credible in the matter under consideration. Such further examination leads to the tests specific to the individual types of data.

The test of external consistency can be used positively to validate data as well as negatively to refute data. When used in the positive sense it becomes the test of "independent corroboration." Historian Louis Gottschalk (166) defines "independent corroboration": "The general rule of historians is to accept as historical only those particulars which rest upon the independent testimony of two or more reliable witnesses." If two unrelated, independent sources provide us with the same premises, facts, or opinions, the credibility of our data is more firmly established.

The Test of Relevancy

The test of relevancy asks the question, Do the data support the conclusion they are asserted to support? This test suggests that data can be credible in every other respect but may still be an insufficient basis for argument because they are tangential to the conclusion being forwarded. It is not infrequent for a conclusion to assert one thing and for the data to establish something slightly different. If, for example, an advocate sets forth the conclusion that no one in America suffers from the problems associated with homelessness and cites expert opinion evidence which claims, "No one in America *need* suffer from homelessness," the evidence must be regarded as irrelevant to the claim. In examining the relevancy of data to any given conclusion, then, one must always ask the question, Does this piece of data really support this conclusion? If any of the data are tangential to the conclusion, it provides no probative force and may be dismissed as irrelevant.

SPECIFIC TESTS OF PERCEPTUAL AND VALUE PREMISES

The claim is frequently made that when we reduce an argument to its underlying perceptual or value premise, we have arrived at a point where no further testing can take place. Such a position ignores the fact that people can and, at times, do accept new perceptions and values. In ancient Greece many people perceived earth to be a cylindrical object floating in a flat sea of water. Today we perceive earth to be a round globe traveling around the sun. Prior to the 1960s few people perceived cigarette smoking to be dangerous. Yet, as the evidence mounted during the 1960s, 1970s, and 1980s, most people today perceive the dangers posed to health by smoking. American society prior to the 1960s accepted segregation of blacks. Today, the values of integration and equal rights have replaced the belief in segregation.

To be sure, our commitment to deeply held values and perceptions is often emotional and thus more difficult to test than externally verifiable data. Nevertheless, it is possible to test the adequacy of perceptual and value premises in particular argumentation situations. Specifically, premises should be tested in three ways: philosophically, pragmatically, and consensually. Since premises are internally established, the tests cannot establish logical validity. Instead, the tests provide us with signs that indicate the adequacy of premises in specific situations.

Philosophical Tests of Premises

Philosophy is concerned with discovering and evaluating the reasons used by human beings to support their beliefs and actions. Philosopher C. J. Ducasse (9) points out that philosophizing involves "the mental activity of searching for those reasons [used to support the validity of a judgment], and of then so editing them as to purge them of inconsistencies or exaggerations or errors that opponents were able to point out." Answers to three philosophical questions provide us with signs indicating the adequacy of premises: (1) Is the premise meaningful? (2) Is the premise based on a clear rationale? (3) Is the premise consistently applied?

Meaningful value *Is the premise meaningful?* Premises, especially those based on values, are highly abstract linguistic constructs. The sanctity of life, for example, is a value premise used by both supporters and opponents of euthanasia. Patriotism has been used both to support and to oppose the same wars. Whenever we use value premises as data, we must be sure that the premises are meaningful. This requires us to precisely define and apply the value or perception.

The lack of a meaningful value premise was an effective argument during the intercollegiate debate proposition that called for curtailing the power of labor unions. Several affirmative teams argued for the need to promote democracy within labor unions. Many of these teams simply argued that democracy is an assumed and cherished value. Several debates were won by a negative team that challenged the value premise on two levels. First, the negative team argued that in order to accept a value position the affirmative team must clearly define the value. The team claimed that merely labeling democracy a cherished value in no way defines the value. Second, the negative team presented considerable evidence that democracy is meaningful only in relation to government and not within the workplace. Many judges found the negative position impressive and indicated on the debate ballot that given the absence of a clearly defined and meaningful value, the proposition should not be affirmed.

Clear rationale *Is the premise based on a clear rationale?* Although premises often become so ingrained in us that we take them for granted, careful introspection should lead us to the reasons why we have adopted a particular perceptual or value premise. Consider, for example, the same value premise used by two individuals.

RON: Abortion is wrong. It just is.
SUSAN: Abortion is wrong. As I think through my position on this issue, I cannot help but recall my religious training and upbringing. I was born and raised a Catholic. In Sunday school I was taught that life is sacred. I respect the Catholic church and have always found church teachings to help me in my daily living. When it comes right down to it, my opposition to abortion is fundamental to my faith.

Notice that Ron's position comes across as a gut-level feeling—a position that does not appear to be carefully formulated. Susan's position, in contrast, is based on a rationale rooted in her religious beliefs.

When asking if a premise is based on a clear rationale we are not testing the validity of the rationale. Instead, we are assuming that premises based on reasons are more likely to be true than premises based on whim.

Consistent application   *Is the premise consistently applied?* The third philosophical test of premises is closely related to the notion of internal consistency. The degree to which an abstract value is consistently applied to various situations helps us determine the relative strength of the value.

Inconsistent application of a value premise was used as an attack strategy in the 1988 presidential debate between Massachusetts Governor Michael Dukakis and Vice-President George Bush. In rebuttal to Bush's statement on the importance of instilling values that prevent drug abuse by the young, Dukakis charged:

> I agree with Mr. Bush that values are important. But it's important that our leaders demonstrate those values from the top. That means those of us who are elected to positions of political leadership have to reflect those values ourselves. Here we are with a government that's been dealing with a drug-running Panamanian dictator. We've been dealing with him; he's been dealing drugs to our kids. . . .
>
>   But I want to be a President of the United States who makes sure that we never again do business with a drug-running Panamanian dictator; that we never again funnel aid to the contras through convicted drug dealers.
>
>   Values begin at the top—in the White House. Those are the values I want to bring to the Presidency and to the White House. . . .[1]

Dukakis's strategy attempted to demonstrate that Bush was guilty of inconsistently applying values. On the one hand Bush condemned drug abuse, on the other hand he was part of an administration that allegedly made deals with a suspected drug dealer.

Pragmatic Tests of Premises

Premises, when used as data, must always be related to factual situations. There frequently exist situations in which a premise cannot be applied without qualification. The value judgment that it is wrong to take another human life, for instance, is modified under conditions of war and self-defense. The perceptual premise that marijuana use is dangerous is modified in cases where the drug is used to provide relief to glaucoma patients. To deny the universal application of a premise, one must show that the premise does not constitute an ultimate good in a specific situation. This requires us to examine the pragmatic implications of applying an abstract principle. Two questions should be asked: Does accepting the premise result in good? Are more important premises sacrificed by accepting the premise?

Result in good   *Does accepting the premise result in good?* Premises can be pragmatically tested by applying them to particular situations in order to determine if they result in good. Consider a perceptual premise held by Jim. Jim perceives the world to be a terrible place. He believes that no matter how hard he tries, failure will necessarily result. In preparing for a job interview Jim takes the attitude that he has no chance for the position. The perceptual premise dooms Jim from the start. In this instance, the perceptual premise is counterproductive.

Value premises should also be pragmatically tested by asking if good results from their application. In the wake of a tragic airline bombing by terrorists, many public officials and private citizens questioned a government policy that withheld notice to the public of terroristic threats. The officials and citizens based their arguments on the value premise of the public's right to know. They argued that informing the public of terroristic threats would allow airline travelers to make their own decisions as to the risk of travel and would heighten public demand for tighter airport security measures. The officials and citizens thus demonstrated that accepting their value premise accomplishes good.

Sacrifice of more important premises   *Are more important premises sacrificed by accepting the premise?* As we learned in Chapter 6, values rarely occur in a vacuum. Instead, values usually occur hierarchically. A premise is frequently tested by asking whether or not a more important or meaningful premise should be applied to a given situation. A value premise, to begin with, is a concept involving "the most important." To suggest that there is another consideration which is even more important is to deny the primacy of the original value as the basis of the argument.

The identification of premise conflicts or value hierarchies is a realistic approach to the controversies we face since the primacy of a specific value often precludes the realization, or at least the maximization, of other values. Students must frequently establish priorities among their desires to get good grades, to participate in extracurricular activities, and to earn money for entertainment and necessities. Married couples must establish priorities among their desires to develop careers, maintain a social life, take care of daily living matters, and raise children.

Consider the case of an advocate who is questioned on her claim that free speech is an absolute value.

DIANE: So, your claim is that freedom of speech is an absolute value, a freedom that should never be denied?

IVY: That is correct.

DIANE: I want to clarify this point so that I'm absolutely sure of what you are claiming. There are no situations in which people should be denied the right to say whatever they want to say? Is that right?

IVY: That's exactly what I am saying.

DIANE: Let us suppose the nation is at war. Let us further suppose that a spy has infiltrated our command center and learned the attack strategy planned by our troops. The spy is caught and demands her right to free speech—she wants to tell the press about the attack plans. Given your value premise she would have the right to speak? Correct?

IVY: That's an extreme case, but, yes, she would have the right to free speech.

Notice that in this example Diane questions the universal value of free speech, suggesting national security to be a more important value. Diane demonstrates that more important values may be sacrificed by accepting Ivy's premise.

Consensual Tests of Premises

Simply because a perceptual or value premise is adopted by a large number of people does not necessarily mean that the premise is true. However, the fact that a premise is widely shared does suggest its usefulness as data. Consensual tests, although failing to establish truth, do help us determine whether or not particular premises should be used. Two consensual tests are especially important: Is the premise widely accepted? Do subject area experts support the premise?

Wide acceptance   *Is the premise widely accepted?* Determining whether or not a premise is widely accepted is an empirical question. Public opinion polls such as those conducted by the Gallup and Harris organizations, as well as survey research reported in newspapers and on television, provide much insight into the degree to which the public accepts particular premises.

Suppose we want to base an argument on the perceptual premise that Americans value democracy. We could find much support for this perceptual premise by turning to public opinion polls which consistently report that the vast majority of Americans, often over 90 percent, support such abstract principles as majority rule, minority rights, equality before the law, and First Amendment freedoms (Corbett, 28–30). However, a caution is in order. When abstract principles are replaced with specific applications, public support often substantially drops. For example, although close to 90 percent of Americans agreed with the right of free expression and equality under the law, less than 50 percent believed that homosexuals should be allowed to teach in college. Less than 40 percent felt that atheists should be permitted to teach (Corbett, 32–41). Simply because an abstract premise is widely accepted, therefore, does not necessarily mean that it will be supported in particular situations.

Expert support   *Do subject area experts support the premise?* A second test of premises is to determine if they are supported by subject area experts. This test is based on the assumption that subject area experts have devoted considerable time to investigating the basis for their beliefs and thus are in a better position to assess the adequacy of premises. For example, if we are testing the adequacy of religious premises in Judaism, we would likely search out writings by learned rabbis rather than statements by individuals who had recently converted to the Jewish faith. Similarly, in testing the adequacy of scientific premises, we should turn to established senior scientists rather than to high school chemistry students.

Throughout this discussion we have emphasized that tests of premises do not establish the truth of a given perception or value. However, the tests do provide us with signs of the strength and pervasiveness of premises. By subjecting premises to philosophical, pragmatic, and consensual tests, we can make reasonable distinctions between premises that should be used as a starting point for argument and those that should not be used. In the next section we examine tests of data external to the advocate.

SPECIFIC TESTS OF FACTUAL AND EXPERT OPINION EVIDENCE

Factual and expert opinion evidence may be specifically tested in a variety of ways. The tests include recency, source identification, source ability, source willingness, and context, along with various tests of statistical evidence.

The Test of Recency

The test of recency asks the question, Is the statement of the evidence based on recent observations of the real situation? Since the world is constantly changing and new information is continually being discovered, most facts and opinions have maximum validity for only a limited period of time. The test of recency simply asks if the evidence is recent enough so that important facts have not changed in the elapsed time. Factual evidence concerning wage levels in a given profession, for example, can be badly dated in even a year or two. The same is true of data on economic growth, population trends, pollution levels, stock market rates, and the like. Expert opinions interpreting such dated facts must also be carefully examined.

The test of recency was used in the final round of the 1983 National Debate Tournament. The affirmative team from the University of Kansas claimed that prohibiting United States military intervention in the internal affairs of Cuba would prevent a U.S.-Cuban war. The negative team from Dartmouth College used the test of recency to attack the evidence presented by the affirmative team: "The evidence [presented by Kansas on the second advantage] is also incredibly old. Most of it is in [19]81 or early [19]82. Changes in the political conditions and the U.S.-Cuban relations have made it different."[2]

In applying the test of recency, the advocate should be especially aware of recent statements of old facts. It is not uncommon for current books or articles to base conclusions on evidence from older sources. Books are especially suspect on this count, since there is frequently a time lapse of several years between the writing of certain sections of a book and its actual publication.

The Test of Source Identification

The test of source identification asks the question, Is the source of the evidence identifiable? This test suggests that each piece of evidence should be traceable to a specific source. Without adequate source identification, complete testing of evidence is impossible. The credibility of factual and expert opinion evidence is, in large part, dependent on the ability and willingness of a source to perceive and interpret the situation accurately and fairly. Without source identification we cannot make these vital credibility judgments.

Frequently we are confronted with general documentation such as "sources close to the president," or "according to *Newsweek*," or "high-ranking government officials say," or "economists believe." Such general documentation renders adequate source evaluation impossible. Every time such general documentation is encountered, one must ask why the documentation was not more specific and must examine whether or not those using the evidence may have reasons for not disclosing the full identity of their sources.

The Test of Source Ability

The test of source ability asks the question, Is the source of the evidence *able* to report or interpret the situation accurately? Because the factual and expert opinion evidence used in argumentation must be reported, it is necessary to examine the source of the evidence as well as the fact or expert opinion itself. In questioning a source's ability to report or interpret the situation accurately, it is vital to consider both the source's accessibility to the situation and the source's expertness.

It is first important to determine a source's geographical and chronological proximity to the elements of the situation being reported or interpreted. Lack of direct accessibility results in a source who is dependent on other sources. When the source is separated from the situation, the facts and opinions must be sifted through a variety of individual perceptions and interpretations and are, therefore, more subject to distortion and misrepresentation. As a general rule, then, the more a source is separated from direct access to the important elements of a situation, the less accurate will be the report or interpretation. In our courts of law, as well as in society in general, eyewitness accounts are considered more credible than hearsay evidence.

In addition to examining source *accessibility* one must also consider source *expertness.* More specifically, we should consider whether or not the source is qualified by experience, training, or position to interpret the situation. These factors of expertness are crucial in determining whether or not the source of the evidence is able to tell the truth. Even superior access to the situation may not be helpful if specialized knowledge or background is necessary to understand the event.

The *experience* test suggests that a source should have worked with the situation sufficiently to enable accurate reporting or interpretation. An experienced diplomat is much better able to interpret the public statements of a foreign power than is a novice news reporter. To the novice news reporter, a foreign policy statement may seem to be the same as previous statements. The experienced diplomat, on the other hand, may be able to read between the lines of the statement to see subtle shifts in policy.

In many situations, *specific training* may be necessary to interpret events or merely even to report them. News reporters receive intensive training before being sent to cover combat situations. Military combat situations are so complex that specialized training is necessary simply in order to report events intelligently. In deciding complex constitutional questions in our society, years of legal training are a vital prerequisite. The average layperson simply lacks the specialized training necessary to permit an authoritative interpretation of complex legal issues.

Another measure of source expertness is that of *position.* The concept of position is closely related to the test of accessibility. A source's position may provide access to information denied to most people. The perfect example, of course, is the position of president of the United States. No matter which individual occupies the office, the position permits access to otherwise classified information. That access enables the president to view and interpret events from a perspective denied to most other people. In much the same way, a senator who is a member of the Senate Foreign Relations Committee has access to important foreign policy information. The senator becomes an expert on these matters because of his or her position, not because of any personal qualities.

In examining a source's ability to report or interpret situations accurately, then, we must consider a source's accessibility to the situation, as well as the source's experience, training, and position with reference to that situation. If a source has problems in any of these areas, we should search for independent corroboration by sources with superior accessibility, experience, training, or position.

The Test of Source Willingness

The test of source willingness asks the question, Is the source of the evidence *willing* to report or interpret the situation fairly? While a source may be in an excellent position to perceive the truth accurately, conditions may exist that cause distorted reporting or interpretation of situations. In examining source willingness to report or interpret accurately, we must consider both the self-interest and writing style of the source.

The first question to ask is, Does the *self-interest* of the source or the source's sponsor prejudice the evidence? If the source of the evidence could profit from a given reporting or interpretation of the situation, we have grounds for questioning the fairness of the source. Self-interest was the basis of an attack made by Soviet Ambassador Ovinnikov in a debate at the United Nations Security Council over condemnation of the Soviet Union for shooting down Korean Airlines flight 007 while it strayed over Soviet airspace. In responding to charges by the United States, Ovinnikov stated:

> As is well known, to get at the truth of various events we need to ask a key question: who stands to gain advantage from them and who can gain from a new wave of anti-Soviet hysteria, under the noise of which they can say that, supposedly, the Soviet Union should not enter the agreements with anyone? Who stands to gain from a situation of hysteria and a whipping up of passions in which demands are made to cut off all types of negotiations with the Soviet Union? Who stands to gain from a military psychosis under cover of which appeals are made to arm and arm?
>
> There can be only one answer to these questions. Such appeals have been made from the very beginning by the current United States Administration, which is waging a crusade against communism.[3]

While bias does not automatically negate the validity of the reporting or interpretation, it causes us to doubt objectivity and to look to the other tests of the evidence's credibility.

We must question not only the self-interest of the source but also the interests of the organization for whom the source works. A source may be consciously restrained from telling the whole truth by the organization which employs her or him if the whole truth conflicts with the interests of that organization. Such may have been the case in a civil trial in which a cigarette smoker sought damages from a tobacco company. Evidence from medical experts was discredited when the plaintiff's attorney revealed that the experts served as consultants to various tobacco companies.

In assessing source willingness to report or interpret events fairly, we must also question whether or not the *writing style* of the source has sacrificed accuracy. Frequently the desire to write in a style thought to be interesting to the public may compromise accuracy. This test is especially important when we evaluate the reporting of sources who write for popular periodicals. The need to make the report simple and interesting to the general reading public frequently leads to overly colorful language and overgeneralization.

The Test of Context

The test of context asks the question, Is the evidence used in a manner consistent with the *meaning and intent* of the source? Inevitably, facts and expert opinions exist in a context broader than that used by the advocate. Since evidence gathering and use are selective processes, it is vital to examine the context of any piece of evidence to ensure that the meaning or intent of the source is not misrepresented. We frequently hear public figures decry that their words have been taken out of context.

The test of contextual accuracy is one of the more difficult tests of evidence to apply because of its inherent subjectivity. The evidence selected for use by an advocate is almost always an incomplete representation of the total argument of the source. A critical measure of whether or not evidence is used in context is its consistency with the overall intent of the source's position.

The test of context was applied by a negative team in a classroom debate. The affirmative speaker presented expert opinion evidence which claimed that ". . .the First Amendment to the Constitution provides an absolute right to free speech—a right that must never be violated, no matter what the situation. . . ." The negative speaker accused the affirmative speaker of violating contextual accuracy. She pointed out that her opponent had conveniently used ellipses to remove important words from the quotation. The full quotation actually read: "Some people argue that the First Amendment to the Constitution provides an absolute right to free speech—a right that must never be violated, no matter what the situation. These people ignore many situations in which permitting absolute free speech would jeopardize more important values." Altering the quotation in this manner clearly violates context and is regarded as unethical.

Tests of Statistical Evidence

When evidence takes the form of statistics, a variety of special tests of the measurement procedures must be applied. These special tests are necessitated by the symbolic nature of statistics. Since items are collected and given a numerical symbol, the resultant statistic exists on a higher level of abstraction than the examples it represents. Because of this symbolic abstraction, statistics are subject to manipulation, and the underlying truth can be lost or distorted. Therefore, in addition to applying other tests of evidence, four special tests should be considered when evaluating statistical evidence.

Adequate sampling *Are the statistics based on adequate sampling techniques?* Many people assume that the figures that they read regarding such matters as the level of unemployment or the rate of inflation represent real numerical counts of all cases within those situations. However, such statistics are usually not true counts, but rather are projections based on limited samples. The validity of such statistics, therefore, rests heavily on the reasonableness of the sampling techniques used in the projections.

Unfortunately, information concerning the size or representativeness of the sample used to arrive at a statistical statement is not always provided. Yet, such information must be sought if intelligent judgments concerning the credibility of statistical evidence are to be made.

If a sample does not adequately represent all of the elements within a class, the resultant statistic will be quite misleading. In a study of homelessness, a group of researchers claimed that the problem was greatly exaggerated. Careful examination of the researchers' survey techniques revealed that they had interviewed only people who had been included in the latest census. Given that the homeless are not likely to be found by census workers, the very people the study sought to find were excluded. An unrepresentative sample made the survey invalid.

Even if the sample is representative, it must be large enough to guarantee the chance that deviation is not operating. The size required depends on the homogeneity of the items being measured and the representativeness of the items within the sample. It is important, therefore, to look for explanation and justification of the sampling techniques when examining statistical evidence. The best sources of statistical evidence are those that provide such explanation and justification.

Appropriate statistical unit *Is the statistical unit an appropriate one?* All statistics view phenomena from a particular perspective, and the statistical unit selected determines the perspective. The answer to so simple a question as What is the average income of an American factory worker depends, in large part, on the statistical unit used to measure "average income." Three statistical measures of average are commonly used: the median, the mean, and the mode. The *median* is the exact middle point; in the number series one through seven it would be the number four. The *mean* is the true numerical average; it is arrived at by adding all the numbers of a series together and dividing by the number of items in the series. The *mode* is the point around which the largest number of items cluster; it is the item which occurs most often. Whether one selects the mean, median, or mode provides a different perspective on the average income of the American factory worker.

The problem of selecting an appropriate statistical unit is by no means limited to the measurement of averages. A variety of potentially appropriate units can be used to describe most situations. If, for example, we wished to discuss unemployment, we could express the extent of this problem in absolute terms (1.2 million unemployed), or as percentages of the total population (6 percent unemployment), or as ratios (one out of every seventeen adult workers is unemployed), or as a percentage increase or decrease from a previous period (a 25 percent decrease from last year), or in a number of other ways.

Officials of the American Council on Education and the College Board used the charge of an inappropriate statistical unit to attack the way in which many colleges attempt to prove their quality. The colleges under attack reported the average scores received by entering students on standardized college admission tests in an effort to prove their quality. The college presidents claimed that reporting the average score "does not necessarily say anything useful about the quality of what goes on in a college or university." The officials requested colleges to report score ranges, claiming that this "could go far towards 'de-hyping' the market for college ratings and related information."[4]

In general, the more we know about what it is we want to measure, and the more we know about appropriate statistical procedures, the more likely we are to select an appropriate unit.

Appropriate time period   *Do the statistics cover an appropriate time period?* Often, statistics are used to describe a situation over a given period of time. It then becomes critical to know whether the time period selected is appropriate for the purposes at hand. In measuring concepts such as economic growth, inflation, and employment, the selection of base years and the length of time measured can have a significant effect on the impression created by the statistic. By selecting an exceptionally high or an exceptionally low base year, an advocate can sometimes suggest the existence of a trend favorable to her or his side. The cause of truth, however, dictates that base years be selected not on the basis of personal advantage but on the basis of representativeness and reasonableness.

Comparable units   *Are comparisons between comparable units?* The old adage that you cannot compare apples and oranges has a significant application to statistical evidence. One of the most common uses of statistical evidence is the attempt to compare conditions. When statistical evidence is used in the comparative sense it is vital to determine whether or not the statistical units are comparable. Before attempting to compare the rates of juvenile crime in two cities, an advocate must determine if the two cities categorize juveniles in the same manner. Some cities define anyone under twenty-one years of age as a juvenile, whereas other cities include only those sixteen and under as juveniles. Similarly, when one is comparing the economic growth of two countries, it is important to determine whether or not these countries measure economic growth in the same way. If one country measures economic growth using only raw gross national product statistics and the other country adjusts gross national product statistics for inflation, a comparison between such statistical units is meaningless.

Each of the following hypothetical pieces of evidence has one of more problems. Identify the problems by applying the various tests of evidence.

1. *Newsworld* magazine, p. 3.

    "According to public opinion polls, 63% of the American public believes that abortion should not be made illegal."

2. John Kramer, citizen, based on a personal interview on December 2, 1988.

    "The Cental Intelligence Agency is engaging in covert action in Europe."

3. Judith H. Carenna, professor of Sociology, Farner University, *Issues in Sociological Inquiry,* 1987, p. 234.

    "Crime and delinquency are serious national problems. My studies of youth in the suburbs of Atlanta clearly demonstrate that crime among our nation's youth is running rampant."

4. Jill D. McMinnow, professor of Political Science, West University, *Journal of Western Political Ideas,* 1965, p. 27.

    "Inflation is at an all-time low. Economic growth, employment, and domestic production are at an all-time high. We can only conclude that our economy is healthy."

5. Kevin Watt, vice-president of IBM, *Washington Gazette,* February 20, 1988, p. 12.

    "The United States needs to invest more money in computerized defense technology in order to stay competitive in the world. The federal government needs to provide massive subsidies to computer-related industries."

6. James F. McMasters, statistical analyst for the FBI, *Special Agent Magazine,* February 1989, p. 232.

    "There can be no doubt that current law enforcement programs are working well. Compared to 1877, we have far less crime."

SUMMARY

There are three general tests of data. The test of internal consistency asks the question, Is the data consistent with other data from the same source? The test of external consistency asks the question, Is the data consistent with other data from unrelated sources? The test of relevancy asks the question, Does the data support the conclusions it is asserted to support?

Perceptual and value premises may be tested in three ways. Philosophical tests ask three questions: (1) Is the premise meaningful? (2) Is the premise based on a clear rationale? (3) Is the premise consistently applied? Pragmatic tests include two questions: (1) Does accepting the premise result in good? (2) Are more important premises sacrificed by accepting the premise? Consensual tests ask two questions: (1) Is the premise widely accepted? (2) Do subject area experts support the premise?

Six tests are unique to factual and expert opinion evidence. The test of recency asks the question, Is the statement of the evidence based on recent observations of the real situation? The test of identification asks the question, Is the source of the evidence identifiable? The test of source ability asks the question, Is the source of the evidence able to report or interpret the situation accurately? The test of source willingness asks the question, Is the source of the evidence willing to report or interpret the situation fairly? The test of context asks the question, Is the evidence used in a manner consistent with the meaning and intent of the source? The tests unique to statistical data require answers to four specific questions: (1) Are the statistics based on adequate sampling techniques? (2) Is the statistical unit an appropriate one? (3) Do the statistics cover an appropriate time period? (4) Are comparisons between comparable units?

NOTES

[1]Commission on Presidential Debates, *Transcript: The First 1988 Presidential Debate—September 25, 1988,* Washington, DC, 1988, p. 2.1.

[2]John K. Boaz, ed., "1983 National Debate Tournament Final Debate: Should the United States Military Intervention into the Internal Affairs of any Foreign Nation or Nations in the Western Hemisphere Be Prohibited?" *Journal of the American Forensic Association* 20 (Summer 1983): 29.

[3]United Nations Security Council, *Provisional Verbatim Record of the Two Thousand Four Hundred and Seventieth Meeting,* English version, September 2, 1983, S/PV.2470-36.

[4]Jean Evangelauf, "Officials Assail Use of Test Scores to Rank Colleges, Call on Institutions to Stop Reporting Averages," *The Chronicle of Higher Education,* November, 23, 1988, p. 1.

SELECTED BIBLIOGRAPHY

CHURCH, RUSSELL T., and DAVID C. BUCKLEY. "Argumentation and Debating Propositions of Value: A Bibliography." *Journal of the American Forensic Association* 14 (1983): 239–50.

CORBETT, MICHAEL. *Political Tolerance in America: Freedom and Equality in Public Attitudes.* New York: Longman, 1982.

CROSS EXAMINATION DEBATE ASSOCIATION. *CEDA Yearbook,* published annually since 1982.

DUCASSE, CURT J. "Philosophy: The Guide of Life." *The Key Reporter* 23 (1958). Reprinted in *Philosophy and Contemporary Issues.* 3d ed. Edited by John R. Burr and Milton Goldinger, 9–16. New York: Macmillan, 1980.

GOTTSCHALK, LOUIS. *Understanding History.* New York: Knopf, 1963.

HUMPHREY, CHRIS. "The Testability of Value Claims." *Journal of Value Inquiry* 3 (1969): 221–27.

MATLON, RONALD J. "Debating Propositions of Value." *Journal of the American Forensic Association* 14 (1978): 194–204.

PERELMAN, CHAIM, and L. OLBRECHTS-TYTECA. *The New Rhetoric: A Treatise on Argumentation.* Translated by John Wilkinson and Purcell Weaver. Notre Dame, IN: University of Notre Dame Press, 1969.

SILLARS, MALCOLM O., and PATRICIA GANER. "Values and Beliefs: A Systematic Basis for Argumentation. In *Advances in Argumentation Theory and Research,* edited by J. Robert Cox and Charles Arthur Willard, 184–201. Carbondale: Southern Illinois University Press, 1982.

SPIKER, BARRY K., TOM D. DANIELS, and LAWRENCE M. BERNABO. "The Quantitative Quandry in Forensics: The Use and Abuse of Statistical Evidence." *Journal of the American Forensic Association* 19 (1982): 87–96.

WARNICK, BARBARA. "Arguing Value Propositions." *Journal of the American Forensic Association* 18 (1981): 109–19.

WILLIAMS, FREDERICK. *Reasoning with Statistics.* New York: Holt, Rinehart, and Winston, 1968.

1. How do the tests of internal consistency and external consistency apply specifically to premises based on perceptions and values?
2. What criteria can be used to determine whether or not an item of data is consistent with the meaning and intent of the source?
3. Some people argue that perceptual and value premises cannot be tested. Do you agree or disagree? Why?
4. How should inconsistency between data sources be resolved?

EXERCISES

1. Examine the editorial and feature pages of your local newspaper and try to find examples of writers applying the tests of data to opposing arguments.
2. Try to discover through library research the statistical bases for the following:
   a. The unemployment statistics released by the Bureau of Labor Statistics.
   b. The population statistics compiled by the U.S. Bureau of the Census.
   c. The public polls taken by the Gallup polling organization.
3. Practice refuting value premises by having one student present an argument based on a value premise and have a second student attack the premise through application of one or more of the appropriate tests.
4. Apply the tests of factual and expert opinion evidence to any evidence that you have collected. Be prepared to discuss any problems you had in applying the tests.

ANSWERS TO PRACTICUM

1. Source identification. No date is provided. Without a date it is extremely difficult to verify the statement. In addition, the quotation does not indicate the specific source of the opinion polls.
2. Source ability. There is no indication that a private citizen would have access to this information. In addition, since a personal interview is not published and therefore difficult to verify, we should not place great credence in the evidence.
3. Inadequate sampling. A conclusion regarding a national problem based on local information uses an inappropriate sample.
4. Recency. The evidence is from 1965.
5. Source willingness or bias. The vice-president of a computer firm has a vested interest in the claim that is made.
6. Inappropriate time period. A claim about the effectiveness of current law enforcement needs to be based on more than crime statistics in 1877. Much has changed since then.

CHAPTER EIGHT
INDUCTIVE ARGUMENTS

We live in a verbal society. Through radio, television, newspapers, magazines, books, direct conversations, public speeches, and a variety of forms of mass advertising, we are subjected to the ideas and claims of many different individuals and groups. Some of these ideas are of no great importance to us and will be largely ignored. Other ideas, however, will require our attention and consideration. In order to evaluate the strength of these claims and to determine to which ideas we should give allegiance, we must have standards for measuring their soundness.

Chapter 5 provided a basic explanation of what an argument is and how it functions. Chapters 6 and 7 considered one of the basic elements of a complete argument, data, and suggested ways in which the various types of data may be examined to determine their adequacy. This chapter and the succeeding one describe the specific forms of inductive and deductive reasoning that are used to relate data to conclusions. It is necessary to be able to identify these different forms of argument because the tests for soundness differ according to which form is used.

Inductive reasoning is used to create three different forms of argument: argument by example, argument by analogy, and argument by causal correlation. Because all of these forms use inductive reasoning, they may be identified by the process of synthesis, beginning with particulars, and probable conclusions. The three forms of inductive argument differ from each other in terms of the *kind of uniformity* (regularity, similarity, or functional correlation) assumed in the inferential

leaps and in terms of the *basic question* (existence, essence, or causation), which is answered in the conclusions.

ARGUMENT BY EXAMPLE

The first inductive form of argument to be considered is the argument by example—or as it is sometime called, argument by generalization.

Characteristics of Argument by Example

The argument by example examines several specific cases in a given class and assumes that if the known cases are alike with regard to a specific characteristic, then other unknown cases in the same class will exhibit the same characteristic. The conclusion of an argument by example rests on the assumption of *regularity of a characteristic within a class.*

If the manufacturers of an automobile discover a defect in the brake mechanism of thirty cars of the same year and model and decide to recall the entire production of that model for replacement of the brake mechanism, they are reasoning by example. Only a limited sample from a given class (thirty cars of the same year and model) has been examined, and a specific characteristic (brake defect) has been discovered to exist in the sample. The decision to recall all of the cars of that year and model for brake replacement is based on the assumption of the regularity of the characteristic of the brake defect in the unknown cases of cars in this class.

Lester Brown and Jodi Jacobson of the Worldwatch Institute illustrate the use of an argument by example.

As cities grow and their material needs multiply, they eventually exceed the supply capacity of the surrounding countryside. Even water sometimes must be transported over long distances. . . . The Greater New York area, for example, which uses 1.9 billion cubic meters of water per year, obtains only 2 percent of it from indigenous underground sources. The remaining 98 percent comes from surface catchments many kilometers from the city proper. Sydney, Australia, a much smaller city that uses only 402 million cubic meters of water per year, obtains only 4 percent of its water from underground sources. Hong Kong has a rather different supply problem. Of the 133 million cubic meters of fresh water used annually, 49 percent comes from underground sources and the rest from surface catchments, mostly from across the border in China. Thus Hong Kong is one of the few cities that depend heavily on water in another country. (51)

In this paragraph the authors provide a limited number of instances from a given class (New York, Sydney, and Hong Kong from the class of cities) and identify a specific characteristic (need for water exceeds immediate supply) which exists in each instance. The conclusion that as cities grow their material needs exceed the immediate supply rests on the assumption of regularity of the characteristic in unknown cases of the class.

The conclusion of an argument by example always extends beyond the cases considered to include other unexamined cases. It is in this sense that the conclusion is a generalization. The generalization does not necessarily have to be a universal statement. The generalization of the conclusion may be limited to include some, but not all, unknown cases. When a generalization is universal and encompasses all members of a class, it answers the question, What is it? (question of essence). The conclusion that all cows give milk, drawn from an examination of fifty cows, is a universal conclusion concerning an essential characteristic of cows. When a generalization is qualified, it answers the question, Is it? (question of existence). If we looked at the same fifty cows and observed that forty-seven of them were brown, we might conclude that most cows are brown. Such a conclusion would be qualified in that it does not include all members of the class, and it would establish the *existence* of a characteristic.

Tests of Argument by Example

The tests of argument by example require us to consider the representativeness and sufficiency of the examples offered in support of the regularity of the class. There are three questions that may be used to determine the soundness of arguments by example.

Typical examples *Are the examples typical?* The assumption of regularity within a class must be based on an examination of typical cases. If unusual or atypical cases are looked at, a faulty pattern will be identified. In order for the generalization expressed in the conclusion to be reliable, it must be based on instances that are representative of the entire class of things being considered. For instance, a survey of the housing needs of the nation based on examples drawn only from the upper economic classes of our society would grossly misrepresent the true housing needs of the total population. In order to have a fair sample, examples from all economic classes need to be considered.

When making judgments about what to believe, most of us, perhaps, are inclined to place too much confidence in our own personal experiences. Although personal experience should not be ignored, we ought to be cautious about generalizing from our limited and, perhaps, atypical experiences. Examples taken from a variety of situations, or over a period of time, or by a number of different people are more likely to represent a class fairly than are examples drawn from a single situation, at one time, by one person.

Negative instances   *Are negative instances adequately accounted for?* When studying a number of specific cases, it is not uncommon to discover one or more instances that do not seem to conform to the general pattern of the class. These atypical instances must not be ignored when drawing conclusions. Sometimes the existence of these negative instances may be taken into consideration through the use of appropriate qualifying phrases such as "many," "most," or "some." The use of such qualifiers results in the identification of nonuniversal conclusions of existence, but precludes the universal conclusion necessary to establish essence.

If the negative instances can be adequately explained in terms of special circumstances, appropriately phrased conclusions of essence may still be warranted. For example, if we discovered that 97 percent of the elementary school teachers in the state of Illinois had college degrees and that the 3 percent who did not have degrees were in nonpublic schools, we might legitimately conclude that all *public* school elementary teachers in Illinois have college degrees. By limiting the conclusion to *public* school elementary teachers, we could still arrive at a universal conclusion that identifies an essential quality of public school elementary teachers. The omission of the qualifying term "public" would result in a conclusion that did not account for the negative (3 percent nongraduates) instances.

Sufficient examples   *Have a sufficient number of examples been examined?* A number of cases must be examined in order to establish regularity within a class. Although a single case may be adequate to *illustrate* a generalization when presenting an argument to an audience, one example is not sufficient proof to *support* the claim of regularity.

The question of how many examples are sufficient is one to which there is no absolute answer. In general, it may be said that the less homogeneous the class, the greater the number of examples that will be needed. If you wished, for example, to draw a reliable generalization about dogs, you would need more supporting cases than if you wished to generalize about female collies. It may also be said that the more universal the conclusion, the greater number of examples required. A generalization that asserts *some* dogs are mean requires fewer examples than one that claims *most* dogs are mean. The term *fallacy of hasty generalization* refers to arguments that are based on too few examples.

ARGUMENT BY ANALOGY

A second inductive form of argument is the argument by analogy. Whereas the argument by example recognizes *regularity* within a class of things, the argument by analogy identifies *similarity* between specific cases.

Characteristics of Argument by Analogy

An argument by analogy examines a limited number of specific cases, usually only two, and compares their essential features. *If the compared cases are alike in all known essential characteristics, it is assumed that they will be alike with regard to a characteristic known in one case but unknown in the other.* The conclusion of an argument by analogy rests on the assumption of the essential *sameness of characteristics within the compared cases.* The argument by example looks at one characteristic within many cases; the argument by analogy examines many characteristics within two cases.

When you reason that you will receive an "A" in a course because your test scores, term-paper grade, and class participation are the same as the test scores, term-paper grade, and class participation of a friend who got an "A" in the same course the previous semester, you are using an argument by analogy. In this argument, the two situations are alike in all known essential characteristics (test scores, term-paper grade, and class participation), and you believe that they will be alike with regard to the characteristic (final grade of "A") known in your friend's case but not yet known in your case.

Senator Edward Kennedy used an analogy to argue that people will not find the licensing of guns a burdensome requirement:

Opponents of firearms laws insist that gun licenses and record-keeping requirements are burdensome and inconvenient. Yet they don't object to licensing automobile drivers, hunters, or those who enjoy fishing. If the only price of gun licensing or record-keeping requirements is the inconvenience to gun users, then the public will

have received a special bargain. Certainly sportsmen will gladly tolerate minor inconvenience in order to protect the lives of their families, friends, and neighbors. (Kennedy, 69).

In his argument, Senator Kennedy asserts that gun licensing is like automobile, hunting, and fishing licensing in an essential characteristic (inconvenience), and he suggests that it will be like the other forms of licensing with regard to the characteristic (tolerance) known in the other forms but not known in the instance of guns.

The form of the argument by analogy calls for specific conclusions. These conclusions do not extend to new cases or classes, but are limited instead to one of the compared instances. The analogy may be used either to establish existence (Is it?) or essence (What is it?). In the first example above, the conclusion, "I will receive an 'A' in this course," was limited to one of the compared instances and did not extend to include new cases. This conclusion was used to establish existence, answering the question, "Is it or is it not going to be an 'A'?"

Sometimes analogies are drawn between *related classes* rather than between *specific cases within a class.* In an analogy between classes, each characteristic of the classes is, itself, a generalization derived from an argument by example. If the class characteristics are all in the form of universally true generalizations, the conclusion will be one of essence. If the class characteristics are in the form of qualified generalizations, the conclusion will establish existence.

In the analogy used by Senator Kennedy the comparison is between different classes (gun users compared to automobile drivers, hunters, and sport fishers). The class characteristic (inconvenience) is presented as a universally true generalization, so the conclusion is an unqualified one of essence (hunters will tolerate). The conclusion is specific to one of the compared classes, but applies universally within the class.

Two kinds of analogies are often presented. The *literal analogy* is the type that we have been describing and the only one that has the force of logical support. The literal analogy involves a comparison between cases, classes, or objects of the same kind. The *figurative analogy,* on the other hand, is concerned with comparisons between unlike categories. Although the figurative analogy is often useful in illustrating an idea, it is generally not considered to constitute proof. That the comparison of the figurative analogy is between unlike categories suggests initially that the objects or cases being compared are fundamentally dissimilar, and this therefore undermines the logical assumption of uniformity.

The following analogy is figurative because the comparison is between a physical characteristic of a mythical character and an intellectual characteristic of modern man. In this example, as in most figurative analogies, the comparison rests more on imaginative and literary similarities than on fundamental likenesses.

The Cyclops was a being of gigantic size and immeasurable strength. He was gifted with acute senses. And his only defect was that he had but one eye placed squarely in the midst of his forehead. This weakness was fatal. For he was brought to his knees by one far smaller in stature than he who was clever enough to deprive him of his eyesight. Thus being blinded, his great strength was useless.

In a way, modern man is an image of Cyclops. For though he possesses two eyes and two ears, he has only one intellect. It is this mind of his that gives man the power to look deep into things and understand them. And yet today millions of men have suffered a cyclopean wound. Their mind's eye is blinded. They are deprived of the vision that their intellect should give them. (McDonald, 154)

Tests of Argument by Analogy

The argument by analogy requires comparisons. The tests of argument by analogy, therefore, require that the comparisons be based on essential characteristics and accurate descriptions.

Compared cases essentially alike   *Are the compared cases alike in all essential characteristics?* The compared cases must be fundamentally alike in order to justify the assumption of the uniformity of the unknown characteristic. It is not necessary to demonstrate absolute similarity. Minor or noncritical differences may exist even among basically similar instances. For example, if you wished to argue for the practicality of a waste recycling program in your city by comparing it to a similar program in another city, you would need to demonstrate that the volume and composition of waste in the two cities are similar. The amount and nature of the waste would be essential factors to consider in comparing the workability of waste recycling in different cities. On the other hand, that one city has a female mayor and the other a male is irrelevant to the question of waste recycling; the sex of the mayors is a nonessential characteristic. The requirement, then, is for fundamental similarity rather than for complete sameness.

The question of what constitutes a critical or essential characteristic requires judgment in the specific situation. If we were to compare two cities in an effort to predict the probable success or failure of a mass transit system, we would need to consider such factors as the size of the metropolitan populations, the degree of concentration of the populations, the extent of express highways, and the geographical location of the downtown area in relation to suburban areas. On the other hand, if we were to compare the same two cities in order to predict the success or failure of specific programs of job training, then different factors—the educational level of the unemployed and the nature of available jobs—would become more critical. In general, the determination of what is essential depends on the nature of the things being compared and on the substance of the conclusion being drawn.

Compared characteristics accurate   *Are the compared characteristics accurately described?* It is particularly important that the data used as a basis for comparison be examined and its accuracy ensured. This is true because the question of what constitutes sameness is as much a matter of judgment as is the question of what constitutes essentiality. To say that two cities have the same needs for public housing because 20 percent of the housing facilities in both cities are more than fifty years old may misrepresent the real situation. If in one of the cities the fifty-year-old housing units are cheaply constructed frame structures, and in the other city the older units were well-constructed brick and stone buildings, the comparison would be invalid.

Even where quantitative comparisons are used, as in the preceding example, questions may be raised regarding the comparability of the units measured or the point at which two measured quantities are similar. When qualitative, rather than quantitative, comparisons are made, the possibilities for misinterpretation of the data are even greater. Moreover, many analogies are developed at fairly abstract levels, so the sameness of the characteristics is only asserted and not demonstrated in detail. The accuracy of the initial comparison, then, should be carefully scrutinized.

ARGUMENT BY CAUSAL CORRELATION

The third inductive form of argument is the argument by causal correlation. This form seeks to establish not simply regularity or similarity but to identify a *functional relationship* between elements.

Characteristics of Argument by Causal Correlation

The argument by causal correlation examines specific cases, classes, or both in order to identify a functional correlation between particular elements. Since a correlation is required, the patterned appearance of at least *two* elements within the cases or classes must be identified. To say that the correlation should be functional means only that the elements should act on one another. It is not necessary to establish that a single element is solely responsible for the other. If it can be shown that under a given set of circumstances, a particular element is either necessary or sufficient to bring forth the other element, a causal correlation has been established. Usually the correlated elements appear in a regular time sequence. When this occurs, the element that appears first is referred to as a cause, and the one that follows is called an effect.

Assumption of causation We noted earlier that all reasoning is based on the assumption of uniformity. Causal reasoning is based on an additional assumption. Not only does causal correlation assume an orderly universe, it also assumes that nothing occurs by chance and that for everything there is a cause. This assumption obviously has profound philosophical implications, so much so that some individuals are unwilling to use the term "causation" and refer only to "correlations." Other individuals are less concerned with the philosophical issues raised by causation and are more disturbed by the practical difficulties involved in genuinely proving the existence of a cause and effect relationship. Some authors of statistics books, for example, avoid the term causation because, they argue, statistics can only establish correlations. Causation, they say, must be inferred.

In spite of these objections, causation is a useful concept. Most of the research in the medical sciences is concerned with the discovery of the causes and cures of diseases. (Notice that the term "cure" really refers to a *cause* of wellness.)

Economists seek to identify the causes of recessions and inflations. Sociologists and criminologists are attempting to learn more about the causes of juvenile delinquency, child abuse, and alcoholism. Causation is, indeed, difficult to establish, but most fields of study are willing to make the assumption of causation, and considerable research continues to be directed to its discovery.

Necessary and sufficient cause   A cause is necessary if the effect will not occur absent that cause. An adequate supply of oxygen, for example, is necessary for human life to exist. Persons whose supply of oxygen is cut off die rather quickly. Thus though oxygen is necessary to support life, it is not sufficient, by itself, to ensure life. There are many places in the universe where oxygen exists, but human life does not. A sufficient cause, on the other hand, may, by itself, be enough to result in a particular effect even though that result might occur under other circumstances as well. For example, high alcohol content in the blood of a driver is sufficient to cause an automobile accident, but automobile accidents also occur even when drivers are sober. Both necessary and sufficient causes involve functional relationships and may be established through arguments by causal correlation.

Mill's canons   The English philosopher John Stuart Mill identified certain procedures (255–66) that can be used to discover causal relationships. These procedures are often referred to as Mill's Experimental Method.

The first of Mill's procedures is the *method of concomitant variation.* According to this method a cause and effect relationship may be assumed to exist whenever it can be established that two elements vary in a consistent and patterned manner. Thus, if the cause increases from time to time by a large amount, the extent of the effect should be expected to vary accordingly. Using this method a cause and effect relationship might be established between the size of a police force and the rate of crime. If it could be shown that the rate of crime in a city increased proportionally as the size of the police force was decreased, or that the crime rate decreased in relationship to increases in the size of the police force, a causal correlation would be indicated.

The second of Mill's procedures is the *method of agreement.* This procedure attempts to discover some common element among essentially dissimilar situations. If the same phenomenon occurs in two or more different situations, and one other common element can be found, that second element may be the cause (or the effect) of the original phenomenon. The method of agreement might be helpful, for example, in attempting to discover the cause of a group's shared food poisoning. By the process of elimination it could be determined that the members of the group had shared only one meal together. By comparing what each person ate at that meal, a single food—clam chowder, perhaps—might be discovered to be the only common element in otherwise dissimilar meals. Thus, the clam chowder could be identifid as the cause of the initial phenomenon, the food poisoning.

Mill's third procedure is the *method of differences.* This method uses a procedure that is essentially the reverse of the method of agreement. The method of differences recognizes one dissimilarity among otherwise identical cases and attempts to discover in the dissimilar case an element to account for the difference. The method of disagreement was used by a town attempting to determine why its new downtown shopping mall had failed to bring the marked increase in retail sales that similar malls had brought elsewhere. Comparisons were made with other towns with successful malls. The towns selected for comparison had similarly designed malls, comparable populations, and stores of approximately equal quality and variety. The one difference that emerged was easy access to parking. Thus, the poor access to parking (the one element different in the compared situations) was assumed to be the cause of the mall's failure to attract more shoppers. By building a new parking structure immediately behind the center of the mall, the city council was able to make the mall successful.

In many instances it is necessary to use a combination of procedures in order to demonstrate a credible cause and effect relationship. The United States Surgeon General's Advisory Committee on Smoking and Health used all three of Mill's methods at various stages of its report on smoking and lung cancer. The report identified the presence of a *concomitant variation* when it reported:

> The systematic evidence for the association between smoking and lung cancer comes primarily from 29 retrospective studies of groups of persons with lung cancer and appropriate "controls" without lung cancer. . . .The 29 retrospective studies. . . varied considerably in design and method. Despite these variations, every one of the retrospective studies showed an association between smoking and lung cancer. . . .
>
> The differences are statistically significant in all the studies. Thirteen of the studies, combining all forms of tobacco consumption, found a significant association between smoking of any type and lung cancer; 16 studies yielded an even stronger association with cigarettes alone. The degree of association between smoking and lung cancer increased as the amounts of smoking increases. (U.S. Department of Health, Education, and Welfare, 230)

The surgeon general's committee used the *method of agreement* to isolate smoking as a sufficient causative factor.

> In lung cancer, we are dealing with relative risk ratios averaging 9.0 to 10.0 for cigarette smokers compared to non-smokers. This is an excess of 900 to 1,000 percent among smokers of cigarettes. Similarly, this means that of the total load of lung cancer in males about 90 percent is associated with cigarette smoking. In order to account for risk ratios of this magnitude as due to an association of smoking history with still another causative factor X (hormonal, constitutional, or other), a necessary condition would be that factor X be present at least nine times more frequently among smokers than non-smokers. No such factors with such high relative prevalence among smokers have yet been demonstrated. (Ibid., 184)

A number of specific research studies cited in the report attempt to factor out, and thereby control, certain specific variables. To the extent that such controls created more homogeneous groups, they allowed for the application of the *method of difference*.

> In a well-conceived analytic study, Sadowsky *et al.,* recognizing that duration of smoking is a function of age, controlled the age variable, and found an increasing prevalence

rate of lung cancer with an increase in duration of smoking among all age groups. (Ibid., 158)

General or specific conclusions of explanation   The conclusion of an argument by causal correlation will be general or specific depending on which of Mill's three methods is used. The method of concomitant variation will provide a class conclusion if a series of instances is observed, or it can render a specific conclusion if a single situation is observed over a period of time. The method of agreement and the method of difference lead to conclusions that are specific to the compared instances. Repeated comparisons of agreement or of difference can, of course, result in generalized conclusions. The food poisoning and shopping mall illustrations provide examples of specific conclusions. The report *Smoking and Health* offers examples of generalized causal conclusions.

Causal correlations render conclusions that answer the question, Why is it? They attempt to explain the existence of one element of a situation in terms of its relationship to another element of the situation. Whereas the conclusion of an argument by analogy identifies the existence of a single element, and the conclusion of an argument by example either describes an essential characteristic of an entire class or indicates the existence of a specific element among many members of a class, the conclusion of an argument by causal correlation establishes an interdependent relationship between two or more elements.

Tests of Argument by Causal Correlation

Because the establishment of a functional relationship is more difficult than the demonstration of regularity or similarity, there are more tests for causal correlation than for the other forms of inductive argument. Several of these tests are drawn from Mill's canons.

Consistent association   *Is the association between the alleged cause and the alleged effect a consistent one?* This criterion suggests that repeated examinations of the association under a variety of circumstances should reveal similar relationships. This test does not demand that the cause and effect appear together in *every* instance. Rather, it requires that a *significant and relatively predictable rate of association must be established.* If a five-year study of juvenile delinquency in Atlanta revealed a high correlation between poverty and juvenile delinquency, we would probably be willing to argue that poverty is a cause of juvenile delinquency. If other studies done in Indianapolis and Dallas found similiar correlations, we would have greater confidence in our conclusion. If still other studies done during periods of both economic prosperity and economic recession also agreed with the correlation, our confidence would continue to increase. The more consistent the correlation the greater assurance we may have that the cause and effect relationship is valid.

When studies made at different times or with different subjects or under different conditions fail to indicate similar correlations, the alleged cause and effect relationship is undermined. Only by accounting for the inconsistent findings through claims of bias or poor study design or other special conditions could the correlation be resubstantiated.

Strength of association *Is the association between the alleged cause and the alleged effect a strong one?* Because a number of causal factors may be operating within a situation, you should be prepared to demonstrate the relative strength of a specific cause. A measure of the strength of a causal correlation can be provided by comparing the extent of the effect in situations where a specific causal factor is present with the extent of the effect in situations where that causal factor is not present. To study the possible effectiveness of a new medicine, for example, you would need to compare the rate of recovery of patients who were given the new medication with the recovery rate of those who were not treated with it. The higher the incidence of the effect (recovery) in those situations where the specific cause (new medicine) operated, as compared to those situations where it did not, the greater the strength of the causal association. If the incidence of the effect was not significantly higher in those situations in which the cause operated, then the causal link would be a weak one.

Regular time sequence *Do the alleged cause and the alleged effect appear in a regular time sequence?* The functional nature of a cause and effect relationship suggests that the two elements should appear in a regular time sequence. As a general rule, the cause occurs before the effect, although in nature the cause and effect sometimes appear to occur simultaneously. In no instance may an effect occur before the cause. A bullet would not be accepted as the cause of a man's death if it were shown that he had died before the bullet was fired. The period of time between the appearance of the cause and the appearance of the effect may vary from case to case, but the same order of appearance must exist.

If it can be shown that an alleged cause and effect relationship is based on an irregular time sequence, the causal correlation is denied. It should be noted, however, that although the irregularity of a time sequence is sufficient to negate a causal association, the mere existence of a regular sequence of events does not, by itself, establish causation. That a black cat crossed your path just before a car

PRACTICUM: TESTING INDUCTIVE ARGUMENTS

Each of the following attempts at inductive argument is flawed in some way. For each, identify the type of inductive argument and apply the appropriate tests.

1. Elementary schools work very well without using the "A" through "F" grading system. Since elementary schools are schools, and colleges are schools too, we should expect that colleges would work very well without an "A" through "F" grading scale.

2. Jeff speaks fast and he wins debates. Jane speaks fast and she wins debates. Ingrid speaks fast and she wins debates. Thus, we can conclude that speaking fast causes people to win debates.

3. Jack went to a dog show and saw fifty dogs. All of the dogs had long, shaggy hair, which was white, grey, and black. None of the dogs had tails. Based on what Jack saw, he concluded that all dogs lack tails and have shaggy hair which is white, grey, and black.

hit you does not mean that the cat caused you to be hit. The assertion of a causal correlation based simply on a temporal relationship is referred to as a *post hoc fallacy* (from the Latin *post hoc ergo propter hoc,* "after this therefore because of this").

Coherence of association   *Is the association between the alleged cause and the alleged effect coherent?* This test suggests that any alleged cause and effect relationship should be consistent with other related data. In every causal situation there is likely to be a body of data that is not directly useful in establishing a causal correlation, but is indirectly related to the causal experience. Such data may be capable of explaining, or of being explained by, the causal correlation. Recent epidemiological studies have revealed more lung problems among marijuana smokers than any other group, including tobacco smokers. At first this finding was surprising since marijuana users generally smoke many fewer cigarettes per day than do tobacco users. Other data, however, helped to explain the association.

> The pot smokers' heightened exposure to tar and carbon monoxide appears to be a function of the way they smoke, Tashkin says. He found that compared with cigarette smokers, marijuana smokers inhale a greater amount of smoke and hold it in almost four times as long. The extra time allows more tar to settle and gives carbon monoxide greater opportunity to be absorbed. (Oliwenstein, 18)

In this instance knowledge about how marijuana smokers inhale and hold the smoke made the causal correlation more understandable or coherent.

When such indirect evidence contradicts the causal correlation, it undermines confidence in the causal relationship. The test of coherence simply asks, Is the causal relationship reasonable in light of other known data?

SUMMARY

Inductive reasoning is used to create three different forms of argument: argument by example, argument by analogy, and argument by causal correlation.

The argument by example seeks to identify a regular characteristic within a given class in order to arrive at a generalized conclusion of essence or existence. There are three tests of arguments by example: (1) Are the examples typical? (2) Have a sufficient number of examples been examined? (3) Are negative instances adequately accounted for?

The argument by analogy attempts to discover similarities of characteristics between cases to establish a specific conclusion of existence. There are two tests of arguments by analogy: (1) Are the compared cases alike in all essential characteristics? (2) Are the compared characteristics accurately described?

The argument by causal correlation tries to establish a functional relationship between certain elements of the cases in order to achieve a general or specific conclusion of explanation. Causal correlation assumes that nothing occurs by chance and that for everything there is a cause. A cause is necessary if the effect will not occur absent that cause; a cause is sufficient if it can produce an effect even though that effect may also occur under other circumstances. John Stuart

Mill's procedures of concomitant variation, the method of agreement, and the method of differences are helpful in establishing causal correlation. There are four tests of arguments by causal correlations: (1) Is the association between the cause and the effect a consistent one? (2) Is the association between the cause and the effect a strong one? (3) Do the cause and the effect appear in a regular time sequence? (4) Is the association between the cause and effect coherent?

SELECTED BIBLIOGRAPHY

BARKER, STEPHEN F. *Induction and Hypothesis.* Ithaca, NY: Cornell University Press, 1957.

BLACK, MAX. "Induction." *Encyclopedia of Philosophy.* 4 vols. Edited by Paul Edwards.

BROWN, LESTER, and JODI JACOBSON. "Accessing the Future of Urbanization." In *State of the World 1987,* Edited by Lester R. Brown, et al., 38–56. New York: Norton, 1987.

KENNEDY, EDWARD. "Tighter Gun Controls—Both Sides of the Dispute." *U.S. News and World Report,* July, 10, 1972; 69.

KRUGER, ARTHUR N. Pp. 146–91 in *Modern Debate: Its Logic and Strategy.* New York: McGraw-Hill, 1960.

MCBURNEY, JAMES H., and GLEN E. MILLS. Pp. 119–34 in *Argumentation and Debate: Techniques of a Free Society,* 2nd ed. New York: Macmillan, 1964.

MCDONALD, DANIEL. *The Language of Argument.* Scranton: Chandler, 1971.

MILL, JOHN STUART. *System of Logic.* London: Longmans, Green and Co., 1900.

OLIWENSTEIN, LORI. "The Perils of Pot." *Discover,* June 1988; 18.

U.S. Department of Health, Education and Welfare. *Smoking and Health.* Washington: GPO, 1964.

VON WRIGHT, GEORG HENRIK. *The Logical Problem of Induction.* Oxford: Basil Blackwell, 1965.

STUDY QUESTIONS

1. After reviewing the three types of conclusions outlined in Chapter 5 (existence, essence, and causation), discuss the following:
   a. Why does an argument by example not reach conclusions of causation or explanation?
   b. Why does an argument by analogy not reach conclusions of causation or explanation?
   c. Why does an argument by causal correlation not reach conclusions of existence or essence?
2. Each of the inductive argument forms involves an inferential leap that takes us beyond our data. How do the various tests of inductive argument help us increase certainty about the conclusions we reach when using inductive argument?
3. In some cultures the figurative analogy is said to constitute acceptable proof. American Indian culture and Far Eastern mysticism, for example, ascribe much power to the figurative analogy. What arguments can be raised to support the idea that the figurative analogy should be accepted as proof? What arguments can be used to reject this position?
4. Suppose that we accepted the position that causation can never be established. What implications does acceptance of this position have on solving such problems as drug abuse, cancer, obesity, or illiteracy?

1. Prepare a notebook in which you collect examples of each form of inductive argument.
   a. Label each argument.
   b. Indicate whether the argument is by example, analogy, or causal correlation.
   c. Is the conclusion of the argument one of essence, existence, or causation?
   d. Are all three elements of a complete argument (data, reasoning process, and conclusion) presented? If not, try to supply the missing element.
   e. Evaluate the argument by applying the appropriate tests .
2. Examine government reports such as those on AIDS, birth control pills, cigarette smoking, asbestos, and the like. Try to determine how each of these reports approached the problem of establishing causation. Note especially any attempt to use the method of concomitant variation, the method of agreement, and the method of differences to demonstrate a cause and effect relationship.
3. Examine basic textbooks in such fields as chemistry, biology, physics, logic, psychology, and sociology. How does the concept of causation differ between the natural sciences and the social sciences?

ANSWERS TO PRACTICUM

1. Analogy. The flaw is that the compared cases are not alike in all essential characteristics. That is, elementary school education is fundamentally different from college education.
2. Causal correlation. One flaw is that the association between the alleged cause and the alleged effect is not coherent. Throughout this book we have learned that there are many factors involved in winning debates. In addition, the association between the alleged cause and the alleged effect is not a strong one. Determining what causes people to win debates requires consideration of many other potential factors.
3. Example. The first flaw is that the examples are not typical. Jack probably attended a dog show limited to Old English sheepdogs! Second, Jack examined an insufficient number of examples. There are millions of dogs in the world. Basing a conclusion on only fifty dogs is inadequate.

CHAPTER NINE
DEDUCTIVE ARGUMENTS

If you are a fan of mystery stories—particularly Sherlock Holmes mysteries—you have an appreciation for deductive reasoning. The use of deductive arguments is not confined, of course, to detectives or mystery writers; deductive arguments are used by all of us, every day. Whenever you use arguments based on principles, definitions, or criteria, you are arguing deductively.

Deductive reasoning is used to create two different forms of argument: argument from causal generalization and argument from sign. Since both of these forms use deductive reasoning, they begin with generalities (class conclusions), use the process of analysis, and arrive at structurally certain conclusions. The two forms of deductive argument differ from each other in terms of the *kind of relationships* (functional or substance and attribute) assumed in the initial premise and in terms of the *basic question* (causation or existence) that is answered in the conclusion.

The deductive process relates parts to the whole or members of a class to the entire class. The mechanism through which this is accomplished is the syllogism. The initial generalizations, on which arguments from causal generalization and arguments from sign rest, are often not expressed when these arguments are used in actual discourse. It is important, however, to be aware of these unstated statements, or premises, and to be able to cast these arguments in complete syllogistic form. Only by casting deductive arguments into syllogistic form is it possible to examine their structural adequacy or formal validity.

ARGUMENT FROM CAUSAL GENERALIZATION

The first deductive form of argument to be examined is the argument from causal generalization.

Characteristics of Argument from Causal Generalization

The argument from causal generalization applies an assumed or inductively established causal relationship to specific cases or classes. By including (or excluding) a specific instance in the category of the general cause (or the general effect), the functioning of the causal relationship in the specific instance can be established.

Because we know that AIDS is transmitted through (caused by) the mixing of bodily fluids and because we know that the sharing of hypodermic needles by drug addicts can result in the accidental transfusion of residual amounts of blood, we may conclude—by the process of causal generalization—that AIDS can be transmitted by the sharing of hypodermic needles. In this example, sharing needles is a specific instance of the general cause—mixing of bodily fluids. The relationship is one of inclusion within the class.

Arguments from causal generalization may also exclude specific causes or effects from the general class of causes or effects. If no one has ever contacted AIDS through merely casual personal contact and if Mary has AIDS, it would be reasonable to conclude that she did not acquire the disease from mere casual contacts.

The conclusions of arguments from causal generalization may be either specific to an individual case or general for a class. When a general conclusion results, the class identified within the conclusion will always be a more specific subset of the original generalization. In the first example above, the conclusion identified a class of causes, sharing needles, which was a subset of the original, more general cause, the mixing of bodily fluids. The conclusion of the second example was specific to an individual case, Mary. Arguments from causal generalization explain why things are as they are by either affirming or denying a functional relationship.

Tests of Argument from Causal Generalization

There are three tests that may be applied specifically to arguments from causal generalization. These tests examine the completeness of the functional relationship by looking at it from broader contexts.

Intervening factors   *Will intervening factors preclude an expected cause and effect relationship?* This test recognizes that cause and effect relationships do not normally function in environments free from other influences. Since other influences may be operating, there is the possibility that a normal cause and effect relationship may be blocked or at least altered. Placing a finger on a hot iron to see if it is ready for use would normally be expected to result in burned flesh. If, however, a bit of saliva is placed on the finger and then the iron is touched, no burn results.

In order to undermine the conclusion of a causal generalization, it is not enough simply to show the possibility of some intervening factor. Both the likelihood that intervening factors exist and that they will negate or significantly change the predicted cause and effect relationship must be demonstrated. It should be noted that this test does not wholly deny the original causal generalization; it only identifies a reservation to its application in a specific situation.

Sufficiency of cause   *Is the cause sufficient to bring about the effect?* This test accepts the idea that a specific cause and effect may be functionally related to each other, but it suggests that the specific cause, acting alone, will not be adequate to bring about the effect. According to this test, other causal forces must be present before the effect will occur. By demonstrating that the effect will not occur in the absence of the other factors, a one-to-one cause and effect relationship is denied, and the significance of the causal force is weakened. Money, for example, may be functionally related to the solution of such domestic problems as poverty and inadequate housing, but if it can be shown that money alone, without effective programs and wise administration, is not sufficient to solve these problems, the causal generalization is undermined. Causal generalizations that fail to meet this test are said to be guilty of the *fallacy of part cause or insufficient cause.*

Other unspecified effects   *Will the cause result in other unspecified effects?* Not only may there be other causes than those suggested by the initial causal generalization, but there may also be other effects. Many causal forces set off a series of reactions rather than result in a single effect. The benefits of certain modern medicines, for example, are sometimes offset by their side effects. Although the identification of such other effects does not directly negate the conclusion of an argument from causal generalization, it does allow for a fairer evaluation of the impact of the cause.

ARGUMENT FROM SIGN

A second form of deductive argument is the argument from sign or argument from circumstantial evidence, as it is sometimes called. Although you may be more familiar with the labels "cause," "example," and "analogy" than you are with the term "sign," arguments from sign are widely used in everyday discourse.

Characteristics of Argument from Sign

The argument by sign is *based on the assumption of a substance-attribute relationship. This assumption suggests that every substance (object, event, person, for example) has certain distinguishing characteristics or attributes (size, shape, sound, color, and the like) and that the presence or absence of either the substance or the attribute may be taken as a sign of the presence or absence of the other.*

When a detective observes small, deep footprints in the snow and a low angle of trajectory of the bullet from the murderer's gun into the victim's body and concludes that the murderer was a short, heavyset person, he or she is reasoning from sign. The detective assumes the existence of a substance (a short, heavyset person) based on the existence of certain attributes (deep, small footprints and low angle of trajectory).

In most sign arguments, the relationship between the substance and the attribute is never explicitly expressed, but the reliability of that relationship is critical. Typically the presence of the attribute (or substance) is noted, and the existence of the substance (or attribute) is stated as a conclusion. In the example below, taken from a letter to the editor of *The Atlantic,* a popular magazine, the underlying substance-attribute relationship is assumed but not expressed.

I am compelled to respond to Ellen Ruppel Shell's astounding statements in her essay "First, Do No Harm" (May *Atlantic*) that physicians receive little formal training in medical school about prescription drugs, and that we get most of our information about new drugs from "detailers."

Pharmacology is one of the seven or so basic sciences taught in medical school as formal courses. It takes up one seventh of Part I of the National Board Exam, taken by most students at the end of their second year of school.

Halfway through medical school we begin prescribing drugs for actual patients, under heavy supervision. We are expected to know why we are recommending a particular drug for a particular patient and condition, and we are expected to be able to anticipate adverse effects and interactions with other drugs. The coursework is done in an academic setting, well isolated from market pressures.

Once we graduate and begin internship and residency, we are still in an academic setting—the teaching hospital. We have available exhaustive reference books, including Goodman and Gilman's *The Pharmacologic Basis of Therapeutics.* Leading journals in every field publish articles in practically every issue concerning the efficacy or side effects of new or commonly used drugs in clinical situations of general interest. Publications like *The Medical Letter* cover drugs exclusively introducing new drugs and discussing new information about older medications. If a doctor associated with a hospital needs information quickly, a hospital pharmacist is often close by to help out.

To state so baldly that we get our information primarily from detailers is an insult to the many physicians who work hard to keep up on the latest drug research and pass their knowledge on to their patients in the form of better care. I do not believe that even the detailers would accept Shell's assertion that doctors do not know much about drugs.

Rose Marie Holt, M.D.
Seattle, Wash.
(August 1988, 7–8)

The unstated initial generalization of Dr. Holt's refutation is that course work, National Board Exams, supervised practice, and the use of reference books are attributes of the substance of training in pharmacology. Since these attributes are shown to exist, she concludes that the substance (training in pharmacology) also exists.

Natural or conceptual basis   The assumed substance-attribute relationship of a sign argument may have either a natural or a conceptual basis. Natural signs are correlations that may be observed in nature and that exist as an inherent part of nature's processes. A farmer who observes hard-crusted soil and concludes that there will be a poor potato crop is reasoning from a natural sign. Arguments from natural signs may ultimately involve unidentified causal relationships. However, the possible existence of a causal relationship is really irrelevant to natural signs because sign arguments only claim coexistence.

Conceptual signs are correlations that exist as a result of custom or of definition. If you point to a Mercedes Benz automobile as an indication of wealth, you are reasoning from a conceptual sign based on custom. If you conclude that a whale is a mammal because it nourishes its young with milk, you are reasoning from a conceptual sign based on the definition of mammals. Dr. Holt's argument that doctors are trained in pharmacology also illustrates the use of conceptual signs based on definition (training is defined as involving course work, Board exams, supervised practice, and the use of reference works). Signs based on definition are particularly important, since all moral and legal questions ultimately depend on them.

Conclusions of existence or essence   The conclusions of sign arguments establish either existence or essence. When the substance-attribute relationship is applied to a specific member or to a specific part of a class, the conclusion demonstrates existence. The detective who observed the deep footprints and the low angle of the bullet's trajectory arrived at a conclusion that identified the characteristics of an individual and that asserted the probable *existence* of a short, heavyset murderer. When the substance-attribute relationship is applied to an entire subgroup within a class, the conclusion asserts essence. The conclusion that whales are mammals because they nourish their young with milk is applied to an entire subgroup of mammals and, therefore, identifies an *essential* quality of whales.

Tests of Argument from Sign

The argument from sign uses the deductive process to apply a general substance-attribute relationship to a more specific situation. The tests of the argument from sign provide different ways of evaluating the reliability of the initial substance-attribute relationship.

Invariable indicators   *Are the substance and the attribute invariable indicators of the presence of each other?* This test seeks to determine if the substance only appears when the attribute is present and if the attribute exists only when the substance is present. When the substance and the attribute are invariable indicators of the presence of the other, the relationship is very strong. It is possible, however, for the attribute to be an invariable indicator of the substance, but for the substance to also exist apart from the attribute. A bullet-ridden body, for example, may be an invariable indication of the existence of a spent firearm, but a spent firearm can exist without indicating the presence of a bullet-ridden body. Similarly, the substance may always signify the presence of the attribute, but the attribute may exist apart from the substance. Thus, a traffic jam always requires the presence of cars, but cars may be present without a traffic jam occurring. If either the substance or the attribute is an invariable indicator of the other, a reliable sign relationship can be drawn. It is important, however, to avoid assuming reciprocal invariability where it does not exist.

Sufficient signs   *Are sufficient signs presented?* If the relationship between a single attribute and the substance is not an invariable one, then it is necessary to offer a number of supporting signs. A series of signs may be considered sufficient when it establishes either invariability or probability. While no one sign may be capable of providing an invariable indicator, a group of signs may often accomplish the same purpose. Most illnesses, for example, require the identification of several symptoms before an accurate diagnosis can be made. Although the presence of chest pains does not necessarily indicate heart disease, chest pains when combined with other symptoms can provide an invariable indication of heart trouble. In other situations, however, it is difficult to establish an invariable relationship between even a group of attributes and a substance or between a group of substances and an attribute. In such instances, the probability of the conclusion rests both on the degree of reliability of the individual substance-attribute relationships and on the number of such relationships presented. If we know that in most periods of history the buildup of weapons and the expression of hostility toward neighboring nations have preceded the outbreak of wars, then we may be willing to predict the future existence of a war based on only these two signs. On the other hand, if only occasionally have the buildup of weapons and the expression of hostility preceded wars, then we would probably require several more supporting signs before accepting the conclusion that war is inevitable in this situation.

Contradictory signs   *Are contradictory signs adequately considered?* The existence of contradicting signs undermines confidence in the conclusion of a sign argument. An asserted sign relationship may be weakened by demonstrating the existence of even one contrary sign. A sign relationship may be completely denied by showing that the preponderance of signs are contrary ones or that the single contrary sign has an inevitable relationship to the substance.

If the existence of an elected government, competing political parties, and universal suffrage were offered as indications that a particular country has a democratic government, the claimed sign relationship could be undermined by pointing to the lack of a free press as a contrary sign. By demonstrating that the existence of a free press was an invariable indicator of democracy or that such other signs of democracy as freedom of speech, freedom of assembly, and fair election procedures were also lacking, the original claim of democracy could be not only weakened but denied.

SYLLOGISTIC FORM OF DEDUCTIVE ARGUMENTS

The tests specific to the argument from sign and the argument from causal generalization, given in the previous sections, are tests of the substantive accuracy or material validity of their initial generalizations. However, since deductive arguments apply these initial statements to new situations, it is necessary to test not only the accuracy of the original statements but also the ways in which they are used. The syllogism, thus, tests the form of the argument or the validity of the *relationship* between the statements.

A syllogism consists of three statements and three terms (words, phrases, concepts). Each statement contains only two of the terms, and each of the statements relates a different set of the terms. The statements of a syllogism are known as the major premise, the minor premise, and the conclusion. The *major premise* states a generalization (All apples are fruit). The *minor premise* relates a specific case or class to the generalization (Jonathans are apples). The *conclusion* follows from the premises (Therefore, Jonathans are fruit).

The terms of a syllogism are known as the major term, the middle term, and the minor term. The *major term* (fruit) appears in the major premise and in the conclusion. It is the term that includes or excludes the middle term. The *middle term* (apples) appears in the major and the minor premises, but not in the conclusion. It is included in or excluded from the major term, and it includes or excludes the minor term. The *minor term* (Jonathans) appears in the minor premise and in the conclusion. It is the term that is included in or excluded from the middle term.

The statements of a syllogism relate the terms to one another based on three logical principles, which are known as Aristotle's laws of thought. These laws are the *law of identity* (A = A), the *law of contradiction* (every A has its non-A), and the *law of the excluded middle* (B is either A or non-A). These laws assume that it is possible to separate phenomena and to define terms categorically. By establishing precise categories, classes are set up that include or exclude other terms.

There are three types of syllogisms based on the structure of the major premise. They are the categorical syllogism, the hypothetical syllogism, and the disjunctive syllogism. All three types are based on the laws of thought, and all involve three premises and three terms. The structure of an argument from sign or an argument from causal generalization may involve any one of these three types.

Tests of Categorical Syllogisms

A categorical syllogism is a syllogism whose major premise classifies without qualifications. Such major premises are characterized by words such as "all," "every," "each," "none," or "no." An example of a categorical syllogism would be:

> All Christians believe in the divinity of Christ.
> John is a Christian.
> John believes in the divinity of Christ.

There are five basic tests of the logical validity of the categorical syllogism.

Middle term universal   *Is the middle term used in a universal or unqualified sense in at least one of the premises?* The middle term must apply universally to every member of the class in order to provide a clear basis for inclusion or exclusion. If the middle term were not universal, and applied only to some members of the class, there would be no basis for predicting whether or not a specific member of the class was included within the generalization of the first premise. The following is an example of an invalid syllogism based on a nonuniversal (or undistributed) middle term:

> Some history professors are poor lecturers.
> Dr. Robinson is a history professor.
> Dr. Robinson is a poor lecturer. (Invalid)

The middle term, "history professors," is not universal, so there is no way of knowing whether or not Dr. Robinson is part of the group of history professors who are poor lecturers.

Terms universal in premise and conclusion   *If a term is universal in the conclusion, was it universal in the premises?* A term that is qualified in one of the premises cannot assume universality in the conclusion. Deductive arguments provide structural certainty because the conclusions do not extend beyond the initial data. To assert universality in the conclusion when the terms of the premises were limited would be an unwarranted extension of the argument and would violate the certainty of the conclusion. Consider the following example:

> All people with poor vision should wear glasses.
> Many college graduates have poor vision.
> All college graduates should wear glasses. (Invalid)

The minor term, "Many college graduates," was not universal in the minor premise, but became so in the conclusion. The inclusion of "many college graduates" in the category of "people with poor vision" does not justify the inclusion of all college graduates in that category.

One affirmative statement   *Is at least one of the premises an affirmative statement?* Affirmative statements are necessary in order to establish class-inclusive relationships. Negative statements indicate relationships of exclusion. If both premises are negative statements, both the major and the minor terms are excluded from the middle term. With the major and minor terms excluded from the middle term, there is no way of relating the major and minor terms to each other. A syllogism with two negative premises is illustrated here:

> No Arabs are Zionists.
> Harry is not an Arab.
> Harry is a Zionist. (Invalid)

The first premise excludes Zionists (major term) from the class of Arabs (middle term). The second premise excludes Harry (minor term) from the class of Arabs. That Arabs are not Zionists does not ensure that non-Arab Harry is a Zionist. Lacking a positive statement of inclusion in at least one premise, there is no way of linking the major and minor terms through the middle term.

Negative premise, negative conclusion   *If one premise is negative, is the conclusion negative?* A negative premise excludes the term of that premise from the middle term. Therefore, the only relationship that can be identified between the major and minor terms is a negative one of exclusion. This rule is violated in the following example:

> No Russian believes in capitalism.
> Ivan is a Russian.
> Ivan believes in capitalism. (Invalid)

In this sample syllogism the first premise is a negative one that excludes all Russians from believing in capitalism. Since Ivan is included in the category of Russians, he must be excluded (along with all other Russians) from the category of those who believe in capitalism.

Terms used the same   *Are the terms of the syllogism used in the same sense throughout?* As was explained earlier, syllogisms are based on precise definitions of terms. If the meaning of a term is not precise and shifts during the development of an argument, a fourth category may inadvertently be introduced. Since the form of the syllogism only permits three terms to be related at a time, the introduction of a fourth term (in the form of a shift in meaning) precludes any valid conclusion. Observe how the shift in the concept of communism creates a fourth term in the following syllogism:

> All Communists were opposed to United States involvement in Vietman.
> All those who believe in the collective ownership of property are Communists.
> All those who believe in the collective ownership of property were opposed to United States involvement in Vietnam. (Invalid)

In this example, the term Communist is used to refer to a political viewpoint in the first premise, but in the second premise it refers to an economic concept. Since the political viewpoint and the economic concept do not necessarily coincide, a fourth term was introduced into the syllogism. When an advocate changes the meaning of a critical term during the course of an argument, he or she is said to be guilty of the *fallacy of equivocation*.

Tests of Hypothetical Syllogisms

A hypothetical syllogism is a syllogism whose major premise is concerned with uncertain or conditional happenings, which may or may not exist or occur. The uncertain condition is usually indicated by such terms as "if," "when," "assuming," or "in the event of." An example of a hypothetical syllogism follows:

> If a system of compulsory health insurance is financed throught the income tax, it will win approval.
> The proposed system of compulsory health insurance is financed through the income tax.
> The proposed system of compulsory health insurance will win approval.

There are two basic tests of the hypothetical syllogism.

Affirms antecedent, affirms consequent *If the minor premise affirms the antecedent, does the conclusion affirm the consequent?* The antecedent is the conditional clause, and the consequent is the independent clause. If the minor premise denies the antecedent, no valid conclusion can be drawn. When the antecedent is denied, the condition of the first premise has not been met, and we have no basis for predicting what will happen. The second premise of the following syllogism denies the antecedent:

> If you have outstanding grades, you will be admitted to law school.
> You do not have outstanding grades.
> You will not be admitted to law school. (Invalid)

The first premise indicates only the positive results of outstanding grades. It does not suggest the possible consequences of less than outstanding grades. The conclusion predicting nonadmission to law school is, therefore, unjustified.

Denies antecedent, denies consequent *If the minor premise denies the consequent, does the conclusion deny the antecedent?* By knowing that the consequent does not exist, we must also know that the condition that would have resulted in its existence does not exist. However, if the minor premise affirms the consequent, we do not necessarily know that the antecedent has occurred. It may be that the condition of the antecedent is only one of many conditions that could cause the consequent to exist. Thus, when the minor premise affirms the consequent, no valid conclusion can be drawn. Observe the following example:

> Whenever I eat too much, I get sick.
> I got sick.
> I ate too much. (Invalid)

Since conditions other than eating too much might cause us to get sick, the conclusion does not necessarily follow.

Tests of Disjunctive Syllogisms

A disjunctive syllogism is one whose major premise presents alternatives. The alternatives are usually indicated by such terms as "either. . .or," "neither. . .nor," or "but." An example of a disjunctive syllogism follows:

> Either the state must keep its spending more in line with its revenue or it will go bankrupt.
> The state will keep its spending more in line with its revenue.
> It will not go bankrupt.

There are three tests of disjunctive syllogisms.

Affirms one alternative, denies the other   *If the minor premise affirms (or denies) one of the alternatives, does the conclusion deny (or affirm) the other alternative?* Since the major premise establishes alternatives, one of the alternatives must be accepted and the other denied. It does not matter whether the minor premise affirms or denies one of the alternatives so long as the conclusion does the opposite. Note the following violation of this test:

> Either I must get a part-time job or else I will have to quit school.
> I did not get a part-time job.
> I will not have to quit school. (Invalid)

In this example, the conclusion is inconsistent with the other two premises. If the choice is truly between working part time or quitting school, then the rejection of part-time work requires the acceptance of the alternative (quitting school).

Alternatives mutually exclusive   *Are the alternatives presented in the first premise mutually exclusive?* The alternatives presented in the first premise must automatically exclude each other. If the acceptance of one alternative does not necessarily force the rejection of the other, the alternatives are not mutually exclusive. A syllogism in which the terms are not mutually exclusive is illustrated below:

> Either we must take plenty of time or we must be unfair.
> We will take plenty of time.
> We will not be unfair.

The conclusion follows consistently, but the first premise is inadequate. It is possible both to take plenty of time and to be unfair; therefore the alternatives are not mutually exclusive.

All possible alternatives   *Does the major premise include all of the possible alternatives?* The major premise of a disjunctive syllogism must not ignore possible alter-

Each of the following attempts at deductive argument is flawed in some way. For each, identify the type of deductive argument or the type of syllogism and apply the appropriate tests.

1. All doctors are good communicators.

   Jane is studying to become a doctor.

   Jane is a good communicator.

2. During a critical fourth down play, the football coach threw his hands up in the air and started shouting. I didn't see the play myself, but based on Coach Osborne's reaction, I'm positive the referee must have made a lousy call.

3. If you spend twelve hours a day studying for debate class, you will earn an "A."

   You do not spend twelve hours a day studying for debate class.

   You will not get an "A" in debate class.

4. Cynthia has been lying in the sun for hours. She will have a painful sunburn later today.

5. Either Jim is for the proposal or he is against the proposal.

   Jim is not for the proposal.

   Jim is not against the proposal.

natives. If other alternatives than those indicated in the first premise exist, the conclusion can be denied by pointing to the incompleteness of the original premise. Note the incompleteness of the disjunction in the following syllogism:

Jay does poor work so he must be either stupid or lazy.
He is not stupid.
He is lazy.

Although the conclusion follows consistently from the major premise, the major premise is faulty. There are many other possible explanations for the poor work—he may have been too busy to do it well, emotional problems may have precluded a good job, and so forth.

SUMMARY

Deductive reasoning is used to create two different forms of argument: argument by causal generalization and argument by sign.

The argument from causal generalization applies an assumed or inductively established causal relationship to specific cases or classes. By including (or excluding) a specific instance in the category of the general cause (or general effect), the functioning of the causal relationship in the specific instance can be established. There are three tests of arguments from causal generalization:

(1) Will intervening factors preclude an expected cause and effect relationship? (2) Is the cause sufficient to bring about the effect (fallacy of part cause)? (3) Will the cause result in other unspecified effects?

The argument from sign is based on the assumption that every substance (object, event, person, and so forth) has certain distinguishing characteristics or attributes (size, shape, color, and the like) and that the presence or absence of either the substance or the attribute may be taken as a sign of the presence or absence of the other. The substance-attribute relationship may have either a natural or conceptual basis. There are three tests of arguments from sign: (1) Are the substance and the attribute invariable indicators of the presence of each other? (2) Are sufficient signs presented? (3) Are contradictory signs adequately considered?

The syllogism may be used to test the validity of the relationship between the statements. A syllogism consists of three premises or statements and three terms (words or concepts). There are three types of syllogisms based on the structure of the major premise. A categorical syllogism places objects or concepts into categories. The tests of a categorical syllogism are (1) Is the middle term used in a universal or unqualified sense in at least one premise? (2) If a term is universal in the conclusion, was it universal in the premise? (3) Is at least one of the premises an affirmative statement? (4) If one premise is negative, is the conclusion negative? (5) Are the terms of the syllogism used in the same sense throughout (fallacy of equivocation)? A hypothetical syllogism is concerned with uncertain or conditional happenings. The two basic tests of the hypothetical syllogism are (1) If the major premise affirms the antecedent, does the conclusion affirm the consequent? (2) If the minor premise denies the consequent, does the conclusion deny the antecedent? A disjunctive syllogism is one whose major premise presents alternatives. There are three tests of disjunctive syllogisms: (1) If the minor premise affirms (or denies) one of the alternatives, does the conclusion deny (or affirm) the other alternative? (2) Are the alternatives presented in the first premise mutually exclusive? (3) Does the major premise include all of the possible alternatives?

SELECTED BIBLIOGRAPHY

COPI, IRVING M. *Introduction to Logic.* 3d ed. New York: Macmillan, 1968.
McBURNEY, JAMES H., and GLEN E. MILLS. Pp. 145–53 in *Argumentation and Debate: Techniques of a Free Society.* 2d ed. New York: Macmillan, 1964.
The Rhetoric of Aristotle. Translated by Lane Cooper. New York: Appleton-Century-Crofts, 1960.
SMITH, WILLIAM S. "Formal Logic in Debate." *Southern Speech Journal* 27 (Summer 1962): 330–38.

STUDY QUESTIONS

1. Is reasoning based on induction superior to reasoning based on deduction? Why or why not?
2. What are the primary differences between inductive and deductive reasoning?

3. How is it possible for the conclusion of a syllogism to be false even if the syllogism is properly structured?
4. What is the difference between a *causal generalization* and a *causal correlation?*

EXERCISES

1. Prepare a notebook in which you collect examples of each form of deductive argument.
   a. Label each argument.
   b. Indicate whether the argument is by sign or by causal generalization.
   c. Is the conclusion of the argument one of existence or causation?
   d. Place the argument in syllogistic form, filling in missing premises or conclusions.
   e. Evaluate the argument by applying the appropriate tests.
2. Provide a valid example for each of the three types of syllogisms (categorical, hypothetical, and disjunctive).

ANSWERS TO PRACTICUM

1. Categorical syllogism. The conclusion is invalid since Jane is not yet a member of the class identified in the major premise.
2. Argument by sign. The conclusion is invalid for a variety of reasons. First, that the coach throws his hands up in the air and shouts is not an invariable sign of a "lousy call" by a referee. Coach Osborne may have been expressing displeasure with the way in which his team executed the play. Second, a sufficient number of signs are not presented. The additional sign of Coach Osborne shouting directly at the referee would establish a stronger conclusion.
3. Hypothetical syllogism. The first premise indicates only the positive outcome of studying for twelve hours a day. It fails to suggest the consequences of *not* studying for twelve hours a day.
4. Causal generalization (the unstated premise is that people who lie out in the sun get sunburned). Although the conclusion seems reasonable, we do not know if intervening factors are operating that will preclude the effect. For example, Cynthia may be using a sunblock lotion to prevent sunburn.
5. Disjunctive syllogism. The conclusion is inconsistent with the other two premises. If the choice is truly between "being for" or "being against," the "being against" requires that Jim be "for" the proposal.

CHAPTER TEN
ORGANIZING
AND BRIEFING
ARGUMENTS

In order to form a reasonable argumentative case or position, you must be able to organize individual arguments in a meaningful and consistent manner. The logical outline and the argumentative brief are the primary means of accomplishing this objective. Logical outlining provides a set of logical, grammatical, and visual concepts that help to ensure that the relationships drawn between individual arguments are appropriate, and briefing offers a practical application of these concepts.

LOGICAL OUTLINING

Although it might be possible to construct an entire argumentative case using an extended chain of deductive reasoning or a series of a single form of inductive arguments, it would, undoubtedly, be difficult to do so. In everyday argument, we generally use many different forms of inductive and deductive arguments in building our analyses. The logical outline provides the most exacting means for structuring both inductive and deductive relationships and for relating the different forms of argument to one another.

The Nature of Outlining

An outline consists of a number of statements that are arranged in a series. There are essentially two kinds of idea relationships that can exist between main points and subordinate points. An idea relationship of "parts-to-the-whole" is the essential characteristic of a topical outline, whereas the idea relationship of support constitutes the essential characteristic of the logical outline.

A topical outline breaks a whole down into its parts for purposes of clarity. In this type of outlining, the subpoints do not support the main point, but rather constitute parts of the main point. This type of outlining is generally used for informative discourse. In Chapter 5, our discussion of the processes of reasoning is broken down into two parts: inductive reasoning and deductive reasoning. Our further division of inductive reasoning—synthetic process, begins with particulars, and probable conclusion—continues the parts-to-the-whole division. In outline form, this topical outline segment appears as follows:

I. Reasoning Processes
   A. Inductive Reasoning
      1. Synthetic Process
      2. Begins with Particulars
      3. Probable Conclusions
   B. Deductive Reasoning

In this chapter our primary concern is with logical outlining rather than with topical outlining. *In a logical outline the relationship between the different levels of statements is one of support.* In other words, each statement in a logical outline provides either data in support of the validity of the statement to which it is subordinate or a reason for the acceptance of that statement. Logical outlines are used for argumentative discourse, and topical outlines are used for informative discourse.

The following sample outline illustrates both the form and the relationships involved in logical outlining.

SAMPLE LOGICAL OUTLINE

I. Money bail is unnecessary to ensure the appearance of a criminal suspect at trial.
   A. In jurisdictions with money bail, 96 percent of the criminal suspects released returned for trial.
   B. In jurisdictions without any system of monetary guarantee, 98 percent of the criminal suspects released returned for trial.
II. Money bail is ineffective in protecting society against the recommission of crimes.
   A. Professional criminals have little difficulty in raising the necessary money for bail.
   B. Many serious crimes are committed by individuals who are out of jail on bond.
      1. In some jurisdictions as much as half of all the crimes committed are the acts of people on bail.
      2. The rate of murder and rapes among those released on bail is particularly high.

III. Money bail is undesirable.
    A. The system of money bail discriminates against the poor.
        1. Many of the poor cannot afford to put up even fifty dollars in bail money.
        2. More affluent citizens can meet bonds of one hundred thousand dollars or more.
           a. Some citizens have enough cash and collateral to pay the bail directly out of their own resources.
           b. Other citizens have at least enough resources to meet the fee of a professional bail agency.
    B. The system of money bail is costly to the state.
        1. It typically costs the state a thousand dollars or more to hold a suspect in custody pending trial.
        2. Prolonged pretrial detention of a family's breadwinner forces the family onto welfare.
    C. The system of money bail is damaging to persons who are detained.
        1. They are subject to assault and homosexual rape.
        2. They are more likely to be convicted.
           a. They are less able to help in the preparation of their own defense.
           b. Studies have shown that those detained in jail during the pretrial period are twice as likely to be convicted as those released during that period.

The Principles of Logical Outlining

The basic principles of logical outlining provide both guidelines for constructing outlines and tests of their logical adequacy. Failure to adhere to any one of these principles when organizing arguments is an indication of an inconsistent, incomplete, or unclear relationship.

Coordination At any given level of the outline form, statements should have some common relationship to one another. The common element or elements connecting such statements are determined by the statement to which they are subordinate. When unrelated or unequal statements appear at the same level of the outline form, an inconsistent relationship is revealed.

In the example below, note that items A, B, and D are all related to one another in that they identify specific manifestations of inflation's harm. Item C, on the other hand, indicates the magnitude of inflation, rather than its effect or harm. Statements A, B, and D are coordinate; statement C breaks the pattern of coordination.

I. Inflation is harmful to the nation. (Because)
    A. Inflation erodes the purchasing power of those on fixed incomes.
    B. Inflation encourages unsound business speculation.
    C. Inflation has been increasing at the rate of 5 percent per year.
    D. Inflation makes the financing of state and local services more difficult.

Subordination Those statements that are placed in a lower order in the outline form should justify, support, or prove the statement to which they are subordinate. Since the support for the higher-order statement may be based on either inductive or deductive reasoning, the subordinate statements may be either more or less specific than the higher-order statements. In the first example below, the higher-order statement is the conclusion of a deductive argument. Since the lower-order statements are the premises on which the conclusion is based, they are more general than the higher-order statement.

II. High unemployment will be necessary to halt our present inflation. (Because)
    A. In the past, inflation has never been halted until after unemployment became severe.
    B. The present inflation is not different from earlier inflations.

In the second example, the higher-order statement is the conclusion of an inductive argument, and the supporting lower-order statements are less general.

I. Inflation has never been halted until after unemployment became severe. (Because)
    A. The inflation of the late 1920s was not stopped until the Depression and high unemployment of the early 1930s.
    B. The inflation of 1956 ended with the high unemployment of 1957.
    C. The inflation of the late 1970s ended with the high unemployment of the early 1980s.

Whether more general or less general, subordinate points must lend support to the claim of the higher-order statement. When they do not, they are out of place in the outline form and logically irrelevant. In the following specimen, both points B and C are irrelevant to the statement of point I because they fail to justify a belief in that statement.

I. Unhealthy diets increase the incidence of disease.
    A. The consumption of large amounts of saturated fats is a primary cause of heart disease.
    B. Millions of Americans fail to eat properly.
    C. Men have worse dietary habits than women.

Division   At least two subordinate points must be presented for each subdivided statement within the outline. That every argument involves two elements other than the conclusion—the data and the reasoning process—suggests that there must be at least two elements of subordination. All deductive arguments derive their conclusions from two premises and, therefore, demand two elements of subordination. The nature of each of the forms of induction requires at least two elements of data. The argument by example requires a minimum of two examples in order to establish the assumption of regularity. The argument by analogy requires the identification of one or more points of similarity and the discounting of all dissimilarities. The argument by causal correlation requires the examination of at least two cases in order to establish concomitant variation, similarities, or differences. Thus, the use of fewer than two subordinate points in a logical outline is contrary to the principles of argumentation.

The appearance of a single subordinate point in an outline indicates an incomplete deductive argument or insufficient support for the conclusion of an inductive argument. When only one subordinate point is presented, it may mean that a premise of a deductive argument has been overlooked. This is the error in the following example.

I. The economy is heading out of its recessionary downturn. (Because)
   A. Car sales have been increasing.

The support for this argument could be made complete by adding a second subordinate point expressing the major premise of the argument.

   B. An increase in car sales is a reliable indicator of an economic upturn.

Single subpoints may also indicate insufficient support for the conclusion of an inductive argument rather than incomplete deductive reasoning. In the following outline segment, one example is not sufficient to support the general claim of the major premise.

I. Nationalism is capable of stopping communism. (Because)
   A. Nationalism has thwarted communism in Thailand.

Other supporting examples should be found or else the claims of the argument should be limited to the one example.

Completeness   Subordinate points should provide support for all of the concepts included within the statement of the superior point. This principle recognizes that the proof requirements of all propositions and arguments flow from their statement and that even sentences that are simple in structure and focus may contain several different concepts. The inclusion or exclusion of a single modifying term may change the proof requirements of any statement and, hence, the number and kind of subordinate points required. The failure of the subordinate points to support the claim of any concept of a statement results in a logically incomplete outline.

In the outline segment below the two subpoints do not provide complete support for the major idea, since the concept of "harmful" is not established.

II. Continued reliance on the property tax harmfully limits the expansion and upgrading of education. (Because)
   A. The property tax continues to be the major source of revenue for education.
   B. The expansion and upgrading of education have been limited by the lack of funds.

The inclusion of an additional subpoint would make the outline segment logically complete.

   C. Failure to expand and upgrade educational opportunities has resulted in the waste of human resources.

Simplicity   Each point in a logical outline should be stated in the form of a simple declarative sentence. A simple sentence is, by definition, a single unit of thought. Any collection of words that is less than a simple sentence does not express a complete idea. Phrases do not focus or limit thoughts, and for this reason it is not possible to determine their relationship to other ideas or concepts. Examine the two outline segments below. Notice how much clearer the relationships are in the second segment because the use of complete sentences has focused and limited the ideas.

I. Pollution
    A. Getting worse
    B. People die
    C. Property damage

I. Increasing levels of air pollution have resulted in serious costs to the nation. (Because)
    A. Air pollution is increasing.
    B. Air pollution results in serious costs.
        1. Air inversions have resulted in many deaths.
        2. Chemical particles in polluted air dirty and decompose physical structures.

Compound and complex sentences are expressions of the relationships between two or more complete units of thought. Compound sentences indicate two independent ideas, whereas complex sentences indicate a dependent or conditional relationship between clauses. Because compound and complex sentences constitute larger units of thought and more varied relationships than do simple sentences, they do not permit the diagramming of clear and consistent relationships. Multiple units of thought should be expressed in two or more simple sentences, and the outline form, rather than the sentence structure, should be used to indicate appropriate relationships between thought units. In the illustration below, the statement of the first outline is a complex sentence. Notice how the second outline segment visually illustrates the subordinate nature of the concept of the dependent clause, while more clearly emphasizing the overall importance of the independent clause.

I. Although a system of mass transit will be expensive to build and operate, Metropolis should begin construction immediately.

I. The cost of a mass transit system should not prevent Metropolis from beginning immediate construction. (Because)
    A. The cost of building the system can be paid off over a period of years.
    B. The cost of operating the system will be offset by the economic benefits to the city.

In the next set of examples, the statement in the first outline is a compound sentence, whereas the two statements of the second outline are simple sentences. Since the two clauses of the statement in segment one are of equal importance, they should be structured as coordinate points.

I. The city is capable of bearing the cost of constructing a mass transit system, and the benefits would be great.

I. The city is capable of bearing the costs of constructing a mass transit system.
II. The benefits of a mass transit system would be great.

Discreteness   The ideas presented in an outline must be expressed so that each statement is a separate and discrete unit of thought. Overlapping statements indicate indistinct and unclear relationships between ideas.

In the first outline segment below, the statement of point A is simply a different way of expressing the idea of I. In the second segment, point C is contained within the ideas of point B. Both outlines are logically unsatisfactory because they violate the principle of discreteness.

I. A Communist monolith no longer exists. (Because)
    A. Unity within the Communist world does not exist.
    B. Russia and China have conflicting economic and political objectives.
    C. Yugoslavia and Albania are not members of the Warsaw Pact.

I. Racial discrimination is socially unacceptable. (Because)
    A. Racial discrimination creates antagonism between the races.
    B. Racial discrimination prevents the maximum development of our human resources.
    C. Racial discrimination denies equal educational opportunity.

Symbolization   Each statement in an outline requires a letter or number that will indicate its relative rank with reference to the other ideas in the outline. Points having similar symbols are expected to be of comparable importance. Common practice recommends the use of roman numerals for main points, capital letters for the first level of subordination, arabic numbers for the second level of subordination, and lower-case letters for the third level of subordination.

When symbols are not used in a consistent manner the logical relationship between points becomes confused. The use of more than one symbol for a single statement reveals an incomplete subordination. Notice how, in the following outline segment, the shift from arabic numbers to lower-case letters confuses the relationship between the three subpoints of B. Notice, also, that the use of two symbols at the A level of the outline reveals an omitted conclusion. The arabic numbers (1 and 2) should be subpoints of a statement (A) such as: "Corruption of state and local officials is widespread."

I. The widespread corruption of state and local officials protects the activities of organized crime. (Because)
    A. 1. The criminal syndicate is alleged to control the state of Louisiana.
        2. The criminal syndicate controls major public officials in all of our larger cities.
    B. Corruption protects the activities of organized crime. (because)
        a. Corrupt officials fail to report illegal activities.
        b. Corrupt officials warn of planned raids.
        c. Corrupt officials thwart the prosecution process.

Benefits of Logical Outlining

The development of skill in logical outlining requires considerable effort and experience, but, once acquired, this skill is of great assistance in the preparation of entire argumentative cases and in the consideration of particular series of arguments. There are three reasons why logical outlining is so helpful.

First, the logical outline offers the only structure available for testing the relationships *among* individual arguments. The principles of logical outlining make it possible to organize all the forms of argument together within a single framework and to examine the relationships in terms of basic logical concepts. The principles of coordination and subordination provide guidelines for consistency of relationships. The principles of division and completeness test the comprehensiveness of the development, and the principles of simplicity, discreteness, and symbolization are directed at the clarity of the relationships. Thus, by working out an outline of arguments, you can help to ensure that you will be prepared to support a given proposition in a consistent, comprehensive, and clear manner.

Second, the logical outline is helpful because it encourages careful attention to the wording of arguments. Within the framework of the logical outline, only as many separate ideas can be related as can be expressed within the structure of a single simple sentence, and every idea expressed within that sentence must be supported by subpoints. Thus, you must develop skill at phrasing conclusions in order to focus relationships while at the same time limiting your claim.

Finally, the logical outline organizes ideas in a manner that can be easily communicated to others. When supporting arguments are presented before more general conclusions, listeners (or readers) may be confused about the purpose of the communication; but when conclusions are set forth before supporting arguments, receivers of the communication can more easily follow the presentation. Since this latter ordering of ideas is required by the logical outline, it helps to develop a pattern of thinking that is conducive to clear communication.

BRIEFING

Logical outlines can be used to provide the basic structure for speeches, written reports, or position papers. One of the most immediately useful applications of outlining, however, is in the preparation of briefs. A brief is an organized set of arguments and evidence designed to attack or defend a position. Briefs differ from logical outlines in that they include the evidence used to support specific arguments.

Role of Briefs

Briefs of one kind or another are used in a variety of argumentation contexts. When lawyers appeal cases to higher courts, the initial arguments are presented to the court in the form of written briefs. These briefs tend to be quite lengthy and include the background for a case as well as all of the major arguments to be advanced. The legal brief is written in paragraph form, but the presentation of arguments basically follows the logical outline pattern. Although lawyers are not always required to present written briefs at the original trial level, most lawyers brief their arguments prior to trial as a means of organizing their thinking for oral argument.

Business leaders and politicians also find briefs helpful in preparing for important meetings or press conferences. As political debates have become more commonplace, political candidates have begun to rely more on brief books prepared by aides to help ready candidates on the major issues to be discussed (White, 322–23). Political candidates in the midst of an election campaign have only limited time to give to studying and preparing for debates, so the focusing and organizing of evidence and arguments provided by briefs is extremely valuable.

In recent years, academic debaters have placed increasing reliance on briefs not only as a means of preparing arguments but also as a means of presenting them in rounds of debate. Today, debaters prepare briefs on almost every argument they expect to confront. These briefs help the debaters order and organize their evidence and arguments prior to the actual contests and provide a quick and easy reference point for their oral argumentation during the debate.

Benefits of Briefing

There are a number of specific benefits that can be derived from the briefing of arguments. First, the process of preparing briefs forces you to anticipate arguments and directs your research. After you have done some research on a topic and begun to think about basic positions, it is easy to feel that you are ready to debate. However, as you begin to prepare direct responses to arguments, you will probably realize that more specific research and analysis is required. You may discover that there are some major arguments to which you have few or no answers and that many of the arguments for which you have answers are not adequately supported by evidence. Thus, because briefing forces you to confront specific arguments with contradicting evidence and analysis, it helps to guide preparation.

A second benefit of briefing is that it helps you to organize your evidence and analysis. If evidence is to be useful for anything more than background on a topic, it must be organized for easy reference and use. The briefing of evidence demands more complete integration of evidence and analysis than is required by the simple development of an evidence file. Because a brief is created over a period of time and prior to the actual moment when it will be used, it can be carefully prepared, and the implications of arguments can be thoughtfully considered. Evidence that is organized in advance is more likely to be consistently and meaningfully ordered, and arguments are more likely to be carefully worded.

Third, briefing saves time during the actual presentation. In nearly all oral advocacy situations—board meetings, press conferences, interviews, formal debates—speakers are under some pressure to respond to arguments and questions in a timely manner. If responses have been briefed in advance, less time will be required during the actual encounter for finding evidence, thinking about what to say, and organizing answers. Responses can be more immediate and concise. With this preparation, whatever time is available during the actual presentation can be used for contemplating the deeper issues and for adapting and selecting responses.

A final benefit of briefing is that it helps to guard against forgetting responses. Sometimes while you are reading and researching, a brilliant—or, at least, good—response to an argument will come to mind. If you fail to make note of that response, however, it may be quickly forgotten. Even if you remember the argument for several days or weeks, you may still fail to recall it at the precise moment you need to, a month or two hence. Briefs should be prepared as soon after a specific issue is researched as possible. When responses are recorded in a systematic way, they will not be forgotten. Briefing arguments means they will be available when needed and that they can be easily retrieved.

Process of Briefing

There are three steps involved in the process of preparing briefs: (1) the identification of topics for briefing, (2) the gathering of materials, and (3) the construction of the briefs. Each of these procedures is fairly simple, but it is important that the process be systematic.

Identifying topics   Although it might be desirable to have briefs on every possible argument that can be raised, it is usually impossible to achieve that level of preparation. It is helpful, however, to have as many briefs ready as possible, and you should, certainly, have all of the major arguments briefed. To help develop priorities, you should prepare a list of the major arguments you expect to encounter. In generating such a list, you should be guided by your research, and you should be sure to consider each of the stock issues. Consultation with friends and advisors is also helpful. Once a fairly comprehensive list of needed briefs is achieved, priorities can be established. The arguments you expect to use most frequently should be briefed first. Over a period of time new arguments will be added to your list, and your priorities may change, but, by keeping such a list, you will always know what brief to prepare next.

Gathering materials   Gathering materials on any topic generally begins with broad research. Such broad research is necessary for gaining a fundamental understanding of the topic. At some point, however, specific issues and arguments must be studied in greater depth. Although general research is sufficient for the identification of topics for briefing, the preparation of specific briefs demands more focused, in-depth research. As research for a specific argument is collected, it should all be kept together so that you can better judge what additional materials are needed. Sometimes a considerable amount of frustrating searching will be necessary before the last few pieces of evidence can be found. Individual pieces of evidence should be kept on separate cards or sheets so that they will be easier to organize once the actual brief preparation begins.

Construction of briefs   In general, briefs should be constructed using the logical outline form. The logical outline helps to ensure that clear and sound relationships are established. Moreover, the system of indentation makes it easier to find specific arguments and evidence on the brief. In recording arguments on a brief, you should be especially careful to state arguments precisely and persuasively.

How deeply to develop the analysis on a brief is often a matter of concern. Sometimes debaters may have as many as twenty or thirty individual responses to an argument. Since all of these responses probably will not be necessary and since time constraints will normally preclude using them all, it is important that

First Negative Brief
Minimization of the Harms of Apartheid in South Africa

1. Measures to end nonpolitical discrimination are being enacted.

    Peter J. Spiro, correspondent for *Johannesburg Financial Mail, USA Today,* January 1988, 70.

    "At the same time it has moved to suppress black unrest, the government also has taken significant and positive steps to eliminate some of the more pervasive facets of the apartheid system. It has moved to abolish most of the race-based laws enumerated above, and smart money would bet that all non-political discriminatory legislation will be scrapped in the near future."

2. Economic empowerment of the black population will lead to political reform.

    a. Many blacks have attained middle-class professions.

        Staff writer, *Time,* February 29, 1988, 56.

        "Increasing numbers of blacks are working in middle-class professions as lawyers, doctors, psychiatrists, engineers, tax consultants and stockbrokers."

    b. Blacks have become increasingly wealthy in the past two years.

        Staff writer, *Time,* February 29, 1988, 56.

        "This newly affluent class is spearheading a peaceful but dramatic revolution in which blacks, who outnumber whites nearly 5 to 1 in South Africa, are starting to flex their economic muscle as earners and consumers. Blacks will pay an estimated total of $350 million in taxes this year, up from $58 million two years ago."

    c. Black economic leverage is growing steadily.

        Staff writer, *Time,* February 29, 1988, 56.

        "The rise in black purchasing power is having a marked impact on the national economy. More and more companies are boosting their sales figures by targeting their products to the black consumer, who now buys almost half of all items sold at retail."

    d. Continued economic prosperity will facilitate gradual political reform.

        Marshall Loeb, staff writer for *Fortune,* July 18, 1988, 90.

        "The blacks' surest hope for gaining political power is to gain still greater economic power. The faster the economy grows, the more rapidly they can do that."

3. Political rights of the South African blacks have already improved dramatically.

    a. Blacks have the right to vote in local elections.

        Staff writer, *The National Review,* November 25, 1988, 17.

        "Fair-minded reporting would have cited the 30 percent black turnout for contested seats, which, in the face of considerable intimidation, was a remarkable sign of civic responsibility. Far-seeing leaders in the church, in law, and in the academy would have seen these first black votes as a resounding blow against the theoretical foundations of apartheid. And a sensible Western policy would have given the elections a qualified welcome as a useful first step."

b. Black leaders are becoming local political officials.

Lynda Schuster, staff writer for *The Christian Science Monitor,* January 26, 1989, 91.

"Part of that plan calls for the installation of 'moderate' black leaders in town councils to neutralize anti-apartheid 'radicals'."

4. Blacks are on the brink of increased political power on the national level.

a. President Botha is ready to bring blacks into the national government.

Staff writer, *The Christian Science Monitor,* February 9, 1989, 3.

"Botha effectively is free to take the relatively radical steps needed to bring disenfranchised blacks into national government. It's a plan, colleagues believe, the President has long been itching to implement."

b. Local autonomy for blacks is leading the way to national power for blacks.

Lynda Schuster, staff writer for *The Christian Science Monitor,* January 26, 1989, p. 2.

"Privately, Mkhwanazi says that 'We're testing the government. Now we'll see if its true that black local authorities really can make their own decisions.'

"As for anti-apartheid activists, the matter is a test case. Regardless of the outcome, they reckon they've won at least provisional concessions from the authorities. We're national leaders, Reverend Chikane has said, and this could have national implications."

your strongest and most universally applicable arguments and evidence be listed first or noted in some special way. Some judgments regarding what are your best arguments and evidence should be made as the briefs are being prepared so that less time will be required for making these choices during the contest.

Although a single level of briefs is frequently sufficient, it is often helpful to have both initial and supporting briefs. The initial brief typically provides a list of several independent responses to an argument; supporting briefs provide in-depth defenses of particular arguments listed on the initial briefs. Suppose you wished to argue that our educational system has failed. Your initial brief might provide a number of different signs of the failure of public education—low scores on standardized tests, high student dropout rates, watered down curriculums, and so forth. Back-up briefs could be developed for each—or, at least, several—of these arguments. A back-up brief on low test scores might provide reasons and evidence explaining why standardized tests are valid and reliable measures of student achievement.

Using Briefs

Although the preparation of briefs can be extremely helpful to advocates, the improper use of briefs can negate many of their benefits. The two most common misuses of briefs involve failures to adapt and update.

All advocates who use briefs need to be especially sensitive to the need for adaptation. A significant complaint raised against candidates in presidential debates has been their nonresponsiveness and tendency to overuse prepared answers (Bitzer and Rueter, 198–204). Debaters and lawyers are also prey to this overreliance on stock responses.

Because briefs provide general responses to arguments, the responses offered on briefs are not always suited to the individual subtleties and nuances that may exist in the particular development of arguments. Advocates who read their briefs without adapting to these subtle differences in development may appear to be irrelevant. Often a slight change in the wording of an argument or some additional explanation is all that is needed to adjust the answers from the brief to the peculiarities of the specific case argument. An additional answer or two may also be required to ensure a complete response to the argument.

Not only must briefs be adapted to the specific situation, but they must also be periodically revised. Briefs are often prepared weeks, or even months, before they are actually used. Such advance preparation is both necessary and desirable. However, this advance preparation sometimes results in arguments and evidence becoming outdated. Circumstances change; new evidence becomes available; additional laws are passed. Advocates who rely on outdated briefs may find that their old arguments no longer apply. For this reason, briefs should be periodically reviewed and revised. The analysis should be reconsidered in the light of changed circumstances, and new arguments and evidence added or substituted.

SUMMARY

An outline consists of a number of statements that are arranged in a series. The idea relationship of a topical outline is one of parts-to-the-whole. The idea relationship of a logical outline is based on the principle of support. In other words, each statement in a logical outline provides either evidence of the validity of the statement to which it is subordinate or a reason for the acceptance of that statement.

Seven basic principles should be observed when preparing logical outlines: (1) The principle of coordination requires that statements at any given level of the outline form have some common relationship to one another. (2) The principle of subordination declares that those statements that are placed in a lower order should support or prove the statement to which they are subordinate. (3) The principle of division states that at least two subordinate points must be presented for each supported statement. (4) The concept of completeness requires that subordinate points must provide support for all of the ideas included within the statement of the superior point. (5) The simplicity principle indicates that each point in a logical outline should be stated in the form of a simple declarative sentence. (6) Discreteness refers to the principle that ideas presented in the outline must be expressed so that each statement is a separate and distinct unit of thought. (7) The principle of symbolization declares that each statement in the outline must have a letter or number that will indicate its relative rank with reference to the other ideas in the outline.

Skill in logical outlining is helpful in preparing for argumentation. The logical outline offers the only structure available for testing the relationships among individual arguments. It encourages careful attention to the wording of arguments. It organizes the ideas in a manner that can be easily communicated to others.

A useful application of logical outlining is in the preparation of briefs. A brief is an organized set of arguments and evidence designed to attack or defend a position. Briefs differ from logical outlines in that they include evidence.

There are three steps involved in the process of preparing briefs: (1) the identification of topics for briefing, (2) the gathering of materials, and (3) the construction of the briefs. It is helpful to prepare both initial and supporting briefs.

The improper use of briefs may negate many of their benefits. The two most common misuses of briefs are the failure to adapt to specific situations and the failure to update the analysis and evidence used in the brief.

SELECTED BIBLIOGRAPHY

BAKER, GEORGE P., and H. B. HUNTINGTON. Pp. 211–70 in *Principles of Argumentation*. Boston: Atheneum, 1925.
BITZER, LLOYD, and THEODORE RUETER. Pp. 198–204 in *Carter vs Ford: The Counterfeit Debates of 1976*. Madison: University of Wisconsin Press, 1980.
PFAU, MICHAEL, DAVID A. THOMAS, and WALTER ULRICH. Pp. 72–85 in *Debate and Argument*. Glenview, IL: Scott, Foresman, 1987.
WHITE, THEODORE H. Pp. 322–23 in *The Making of the President: 1960*. New York: Atheneum, 1961.

STUDY QUESTIONS

1. In preparing argumentative discourse, why is a logical outline preferable to a topical outline?
2. Why does the appearance of a single subordinate point in an outline indicate an incomplete deductive argument or insufficient support for the conclusion of an inductive argument?
3. Why is it important to take special care in "wording" the statements of arguments in a logical outline?
4. What problems will the advocate confront by relying on briefs? What steps can be taken to overcome these problems?

EXERCISES

1. Select a proposition for debate and prepare a logical outline of the issues and supporting arguments on one side of that controversy. Be sure your outline conforms to the principles of logical outlining.
2. Prepare a one- or two-page logical outline on any controversial topic. Make most of the outline conform to the principles of logical outlining, but deliberately violate two or three of the principles at certain points in the outline. Exchange outlines with other class members and see if you can detect the errors.
3. Turn to one of the sample debates in the appendixes of this book and

try to prepare a logical outline of the first affirmative speech. What does your outline tell you about the completeness, consistency, and clarity of the arguments presented?

4. Obtain a basic law textbook that discusses legal briefs. Is the advice on briefing in the law textbook consistent with the advice offered in this text?

5. Pair up with another class member. One of you should prepare an affirmative brief that demonstrates an ill issue on a particular controversy. The other should prepare a negative brief that denies or minimizes the same ill issue. Present these briefs orally in class.

CHAPTER ELEVEN
FIELDS, FORUMS, AND FORMATS

Fields, forums, and formats comprise the situation within which advocacy occurs. Effective argumentation requires us to recognize *the shared purpose that guides the community in which our inquiry and advocacy occurs* (the *field*), to understand *the arena in which our arguments are presented* (the *forum*), and to be aware of *the conventions that influence the presentation of our arguments and those of our opponents* (the *format*). Fields, forums, and formats represent a bridge between inquiry and advocacy. In a sense, analysis of the situations in which our arguments occur is still very much within the framework of inquiry since the process continues to be investigative. That investigation, however, no longer focuses on the discovery of the probable truth within a given controversy, but rather becomes an analysis of the specific situation in which that truth is presented. This chapter explains the perspective of argument fields, identifies a continuum of advocacy forums, and details several specialized formats for educational debate.

THE PERSPECTIVE OF ARGUMENT FIELDS

The concept of argument fields provides an important perspective on advocacy situations. This section defines argument fields and identifies the implications of using such a perspective.

Definition of Argument Fields

Contemporary scholars of argumentation have devoted considerable effort to debating the standards that should be used to judge arguments. Most of these scholars have rejected the idea that arguments should be judged on the basis of the formal validity required by the discipline of logic. They have also rejected the notion of relativism—the belief that there is no appropriate way to assess arguments. In an effort to propose judgmental standards, argumentation scholars have increasingly turned to the concept of argument fields.[1]

As originally presented by Stephen Toulmin in 1958, *an argument field involves a community that subscribes to a common set of standards for judging the worth of arguments.* Toulmin claimed that argument is either *field-invariant* or *field-dependent.* Argument is field-invariant in the sense that basic concepts such as burden of proof, presumption, argument components (data, reasoning process, conclusion), and burden of rebuttal occur in *every* argument field. For example, regardless of the field in which we argue, reasonable people expect us to respond when our claim is challenged (the burden of rebuttal). Many of the basic concepts we presented in Chapter 2 (for example, presumption, burden of proof, and burden of rebuttal) are field-invariant concepts. Argument is field-variant in the sense that *different fields* use *different standards* to assess the *validity* of arguments and to operationalize such concepts as presumption and burden of proof. For example, a conclusion that we reach about someone else based on gossip may be perfectly acceptable to ourselves and to our friends. However, that same conclusion would be rejected as hearsay in a court of law.

Argumentation scholars embraced Toulmin's notion of argument fields. However, they encountered much difficulty in agreeing on a precise definition of an argument field. Some scholars believe that the form of argument determines the field. Other scholars suggest that subject matter is the key to defining a field.[2]

The approach to argument fields that we find most persuasive is advanced by Robert Rowland. Rowland ("Influence of Purpose," 233–34) contends that "shared disciplinary purpose" is the unifying characteristic of argument fields:

> All of the important defining characteristics of fields develop out of the shared problem-solving purpose unifying a group of arguers. . . . A community of scholars or scientists develops around a shared goal of solving a problem—this goal becoming the purpose which energizes the community. Here it should be noted that the purpose of a field is the goal shared by a group of arguers in an area. It is their aim or reason for building arguments.

The American legal system illustrates the argument field concept. Although the law has many purposes, its primary function is to dispense justice. Justice, in criminal law, includes protecting innocent people from being punished, as well as punishing people who violate the law. This shared purpose dictates the standards used to evaluate arguments in our courts, the procedures which must be followed by participants in the courtroom, the stringent proof requirements placed on prosecutors, and the form which arguments must take.

Implications of Argument Fields

The shared purpose approach to argument fields has a number of important implications as we enter various advocacy situations. As the definition of argument fields suggests, the shared purpose of a field determines all components of that field—from the standards used for argument evaluation to the accepted style of delivery. Three implications of the shared purpose approach are especially useful.

First, the fields approach emphasizes the *we must study the field in which we will be arguing*. Law Professor Kingsfield, a character in the popular television series "The Paper Chase," addressed his law students on the first day of class with the following words: "The study of law is something new and unfamiliar to most of you, unlike any other schooling you have ever known. You teach yourselves the law. But I train your minds. You come in here with a skull full of mush and, if you succeed, you leave thinking like a lawyer." Kingsfield expresses a view shared by many successful law school graduates. To succeed in law it is not enough to know the law. One must reason in a manner consistent with the demands of the field of law.

Studying the field in which we will argue helps us understand the specific role played by the basic concepts discussed throughout this text. The concepts of presumption and burden of proof are fundamental concepts that are central to inquiry processes. Their application in argument fields, however, is by no means uniform. In fields designed to keep advocacy within a rigorous, rational framework, such as legal situations and academic debates, the concepts of presumption and burden of proof are directly relevant. In other argument fields, however, these concepts cannot be so strictly applied. For example, the overwhelming support of a particular audience for a proposed new policy may render the present policy's presumed "preoccupation of ground" as largely irrelevant. The argument field, therefore, must be analyzed to determine the extent to which such concepts as presumption and burden of proof are functionally relevant.

A second implication of the fields approach is the realization that *argument evaluation is at least partially field-dependent, not solely advocate-dependent.* Advocates often find themselves in situations where the purpose of the field in which they argue is not completely compatible with their own purpose. The first consideration of defense attorneys, for instance, is to secure a not guilty verdict for their clients. However, the primary goal of the courtroom situation in which the advocacy takes place is to determine the truth of the question under consideration. The rules and procedures that characterize legal advocacy respond to the situational goal, not to the goal of the individual advocate. In much the same way, the goal of politicians on press interview programs is to build their own political support, but the institutional purposes and procedures of these programs encourage questions that may embarrass the politician. In approaching advocacy, therefore, we must consider not only our personal goals. We must also analyze the purpose of the argument field in order to determine its influence on our advocacy.

The third implication of the argument fields perspective is the recognition that *standards and practices of argument are not completely transferable between fields.* The frustrating experience of a first year college debate student helps illustrate this point. John had just completed a beginning debate class when he was asked to participate in a public debate at the downtown Rotary club. John carefully studied and researched the topic, applying many of the concepts he had learned in class. After the debate John felt dejected. He went back to his debate teacher and complained: "I just don't know what happened. My opponent didn't meet her burden of proof and nobody in the audience seemed to care that I had presumption and should have won. She used almost no evidence to support her case. It's just not fair that she won." John failed to realize that the advocacy situation in which he participated was quite different from that of collegiate debate. The argument field in which our arguments occur determines the amount and kinds of proof we must present. Some fields impose strict proof requirements on the advocate. The legal field, for instance, severely limits the types of evidence that may be presented as proof. In less structured fields before less specialized audiences, on the other hand, proof requirements may be significantly altered. More time may have to be spent in illustrating concepts than in proving them. Such situations may also demand that the proof we use be derived from the premises of our audience rather than from external evidence.

Because argument standards are not completely transferable between fields, we can see why an argument that is perfectly acceptable in one field is completely unacceptable in another field. Superior advocates are guided by the purpose of the field in which they argue.

Consider the following illustrative example. Dr. Mary Phillips, a biological scientist who specializes in the study of the effects of prescription drugs on human tissue, begins her day by presenting a research paper at a symposium. She tells the audience of scientists that the research on the relationship between using birth control pills and developing breast cancer contains numerous uncertainties and inconsistencies. She concludes that the relationship between the pill and breast cancer must remain a hypothesis rather than a fact. Later that afternoon, Dr. Phillips testifies at a hearing of the Food and Drug Administration (FDA). The purpose of the hearing is to determine whether or not birth control pills should be accompanied by a printed FDA warning label. Dr. Phillips testifies that uncertainty does exist in the scientific community, but, based on the evidence she has reviewed as well as the availability of safer birth control measures, the FDA should act immediately and require a warning. That evening, Dr. Phillips is the guest speaker at a Catholic church youth group meeting. She tells the teenagers: "Sure, there is scientific evidence that suggests there may be some danger to using birth control pills. But what is really important is our faith. Our belief in God and in our church is what should guide us."

At first glance Dr. Phillips appears quite inconsistent. How can she claim that the evidence is insufficient if she believes birth control pills are dangerous enough to require a warning label? Furthermore, since she is a scientist, why should she not encourage teenagers to look at the scientific evidence? The point is, however, that Dr. Phillips acted in three different argument fields, and each field is guided by a different purpose. At the scientific symposium Dr. Phillips adopted the proof standards of science, which require exhaustive testing and exclusion of all alternative hypotheses. Such proof was not necessary in the policy-making field of the FDA, a field in which risks and benefits must be weighed and action must be taken. Finally, in the religious field, the premise of faith made the proof standards of science and policy-making irrelevant.

Argument fields, therefore, exert a controlling influence on us as advocates. We must understand the components and reasoning patterns of the field in which our advocacy takes place. Failure to understand the nature of the specific advocacy situation and failure to adapt appropriately to the demands of that field significantly reduce the likelihood of successful advocacy.

CONTINUUM OF ADVOCACY FORUMS

The forum of advocacy is the particular arena in which arguments are presented. Courtrooms, legislative chambers, and televised political debates are examples of forums. It is useful to view advocacy forums on a continuum according to their purposes, the nature of their procedures, and the nature of their audiences. On one end of this continuum are advocacy forums characterized by highly formalized procedures and specialized audiences. On the other end of the continuum exist advocacy forums with no formal procedures and nonspecialized audiences. In the model below, the advocacy situations have been placed on this continuum and have been grouped according to three situational purposes: (1) immediate truth determination, (2) information-seeking, and (3) audience activation.

Truth Determination Forums

The guiding purpose of those advocacy forums with the most specialized audiences and rules of procedure is to determine truth in the immediate situation. Included within this grouping are legal advocacy, academic debate, and parliamentary debate. In these forums specific rules of procedure are drawn up and decision-making is left to specialized audiences in order to ensure that the goal of truth determination is not subverted by the individual advocates who participate within the forum. Since such forums are designed to encourage rational decision-making, the standards of argumentative inquiry can be expected to be most relevant here.

Model of the Continuum of Advocacy Forums

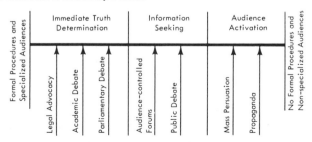

Legal advocacy forums   More than any other single advocacy forum, courtroom advocacy is structured to attempt to determine the truth in the immediate situation. All of the rules of procedure in legal advocacy are designed to ensure that the situational goal of truth determination prevails over the individual goals of the participants in the forums. The rules of procedure call for a precise statement of the proposition for debate (indictment) and rigidly apply the concepts of presumption and burden of proof. Direct and thorough refutation of ideas presented by participating advocates is guaranteed. Strict rules of evidence severely limit the types of supporting materials that are allowed. The trial takes place in front of a judge trained in the law. Juries receive specific instructions concerning the criteria by which they must evaluate the advocacy.

The concepts and standards of argumentative inquiry apply most directly to legal advocacy forums because such situations are characterized by rules of procedure and specialized audiences, which ensure that rational standards will be applied in the evaluation of advocacy. To be sure, motivational elements are present even within the restrictive framework of legal advocacy. Despite the existence of rigid procedures and trained audiences, judges and juries are human and subject to emotive appeals. Yet, within the framework of free human decision-making, legal advocacy forums come the closest to the ideal of guaranteeing immediate truth determination.

Academic debate   An examination of the advocacy forums for academic debate reveal striking similarities to legal advocacy. Like legal advocacy, academic debate requires a statement of proposition, which provides the framework within which advocacy must take place. The concepts of presumption and burden of proof are applied in a manner similar to their usage in legal advocacy. As in the legal advocacy forum, academic debate forums are designed to encourage direct and thorough clash of ideas. Evidence rules are also applied, although not as rigidly as in legal advocacy. Academic debate usually uses expert judges to adjudicate decisions. However, since academic debate forums function as training grounds for reasoned advocacy, debate judges are likely to judge as much on the techniques and strategies of argument as on the specific subject matter.

Parliamentary debate forums Parliamentary debate forums include a variety of bodies that are governed by the rules of parliamentary procedure, including the U.S. Congress, state legislatures, and student councils. Even though parliamentary debate can be characterized as a truth determination forum, its rules of procedure and its audiences do not ensure the same level of rigor as do legal advocacy forums and academic debate forums. Generally, parliamentary debate may occur only after a specific motion or resolution has been made and seconded. Attempts are made to keep debate relevant to the specific motion or resolution at hand by empowering the chairperson to declare irrelevant debate out of order. Parliamentary debate guarantees the opportunity for the presentation of opposing views, but the rules of procedure do not guarantee direct clash of ideas. The concept of presumption is institutionalized through voting procedures, but evidence rules are notably absent.

Information-Seeking Forums

In the middle of the continuum are advocacy forums, which have been classified as essentially information-seeking in nature. Such forums have elements of truth determination and audience activation in them but are designed to achieve the primary objective of gathering information. Within this classification are included audience-controlled forums and public debates. They are placed in the middle of the continuum because they have either less rigorous rules and procedures or less specialized audiences than do truth determination forums.

Audience-controlled forums Audience-controlled forums are public advocacy situations in which the direction of the advocacy is strongly controlled by the immediate audience in order for it to obtain desired information. Such forums include committee hearings, press conferences, and the full range of broadcast programs in which an advocate is questioned by a professional interviewer or by a panel of media representatives.

When compared with truth determination forums, audience-controlled forums lack rigid rules of procedure. Such forums, for instance, frequently operate from open-ended questions rather than from precise statements of proposition. The formats do not guarantee an in-depth discussion of a single question, but instead frequently permit the discussion to wander from question to question with a minimal degree of purposefulness. The concepts of burden of proof and presumption are not consistently applied, and rules of evidence are also not characteristic of such forums.

Public debate forums   Public debate refers to all advocacy forums that guarantee presentation of both sides of a controversy before general public audiences. Debates between candidates for political office are examples of the public debate forum. Such advocacy forums are classified as essentially information-giving rather than as truth determination situations because of their less institutionalized rules of procedure and because they occur before nonspecialized audiences. They differ from audience-controlled forums in that they guarantee pro and con advocacy. The audiences for public debates, however, tend to be more passive than those of audience-controlled forums.

There are great variation in rules of procedure among public debate forums. Frequently, for instance, the essence of the controversy is not clearly stated beyond the identification of a topic area. The concepts of presumption and burden of proof are not formally recognized and specific rules of evidence seldom exist. The advocacy forum is totally dependent on the specific debate format used and on the refutation skill of the individual advocates. The audience becomes a variable in the rules of procedure only to the extent that the format permits direct questioning from the audience.

Audience Activation Forums

Audience activation is the goal of those advocacy forums at the extreme end of the continuum. In these forums few, if any, formal procedures exist, and the goal becomes the motivation of a nonspecialized, nonparticipating audience. It is hoped that advocates in these forums will use the standards of reasoned inquiry to arrive at their positions, but, in seeking to activate audiences, they tend to place greater emphasis on motivational factors as opposed to purely rational forms of proof and development.

Mass persuasion, propaganda, and advertising are terms that can be used as synonyms for audience activation. In such forums none of the rules of procedure that encourage rigor can be guaranteed. In fact, a distinguishing feature of audience activation forums is the complete lack of predictable rules of procedure. Nothing exists within the advocacy forum to guarantee that advocacy will remain focused on a specific proposition. Presumption, burden of proof, and specific evidence rules are almost totally absent. Whereas other advocacy forums permit and even encourage the presentation of opposition views, audience activation forums are characterized by one-sided presentations.

In addition to understanding the general nature of the fields and forums in which we argue, we must also have knowledge of the specialized procedures for conducting argument—the formats demanded by the forum. In the next section we examine several formats used in educational debate.

SPECIALIZED FORMATS FOR EDUCATIONAL DEBATE

This final section of the chapter is devoted to a more detailed examination of the formats that students most frequently encounter in educational debate training.

Such formats are used in advocacy forums designed to teach the skills of reasoned inquiry and reasoned advocacy. These formats include the traditional academic debate formats along with audience debate, parliamentary debate, and mock trial competition.

Traditional Educational Debate Formats

Any student who anticipates participating in interscholastic debate will soon have to become familiar with the standard debate formats, which constitute the framework of the advocacy situation for academic debate. Although a variety of debate formats are in use in college and high school debating, the three formats outlined below are encountered most frequently. They are known as team policy debate, team value debate, and Lincoln-Douglas debate.

TEAM POLICY DEBATE FORMAT

1st Affirmative Constructive	9 minutes
Negative Speaker Cross-examines 1st Affirmative	3 minutes
1st Negative Constructive	9 minutes
Affirmative Speaker Cross-examines 1st Negative	3 minutes
2nd Affirmative Constructive	9 minutes
Other Negative Speaker Cross-examines 2nd Affirmative	3 minutes
2nd Negative Constructive	9 minutes
Other Affirmative Speaker Cross-examines 2nd Negative	3 minutes
1st Negative Rebuttal	6 minutes
1st Affirmative Rebuttal	6 minutes
2nd Negative Rebuttal	6 minutes
2nd Affirmative Rebuttal	6 minutes

Preparation Time Used by Affirmative throughout the Debate	10 minutes
Preparation Time Used by Negative throughout the Debate	10 minutes

TEAM VALUE DEBATE FORMAT

1st Affirmative Constructive	8 minutes
Negative Speaker Cross-examines 1st Affirmative	3 minutes
1st Negative Constructive	8 minutes
Affirmative Speaker Cross-examines 1st Negative	3 minutes
2nd Affirmative Constructive	8 minutes
Other Negative Speaker Cross-examines 2nd Affirmative	3 minutes
2nd Negative Constructive	8 minutes
Other Affirmative Speaker Cross-examines 2nd Negative	3 minutes
1st Negative Rebuttal	4 minutes
1st Affirmative Rebuttal	4 minutes
2nd Negative Rebuttal	4 minutes
2nd Affirmative Rebuttal	4 minutes
Preparation Time Used by Affirmative throughout the Debate	8 minutes
Preparation Time Used by Negative throughout the Debate	8 minutes

LINCOLN-DOUGLAS DEBATE FORMAT

Affirmative Constructive	6 minutes
Negative Cross-examines Affirmative	3 minutes
Negative Constructive	7 minutes
Affirmative Cross-examines Negative	3 minutes
First Affirmative Rebuttal	4 minutes
Negative Rebuttal	6 minutes
Second Affirmative Rebuttal	3 minutes
Preparation Time Used by Affirmative throughout the Debate	3 minutes
Preparation Time Used by Negative throughout the Debate	3 minutes

The three traditional educational debate formats share a number of characteristics. All three provide the affirmative and negative sides equal time to present arguments. The affirmative side is given the first and last word. All three formats distinguish between constructive speeches in which debaters initiate and develop arguments and rebuttal speeches in which they refute and focus arguments. The formats all provide for cross-examination periods in which questions are used to clarify, commit opponents to a position, refute, set up arguments, and to undermine opponent credibility. Preparation time provided to each side limits the time that can be used between speeches.

We next examine the variations between the three standard academic formats. The variations are best understood by examining their philosophical and educational underpinnings, the types of propositions used, and the basic speaker duties.

Team policy debate format   Team policy debate involves four persons, two affirmative speakers and two negative speakers. The format is used at the American Forensic Association's National Debate Tournament as well as at many invitational college debate tournaments. A slight variation of this format is used at college tournaments sponsored by the American Debate Association (nine-minute contructives, two-minute cross-examination periods, six-minute rebuttals) and at high school policy debate tournaments sponsored by the National Forensic League (eight-minute constructives, three-minute cross-examination periods, four-minute rebuttals).

Philosophical and educational underpinnings: The stock issues approach dominated academic debate until the early 1970s. Although the stock issues approach remains popular, a number of other models or paradigms are also used. The policy-making paradigm, for example, uses a legislative analogy. Debaters are viewed as legislators who debate public policy controversies in an effort to discover the best policy.[3] Another policy debate paradigm is hypothesis-testing. Using the analogy of science, the proposition is viewed as a hypothesis to be tested by comparing it to all other relevant hypotheses. As in the scientific community, a hypothesis is accepted only after determining all other hypotheses to be incorrect.[4] Although there are different emphases in the various policy debate paradigms, all of them are similar in their truth-seeking function.

Type of proposition: Team policy debate uses propositions of policy. The propositions call for the affirmative team to defend a plan of action that embodies the proposition. The following are examples of policy propositions debated in recent years:

> *Resolved:* That the federal government should guarantee retirement security for all U.S. citizens over age sixty-five.
>
> *Resolved:* That the federal government should implement a comprehensive, long-term agricultural policy in the United States.
>
> *Resolved:* That the federal government should significantly curtail its arms sales to other countries.
>
> *Resolved:* That the United States should reduce substantially its military commitments to NATO member states.
>
> *Resolved:* That more rigorous academic standards should be established for all public elementary and/or secondary schools in the United States in one or more of the following areas: language arts, mathematics, natural sciences.
>
> *Resolved:* That the United States federal government should significantly increase exploration and/or development of space beyond the earth's mesosphere.

Notice that each of these topics contains the word "should." This word is commonly defined as "ought to, not necessarily will." The proposition requires the affirmative team to demonstrate the desirability of implementing a particular plan of action. It does not require the team to prove that its plan *will* be adopted.

Speaker duties in constructive speeches: In the *first affirmative constructive speech* it has become standard practice for the speaker to develop the basic outline of the entire affirmative case. This outline generally includes the affirmative's plan, the rationale for change (ill and blame), and proof that the plan is desirable (cure and sometimes cost). The plan is usually an operationalization or example of the debate proposition. For example, the affirmative might operationalize increased exploration and/or development of space (the proposition) by presenting a plan that establishes a space colony on the moon. The plan operationally defines how the affirmative team interprets the proposition.

The *first negative constructive speech* has two major duties. These are to present the negative position and to attack what the affirmative has presented. The type of position taken by the negative team determines the precise duties of this constructive speech. A traditional approach to the first negative constructive speech concentrates on the issues of ill and blame, leaving the cure and cost issues to the second negative speaker. The speaker begins with a brief statement of the negative philosophy on the proposition and then follows the organization of the first affirmative constructive speech to refute the ill and blame issues. There are times when an approach other than the traditional one should be used. For example, if the negative position emphasizes the cost issue, the first negative speaker may present disadvantages to the plan. Similarly, the negative team may feel that the affirmative plan is especially weak and therefore attacks the cure issue during the first negative speech. If topicality or jurisdiction is an issue, the first negative constructive speech presents this issue.

The *second affirmative constructive speech* generally focuses on rebuilding the affirmative analysis in light of the refutation presented in the first negative constructive. Although this speech usually follows the organizational structure set up in the first affirmative speech, its initial few minutes may have to be spent dealing with the negative philosophy, the refutation of negative cost arguments, and clarification of definitional questions. Wherever possible, the speech deals with negative refutation within the affirmative organizational framework and attempts to advance the basic affirmative analysis by providing more details and more supporting material.

The content of the *second negative constructive speech* depends on the overall position taken by the negative team. In situations where the negative team takes a traditional approach, this speech is devoted exclusively to an analysis of the affirmative proposal for change. The second negative speaker sets up her or his own organizational structure built around the stock issues of cure and cost. The speaker demonstrates that the affirmative plan fails to solve the ills (cure) and causes greater problems (cost). If a different negative position is taken, the second negative constructive speaker may find it necessary to further develop cost arguments initially presented by her or his partner, to attack the ill or blame issues, or to attack other affirmative arguments.

Speaker duties in rebuttal speeches: The time allocated for rebuttal speeches is considerably less than that devoted to constructive speeches, indicating that the rebuttal speeches are used more for focusing of the debate rather than for the thorough development of initial arguments. A standard convention in academic debate is not to allow new arguments to be raised in rebuttals. All rebuttal arguments should be extensions of arguments presented in the constructive speeches. This does *not* preclude additional evidence from being presented. Rebuttals should be viewed as the most important speeches in the debate round. No matter how strong your constructive arguments are, they become meaningless if they cannot be extended and advanced in rebuttals. The precise duties of each speaker in rebuttal depends on the positions taken in the constructive speeches.

The *first negative rebuttal* can really be viewed as an extension of the second negative constructive speech. Since no affirmative speech comes between these two speeches, the two are usually treated as one complete speech delivered by two advocates. When the second negative constructive speech focuses exclusively on the affirmative plan, the first negative rebuttal returns to the arguments raised against the affirmative rationale for change in order to complete the negative attack. Using the structure of the first affirmative constructive speech, the first negative rebuttal attempts to reestablish the focus of the attack, which was outlined in the first negative constructive speech. The speech must be responsive to the arguments developed in the second affirmative constructive speech.

The *first affirmative rebuttal* is the most difficult speech in the debate because it must deal with a block of negative speaking more than twice its own length. It must respond to the negative analysis of the affirmative proposal as well as attempt to rebuild the affirmative rationale for change. Because of the short amount of time allotted to this speech, organization must be tight and argument development precise. The general practice is to begin the speech by dealing with the plan attacks outlined in the second negative constructive and then to move to the rebuilding of the affirmative case structure.

The *second negative rebuttal* climaxes the focusing of the debate for the negative. Like the first affirmative rebuttal, this speech must also cover the major clashes, both on the affirmative rationale for change and on the negative analysis of the affirmative plan. In addition to covering the total argumentative ground, however, this speech must also narrow the negative attack to a focus on the crucial issues in the debate. The second negative rebuttal generally emphasizes the negative objections to the plan before moving to a concluding emphasis on the affirmative rationale for change.

The *second affirmative rebuttal*, as the final speech in the debate, summarizes the debate from the affirmative point of view. Although the speech must be responsive to significant negative arguments that have developed throughout the debate, it also must focus the debate on the clashes that the affirmative finds crucial to the proposition. As in the last two speeches, its consideration of negative plan attacks follows the structure established by the second negative constructive, and its rebuilding of the affirmative analysis returns to the structure outlined in the first affirmative constructive speech.

Team value debate format   Team value debate also involves four persons, two affirmative speakers and two negative speakers. The format is used at the college level by students participating in tournaments sponsored by the Cross Examination Debate Association.

Philosophical and educational underpinnings: The Cross Examination Debate Association was founded in the early 1970s by a group of debate teachers who had become dissatisfied with certain practices in policy debate. In particular, the teachers felt that policy debate had become too stylized and overemphasized the logical dimension of argumentation at the expense of the communicative dimension. They sought to obtain "a better balance among evidentiary support, sound analysis, and effective delivery in debate than is currently encouraged by national propositions that emphasize evidence almost to the exclusion of these other areas" and "to try and arouse an interest in debate among college students for whom a current national topic might have little appeal."[5]

Type of proposition: The Cross Examination Debate Association believes that the proposition selected for debate plays a major role in determining the quality of the educational experience students receive. Although for several years the association selected policy propositions, fact/value propositions have been used since 1975. The propositions require the affirmative team to defend a particular value application or judgment. The following are examples of fact/value propositions debated in recent years:

> *Resolved:* That membership in the United Nations is no longer beneficial to the United States.
> *Resolved:* That significant government restrictions on coverage by the U.S. media of terrorist activity are justified.
> *Resolved:* That individual rights of privacy are more important than any other Constitutional right.
> *Resolved:* That protection of the national environment is a more important goal than the satisfaction of American energy demands.
> *Resolved:* That activism in politics by religious groups harms the American political process.
> *Resolved:* That federal government censorship is justified to defend the national security of the United States.

Notice that each of these topics implicitly or explicitly identifies a value (e.g., privacy, national security, environmental protection) and applies that value judgment to a particular context. Many of the topics involve value judgments about particular policies.

Speaker duties in constructive speeches: There is not as much agreement on the standard speaker duties in value debate as there is in policy debate. The speaker duties we present here reflect one method of approaching value debate. As in debate on any subject, the duties must be adapted to the particular demands of the advocacy situation and to the strategies used by your opponent.

The *first affirmative constructive speech* presents an outline of the entire affirmative case. This outline generally includes identification of the specific fact/value judgment presented in the proposition (frame of definition) and the presentation of the benefits of applying the fact/value judgment to a particular situation (frame of existence of fact). For example, in defending the proposition that censorship of extreme political views is wrong, the first affirmative constructive speech should define the terms "censorship," "extreme political views," and "wrong," demonstrate that censorship *is* wrong, and prove that *not* censoring "extreme political views" is desirable. The first constructive speech often presents and defends criteria for making value judgments.

The *first negative constructive speech* has two major duties. These are to present the negative position and to attack what the affirmative has presented. Typically, the first negative speaker challenges the definitions and criteria presented in the first affirmative constructive, following the organization of that speech. The speaker generally concentrates on the frames of definition and existence of fact. The first negative speaker may also present the negative case, identifying specific reasons why the negative team believes that the proposition is not true. This frequently requires the speaker to establish an organizational pattern different from that presented in the first affirmative constructive.

The *second affirmative constructive speech* reestablishes the affirmative analysis in light of the refutation presented in the first negative constructive. If the negative has presented arguments that do not fit into the organizational pattern used in the first affirmative speech, the second affirmative constructive speaker may need to spend time directly answering these arguments. In addition to refuting negative arguments, the speaker should advance the affirmative analysis by providing additional supporting material.

The *second negative constructive speech* generally concentrates on examining the effects of accepting the judgment reached in the proposition. Primarily, this involves the stasis of quality. It has become customary for the second negative constructive speaker to present *value objections* to the affirmative value choice. Value objections are the disadvantages of accepting the value choice reached in the proposition. The second negative speaker applies the affirmative value to particular situations and shows how the value objections outweigh the affirmative value.

Speaker duties in rebuttal speeches: Rebuttals, as in policy debate, involve extending, focusing, and summarizing arguments. The best rebuttalists in team value debate are those who take an issues orientation, demonstrating how the arguments raised in constructive speeches translate into issues that justify accepting or rejecting the proposition.

The *first negative rebuttal* concentrates on extending the arguments raised in the first negative constructive speech, taking into account the refutation by the second affirmative constructive speaker. The speaker should demonstrate how the arguments become issues that warrant rejecting the proposition. The first negative rebuttalist frequently concentrates on proving that the affirmative has imprecisely defined and inappropriately applied its value judgment.

The *first affirmative rebuttal* generally begins by refuting the value objections and other arguments presented in the second negative constructive speech. Next, the speaker covers the case arguments extended in the first negative rebuttal. The speaker must be concise because she or he is covering twelve minutes of negative argument in the space of four minutes.

The *second negative rebuttal* is the last chance for the negative to refute the affirmative case and to advance its own case. This speech should address issues and demonstrate how the affirmative team has failed to meet its burden in winning those issues. The speaker generally begins on the value objections and other arguments presented in the second negative constructive, showing how they warrant rejecting the proposition. The speaker then extends the issues advanced in the first negative rebuttal.

The *second affirmative rebuttal* is the affirmative team's last chance to convince the audience that the proposition should be affirmed. The speaker must deal with all the issues raised by the negative throughout the debate. In addition, the speaker must focus the debate on the major issues he or she believes to justify affirming the proposition. The speaker usually begins by dealing with the value objections and other arguments advanced during the first part of the second negative rebuttal speech. Next, the speaker covers the case arguments and other issues advanced in the second part of the second negative rebuttal speech.

Lincoln-Douglas debate format   In contrast to team policy debate and team value debate, the Lincoln-Douglas debate involves two people instead of four, one affirmative speaker and one negative speaker. The format is popular at the high school level and is becoming increasingly popular in college.

Philosophical and educational underpinnings: The Lincoln-Douglas format is named in honor of the famous debates held between Abraham Lincoln and Stephen Douglas in 1858. Lincoln and Douglas confronted each other in seven three-hour debates on the values of slavery, freedom, and states rights. Educators saw many educational benefits that students could gain from one-on-one debating of important value issues and developed the Lincoln-Douglas format in the early 1970s. The format emphasizes communicative delivery in presenting philosophical and value judgments to audiences composed of laypersons.

Type of proposition: A Lincoln-Douglas debate uses fact/value propositions. The propositions call for the affirmative speaker to defend a particular value. The following are examples of fact/value propositions debated in recent years:

> *Resolved:* That political tolerance is the most important value on which a democracy should be based.
> *Resolved:* That there is no such thing as a just war.
> *Resolved:* That liberty is more precious than law.
> *Resolved:* That the right to die should be as important as the right to live.
> *Resolved:* That public safety justifies restricting media coverage of terrorism.
> *Resolved:* That mandatory drug testing in the workplace unjustifiably violates the individual's right to privacy.

Lincoln-Douglas debate propositions generally require the affirmative to defend the absolute primacy of a value (as in the first and second topics above), to compare the primacy of two or more values (as in the third and fourth topics above), or to apply a value to a particular situation (as in the last two topics above).

Speaker duties: The *affirmative constructive* details the arguments justifying the proposition. The arguments concentrate on definition, existence, and quality. The speaker begins with a brief introduction during which the proposition is presented and its importance is explained. Next, definitions of key terms are presented. The speaker then identifies the reasons why the proposition is true. This is frequently accompanied by presenting criteria by which value judgments can be made, compared, and applied.

The *negative constructive speech* usually involves two major duties. The speaker refutes the affirmative case as well as builds her or his own case. The speaker must give particular attention to the criteria presented in the affirmative constructive. Negative speakers frequently reject the affirmative criteria and propose superior criteria or argue that the affirmative misapplies the criteria. The speaker may also present pragmatic implications of applying the affirmative value judgment in particular situations.

The *first affirmative rebuttal* reestablishes the affirmative analysis in light of the refutation presented in the negative constructive speech. The speaker must concentrate on extending and advancing her or his initial case as well as refuting the negative case.

The *negative rebuttal* is the last opportunity for the negative speaker to refute the affirmative rationale for the proposition. This speech should concentrate on extending the most important issues developed in the constructive speech. The speaker must leave the audience with clear reasons why the proposition has not been and should not be affirmed.

The *second affirmative rebuttal* is the last speech of the debate. Here the speaker has three minutes in which to respond to the issues raised in the six minute negative rebuttal. The speaker must concentrate on refuting negative arguments as well as advancing and summarizing the affirmative case. Generally, the speaker begins by refuting the negative case and ends by reestablishing the affirmative case. The short time span of the rebuttal requires the speaker to concentrate on the most important issues.

Alternative Educational Debate Formats

Debate is very much a part of cocurricular and extracurricular activities in colleges and high schools. There are many formats other than the traditional ones presented above. Teachers use classroom debate to teach literature, science, and economics. Students spend a great deal of time debating in such activities as student government, Model United Nations, Future Problem Solving, and mock trial competition. Many debate programs involve students in public debates in front of such organizations as Rotary and Kiwanis clubs. In this section we briefly examine two alternative forums for academic debate: audience debate and mock trial competition.

Audience debate   Many educational debate programs involve students in audience debate activities as well as in interscholastic activities. Unlike interscholastic debate, however, there are no standard formats for audience debate situations. Formats for audience debating must be developed to adapt to the uniqueness of the advocacy situation involved. When developing formats for audience debate activities, we must realize that general audiences differ from the critic judges of competitive debate in terms of their comprehension levels, their interest levels, and the propensity to allow their personal attitudes and values to influence their evaluation of the debate.

The first consideration in building formats for public debate is to adapt to audience comprehension levels. Most public audiences have difficulty following a debate that uses the standard format for team value debate or team policy debate. There are generally too many lines of argument and too many speeches for non-specialized audiences to follow in these formats. Formats for audience debate must be simplified and must encourage a clearer focusing of the arguments for the sake of clarity and ease of comprehension. The Lincoln-Douglas format works well for audience debating.

Second, formats for audience debating should adapt to audience interest levels. In a sense, this is closely related to the comprehension criterion, because an audience that fails to comprehend the development of arguments in a debate is unlikely to sustain interest in the debate. Few audiences can bear a full hour of uninterrupted debate. For this reason, consideration should be given to shortening the time limits of the format. Cross-examination is another way of adapting to audience interest levels.

Finally, formats for public debate should permit advocate adaptation to specific audience attitudes and values. This is important because the whole reason behind placing students in audience debate situations is to teach them how to deal with audiences who evaluate what they hear in terms of their own attitudes and values. One way of guaranteeing audience input is to set aside a block of time within the debate for direct questions from the audience. This not only gives the advocates a chance to adapt to audience attitudes and values, but also adds an additional interest factor for the audience.

Below we outline a sample format for use in audience debate situations. Although this format is not presented as a standard audience format, it is useful in illustrating some of the changes in interscholastic formats that can be made to adapt to audience debate advocacy situations.

SAMPLE AUDIENCE DEBATE FORMAT

Affirmative Opening Statement	2 minutes
Negative Opening Statement	2 minutes
Affirmative Constructive Case	6–8 minutes
Negative Cross-examination	2–3 minutes
Negative Constructive Case	6–8 minutes
Affirmative Cross-examination	2–3 minutes
Audience Question Period	10–15 minutes
Affirmative Summary	3–5 minutes
Negative Summary	3–5 minutes

The format adapts to audience comprehension levels in several ways. The short opening statements permit the advocates to give the audience a summary of the case philosophy and structure before moving into detailed argument development. The shorter speeches, cross-examination, and audience question period also provide mechanisms for simplifying the debate and assisting audience comprehension. The format gives advocates the opportunity to respond directly to audience attitudes and values. Even though the advocates may adapt to audience beliefs throughout the debate on the basis of prior knowledge about the audience, the direct question period adds an element of spontaneity that will test adaptation abilities.

Mock trial competition   Bar associations in many states sponsor mock trial competitions for students. This event introduces students to the legal system and fosters such skills as case construction, argument selection, cross-examination, and oral advocacy.[6]

Mock trials use a variety of formats. One format involves two teams of six students each. Each team consists of three student attorneys and three student witnesses. The students work with a faculty advisor, who coaches them on oral presentation skills, and an attorney, who works with them on understanding and developing legal issues. Coaching takes place prior to, but not during, the mock trial. Several days before the mock trial takes place, teams are assigned to the prosecution or defense. Each team is given an outline of a legal case that has been previously heard in a real court. The outcome of the case is not revealed. Cases are selected to provide a fairly equal balance between the strength of prosecution and defense arguments. Witness affidavits are also provided to identify what the witnesses may and may not claim. Each team prepares its own case. At the mock trial one student attorney for each side presents an opening statement. The student attorneys then take turns questioning the student witnesses. Each side then designates one student attorney to present the closing statement. A decision in the trial is rendered by a real attorney or judge who presides at the mock trial. The mock trial typically lasts between one-and-a-half and two hours. The following mock trial format is adapted for use in the classroom. Each side has two student witnesses.

SAMPLE MOCK TRIAL FORMAT FOR CLASSROOM USE

Opening Statement for Prosecution by Attorney 1	6 minutes
Opening Statement for Defense by Attorney 1	6 minutes
Direct Examination of Prosecution Witness 1 by Prosecution Attorney 2	5 minutes
Cross-examination of Prosecution Witness 1 by Defense Attorney 2	3 minutes
Direct Examination of Prosecution Witness 2 by Prosecution Attorney 1	4 minutes
Cross-examination of Prosecution Witness 2 by Defense Attorney 1	2 minutes
Direct Examination of Defense Witness 1 by Defense Attorney 2	5 minutes
Cross-examination of Defense Witness 1 by Prosecution Attorney 2	3 minutes
Direct Examination of Defense Witness 2 by Defense Attorney 1	4 minutes
Cross-examination of Defense Witness 2 by Prosecution Attorney 1	2 minutes
Recess for Planning Closing Arguments	10 minutes
Defense Closing Arguments by Attorney 2	5 minutes
Prosecution Closing Arguments by Attorney 2	5 minutes

SUMMARY

Fields, forums, and formats may be thought of as the bridge between inquiry and advocacy. An argument field involves a community of individuals who share a problem-solving goal. This shared purpose establishes standards by which arguments within the field are evaluated.

The fields approach to argument suggests that we must study the field in which we will be arguing, that we should realize that argument evaluation is partially field-dependent, and that standards and practices of argument are not necessarily transferable between fields. Argument fields exert a controlling influence on us as advocates. We must understand the components and thinking patterns of the field in which our advocacy takes place.

Advocacy forums may be thought of as existing on a continuum according to their goals, the nature of their procedures, and the nature of their audiences. At one end of the continuum are truth determination forums, which are characterized by formal rules of procedure and highly specialized audiences. Included within the grouping are legal advocacy forums, academic debate, and parliamentary debate. In the middle of the continuum are information-seeking forums, whose rules and procedures are less formal and whose audiences are generally less specialized than those of truth determination forums. This grouping includes audience-controlled forums and public debate. At the far end of the continuum are audience activation forums, which are characterized by a lack of formal procedures and nonspecialized audiences. Mass persuasion, propaganda, and advertising are included as audience activation forums. Because there are no rules of procedure and because audiences are characteristically nonspecialized, the standards of argumentative inquiry are the least relevant at this end of the continuum.

Within educational debate training, students are most likely to encounter the advocacy situations of traditional and educational debate formats and alternative educational debate formats. Traditional debate formats include team policy debate, team value debate, and Lincoln-Douglas debate. Each format has its own philosophical and educational underpinnings, uses a particular type of proposition, and specifies different speaker duties. Alternative debate formats include audience debate and mock trial competition.

NOTES

[1]An excellent discussion of the theoretical grounding of argumentation is provided by Cox and Willard, and by Zarefsky.

[2]See the review of argument fields by Zarefsky.

[3]An excellent discussion of the policy-making paradigm is provided by Rowland ("Policy Dispute"), Thomas, and Lichtman and Rohrer.

[4]For a more complete explanation of the hypothesis-testing paradigm, see Zarefsky and Henderson, Hollihan, and Corsi.

[5]Quotations are from a "statement of principles" issued by Jack Howe and distributed in letter form to members of the Southwest Cross Examination Debate Association, September, 13, 1971.

[6]An excellent discussion of the practical demands of argumentation in the field of law is provided in Rieke and Sillars (216–42).

SELECTED BIBLIOGRAPHY

CORSI, JEROME R. "Zarefsky's Theory of Debate as Hypothesis Testing: A Critical Re-Examination." *Journal of the American Forensic Association* 19 (1983): 158–70.
COX, J ROBERT, and CHARLES A. WILLARD, eds. Pp. xiii–xlvii in *Advances in Argumentation Theory and Research*. Carbondale: Southern Illinois University Press, 1982.

HERBECK, DALE, and JOHN KATSULAS. *Paradigms of Debate*. Kansas City, MO: National Federation of State High School Associations, 1988.

HILL, BILLY J. "Improving the Quality of CEDA Debate." *National Forensic Journal* 4 (1986): 105–21.

HOLLIHAN, THOMAS A. "Conditional Arguments and the Hypothesis Testing Paradigm." *Journal of the American Forensic Association* 19 (1983): 171–78.

HULTZEN, LEE S. "Status in Deliberative Analysis." In *The Rhetorical Idiom: Essays in Rhetoric, Oratory, Language, and Drama,* edited by Donald C. Bryant. Ithaca, NY: Cornell University Press, 1958.

HUNSAKER, RICHARD. *Lincoln-Douglas Debate: Defining and Judging Value Debate*. Kansas City, MO: National Federation of State High School Associations, 1988.

LICHTMAN, ALAN J., and DANIEL M. ROHRER. "The Logic of Policy Dispute." *Journal of the American Forensic Association* 16 (Spring 1980): 236–47.

RIEKE, RICHARD D., and MALCOLM O. SILLARS. *Argumentation and the Decision Making Process*. 2d ed. Glenview, IL: Scott, Foresman, 1984.

ROWLAND, ROBERT C. "The Influence of Purpose on Fields of Argument." *Journal of the American Forensic Association* 18 (1982): 228–45.

ROWLAND, ROBERT C. "The Relationship Between Realism and Debatability in Policy Advocacy." *Journal of the American Forensic Association* 22 (1986): 125–34.

THOMAS, DAVID A., ed. "Forum on Policy Systems Analysis." *Journal of the American Forensic Association* 22 (1986): 123–66.

TOMLINSON, JAMES E. "Current Issues in the Cross Examination Debate Association." *National Forensic Journal* 4 (1986): 91–103.

ULRICH, WALTER. *Rebuttals and Extensions in Debate*. Kansas City, MO: National Federation of State High School Associations, 1987.

WILLARD, CHARLES A., ed. "Special Issue: Review Symposium on Argument Fields." *Journal of the American Forensic Association* 18 (1982): 191–257.

ZAREFSKY, DAVID. "Persistent Questions in the Theory of Argument Fields." *Journal of the American Forensic Association* 18 (1982): 191–203.

ZAREFSKY, DAVID, and BILL HENDERSON. "Hypothesis-Testing in Theory and Practice." *Journal of the American Forensic Association* 19 (1983): 179–85.

STUDY QUESTIONS

1. Should we define an argument field on the basis of the standards of proof used by a community of arguers? How does the study of argumentation benefit by defining an argument field in this manner?

2. What conditions might justify the classification of a committee hearing as closer to *truth determination* than *information-seeking*?

3. Is the responsibility for advocates to conduct thorough inquiry reduced when they are preparing for advocacy in *audience activation* forums?

4. Which of the three traditional educational debate formats identified in this chapter (team policy debate, team value debate, and Lincoln-Douglas debate) do you think provides the better educational experience?

EXERCISES

1. Observe a public advocacy situation, either live or televised, and discuss the following elements of that situation:
   a. In what ways does the situational goal differ from the advocacy goals of the individual advocates?
   b. To what extent are the concepts of presumption and burden of proof relevant in this advocacy situation?

c. What demands does the advocacy situation make in terms of the kinds of proof that the advocates must present?

d. Where would you place this advocacy situation on the continuum outlined in this chapter? Justify your decision.

2. Obtain a transcript of a presidential debate and answer the following questions:

a. Do concepts such as presumption and burden of proof operate in this debate?

b. Discuss the following claim: "Presidential debates are not really debates at all; at best, they are press conferences. Presidential debates are pseudo-debates."

3. Observe an interscholastic debate and discuss the ways in which it falls short of the goal of *truth determination*.

4. Structure a format for a two-hour televised debate between two political candidates that would guarantee maximum application of the standards of reasoned inquiry. Do you think that contemporary political candidates would agree to debate within this format? Do you think that the public would watch the debate?

5. Observe a courtroom trial. Identify the ways in which the format is designed to discover truth.

CHAPTER TWELVE
STRATEGIES FOR FACT/
VALUE CONTROVERSIES

The inquiry process, as we have learned, provides us with data that we relate through the reasoning process to a conclusion. The advocacy process requires us to *present* our arguments within a particular field, forum, and format. Few forums provide advocates with the opportunity to carefully present *everything* that they have learned in the inquiry stage. Such factors as time constraints, audience interest, and audience perceptions require us to be *selective* in what we present in a particular forum. This chapter identifies various strategies that can be used in selecting the issues to emphasize when debating fact/valve propositions.

THE NATURE OF STRATEGIES

Advocacy strategies are broad plans that determine how advocates will adapt the presentation of their analysis to the constraints and opportunities of a particular communication situation. A strategy is designed to heighten the persuasive impact of the analysis by altering perception, emphasis, or both. An examination of this definition suggests that there are five important elements to the concept.

First, *strategies are broad plans*. They involve overall argumentative and rhetorical choices. Advocacy strategies are concerned with how major constraints should be dealt with and how fundamental issues should be developed. The concept of strategies is not concerned with specific ways of refuting individual arguments except to the extent that such refutation is part of a larger strategic consideration.

Second, *strategies determine how advocates adapt the presentation of their analysis.* *Adapt* and *presentation* are the critical terms here. The development of an appropriate strategy does not require you to abandon your basic analysis of a proposition. A strategy does suggest ways in which you should alter the *presentation* of your analysis. Without changing your overall position on the issues, you must decide how thoroughly to develop each issue, which arguments to select in support of those issues, what order of presentation to use, and so on. The use of strategies ought not to imply the compromise of ethical principles or basic obligations. Rather, strategies simply recognize the fact that the same overall position may be presented in various ways.

Third, *strategies call for adaptation to the constraints and opportunities of the particular communication situation.* In determining how to adapt your analysis for presentation, you must examine the total circumstances of the immediate communication situation. The degree to which your audience respects you and supports your cause are important elements that must be analyzed. The nature of the occasion, specific rules of procedure, and audience expectations are additional factors that require consideration. In general, the more thoroughly you understand the demands of the *total situation,* the better prepared you will be to make the restraints of the situation work to your advantage.

Fourth, *the aim of strategies is to heighten the persuasive impact of your analysis.* No matter what the context, the purpose of a strategy is to increase the chances of achieving the goal in that particular situation. In military conflict the goal of a

strategy is victory over the enemy. In political contests the purpose of a strategy is to gain enough votes to win the election. Since the immediate goal of communication situations is acceptance of the message, the purpose of advocacy strategies is to increase the chances of your ideas being accepted by the audience.

Fifth, *strategies seek to achieve their objective through alterations in perception, emphasis, or both.* Professional photographers know how important perspective and emphasis are in making a picture interesting and meaningful. A dandelion growing through a crack in the sidewalk may not strike us as very attractive when used as part of a total backyard scene. But when that same dandelion is photographed against a more limited background with soft shadows forming patterns on the sidewalk, it can become an object of striking beauty and symmetry. Similarly, the impact of a given argument may be significantly increased or decreased by relating it to different values, premises, or conclusions. Skilled advocates, like other artists, can stimulate excitement, not by ignoring reality, but by viewing reality from strikingly different, yet appropriate, frames of reference.

There can be little doubt that the advocacy strategies we use have important effects on the outcome of the arguments in which we participate. Most of us have learned, for example, that when disagreeing with a friend or loved one, it is usually best to avoid starting out the dispute with the statement "you are wrong." Such an approach usually does little more than create a defensive response. A better strategy is to start out with a statement that establishes common ground.

The remainder of this chapter examines case strategies useful in debating fact/value propositions. The following chapter presents case strategies specific to policy controversies. A *case* may be thought of as *a specific pattern of relationships used to support or oppose a proposition.* Strategic case-building requires the selection of certain arguments and the exclusion of others and the relating of the selected arguments in a particular way.

AFFIRMATIVE CASE STRATEGIES FOR FACT/VALUE PROPOSITIONS

The affirmative side of any controversy is composed of those people who support the change in fact/value or policy judgment recommended by the proposition. The affirmative side is obligated to present arguments sufficient to fulfill its burden of proof and, thus, to overcome the present system's presumption. The affirmative seeks to accomplish this by providing positive responses to each of the issues.

The issues may be developed and related to one another in a number of different ways, but there are certain basic approaches. This chapter presents three basic affirmative case strategies and three basic negative case strategies for fact/value propositions. These approaches are simply ways of developing detailed arguments into an adequate case.

As we learned in Chapter 3, the stasis formula is a useful method for analyzing fact/value controversies. Specifically, the stasis formula suggests that potential issues in fact/value controversies may be discovered by exploring four frames:

jurisdiction, definition, existence of fact, and quality. As we prepare to present a case which affirms a fact/value claim, we must decide which frame or frames to emphasize as well as the specific arguments within each frame that deserve particular attention.

There are three basic strategies that may be used in developing affirmative cases for fact/value propositions. They are (1) the stasis formula case, (2) the criteria establishment case, and (3) the criteria application case. These three case strategies differ from one another in terms of the emphasis that they give to the frames of stasis analysis. No matter which case strategy affirmative advocates select, they are obligated to consider all of the relevant circumstances and to attempt to interpret them in light of the appropriate argumentative responsibilities.

The Stasis Formula Case

The *stasis formula* approach to case development directly addresses three of the four frames contained in the stasis formula. Specifically, the affirmative presents major points that answer the questions of definition, existence of fact, and quality. This case strategy is useful in situations where your audience has very limited knowledge of the controversy or when you have limited knowledge as to the issues on which your opponent will disagree with your analysis.

The stasis formula case strategy begins with the frame of definition. The advocate carefully identifies the nature of the fact or value being considered. Next, the frame involving existence of fact is developed. Here the advocate applies the definition to a particular circumstance. Finally, the advocate presents the frame of quality, showing that special circumstances do not mitigate against accepting a fact/value claim.

The stasis formula approach to case presentation is frequently used by student prosecuting attorneys in mock trials. The stasis formula case is a particularly appropriate strategy in this format since the mock trial is designed to help students understand the legal process. The following opening statement of a student attorney at a mock trial shows that the prosecution will use a stasis formula case:

> The case against Kevin Jones is quite simple. Mr. Jones is accused of first degree murder. We are all aware of the legal definition of first degree murder. This crime involves the deliberate, premeditated termination of a human life [frame of definition]. The prosecution will demonstrate that Mr. Jones arranged for his wife to purchase a one-million-dollar life insurance policy, naming himself as beneficiary. We will further demonstrate that acquaintances of Mr. Jones heard him say that he wanted his wife dead. We will also prove that the gun used to terminate the life of Mrs. Jones displays only the fingerprints of Mr. Jones. In short, your Honor, we will demonstrate beyond all reasonable doubt that Mr. Jones deliberately, and in a premeditated manner, murdered his wife [frame of existence of fact]. Finally, your Honor, the prosecution will prove that Mr. Jones did not act in a fit of temporary anger or in a moment of insanity. Nor did he act in self-defense. There were no circumstances that in any way mitigate against returning a guilty verdict [frame of quality].

Notice that the student prosecuting attorney specifically addresses three of the four frames of stasis analysis. The frame of jurisdication is omitted since the preliminary hearing already established the court's jurisdiction to hear the case.

SAMPLE STASIS FORMULA AFFIRMATIVE CASE

Resolved: That the U.S. military invasion of Grenada was unjustified.	Proposition
I. Military invasion is justified only when a nation engages in actions that endanger the national sovereignty of another nation.	Frame of definition
A. This principle is established by international law.	
B. This principle was used by the United States in every military invasion prior to the Grenada invasion.	
II. The Cuban military presence in Grenada in no way endangered the security of the United States or its allies.	Frame of existence of fact
A. Cuban troops in no way endangered U.S. sovereignty.	
B. Cuban troops in no way endangered the sovereignty of U.S. allies.	
III. Noninvasive measures could have been used to counter any potential Cuban threat.	Frame of quality
A. Diplomatic measures would have been superior to military action.	
B. Pressure by U.S. allies would have been superior to military action.	

The Criteria Establishment Case

The *criteira establishment* approach to case development emphasizes the stasis of definition. The major focus of this affirmative case strategy is justification of the particular definitions or criteria used to affirm a factual or value judgment. The criteria establishment case is an excellent strategy in situations where the criteria to be applied are not commonly understood or when the criteria are not likely to be readily accepted by an audience or an opponent.

The criteria establishment case begins with presenting the criteria or definitions that are to be applied. The nature of the criteria or the definitions are prescribed, and the relevance of those criteria to the nature of the judgment expressed in the proposition is justified. This justification may rest on the expert opinion of an authoritative individual or group, or it may be based on a comparison with related situations. After the nature and relevance of the criteria have been explained, the facts of the specific circumstances under consideration are examined in light of the criteria. The affirmative application of the criteria to the situation is, of course, done in such a way as to justify the acceptance of the proposition. In those circumstances where the criteria establishment case is used, the justification of the criteria usually becomes the focus of the controversy, and the application step may receive only minor consideration.

The criteria establishment approach was used by the lawyers for the plaintiff in the famous Supreme Court case of *Brown v. Topeka Board of Education.* This was the case that challenged the previously established doctrine that separate facilities for black students could provide equal educational opportunities. The specific charge against the Topeka Board of Education was that it had denied the Constitutional rights of a black child by denying him the right to attend a school with white children. In order to establish that the black child's Constitutional rights had been violated, the representatives for the plaintiff defined *equal* facilities as being the *same* facilities. The criterion of sameness was justified by expert testimony and sociological and psychological data that indicated that separate facilities were not equal in terms of their sociological and psychological effects. Once this criterion was established its application to the separate but similar practices of the Topeka Boad of Education made it possible to establish the claim that Brown's Constitutional rights had indeed been denied.

SAMPLE CRITERIA ESTABLISHMENT AFFIRMATIVE CASE

Resolved: That air bags are a better automobile safety device than seat belts.		Propostion
I.	Automobile safety systems should meet three criteria:	Frame of definition (stating the criteria)
	A. They should save lives.	
	B. They should require minimum activation and effort by the passenger.	
	C. They should be cost-beneficial.	
II.	The criteria are the best criteria for evaluating automobile safety systems.	Frame of definition (justifying the criteria)
	A. The criteria are supported by government safety institutes.	
	B. The criteria are supported by private industry safety experts.	
III.	Air bags meet the criteria better than do seat belts.	Frame of existence of fact (applying the criteria)
	A. Air bags can save more lives than seat belts.	
	B. Air bags require less consumer activation and effort than do seat belts.	
	C. Air bags are more cost-beneficial than are seat belts.	

The Criteria Application Case

The *criteria application* strategy emphasizes the existence of fact stasis. Unlike the criteria establishment case, this case strategy does not offer direct justification of the criteria. Instead, the criteria application strategy focuses on the application of the criteria in a particular situation. This approach to case development should be used when the criteria or definitions are commonly accepted ones and are not likely to be challenged.

The criteria application case does not begin with an explanation of the relevance of the criteria. Rather, it assumes that the criteria or elements of the definition are relevant and begins immediately to demonstrate that the facts of the situation conform to the criteria. The criteria are the substances whose existence must be established, and the facts of the situation are used as signs or attributes of those substances. Thus, the basic form of argument used in developing the criteria application case is argument from sign.

The criteria application approach was effectively used by an intercollegiate debate team defending the claim that Samuel L. Morison was unjustly convicted of espionage. Morison was convicted of violating the Espionage Act of 1917. Specifically, Morison was accused of sending classified photographs of the Soviet Union's first nuclear-powered aircraft carrier to the journal *Jane's Defense Weekly.* The affirmative team focused its case on demonstrating that Morison's action in no way violated the specific criteria established in the Espionage Act. They presented evidence that Morison had not acted as a spy, that he did not intend to compromise national security, and that his action in no way jeopardized U.S. security interests. Since the criteria for espionage are clearly established in law, the affirmative team recognized that they should concentrate on applying the criteria to the facts of the situation.

SAMPLE CRITERIA APPLICATION
AFFIRMATIVE CASE

Resolved: That the space program has benefited humanity.		Proposition
I.	Medical discoveries promoted by the space program have decreased human death and suffering.	Frame of existence of fact (implied criteria)
II.	Engineering discoveries promoted by the space program have improved the quality of human life.	Frame of existence of fact (implied criteria)
III.	Scientific discoveries promoted by the space program have advanced scientific knowledge.	Frame of existence of fact (implied criteria)

NEGATIVE CASE STRATEGIES FOR FACT/VALUE PROPOSITIONS

The negative side of a controversy is the side that opposes the proposition. The nature of negative advocacy differs from that of affirmative advocacy in two important ways. First, *the negative normally has the advantage of presumption.* If the negative wins a single issue in the controversy, it has defeated the proposition. Unlike the affirmative, then, the negative is not bound to clash on all potential issues. While a strong negative advocate is prepared to clash in all potential areas of affirmative weakness, the application of the concepts of presumption and burden of proof permits opponents of change greater flexibility in choosing areas of clash.

Second, *negative advocacy,* almost by definition, *is argumentation in response to an attack.* Before negative advocates can decide which specific lines of argument will be appropriate in a given situation, they must wait until an affirmative rationale or proposal has been presented. Negative advocates can, however, determine in advance the general philosophical position that they will take in responding to affirmative arguments and work out a variety of possible arguments consistent with that position. In this context, therefore, negative approaches to advocacy should not be thought of as specific types of cases in the same sense as are affirmative approaches. Rather, the concept of negative approaches to advocacy describes certain philosophical positions that condition the general nature of negative responses to affirmative cases.

The advocate speaking against a proposition must also make strategic case choices. These choices are influenced by the analysis of the proposition and by the specific case strategy used by the affirmative. There are three philosophical positions from which negative speakers may argue fact/value propositions. These are (1) rejecting the affirmative definition or criteria, (2), denying the affirmative application, and (3) establishing an alternate value hierarchy. These three approaches differ in terms of the degree to which they accept portions of the affirmative analysis.

Rejection of Criteria

The *rejection of criteria* strategy requires the negative to clash directly with the crucial criteria on which the affirmative case rests. The approach argues that the criteria selected by the affirmative team are inappropriate, insufficiently supported, or in some other way wrong. The use of the rejection approach does not imply that the affirmative is lying or deliberately misrepresenting the situation. In most instances, negatives take this position because they believe that the affirmative has misanalyzed the appropriate criteria, overlooked important facts, given too much significance to certain facts, or, in other ways, drawn unwarranted conclusions from available data. The rejection of criteria strategy is especially effective in refuting affirmative cases based on criteria establishment, although it can be used against all three affirmative fact/value case approaches.

The rejection approach was used by attorneys in the famous euthanasia case involving Karen Ann Quinlan. Ms. Quinlan lay in a coma in a Danford, New Jersey, hospital. Medical experts agreed that she would never regain consciousness. Attorneys representing the parents of Ms. Quinlan sought the court's permission to allow doctors to disconnect the machinery that sustained Ms. Quinlan's existence. Attorneys for the state of New Jersey argued against removing the life-support machinery. They claimed that even though Ms. Quinlan was doomed to a vegetative existence, she still met all the criteria for life established by accepted legal and medical definitions. She was not brain-dead, and, thus, deliberately removing the life-support equipment would constitute murder. The attorneys for Ms. Quinlan's parents directly attacked the criteria, claiming that brain activity is an inadequate measure of life and death. They argued that criteria should be used that take into account the quality of one's life, not just the existence of physical signs of life. The courtroom debate thus focused almost exclusively on what criteria should be used to determine whether or not a person is alive.

The rejection of criteria strategy is a strong one because it can lead to total rejection of the affirmative judgment. The approach should be used, however, only when the affirmative criteria are inappropriate or unjustified. Ethical advocates will avoid any temptation to distort the criteria in order to secure an unjustified rejection.

Denial of Application

Negative advocates may encounter situations where the affirmative criteria are clearly justified and appropriate, but are in some way misapplied. Such circumstances warrant using the *denial of application* strategy. This approach accepts the basic criteria identified by the affirmative. However, the approach argues that the affirmative incorrectly applies the criteria to the specific event under consideration. Denial of application is the most common case strategy used by defense attorneys in routine criminal trials. The defense attorney usually accepts the definition of the crime and the criteria that must be met to establish guilt. However, the defense attorney denies that the crime was committed by her or his client.

The denial of application approach was used by the defense lawyers for a well-known professional football player who was charged with drunken driving. The prosecution attempted to establish that the defendant was drunk by demonstrating that he had spent several hours drinking in a bar. The defense lawyer denied that drinking in a bar over a period of several hours was sufficient evidence to prove that the defendant was legally drunk (a technical matter involving a specific percentage of alcohol in the blood). The defense offered several witnesses who testified that the defendant had consumed only one glass of beer during his three hours in the bar, and it presented evidence that indicated that the alcohol content of the blood from one glass of beer would not, after three hours, be sufficient to meet that state's criterion of drunkenness. In this case the defense lawyer accepted the prosecution's criteria, but denied that the actual situation conformed to those criteria.

Like the rejection of criteria approach, the denial of application strategy is powerful. The approach directly refutes a basic affirmative burden. Again, the responsible advocate will take care not to distort the facts of the situation in order to gain an unjustified denial.

Establishment of an Alternate Value Hierarchy

The *alternate value hierarchy* strategy is based on a tacit acceptance of the affirmative's criteria and description of facts. This position does not reject the affirmative's analysis as false; rather, it suggests that the affirmative's judgment is based on a limited perspective. The alternate value hierarchy position argues that there are unusual factors operating within the total situation that ought to be considered. If these extraordinary elements are accepted as relevant, the judgment in question must be tempered or changed. The alternate value hierarchy approach can be used in two ways: (1) by *demonstrating extenuating circumstances* that justify tempering or suspending the value judgment, and (2) by *proposing alternate values* that serve as value objections to the affirmative judgment.

The notion of extenuating circumstances is well established in our criminal courts. Individuals who readily admit that they committed a crime may be acquitted by reason of insanity or because the exclusionary rule results in vital evidence being disallowed in the trial. They are acquitted because our judicial system subscribes to certain values that outweigh the discovery of truth in a particular situation. The exclusionary rule, for example, is designed to ensure that law enforcement officers follow rules that protect individual rights. Our courts operate with the value assumption that it is better that guilty persons go free than for innocent people to be denied liberty.

In 1970 the U.S. Army brought charges against a number of American combat soldiers for allegedly having taken part in the mass murder of hundreds of South Vietnamese civilians. Although the details of each case varied, the lawyers for most of the defendants based their defense efforts on extenuating circumstances. They attempted to show that the defendants were either acting on orders from above or were suffering from extreme fatigue and severe emotional strain. Awareness of these factors did not, of course, alter past events, but they did help to explain them and temper the court's judgment of the soldiers.

The second way in which the value hierarchy position can be used is by proposing alternate values that serve as value objections to the affirmative judgment. Affirmative case approaches to value questions frequently emphasize the application of a value to one or more specific situations. For example, in supporting the claim that the public has a right to know what its government is doing, an affirmative advocate might concentrate on demonstrating the benefits derived from public knowledge of the social security program, income taxes, and government support of education. The affirmative thus restricts the total context in which the value judgment is made. The notion of a value hierarchy suggests that value judgments must be made in a rather broad context. That is, a particular value may seem important in a limited context but may be subordinated to another value in a larger context. For example, a negative advocate may agree that public knowledge about social security is beneficial, but argue that public knowledge of what its government is doing in military research and planning endangers a more important value—the country's national security. The negative advocate thus establishes a value heirarchy in which national security is of greater value than the public's right to know. In essence, the negative raises a value objection to the affirmative judgment, arguing that if we accept the affirmative judgment, we undermine a more fundamental value. Often, this approach requires the negative advocate to demonstrate the pragmatic implications of accepting the affirmative's value judgment.

The value hierarchy position thus does not directly clash with the outline of the affirmative case but suggests that the case must be considered in a broader context. The position is especially useful when the affirmative case adopts a narrow viewpoint.

SUMMARY

Advocacy strategies are broad plans that determine how advocates will adapt the presentation of their analysis to the constraints and opportunities of a particular communication situation. Strategies are designed to heighten the persuasive impact of the analysis by altering perception, emphasis, or both.

A case involves the presentation of a specific pattern of relationships used to support or oppose a proposition. Case-building is a selective process in which advocates emphasize certain issues and deemphasize other issues.

The affirmative side of any controversy is composed of those people who support the change in fact/value or policy judgment recommended by the proposition. The affirmative side is obligated to present arguments sufficient to fulfill its burden of proof and, thus, to overcome the negative presumption. The affirmative seeks to accomplish this by providing positive responses to each of the issues.

The three basic affirmative case strategies for fact/value propositions are: (1) the stasis formula case, (2) the criteria establishment case, and (3) the criteria application case. Although these approaches differ in terms of issue emphasis, they require the advocate to consider all of the relevant circumstances and to interpret them in light of appropriate constructs.

The negative side of a controversy is the side that opposes the proposition. Negative advocacy differs from affirmative advocacy in two ways: (1) the negative normally has the advantage of presumption and (2) negative advocacy is argumentation in response to an attack.

Negative cases involve philosophical positions that condition the general nature of negative responses to affirmative cases. There are three philosophical positions from which negative speakers may argue fact/value propositions: (1) rejecting the affirmative definition or criteria, (2) denying the affirmative application, and (3) establishing an alternate value hierarchy. These three approaches differ in terms of the degree to which they accept portions of the affirmative analysis.

SELECTED BIBLIOGRAPHY

CIRLIN, ALAN. "On Negative Strategy in Value Debate." In *CEDA Yearbook 1984,* edited by Don Brownlee, 31–39. Northridge, CA: Cross Examination Debate Association, 1984.

FRYAR, MARIDELL, and DAVID A. THOMAS. *Student Congress & Lincoln-Douglas Debate.* Lincolnwood, IL: National Textbook, 1981.

HUNSAKER, RICHARD A. *Lincoln-Douglas Debate: Defining and Judging Value Debate.* Kansas City, MO: National Federation of State High School Associations, 1988.

MATLON, RONALD J. "Debating Propositions of Value." *Journal of the American Forensic Association* 14 (1978): 194–204.

PRENTICE, DIANA, and JACK KAY. *The Role of Values in Policy Debate.* Kansas City, MO: National Federation of State High School Associations, 1986.

SHAW, WARREN C. *The Art of Debate.* New York: Allyn and Bacon, 1922.

ZIEGELMUELLER, GEORGE W., and CHARLES A. DAUSE. *Argumentation: Inquiry and Advocacy.* 1st ed. Englewood Cliffs, NJ: Prentice-Hall, 1975.

STUDY QUESTIONS

1. Strategies, by their very nature, require us to be selective in the arguments we present. What ethical concerns should guide our use of strategies?

2. What criteria can be used to determine whether to use a criteria establishment or a criteria application case?

3. Should negative advocates always reject the criteria presented by affirmative advocates?

4. Is the alternate value hierarchy strategy weaker than the strategies of denial and rejection?

EXERCISES

1. Develop brief case outlines for each of the affirmative case approaches discussed in this chapter. Be sure to select a proposition of judgment for each of the case approaches.
2. Develop brief negative case outlines which respond to the affirmative case outlines developed for Question 1.
3. Examine the newspaper accounts of two or three recent court cases and characterize the approaches taken by the prosecution and by the defense. What factors led the lawyers to select the approaches they used?

CHAPTER THIRTEEN
STRATEGIES FOR POLICY
CONTROVERSIES

Every policy controversy involves a multitude of factual and value judgments. Therefore, the case strategies for fact/value controversies discussed in the previous chapter are certainly relevant to policy questions. But because policy questions require the additional consideration of a plan of action, more comprehensive case strategies are necessary. This chapter discusses a variety of case strategies useful in policy controversies.

AFFIRMATIVE CASE STRATEGIES FOR POLICY PROPOSITIONS

The five basic strategies that may be used in developing affirmative cases for policy propositions are (1) the traditional case, (2) the comparative advantages case, (3) the goal/criteria case, (4) the effect-oriented case, and (5) the on-balance case. These five case strategies differ from one another in terms of their levels of analysis, in terms of the ways in which stock issue concepts are related, or both.

No matter which one of the five approaches is used, affirmative advocates are obligated to address—or at least to be prepared to address—each of the concepts suggested by the stock issues. Affirmative advocates must be prepared to demonstrate that their interpretation of the proposition is topical, as required by

the stock issue of jurisdiction. They must be able to show a signifiant past, present, or future problem or harm as suggested by the ill issue. They must be able to causally relate that ill to the basic philosophy of the present system as suggested by the blame issue or inherency concept. They must be prepared to outline a specific plan and demonstrate how it would solve the problem of the ill as required by the cure issue. And they must be prepared to respond to disadvantages to their proposal as indicated by the cost issue. These basic requirements are in no way circumvented by any of the five case strategies.

The Traditional Case

The *traditional approach* to case analysis begins with the identification of the stated or implied goal of the proposition. Once this goal has been determined, each of the stock issues is developed in accordance with the goal. The analysis of the traditional case therefore occurs at the level of the proposition's goal. The ill issue of the traditional case is a direct outgrowth of the failure of the present system to achieve the suggested goal of the proposition. The existence of ills or harms is an indication both that the goal of the proposition has not been achieved and that its attainment is warranted. The blame issue argues that the basic philosophy of the present system is the cause of the ill, or the reason why the goal of the proposition has not been accomplished. The cure issue offers a plan based on philosophical and structural principles consistent with the proposition but different from those of existing policies. The plan, it is claimed, will remove the cause (the philosophy of present policies) of the harms and, thus, remove the harms and accomplish the goal of the proposition.

Affirmative advocates of compulsory health insurance typically develop their arguments in accordance with the traditional approach. They generally identify the goal of compulsory health insurance to be the provision of adequate medical care to all citizens without severe economic hardship. In order to justify this goal, the ill issue is developed to demonstrate that many people receive inadequate medical care as shown by delayed treatment, incomplete treatment, and the denial of treatment. Even when treatment is received, it is claimed, the expenses incurred from a prolonged illness erode savings, create severe indebtedness, and lead to bankruptcy. Thus, the ills flow directly from the goal of the proposition. The blame issue argues that the goal of the proposition cannot be achieved through existing programs of voluntary health insurance and government assistance. Advocates of compulsory health insurance claim that the private, competitive nature of voluntary insurance means that increased insurance coverage must be reflected in higher prices. Therefore, under voluntary health insurance those who most need comprehensive protection are those who are least able to afford it. Government assistance programs, under a system of private medicine, must be limited to those in real need so that people must first suffer severe economic hardship before they can receive government aid. As a substitute for the private, noncomprehensive, and restrictive policies of the present system, advocates of compulsory health insurance offer a cure based on the contrary philosophical concepts of public policy, comprehensiveness, and universality. By eliminating the alleged causes (the private, noncomprehensive, and restrictive nature of present programs) of the ills (inadequate care and economic hardship), compulsory health insurance would presumably eliminate the ills and achieve the goal of the proposition (adequate medical care without economic hardship).

Not all propositions lend themselves to development according to the traditional approach. Two conditions must exist before a traditional case can be formulated: (1) the goal of the proposition must be thwarted by the principles of the present system and (2) both the ill and the cause of the ill must be capable of being eliminated by the affirmative plan. The traditional approach is the most fundamental framework for case analysis because it is based on a single level of goal analysis and because its causal links are direct.

SAMPLE TRADITIONAL AFFIRMATIVE CASE

Resolved: That the U.S. federal government should establish a comprehensive program to combat ozone depletion.   Proposition

1. The federal government will sponsor a major research and development effort for solar energy.   Plan
2. Fossil fuel usage will be taxed so as to ensure a 25 percent decrease in consumption by the year 2000.
3. Tax incentives will be given to utility and manufacturing companies to encourage the shift to solar energy.
4. The Department of Energy will oversee and enforce the plan provisions. Necessary enforcement powers will be provided.
5. Funding for the plan will come from a tax on fossil fuels.

I. Environmental disaster results from ozone depletion.   Ill
   A. Global warming produced by ozone depletion will turn the earth into a useless desert.
   B. Millions will die from cancer resulting from ozone depletion.

II. The U.S. commitment to fossil fuels guarantees increased   Blame
    ozone depletion.
    A. Current energy policy makes fossil fuel consumption
       more profitable than safer energy sources.
    B. Continued reliance on fossil fuels guarantees increased
       ozone depletion.
III. A government program promoting solar energy protects   Cure
    against ozone deplection.
    A. Solar energy does not deplete ozone.
    B. Taxes and incentives can achieve a 25 percent decrease
       in fossil fuel consumption by 2000.
    C. A 25 percent decrease in fossil fuel consumption
       prevents ozone depletion.

The Comparative Advantages Case

The *comparative advantages* case strategy requires the determination of a secondary level of goals and the establishment of all its causal links on this secondary level. This case strategy should be used when *both* the present system and the affirmative proposal are capable of achieving the primary goal of the proposition or when *neither* the present system nor the affirmative proposal are fully capable of achieving the primary goal of the proposition.

When differences do not exist at the primary goal level, then subordinate criteria must be applied in order to evaluate the two systems. These secondary goals (values, criteria) may be special qualitative factors such as speed, efficiency, fairness, or flexibility, or they may involve the application of such quantitative measures as more or less.

To develop a case based on the comparative advantages strategy, an advocate begins by selecting subgoals appropriate to the situation. The wording of the arguments should clearly reveal what those secondary goals are. The ill issue is established at the subgoal level so that the harms cited justify the subgoals rather than the primary goal of the proposition. The blame issue is also developed at the level of the subordinate goals. The principles of present policies are shown to be responsible for the harms and the reason why the subgoals have not been met. The cure issue establishes that the affirmative plan will remove the harms and establish the subgoals by eliminating the cause of the harms (the principles of the present system) and by substituting a new plan based on the principles of the proposition.

Many city councils have considered or adopted proposals that require citizens to separate their trash into different categories—newspapers, glass, cans, and the like—so that some of it can be recycled for future use. The advocates of such proposals are not concerned with the primary goals of sanitation work, that is, the removal of unwanted materials. They concede that existing systems of trash pickup achieve this primary objective, but their concern is with such secondary objectives as the conservation of resources and the production of additional revenue. To justify a new system of trash collection, the advocates of recycling attempt to demonstrate that the failure to conserve our resources will result in future shortages (ill of the first subgoal) and that the failure to find new sources of revenue will result in less government services (ill of the second subgoal). The blame analysis rests on the charge that to attempt to separate the trash after its collection would be structurally impractical because of the amount of time and number of workers required. The cure issue suggests that the structural impracticality of the present system is removed by having private citizens separate their own trash, and, thus, the benefits of conservation and revenue production can be realized.

In the preceding illustration, both the conventional system of trash collection and the proposed system of trash separation could accomplish the primary goal of waste removal. A past intercollegiate debate proposition illustrates a situation in which neither the present system nor the affirmative proposal could fully achieve the primary goal. When college debaters argued the proposition that "law enforcement agencies should be given greater freedom in the investigation and prosecution of crime," neither side could claim that their system would fully meet the implied goal of successfully prosecuting all criminals. Affirmative debaters, therefore, offered secondary criteria as a basis for comparing the two systems. Frequently, quantitative goals such as "greater effectiveness" were selected. The ills of not having greater effectiveness were identified as rising crime rates, more violent deaths, and increasing property losses. Restrictive Supreme Court decisions in the areas of interrogation, search and seizure, or wiretapping were blamed for the increased ills. The removal of these restrictions through the affirmative plan was suggested as the cure and the means of achieving the goal of "greater effectiveness."

SAMPLE COMPARATIVE ADVANTAGES AFFIRMATIVE CASE

Resolved: That the federal government should require all U.S. citizens to serve in the military. — *Proposition*

1. All U.S. citizens between the ages of eighteen and thirty will be required to serve for two years in the U.S. armed forces. — *Plan*
2. Conscientious objectors will be permitted to serve in a non-military capacity.
3. All necessary implementation and enforcement procedures will be provided by the Department of Defense.
4. The plan will be funded by an increase in the federal income tax.

I. Greater equity is guaranteed by universal military conscription. — *Advantage*
   A. Economic necessity ensures that minorities and the poor will constitute a disproportionately large segment of a volunteer army. — *Blame*
   B. Equity is violated by placing minorities and the poor in the position of bearing the brunt of our nation's defense. — *Ill*
   C. Universal military conscription is more equitable than the volunteer army. — *Cure*

II. A more effective military is guaranteed by universal military conscription. — *Advantage*
   A. Serious skill shortages in the military weaken U.S. defense. — *Ill*

B. Skill shortages will continue because the private sector can always pay more to attract skilled personnel.	Blame
C. Universal military conscription guarantees the skilled personnel necessary for a strong military.	Cure

The Goal/Criteria Case

The *goal/criteria case* strategy is based on the same principle as the criteria establishment and the criteria application cases discussed in the preceding chapter on fact/value controversies. The only difference is that the goal/criteria case includes a plan.

There are two types of goal/criteria cases. The first identifies certain objectives or goals that have been accepted by the present system and argues that the proposition better achieves these objectives than does the present system. This approach is similar to the criteria application approach to fact/value questions. For example, affirmative advocates debating a proposition calling for restricting arms sales to foreign countries may decide to base their case strategy on the goal of enhancing U.S. security, a goal accepted by the present system. The strategy of the goal/criteria case is to decrease the amount of time spent in the debate on the ill issue. Negative teams who defend the present system will likely concede that U.S. national security is a significant concern.

The second type of goal/criteria case selects a goal or objective on which the present system has not acted. In a sense, this strategy is similar to the criteria establishment case discussed in the preceding chapter. The affirmative advocate identifies a particular goal, objective, or criteria and defends it as important. For example, in debating the curtailment of arms sales, the affirmative advocate might argue that U.S. arms sales should be governed by two criteria: (1) weapons should be sold only for strategic consideration and (2) no weapon should be sold that may end up being used by an enemy. The affirmative advocate would then justify the importance of these criteria.

SAMPLE GOAL/CRITERIA AFFIRMATIVE CASE

Resolved: That the United States should significantly curtail its arms sales to other countries.	Proposition
1. The federal government will establish an Arms Sales and Transfer Board to review and approve arms sales and transfers to foreign countries.	Plan
2. Arms sales and transfers will be approved only when the board certifies that the weapons will be used only in a defensive manner and when the receiving government is committed to the protection of human rights.	
3. The board will be given all necessary funding and enforcement powers.	
4. The plan will be financed by an arms sales tax.	
I. U.S. arms sales should be subject to two criteria.	Goal/Criteria establishment
A. Only defensive weapons should be sold.	
B. Human rights should be promoted.	

II. Present U.S. arms sales policy violates these criteria.   Blame
  A. The United States is committed to the sale of offensive
    weapons.
  B. U.S. arms sales policy inherently ignores the
    consideration of human rights.
III. Violating the criteria is disastrous.   Ill
  A. The sale of offensive weapons increases dangerous
    regional conflict.
  B. Arms sales to totalitarian regimes promote the
    violation of human rights.
IV. Curtailing U.S. arms sales meets the criteria.   Cure
  A. Regional conflict is decreased.
  B. Human rights are promoted.

The Effect-Oriented Case

The *effect-oriented case* strategy eliminates the ills of the present system without removing the philosophical or structural cause of those ills. This case treats symptoms or effects rather than causes. The effect-oriented strategy should be used whenever the analysis of a proposition suggests that it would be impossible or undesirable to eliminate the basic cause of the ill.[1]

The ill and blame analysis of an effect-oriented case may be developed in terms of either a traditional or a comparative advantages approach. That is, its ill and blame analysis may occur at either the primary or secondary goal levels. The ill issue must demonstrate that because either the primary goal of the proposition or certain secondary goals have not been realized, significant harms exist. The blame issue must establish that the underlying philosophy of present programs is the inherent cause of the harms and the reason why the goals have not been met. The cure issue differs from that of earlier cases in that it does not change the philosophy of the present system (it does not remove the cause of the harms). Rather, it offers a plan that, though different in principle from the present system, is capable of operating within the framework of the present system's philosophy. The affirmative plan alleviates the ills of the present system while, at the same time, permitting the cause of that ill (the philosophy of the present system) to continue.

The effect-oriented case strategy was used by some intercollegiate debaters to justify a guaranteed annual income. These debaters identified the elimination of poverty as the goal of the proposition, and they described the starvation and poor health of poverty victims as manifestations of an ill. The cause of these continued ills was identified as the present system's philosophical assumption that a free market economy can provide an adequate job for all people willing, able, and trained to work. By pointing out that factors such as age, geography, and changing technology make it impossible in an unplanned economy to guarantee that the right kinds of jobs will occur in the right places at the right times, the affirmative developed its blame issue and attempted to demonstrate the inadequacy of the present system's assumption. In this way, the free market system was indicated as the cause of poverty. The affirmative presented its cure issue by offering a plan that guaranteed enough money to everyone to keep them from suffering the hardships of illness and starvation but that did not restructure the economic system of job creation. Thus, the affirmative plan only alleviated the ill of the present system (starvation and ill health) but permitted the cause of those ills (the free market economy) to continue. The affirmative chose this approach to case analysis because they believed that although the free market economy had been harmful to a specific segment of society, its overall effects on society were beneficial.

SAMPLE EFFECT-ORIENTED AFFIRMATIVE CASE

Resolved: That the U.S. federal government should ensure adequate medical care for rural Americans.	Proposition
1. The U.S. Public Health Service will create medical care centers throughout rural America.	Plan
2. Funding to the Public Health Service will be increased so that attractive wages can be offered to medical personnel employed by the centers.	
3. Funding will come from decreasing the defense budget.	
I. Rural medical care in the United States is a national disgrace.	Ill
A. Millions of rural American cannot get needed medical care.	
B. Delay in access to medical care in rural settings results in death and suffering.	
II. The free market system of medical service allocation ensures that rural Americans will go without care.	Blame
III. Government-sponsored rural medical centers guarantee needed care without eliminating the freedom of doctors to choose where to practice.	Cure (cures the ill without changing the structure)

The On-Balance Case

The chief characteristic of the *on-balance case* strategy is its use of the cost issue as part of the affirmative's constructive warrant for change. None of the four preceding approaches to case analysis called for the presentation of the cost issue as part of the affirmative's constructive case. Although affirmative teams using the earlier approaches are required to respond to cost arguments raised by the negative, they are not expected to develop the cost issue as a major part of their rationale for change. The on-balance approach is an appropriate one to use whenever the harms of the ill issue need to be maximized. Maximization may be necessary when the harms are abstract or difficult to quantify, when they are chance happenings rather than universal occurrences, or when they are future prospects rather than immediate realities.

The on-balance approach attempts to maximize the seriousness of the ill issue by comparing it to the minimum cost (slight disadvantage) of adopting the affirmative proposal. The cost issue is developed by demonstrating that present policies are either unnecessary or ineffective. Affirmatives using the on-balance approach may claim that present policies are unnecessary because their alleged benefits could be achieved in other ways. They may argue that present policies are ineffective because they have not achieved and cannot achieve the alleged benefits attributed to them. If, in this way, the cost of abandoning present policies can be shown to be nil, then even a relatively small or abstract ill may be sufficient reason for changing policies.

In general, the ill, blame, and cure issues of the on-balance case are developed according to either the traditional or the comparative advantages approach. If the harms of the ill issue are derived from the primary goal of the proposition, then the traditional approach is used. If the harms result from the failure to meet secondary goals, then the comparative advantages approach is used. It should be noted that if the harm is concerned with a chance (nonuniversal) happening, the causal link of the blame issue must be between the unpredictable risk of the harm and the principles of the present system rather than between the harm itself and the principles of the present system.

The on-balance approach has been used by most of those foreign policy experts who have opposed the U.S. policy of military intervention in the internal conflicts of other countries. The fundamental thesis of these experts is that, on balance, the costs of such interventions have outweighed any possible gains. They contend that the basic harm of our interventionist policy is the waste of lives and resources. Every intervention is said to require some outlay of money that could be better spent on more constructive policies. Moreover, it is claimed that every intervention involves some risk to human lives and that certain interventions— notably Vietnam—have in fact resulted in the loss of many lives. The policy of intervention is inherently blamed for these ills. By its nature intervention requires the movement of troops and supplies, and the movement cannot be accomplished without the expenditure of money. Every intervention is said to involve the risk of some loss of life since it is impossible to predict the exact nature and extent of the opposition's response to our military action. Balanced against these inherent harms are the allegedly minimal benefits of military intervention. The opponents of U.S. interventionists policies develop the cost issue by contending that military interventions are either unnecessary or ineffective. It is claimed that military intervention is unnecessary to stop the spread of communism because, where there is a strong spirit of nationalism, communism cannot succeed. Where there is not a strong spirit of nationalism, it is contended, U.S. intervention will be ineffective. Thus, on balance, the potential harms of intervention are said to counterbalance any possible benefits.

SAMPLE ON-BALANCE AFFIRMATIVE CASE

Resolved: That the federal government should increase the safety of energy use in the United States.　　　　　Proposition

1. The federal government will phase out all nuclear power plants over the next fifteen years.　　　　　Plan
2. Existing nuclear power plants will be dismantled, with nuclear cores being sealed in concrete.
3. Incentives will be given to promote solar power.
4. Funding will come from a tax on fossil fuel energy.

I. Nuclear power is unnecessary.   Cost
   A. Nuclear power provides very little of our nation's
      energy supply.
   B. Alternative energy supplies exist.
II. Nuclear power is dangerous.   Ill
   A. There is a signifiant risk of a nuclear power plant
      accident.
   B. A nuclear power plant accident would be devastating.
III. U.S. energy policy is committed to nuclear power.   Blame
IV. Replacing nuclear power plants with solar energy plants   Cure
    is desirable.

NEGATIVE CASE STRATEGIES FOR POLICY PROPOSITIONS

The four basic philosophical positions from which negatives may argue policy propositions are (1) defense of the present system, (2) repair of the present system, (3) straight refutation, and (4) counterplan. These four strategies differ primarily in terms of their degree of commitment to present policies. All of these approaches may be used in opposition to any of the five affirmative policy case strategies. All of them permit the negative to advance arguments under each of the stock issues, although the demands of particular advocacy situations may not require that certain issues actually be presented.

Defense of the Present System

Defense of the present system (sometimes referred to as the *status quo*) provides the greatest philosophical commitment to present policies. This strategy supports both the principles and the implementation of present policies. Advocates who defend the present system do not necessarily believe that present policies are the wisest and best imaginable. They do believe, however, that they are the wisest and best possible in light of total circumstances. Defense of the present system should be used whenever existing policies can be shown to have considerable success and when alleged failures can either be denied or be shown to be temporary or unavoidable.

Defense of the present system was used by many negative debate teams who argued against the withdrawal of U.S. military forces from Western Europe. In presenting the ill and blame analysis in favor of U.S. withdrawal, affirmative teams often argued that the continued presence of large U.S. military forces in Western Europe encouraged Communist hostility and prevented the evolution of more harmonious East-West relations. Negative teams responded to this by denying both that harmonious relations were desirable (ill issue) and that the lack of better relations was caused by U.S. military presence (blame issue). Harmonious relations were said to be undesirable because Communists view harmonious relations, not as an end in itself, but as a means of lulling the West into a false sense of security. Negatives denied that U.S. forces were the cause of poor relations. Instead, they contended that the Communists' ideological commitment to the destruction of democratic capitalism was the real cause. The cure issue argued that U.S. military withdrawal would not be sufficient to result in improved relations because of such other sources of antagonism as U.S.-Soviet conflict of interest in other parts of the world. The cost issue served to justify the existing policy by pointing out advantages that would be lost by U.S. withdrawal. It was argued, for example, that the U.S. presence in Europe encouraged neutral nations such as Finland and Yugoslavia to keep out of the Soviet sphere of influence and that U.S. withdrawal would cause them to fall under Soviet domination.

Where it can be used, the defense of the present system strategy is a strong one because it places the negative in the position of upholding a concrete policy. It is a positive approach which stands for something. And since both the principles and the implementation of present policies are defended, the distinction between the affirmative and the negative is sharp and clear.

Repair of the Present System

Repair of the present system involves an unqualified commitment to the fundamental principles or basic structure of present policies, but it recognizes that the implementation of those principles can be improved. Advocates who use the repair strategy support minor administrative or mechanistic changes in present policy but oppose fundamental changes. In order to decide if a change in policy is minor or fundamental, the nature of the present system must be examined in light of the proposed affirmative change. A repair, to be legitimate, must be different from the philosophical principle of the affirmative proposition and must be consistent with the essential features of the present system. As a general rule, negative advocates tend to limit the number and extent of repairs that they offer, since the support of sweeping repairs may have the psychological effect of compromising present principles. The repairs approach should be used when the cause of those minor harms can be shown to be not inherent and, thus, repairable.

Opponents of compulsory health insurance have generally assumed the repairs strategy. They accept the existing philosophy of private financing and control of medical care supplemented by limited government programs, but they also recognize that the implementation of this mixed philosophy requires improvement through repairs. When supporters of compulsory health insurance have pointed to delayed care, incomplete care, and denied care as harms of the present system, opponents have generally sought to minimize the argument. In order to do this, they have referred to the overall trend toward improved care and have contended that if a person truly seeks needed care, it will not be denied. A variety of repairs have been suggested by opponents to compulsory health insurance in response to its advocates' blame analysis that under voluntary health insurance, broader coverage results in higher premiums, and that under limited government programs, some needy will always be excluded. In 1988, for example, the U.S. Congress debated a repair to the present system that provided for government-supplemented catastrophic medical care insurance. Although this repair involves a change in the operation of the present system, it is consistent with the philosophy of private financing enhanced by limited government assistance. In developing the cure issue, opponents of compulsory health insurance often argue that the proposal could not significantly improve health standards because fear and ignorance would still keep many people from seeking medical attention. The primary cost arguments raised against compulsory health insurance generally assert that the quality of care would deteriorate under a government system and that dollar costs would be uncontrollable.

The repair position is a realistic one in that it recognizes the possibility for improvement within the system. In offering repairs, however, it is necessary to be careful not to suggest changes that are inconsistent with the cost arguments.

Straight Refutation

Advocates who assume the strategy of *straight refutation* make no real commitment to either the principles or the mechanisms of the present system. Any preference shown to the present system is based solely on its existence and not on any belief in its adequacy. The straight refutation strategy allows the negative to respond to the claims of the affirmative without assuming the responsibility for defending any alternative policy. Affirmative arguments are responded to in many different ways, and extreme concern for consistency is often ignored. In effect, those who argue from this position are saying that they do not know what should be done, but they do know that the affirmative analysis is unsatisfactory.

The straight refutation position is useful when an advocate has not had an adequate opportunity to analyze the fundamental rationale for present policies or to formulate alternate proposals. This position allows the advocate to oppose a specific proposal for change without committing to any alternative.

Many of those who have opposed the legalization of marijuana have argued from the position of straight refutation. Rather than defending existing marijuana laws, these opponents of change have attacked the adequacy and significance of the legalizers' charges. They have taken the position of straight refutation by attacking the scientific accuracy of those affirmative studies that suggest only limited dangers from the use of marijuana. They have sought to minimize the significance of the loss of free choice to the marijuana user and have attempted to deny the need for anyone being subjected to severe criminal penalties. In general, they have argued that more time and more study are needed before any changes should be instituted.

The pure negativism of the straight refutation strategy tends to make it psychologically unsatisfactory and emotionally unappealing. Ultimately, problems require solutions, and those whom we seek to persuade may come to feel that even a bad solution is preferable to doing nothing. Nevertheless, the straight refutation approach may be the only honest option open to some advocates during the early stages of a controversy when they have not yet formulated a clear stand on a proposition. The straight refutation position is most appropriate as a means of delaying action in the hope that better solutions will be forthcoming.

Counterplan

The *counterplan* negative strategy rejects any philosophical commitment to present policies. This position admits that the present system has created serious problems which it cannot alleviate. In response to these inherent problems, the counterplan negative offers a solution that is philosophically and structurally different from both the present system and the affirmative proposal. The counterplan is distinct from negative repairs in that it is neither a part of the present system nor is it philosophically compatible with the present system. The counterplan is distinct from the affirmative in that it is not included within the affirmative proposition and it is not philosophically consistent with the affirmative proposition. Thus, the counterplan negative becomes an advocate for a different kind of change rather than a defender of the present system. Debaters who assume the obligations of a counterplan may minimize certain of the ills cited by the affirmative, or they may challenge the affirmative on the cause of the ills, but normally the cure and cost issues become the central areas of clash between affirmatives and counterplan negatives.

The counterplan should be used when an advocate feels that there is a third approach that is better than either the present system or the affirmative proposal. The counterplan position recognizes that our policy options are open-ended.

The counterplan strategy is used by groups who believe that the present social security system fails to provide for adequate retirement security.[2] The present system of social security mandates that most employers and wage earners contribute a set portion of wages to a fund from which employees may draw on retirement. Most experts agree that although the social security system is presently solvent, it will be unable to meet the future needs of the nation's increasingly elderly population. The present system position is that the social security system is fundamentally sound and that all that is needed to guarantee long-term solvency of the fund is minor tinkering in the form of modest increases in social security taxes, benefit restrictions, and delays in cost-of-living increases provided to retirees. The major opposition to this position comes from groups who believe that minor tinkering is not enough. These groups call for enactment of legislation that supplements the social security system by providing additional retirement security programs such as catastrophic health care benefits, housing allowances for the elderly, nursing home benefits, and nutrition programs. Since much of the congressional activity in this controversy involves new government programs for the elderly, this position may be regarded as the affirmative position in the controversy. A third, less frequently considered, policy option is presented by those on the political right. Their proposal calls for the federal government to get out of the social security business by making contributions to the system voluntary instead of compulsory. This proposal is fundamentally different from existing policies since it rejects forced contributions. It is also fundamentally different from the principles of expanded government involvement called for in the congressional proposals. The federal withdrawal position, therefore, constitutes a counterplan within this controversy.

The defenders of the federal withdrawal from social security counterplan generally agree with the ill and blame analysis of those advocating additional government programs. Supporters of both positions believe that the present social security system will not provide for meaningful retirement security in the long term. However, the federal withdrawal negatives charge that adding new programs will not permanently remove the ills and will eventually lead to expanded federal deficits that will bankrupt the United States. They further claim that citizens can establish much greater retirement security by investing their funds privately rather than through government. Philosophically, federal withdrawal advocates believe that the private insurance and investment are fundamentally preferable to government involvement. In this controversy, as in most debates between affirmatives and counterplan negatives, the clash largely revolves around the advantages and disadvantages of the two plans rather than around present policies.

In recent years the counterplan has been increasingly used in interscholastic debate. Along with its increasing use have come a host of theoretical concerns as to the standards and burdens associated with counterplan usage. In general, most theorists believe that a counterplan must meet two standards: the counterplan must be *nontopical* and *competitive*.[3]

The standard that the counterplan must be *nontopical* (outside the jurisdiction the proposition provides to the affirmative) is necessary to divide affirmative and negative ground. Absent this standard, we would have debates in which, in effect, both the affirmative and the negative acted as affirmatives. For example, if we were debating the proposition "Resolved: That the federal government should decrease its military commitment to NATO member states," we would not see much clash if the affirmative chose to eliminate U.S. military commitments to Great Britain and the negative team chose to eliminate U.S. military commitments to West Germany. The negative in this instance would be using a topical, and thus illegitimate, case.

The second standard for determining the legitimacy of a counterplan is that it must directly *compete* with the affirmative plan. Two criteria are used to assess the competitiveness standard: *mutual exclusivity* and *net benefits*.

The clearest criterion for determining competitiveness is *mutual exclusivity*. That is, the plan and the counterplan cannot simultaneously exist. Suppose that we were debating a proposition calling for air bags to be installed on all new vehicles. The affirmative argues that many lives are lost in automobile accidents and that lives could be saved by air bags. A negative might counter with a plan to require everyone to use seat belts. Although this plan is nontopical, it fails to meet the standard of mutual exclusivity because both the air bag plan and the seat belt plan could exist at the same time. Using this analysis, the negative counterplan does not serve as a reason to reject the affirmative plan.

A second commonly used criterion for determining competitiveness is *net benefits*. The net benefits standard argues that we should favor the counterplan if it can be shown that the counterplan adopted *alone* would be better than enacting *both* the counterplan and the affirmative plan. This criterion is often used by negatives when they advocate a counterplan that can be enacted simultaneously with the affirmative proposal. For example, an affirmative might call for the establishment of more stringent pollution controls on fossil fuel energy production facilities. A negative counterplan to this proposal might call for the government to directly promote the use and development of solar energy. Although both the affirmative plan and the negative counterplan *could* be adopted at the same time, the counterplan advocate might be able to demonstrate that both *should not* be adopted because promoting solar energy without changing existing pollution control laws is superior (net-beneficial) in two ways. First, promoting solar energy while maintaining *existing* pollution control laws avoids the economic problems that industry would face by being required to purchase new pollution control devices. Second, increasing pollution control regulations will delay the shift to solar energy because it requires industry to tie up its capital investment funds is fossil fuel control devices rather than to shift capital funds to solar energy. The net benefits of the counterplan adopted alone thus involve decreased economic dislocations and a more rapid shift to a safer energy supply.

Negatives who assume the counterplan approach do not necessarily abandon presumption. That is, at the end of the debate, if neither the affirmative plan nor the negative counterplan is judged worthy, we will continue with present policies and the proposition will not be affirmed.[4] Thus, a negative advocate can lose the counterplan and still win the debate. However, by using the counterplan, the negative advocate assumes a burden of proof equal to, but distinct from, the affirmative's burden of proof. The negative advocate must prove the counterplan's desirability.

SUMMARY

There are five standard case approaches to policy propositions. They are (1) the traditional case, (2) the comparative advantages case, (3) the goal/criteria case, (4) the effect-oriented case, and (5) the on-balance case. No matter which of these case strategies is used, the advocate is obligated to consider each of the concepts suggested by the stock issues.

The traditional case identifies the stated or implied goal of the proposition and develops each of the stock issues at that level. The comparative advantages case requires the identification of a secondary level of goals and the establishment of all of the stock issue concepts on the secondary level. The goal/criteria case establishes a particular goal or applies a goal accepted by the present system. The effect-oriented case eliminates the ills of the present system without removing the inherent cause of those ills, thereby treating effects rather than causes. The on-balance approach seeks to maximize the ill issue by comparing it to the minimal disadvantages of the cost issue.

There are four basic philosophical positions from which negatives may argue propositions of policy. The defense of the present system approach provides the greatest philosophical commitment to present policies by supporting both the principles and implementation of those policies. The repair of the present system strategy involves an unqualified commitment to the fundamental principles or basic structure of present policies but recognizes that the implementation of those principles can be improved. The straight refutation strategy makes no real commitment to either the principles or the mechanisms of the present system; it allows the negative to respond to the claims of the affirmative without assuming the responsibility for defending any alternative proposal or policy. The counterplan strategy rejects any philosophical commitment to present policies and presents a solution that is philosophically and structurally different from both the present system and the affirmative proposal.

NOTES

[1]Cases built on so-called attitudinal inherency arguments should use the effect-oriented approach. Attitudinal inherency arguments identify an unchanging attitude as the cause (blame) of the ill. Since the attitude is allegedly inherent, it cannot be removed and must be circumvented.

[2]For a more complete discussion of the social security controversy, see Ulrich (*Forensic Quarterly*, 41-50); Peter J. Ferrara, *Social Security: Prospects for Real Reform* (Washington: Cato Institute, 1985); Loren Lamansky, "Buying Out Social Security," *Reason* (January 1984): 33-36.

[3]Many articles have appeared that discuss the standards for counterplans. In particular, see Gossett; Herbeck; Kaplow; Lichtman and Rohrer; Ulrich.

[4]This claim assumes a traditional view of presumption as presented in this text. Some debate theorists believe that when a negative team advocates a counterplan, they abandon the advantage of presumption since they admit that present policies are fundamentally flawed. Using this perspective the judge must, at the end of the debate, select *either* the affirmative plan or the negative counterplan, based on which system is better. A difficulty we see in this approach is that it provides no guidance as to how to resolve controversy if the advantages and disadvantages of both the affirmative plan and the counterplan are identical.

SELECTED BIBLIOGRAPHY

FADELY, DEAN. "Fiat Power and the Mirror State Counterplan." *Speaker and Gavel* 24 (1987): 69-76.

FLANNINGHAM, CARL. "Concomitant Vs. Comparative Advantages: Sufficient vs. Necessary Conditions." *Journal of the American Forensic Association* 18 (1981): 1-8.

GOSSETT, JOHN S. "Counterplan Competitiveness in the Stock Issues Paradigm." In *Dimensions of Argument: Proceedings of the Second Annual Summer Conference on Argumentation,* edited by George W. Ziegelmueller and Jack Rhodes, 568-78. Annandale, VA: Speech Communication Association, 1981.

HERBECK, DALE A. "A Permutation Standard of Competitiveness." *Journal of the American Forensic Association* 22 (1985): 12-19.

HERBECK, DALE A., and JOHN P. KATSULAS. *Writing the Affirmative Case.* Kansas City, MO: National Federation of State High School Associations, 1987.

KAPLOW, LOUIS. "Rethinking Counterplans: A Reconciliation with Debate Theory." *Journal of the American Forensic Association* 17 (1981): 215-26.

LICHTMAN, ALLAN J., and DANIEL M. ROHRER. "A General Theory of the Counterplan." *Journal of the American Forensic Association* (1975): 70-79.

LING, DAVID, and ROBERT V. SELTZER. "The Role of Attitudinal Inherency in Contemporary Debate." *Journal of the American Forensic Association* 7 (1971): 278-83.

SHAW, WARREN C. *The Art of Debate.* New York: Allyn and Bacon, 1922.

ULRICH, WALTER. "Alternative Systems of Care for the Elderly." *The Forensic Quarterly* (1988): 41-50.

ULRICH, WALTER. *Understanding the Counterplan.* Kansas City, MO: National Federation of State High School Associations, 1986.

ZAREFSKY, DAVID A. "The 'Traditional Case'—'Comparative Advantages Case' Dichotomy: Another Look." *Journal of the American Forensic Association* 6 (1969): 12-20.

ZIEGELMUELLER, GEORGE W., and CHARLES A. DAUSE. *Argumentation: Inquiry and Advocacy,* 1st ed. Englewood Cliffs, NJ: Prentice-Hall, 1975.

STUDY QUESTIONS

1. Some people argue that the use of a comparative advantages case reduces the affirmative's burden of proof. Do you agree?

2. In which of the stock issues frames of analysis is the effect-oriented case most different from the traditional case and the comparative advantages case?

3. Does the use of the on-balance case reduce the affirmative's burden to demonstrate that significant problems or harms exist within the present system?

4. What circumstances would make use of a goals/criteria case strategy especially appropriate?

5. When a negative adopts the "repair of the present system" approach as opposed to the "defense of the present system" approach, is the affirmative's burden of proof altered?

6. How does a "repair" differ from a "counterplan"?

7. Who should win a debate if the affirmative plan and the negative counterplan are *equally* disadvantageous and no other issues are contested? In answering this question consider what you have learned about the concept of presumption.

EXERCISES

1. Trace the account of a recent policy controversy in any of the weekly newsmagazines. What approach did the advocates of change take? Why did they select this approach? What approach did the opponents of change take? Why did they select this approach?

2. Develop brief case outlines for each of the affirmative approaches discussed in this chapter.

3. Develop brief case outlines that can be used by negative advocates to respond to the affirmative case outlines developed for Question 2.

CHAPTER FOURTEEN
REFUTATION

Oftentimes advocates can present their cases without immediate concern for refutation by those with opposing points of view. In many other situations, however, advocates must be prepared not only to present their own constructive analysis but also to attack opposing views and to defend their own positions against attack. Parliamentary debates, courts of law, academic debates, press conferences, negotiating sessions, and political campaigns place a high premium on refutational skills. Even when an opposing advocate is not physically present, advocates should anticipate what arguments are in the minds of their audiences and attempt to address them. Whenever you attempt to respond to arguments forwarded by those who disagree with your position, you are engaging in refutation.

THE NATURE OF REFUTATION

Refutation can be defined as the *process of attacking the arguments of an opponent in order to weaken or destroy those arguments*. This definition suggests that refutation is essentially a *tearing down* process which begins with arguments presented by an opposing advocate. Skill in refutation lies at the very heart of reasoned advocacy because it is through the give-and-take and clash of refutation that audiences, judges, and other third parties ultimately gain insight into the truth of an issue.

Refutation may be compared to the defensive efforts of a football team. A football team must spend approximately half of its time warding off the offensive efforts of the opposition. Football history is filled with teams that had outstanding offensive units but failed to become champions for lack of an adequate defense. In argument, refutation is the defensive half of the game. If you are skilled only in forwarding your own analyses, then you are only half prepared. You must also be able to examine the analysis of your opponents and understand its weaknesses, and you must be skilled in the methods of refutation. Many football games are lost for lack of an adequate defense, and many arguments are lost because an advocate was not skilled at refutation.

CHOICES IN REFUTATION

It is generally impossible and usually unnecessary for you to refute all of the arguments presented by your opposition. In addition to engaging in refutation, you must also develop and extend your own constructive arguments. Selectivity, therefore, is necessary if you are to maximize the available time and focus the controversy on those arguments and values that you consider most important. The ability to make proper choices regarding which arguments to refute and how much time to devote to refuting each argument is an essential part of the process of refutation.

The basis on which this necessary selection is made will vary to some extent depending on the specific situation. In audience situations where there are no specific procedural rules, refutation choices should be guided by anticipated audience attitudes and values. In advocacy settings with more formal procedures, such as courts of law and academic debate, greater consideration must be given to such concepts as presumption, burden of proof, and issues. Issue orientation in refutation is especially important to advocates of change because of their obligation to establish each contested issue. Only arguments that are tangential to the issues or that have no potential for winning an issue can be safely ignored by advocates of change. Opponents of change, on the other hand, have greater freedom in their choice of arguments for refutation since they need only carry one issue to win the controversy. Opponents of change will sometimes grant one or more potential issues in order to spend more refutation time, and to focus more clearly, on issues that they perceive as being of greater importance.

In making refutation choices you should be guided not only by the issues and the demands of the specific situation, but also by the adequacy of opposing arguments. It is important to distinguish between attacks that pick annoyingly at the wording of conclusions and presses for more evidence. Unfortunately, inexperienced advocates sometimes become overwhelmed and frustrated by presses and unsupported assertions. An asserted response that is not thoroughly explained or supported with evidence is difficult to convert into a winning issue. Minimal attention should be given to such responses. In general, a good indication of the likely importance of an argument is the amount of time and emphasis given to it by your opposition. If a response is fully developed and well supported by evidence, it is likely to be viewed as critical by opponents and audience. In such instances, a thorough rejoinder is probably required.

Although refutation is essentially a tearing down process, it must take place within the framework of your total analysis of the proposition. Your prior analysis must be thorough enough to permit you to judge the importance of your opponent's responses in relation to the issues of the controversy. You must be able to perceive common premises and underlying opposition assumptions so that you can group arguments for refutation. Only within such a broad framework can appropriate refutation choices be made. It is important that you be willing to make choices in refutation. When conscious choices are not made, factors of audience fatigue or formal time limitations impose unplanned choices. Even poor choices are often better than no choices. Poor choices, at least, allow some focusing of the clash.

PRESENTATION OF REFUTATION

Both the demands of analytical clarity and the need to communicate with others require that refutation be systematically presented. A systematic approach is facilitated by (1) organization of the overall refutation effort and (2) use of a four-step formula for responding to specific arguments.

Organization of Refutation

There are no fixed rules to tell you where to begin and end refutation and how to organize your responses. It is important, however, that you have a clear plan of attack in mind and that you communicate your overall organization scheme to your audience. It is generally easier for listeners to follow your refutation if you respond to opposition arguments in the order in which they were originally presented. If you plan to introduce constructive positions of your own, you should notify the audience of this and explain at what point these arguments will be introduced. Strategic or persuasive consideration may sometime dictate that certain arguments be dealt with out of their regular order. When this occurs, the audience should be alerted to this fact, and a clear road map set forth. It is not enough simply to explain initially to an audience how you will proceed; you should also establish clear signposts as you go so that listeners know to which argument you are moving next. It is generally advisable to organize at the issue level and not to become involved in reorganization of the details of arguments.

Refutation Format

Adherence to a four-step presentational format helps to identify the focus of the clash over specific arguments. The four recommended steps are (1) name the argument to be refuted, (2) state your position, (3) support your position, and (4) conclude by relating to the issue. The first step asks that the argument to be refuted be identified. Failure to identify the specific argument being refuted may cause the audience to become confused and to miss the point of the refutation. Clear identification, on the other hand, helps listeners to focus on the appropriate argument and to understand where the refutation is directed. The second step calls for a statement of your own position in relation to the argument being attacked. What is your claim? What do you perceive as the weakness in the opposing argument? The statement of position should indicate the specific flaws in the argument being attacked. Examples of statements of position would include the following: "The response is irrelevant"; "The evidence doesn't support the conclusion"; "The comparison is invalid"; and so forth. The third step requires that the position set forth be supported by explanation and argument or evidence—or both. Occasionally, explanation alone is sufficient to support a claim. When the claim is made that two arguments are inconsistent, an explanation of why this is so may be all that is needed to support the claim. More frequently, however, claims will necessitate both supporting evidence and arguments. If the refutation position is that the author of a particular piece of evidence is not qualified, specific standards for a qualified authority and evidence that the author fails to meet these standards will be needed. The final step in the form for refutation is to conclude the argument by relating it to the issue. In their eagerness to move on to other arguments, advocates, unfortunately, often omit this step. This step requires more than the mere restatement of the refutation position. The importance of the refutation to the issue under examination must be shown. The individual act of refutation is thereby placed within the overall framework of analysis. The following statements illustrate how arguments can be concluded by relating them to the issues.

> "The evidence indicates that the problem was caused by human misjudgment and not by a fundamental failure of our present programs. Thus, there is no inherent weakness to warrant a change."

> "The disadvantage did not occur in any of the five states when our plan was tried. The disadvantage is empirically untrue. There is no risk in adopting the proposal."

NOTE-TAKING FOR REFUTATION

Refutation may be found on the editorial pages of magazines and newspapers, but it most frequently occurs in oral contexts. In these oral situations, careful note-taking is absolutely essential to effective refutation. Even persons with keen memories cannot be certain they will remember the order in which opposing arguments were presented and not forget important arguments. Random and unsystematic notes provide little help because they do not give a complete record of what was said. Only when opposing arguments are fully and accurately recorded is responsible and effective refutation likely.

The most appropriate form of note-taking will depend on many factors including the situation, the audience, the amount of time available, and the experience of the advocates. Regardless of their specific form, however, notes should always fairly represent opposing arguments, be systematically recorded, and be easy to read. In order to record arguments fairly, it is necessary that you listen to *understand* arguments before attempting to record them. Arguments can be easily misunderstood, especially when you are concentrating on refuting them.

Misrepresentation of opposing arguments is not only unfair, but ultimately, unproductive. The systematic recording of opposing arguments helps to guarantee that important arguments are not overlooked and that your own responses are organized. The suggestion that notes be easy to read recognizes that oral argument usually occurs in pressured situations. While scribbled notes may be easier and faster to record, they are more difficult—sometimes, even impossible—to read. Illegible notes fail to serve their purpose and may even contribute to greater confusion.

Flow Sheets

One specialized form of note-taking used by academic debaters—and in modified form, by other advocates as well—is the flow sheet. The flow sheet provides a means of visually organizing the arguments presented in speeches so that the status of any individual argument can be quickly and easily identified. In order to take notes according to the flow sheet format, a legal pad or a larger artist's sketchpad is required. Although the mechanics of preparing flow sheets are fairly simple, some practice is usually necessary before proficiency is developed. Four general guidelines help to explain the format and use of flow sheets.

First, the flow sheet should be divided into vertical columns corresponding to the number of speeches in the debate, and each speech should be recorded in a separate column. The first affirmative constructive speech is recorded in the first column. The structure of this speech sets the structure for the rest of the case arguments. First negative constructive case arguments are recorded in the second column, second affirmative case arguments in the third column, and so on. Negative plan attacks or value objections, topicality arguments, and counterplans should be noted on separate flow pads with alternating columns for negative and affirmative speeches. The use of separate flow pads for each of these negative arguments makes it easier to reorder the issues, as necessary, as the debate progresses. Some debaters find it helpful to record affirmative and negative arguments in different colored inks to distinguish more clearly between affirmative and negative columns.

Second, notes should be taken in outline form and individual arguments assigned a number or letter. Most debaters present their arguments in outline form so recording them in this form is appropriate. The outline form helps to differentiate between major and minor arguments, and it emphasizes the supporting relationship of arguments to conclusions. The numbering and lettering of individual arguments help ensure that specific responses are not missed, and it facilitates easy reference during the speeches.

Third, responses should be recorded directly opposite the arguments they are intended to answer. In order to guarantee that there will be enough room to record all of the responses that might be generated by a particular argument, it is a good idea to leave plenty of room between arguments in your initial columns. The primary advantage of the flow sheet is that it permits you to see at a glance if an argument has been responded to or extended. If an argument has not been answered, there should be a blank space in the column opposite it. Failure to leave enough space between arguments may result in multiple responses to one argument being recorded in the space presumably reserved for the succeeding argument. When this occurs, it becomes more difficult to tell which arguments have been answered and which have not and to determine which responses belong to which arguments. Crowding arguments may save paper, but it makes the flow sheet less functional.

Fourth, evidence should be recorded whenever possible. Those inexperienced at using flow sheets may find it difficult, at first, to note both the evidence and the arguments. With increased experience, however, it should become possible to do both. It is important to record the evidence in order to evaluate its adequacy. If it is not possible to record all of the evidence, at least some system should be developed for noting possibly suspicious data. Any evidence that seems questionable can be examined in greater detail during cross-examination or in preparation time. Since comparisons of source qualifications, biases, and recency can play a critical role in determining who wins an argument, the more information recorded regarding evidence, the better prepared you will be to argue the issue.

Abbreviations One way of facilitating faster, easier, and more comprehensive note-taking is by using simple abbreviations for commonly used words or terms. The chart on p. 206 provides a list of frequently used phrases and some suggested abbreviations. You may, of course, wish to develop your own system. Whatever abbreviations you use, however, should be simple and easy to remember and comprehend. In addition to a system of abbreviations for general terms, you will also want to use abbreviations for those basic concepts and programs peculiar to a given topic. For example, if the topic under discussion concerned environmental protection, abbreviations such as the following might be used: HW for hazardous wastes, AR for acid rain; GW for groundwater, and EPA for Environmental Protection Agency.

SPECIAL METHODS OF REFUTATION

Although the mechanics of presenting and preparing for refutation are important, the most essential aspect of refutation is, of course, the actual attack on the opposing argument. Previous chapters have already explained certain basic tests that can be used not only to evaluate your own data and arguments, but also to attack the data and arguments of your opponents. In general, the tests of premises provide a basis for refuting the soundness and acceptability of your opposition's fundamental assumptions; the tests of evidence assist you in examining the reliability and validity of opposing evidence; and the tests of argument examine the adequacy of the relationships drawn between the elements of individual arguments. It is essential that you know and understand all of these various tests if you are to be effective in refutation. Asserting that an opposing argument is false is not sufficient; you must also be able to identify the specific weakness in the argument and to explain how this weakness undermines the conclusion drawn. The tests of premises, evidence, and argument are primary means for accomplishing this.

In addition to these tests there are other special methods of refutation. These special methods focus less on individual arguments and look more at the overall relationships between and among arguments. Many of the individual arguments of the opposition will undoubtedly be sound, but when they are looked at from a broader perspective, different kinds of weaknesses in the analysis may appear. The special methods of refutation are intended to help you discover such larger failures.

Exposing Inconsistencies

This method of refutation examines the statement of an advocate to determine if the positions taken and the conclusions drawn are consistent with one another. Inconsistent or contradictory positions cannot both be correct. The presence of inconsistent arguments suggests unclear thinking and a weakness in the overall analysis presented. Exposing an inconsistency does not automatically identify which of the two contradictory positions is false, but it will ultimately force the opposition to abandon or modify one of the two arguments.

Charges of inconsistency are a frequent tactic in American politics. Political figures carefully search for inconsistent statements by their opponents in the hope of reducing the opposition's credibility. Interscholastic debaters also find the exposing of inconsistencies to be an important method of refutation. Whenever a contest involves more than one spokesperson on a side, the risk of inconsistencies becomes greater.

Minimizing

Minimizing the significance of opposition arguments is one of the most useful of all the methods of refutation. Although the validity of some arguments can be attacked directly, most opposing arguments are, at least, partially true and cannot be completely denied. Minimization implies that a conclusion may be correct but denies its significance in relation to other facts or other arguments. Minimization may be used to refute all types of arguments, but it is particularly useful when dealing with conclusions based on statistical data. The objective of minimization is to place an argument in a more favorable perspective. Because so many decisions ultimately require weighing costs versus benefits, minimization is an especially important form of refutation. Minimization may be accomplished in a variety of ways including the establishment of favorable trends, the demonstration of comparisons, and the use of factor analysis.

One method of minimizing an argument is to demonstrate that it is insignificant when viewed within the framework of a trend. Statistics that appear to be important in isolation can be minimized by placing them in the context of a favorable trend. In arguing against more government financed day-care centers, a feature writer for the *New Republic* employed a trend argument to minimize the need for government action.

> There's no doubt that it takes time, especially in a young industry, for supply to catch up with demand. Still, the number of licensed day-care centers has more than doubled since 1976, and the number of home-based day-care providers has grown by more than half. (Wright, 13)

Another method of minimization is that of comparison. An argument or statistic may be minimized by comparing it to another argument or statistic that is considerably more significant. The trend method involves the examination of the same situation or circumstance over a period of time, and the comparison method minimizes by contrasting different things (regions, products, peoples) during the same time frame. You may, for instance, hear an argument that attempts to minimize the cost of some proposed public program by comparing that cost to the amount of money Americans spend on cosmetics or cigarettes or liquor.

A third method of minimization is factor analysis. With this method minimization is accomplished by isolating a single factor from a larger statistic or broader conclusion in order to achieve a desired perspective. For example, a conclusion concerning an increase in crime could be minimized if it were possible to demonstrate that a less serious crime, such as car theft, accounted for the bulk of the increase. By removing the element of auto theft from the overall crime figure, it could be argued that *serious* crimes had not increased significantly.

Maximizing

Maximizing is the flip side of the method of minimization. Just as it is sometimes necessary to minimize an argument you cannot directly deny, so it is often necessary to maximize the importance of a position that the opposition has argued is insignificant. The same basic techniques used for minimization— reference to favorable trends, use of comparisons, and application of factor analysis—can also be used to enhance the importance of your own claim. Obviously different sets of statistics and comparisons would be used. Sandra Postel and Lori Heise of the Worldwatch Institute used comparative statistics to demonstrate the significance of the world's loss of tropical forests.

> The most worrisome finding of FAO's assesment was that tropical trees were being cut much faster than reforestation or nature were replacing them. For tropical regions as a whole, 11.3 million hectares were cleared annually in the early eighties, while only 1.1 million hectares of plantations were established. Thus 10 hectares were being cleared for every 1 planted. In Africa, the ratio was 29 to 1; in Asia, 5 to 1. (p. 85)

Reducing to Absurdity

This method (*reduction ad absurdum*) involves extending the analysis to the point where the conclusion is absurd or otherwise unacceptable. In extending an argument an analogy is often used. The argument is, thus, taken out of its situational context and extended analogically to a different set of circumstances where its application appears ridiculous.

Opponents of drug legalization sometimes use this method of refutation to respond to the argument that certain drugs should be legalized because existing laws are difficult to enforce. In order to ridicule this argument, opponents suggest that by extension the analysis implies that laws against speeding, rape, and murder should also be repealed because of enforcement difficulties.

Denying Inherency

This method of refutation responds to an opposition argument by attempting to demonstrate that the particular problem identified is not fundamental to the system. Sometimes the inherency of the problem can be denied by demonstrating that the system is already working to alleviate the problem. If the program is confronting the problem, so the analysis goes, there is no reason to reject it. At other times it may be impossible to show that a program as currently constituted is solving the problem, but it can be demonstrated that the problem could be dealt with in ways consistent with the philosophy and structure of the program. If the problem results from misadministration or from factors external to the system, then the problem can be alleviated without resorting to a different program or system.

In policy debates the denial of inherency is useful in response to arguments within the ill, blame, and cost frames of analysis. The harms of the present system and the disadvantages of the proposed change must be defended as inherent. Denial of inherency is also used as a method of refutation in fact/value debates, since value judgments must be based on essential features of whatever is being evaluated. In the CEDA National Championship Debate on the topic "Resolved: That regulations in the United States requiring employees to be tested for controlled substances are an unwarranted invasion of privacy," Mike Stanley from the University of New Mexico argued that the alleged unreliability of drug tests was not inherent:

> They tell you that there are administrative problems. Of course, I would argue, number one, that is justification for more regulation. We have more labs. Now he argues that as the volume increases so the problems would increase. That card [evidence cited by the opposition] does not mean more labs, it means you'd have one lab with more tests going to them. [It] indicates you should have more labs, more regulations. (Boaz and Brey, 62)

Identifying Irrelevancies

Just as evidence must be relevant to the argument it is used to support, so arguments must be relevant to the issue being considered. When you label an argument is irrelevant, you are saying that it is unrelated to the issue and that it should have no bearing on the final judgment. Irrelevant responses to arguments usually result from misunderstandings of opposing positions. By identifying the misunderstanding and refocusing the original position, the irrelevant argument can be dismissed.

In the CEDA Championship Debate referred to earlier, Mike Stanley used the method of identifying irrelevancy:

> They argue accuracy [of drug testing] is a priority and you must look at that first. I would argue number one, testing can be implemented to deter, so accuracy would actually be irrelevant. Robert Lindsey tells us in 1986: "Many employers acknowledge that a major reason they initiated drug testing programs was not to catch drug users but to deter employees from using illicit drugs and to discourage drug-using job applicants, a plan, that seems to be working, they say." (Boaz and Brey, 61)

Establishing Dilemmas

This method of refutation reduces the opposition argument to two alternatives, neither of which is acceptable to the opponent or to the audience. To be effective, the two choices (the horns of the dilemma) must cover all of the possible alternatives and each must be damaging to the opponent's cause. If the dilemma does not exhaust the possibilities, the opponent may sustain his or her argument by indicating an alternative that is not damaging to the position being defended.

Opponents of government-supported health care programs frequently use the dilemma approach in discussing the freedom of doctors to set their own fees. On the one hand, they argue, when doctors are permitted to establish their own fee systems, the cost of government-financed health care skyrockets and becomes uncontrollable. On the other hand, government efforts to set maximum fees for medical services cause fewer doctors to participate in the program and reduce the quality of medical services available. The dilemma attempts to place the defenders of government-supported medical care in a situation in which they must choose between two equally undesirable alternatives.

Turning the Tables

One of the most effective means of refutation is to "turn the tables" or to claim a "turnaround." When using this method of refutation, you admit the validity of part of an opposing argument and claim that the admitted part actually supports, rather than denies, your claim. A turnaround may admit the causal link but deny that the effects will be harmful, or it may admit the harm but point to opposite circumstances as the cause.

In the final round of the 1987 National Debate Tournament, the negative team argued that the adoption of the affirmative plan would set back the cause of feminism. Lyn Robbins of Baylor University responded to this argument with a series of turnarounds.

> The twelfth argument is that it [feminism] destroys culture. Schlafly in '81: "It is no gain for women, children, for families, or for America to propel us into a unisex society. Our strength is in our diversity, not in our sameness." Thirteenth argument is [feminism] destroys justice. Amiel in '84: "But what the women's movement has insisted upon is not the idea of individual equality but the dreadful concept of group parity. This is an insidious, dangerous, and unfair suggestion which is not a logical extension of equality but its very opposite."
>
> Fourteen [feminism] destroys religion. Schlafly in '81: "Feminism puts women, rather than God or man, at the center of the universe, and it subordinates all religious, cultural, and social values to the achievement of the paramount goal of women's self-fulfillment." Gilder says in '83: "Complete repudiation of religious values leads to economic collapse as well as moral failure." (Boaz and Brey, 17)

Exposing Fallacies of Composition and Division

The fallacies of composition and division are twin fallacies in which relationships between wholes and their parts are erroneously asserted. The *fallacy of composition* consists of assuming that what is true of separate parts is necessarily true of the collective whole. The fallacy is exposed by demonstrating that the characteristics of the parts cannot logically be extended to the whole. In other words, it argues that the whole is more than the sum of its parts. A basketball team, for instance, may not necessarily be judged to be superior to another team because it has a higher percentage of all-star players. Factors of team balance, teamwork, and coaching competence must be considered. In such a situation, the whole is more than the sum of its parts.

The *fallacy of division* consists of assuming that what is true of the collective whole is also true of all of the separate parts. The fallacy is exposed by demonstrating that the characteristics of the whole may not be present in all of the individual parts. A political party, for instance, may be identified as conservative as a collective whole. It does not necessarily follow, however, that all of the members and candidates of that party are also conservatives.

Identifying Fallacious Appeals

All of the preceding special methods of refutation have been based on the identification of certain limitations of perspective or inference. Sometimes, however, the weakness in an argument may result from faulty assumptions regarding what are appropriate bases for belief. We will describe four such fallacious appeals.

The argument *ad misericordiam* is an argument whose claim for acceptance is based not on evidence and reason but on appeals to pity and sympathy. Appeals to sympathy may be acceptable when they are used to energize and complement more factually based arguments, but when they are offered as the sole reason for supporting a position, they are inappropriate. Every parent knows the power of a child's tears as a persuasive appeal, but good parents also understand that repeatedly giving in to such emotional responses can result in a very unruly, spoiled child. Compassion and empathy are important qualities, but as advocates you should be prepared to warn your listeners against substituting feeling for analysis.

A second inappropriate basis for belief is one that places undue reliance on the authority of a person or institution. The usefulness of expert opinion evidence has been recognized in previous chapters. The argument *ad verecundiam* differs from the use of expert opinion evidence in that it seeks approval of a position, not because of the specific analysis presented by a person with special knowledge and training, but rather because of the generalized revered status of the individual or institution. When the primary reason offered in behalf of a position is "that's what the Constitution says" or "that's what your father said"—the argument is based on a fallacious appeal ad verecundiam. The Constitution and your parents are good sources of expert opinion on certain matters, but their opinions should be accepted or rejected based on the soundness of their judgments and not solely because of their revered status. Appeals to authority that are vague and seek unquestioned conformity are fallacious.

A third fallacious basis for belief are appeals to join the crowd, to get on the bandwagon, or to follow the mob. Such appeals are known as *ad populum* arguments. Ad populum arguments seek to gain adherence by relying on the judgment of a vague group or mass of others. The typical teenager's assertion that "all the other kids are doing it" is an example of an ad populum argument. The mob appeal is unacceptable because the size and composition of the crowd are generally not specified and, more importantly, because the basis of their judgment and the degree of their understanding are unknown.

A final fallacious appeal is based on attacks against a person instead of his or her ideas. The argument *ad hominum* uses name calling and personal abuse

Identify the fallacy *or* the special method of refutation revealed in each of the following argument samples.

1. Johnson State University has more students who are National Merit Scholars than any other state university. Therefore Johnson State is a superior state university.

2. It may be true that ten people died last year because of faulty garage door openers, but if you examine the trend within the last five years the deaths are decreasing.

3. Frank claims to be a very strong advocate for freedom of speech. However, he also claims that individuals exposing racist rhetoric should not be allowed to speak in public.

4. James Stapleton is a great author. Therefore, all his novels are great.

5. John argues that we should allow doctors and families to make decisions to stop all life support and let a terminally ill patient die with dignity. Judy counters with argumentative questions such as: "Who will be next? Will we choose to eliminate all the old, the disabled, the poor, the sick, people with brown hair, people with low intelligence, or people whose last name begins with R? Where will it stop?"

6. Senator Parker claims that a system of merit pay will lead to more effective teaching. The National Education Association argues that since there is no effective way to administer merit pay, the result will be a decline in teacher effectiveness because of the tremendous morale problems created by the merit pay system.

7. I don't care whether he is an expert on social security. He's a jerk.

as a means of diverting attention from the substance of the controversy. Unfortunately, such attacks are not uncommon in the worlds of business and politics. Even when personal attacks against the supporters of a particular position are true, such attacks do not establish anything about the validity of the arguments themselves. The character or personality of the supporters of an idea is irrelevant to the adequacy of the idea itself.

Whenever anyone seeks your or another's support based on any of these fallacious appeals, you should be prepared to expose the unsound nature of the argument. In doing this, you must do more than simply name the fallacy, you must also explain *why* it does not provide an adequate basis for belief.

SUMMARY

Refutation is the process of attacking the arguments of an opponent in order to weaken or destroy those arguments. Choices must be made regarding which arguments to refute and how much time to devote to refuting each selected argument. Issues, the demands of the specific situation, and the adequacy of the opposing arguments should guide the selection of arguments for refutation.

Refutation should be presented in an orderly manner and the audience should be informed of your overall organizational plan. Adherence to a four-step format helps to focus the clash over specific arguments. The four recommended steps are (1) name the argument to be refuted, (2) state your position, (3) support your position, and (4) conclude by relating to the issue.

Systematic and accurate note-taking facilitates effective refutation. The flow sheet provides a means of visually organizing arguments in a debate so that the status of individual arguments can be quickly and easily identified.

The test of premises, evidence, and argument are important means of refutation. In addition to these tests, there are other special methods of refutation that focus less on individual arguments and more on the overall relationships between and among arguments. The special methods of refutation include (1) exposing inconsistencies, (2) minimizing, (3) maximizing, (4) reducing to absurdity, (5) denying inherency, (6) identifying irrelevancies, (7) establishing dilemmas, (8) turning the tables, (9) exposing fallacies of composition and division, and (10) avoiding fallacious appeals—*ad misericordiam, ad verecundiam, ad populum,* and *ad hominem.*

SELECTED BIBLIOGRAPHY

BLACK MAX. Pp. 209–21 in *Critical Thinking: An Introduction to Logic and Scientific Method.* Englewood Cliffs: Prentice-Hall, 1946.

BOAZ, JOHN K., and JAMES R. BREY, eds. *1987 Championship Debates and Speeches.* Annandale, VA: Speech Communication Association, 1987.

CHASE, STUART. *Guides to Straight Thinking.* New York: Harper, 1956.

PFAU, MICHAEL, DAVID A. THOMAS, and WALTER ULRICH. Pp. 262–78 in *Debate and Argument.* Glenview, IL: Scott, Foresman, 1987.

POSTEL, SANDRA, and LORI HEISE. "Reforesting the Earth." *State of the World 1988,* edited by Lester R. Brown, et al., 81–100. New York: Norton, 1988.

WRIGHT, ROBERT. "Kids R Us." *New Republic* August 22, 1988, 13.

STUDY QUESTIONS

1. It is possible to have refutation in the initial presentation by an affirmative advocate?

2. Why must refutation be selective?

3. What are the dangers of using the special method of refutation that reduces an argument to absurdity?

4. Why is it important to expose inconsistency in an opponent's argument?

EXERCISES

1. Read one of the debate transcripts contained in the appendixes of this text and identify the special methods of refutation used.

2. Select a major ill argument of a current policy question and try to develop ways of minimizing its importance.

3. Listen to an interscholastic debate and try keeping a flow sheet. After the debate compare your flow sheet with those of the debaters and the critic of the debate.

4. Using whatever topic you desire, try to develop an argument using each of the special methods of refutation discussed in this chapter.

5. Read a congressional debate in the *Congressional Record.* What special methods of refutation are used by the speakers?

6. Read the first affirmative speech of one of the debates contained in the appendixes of this book. Use the special methods of refutation to argue against a major section of the speech.

ANSWERS TO PRACTICUM

1. Fallacy of composition. The argument assumes that what is true of the separate parts (National Merit Scholars in the student body) is true of the whole (the student body along with the faculty, programs, and the like).

2. Minimization. The argument's impact is reduced by considering the trend toward decreased deaths.

3. Exposing inconsistency. A fact is exposed that leads to questioning Frank's true belief in freedom of speech.

4. Fallacy of division. The argument assumes that what is true of the whole (James is a great author) is true of the separate parts (all the individual novels James has written).

5. Reducing to absurdity. Judy expands the argument beyond its immediate scope to demonstrate the absurd results of the argument.

6. Turning the tables. The National Education Association argument shows that the advantage of merit pay is actually a disadvantage.

7. *Ad hominum.* The attack is against the person, not the argument.

CHAPTER FIFTEEN
CROSS-EXAMINATION

The cross-examination of witnesses in courtrooms and in courtroom dramas often provides moments of great interest. Similarly, in academic debate the use of cross-examination enhances the attention of audiences and judges. Much of the appeal of cross-examination is related to the direct confrontation that it provides between the questioner and the witness. Although the presentation of individual speeches may result in a clash of arguments, it does not offer the opportunity for direct person-to-person verbal exchanges. Only during cross-examination do two individuals jointly share the focus of attention.

Cross-examination is useful, not just for the drama it creates, but because it provides a means, not otherwise available, for clarifying arguments and pinning down opponents. It is much more difficult for an advocate to ignore evidence or evade a line of analysis when questioned about them during cross-examination.

Although the specific techniques of cross-examination are most applicable to academic debate and courts of law, many of the skills involved in asking and answering questions are not limited to these advocacy situations. Press conferences and public forums rely heavily on the ability of participants to question and to respond to questions skillfully. Question and answer skills are also important in classrooms, job interviews, and counseling situations. Thus, while the focus of this chapter will be on cross-examination in formal advocacy situations, particularly academic debate, many of the concepts apply beyond these settings.

DIRECT EXAMINATION AND CROSS-EXAMINATION

Lawyers generally distinguish between the direct examination of witnesses and cross-examination. Direct examination occurs when lawyers question witnesses whom they have selected to help in presenting their side of the case. Because witnesses used in direct examination are generally friendly to a lawyer's case, they may be told in advance what questions will be asked during direct examination, and the answers to these questions may even be rehearsed. Questions used in direct examination are usually fairly open-ended. Direct examination questions are used simply to stimulate the presentation of known responses in order to build a constructive case.

Cross-examination, like direct examination, involves a cross-examiner or questioner, who controls the situation through the asking of questions, and a respondent or witness, who is under obligation to answer the questions posed by the cross-examiner. Cross-examination differs from direct examination in that the witness being cross-examined is likely to be less friendly to the questioner's cause and to hold fundamentally different opinions regarding the case being debated. Therefore, cross-examination requires the questioner to exert more careful control over the examination process. Whereas direct examination is more likely to encourage witnesses to tell their own stories, cross-examination is more focused on eliciting specific individual facts that will later be constructed into an opposing narrative.

In order to be genuine cross-examination, sufficient time must exist for the questioner to ask more than one question. Situations that permit the asking of only a single question per person cannot really be considered cross-examination. The ability to ask a series of questions, each of which grows out of the answer to previous testimony, is an essential feature of cross-examination. Courts of law generally provide unlimited time for cross-examination, but academic debate is not nearly so generous. In spite of these time limits, however, skilled debaters can accomplish much during cross-examination.

PURPOSES OF CROSS-EXAMINATION

There are five primary purposes for which cross-examination is used: (1) to clarify previous statements of the witness, (2) to commit the witness to a particular position on an issue, (3) to refute the validity of a previous statement, (4) to prepare the way for constructive arguments, and (5) to undermine the credibility of respondents. The approach taken in developing questions will vary considerably depending on the specific goal of the questioner. It is important, therefore, to have a clear conception of the kind of answers desired before proceeding with the questioning.

Clarify Previous Statements

Sometimes the meaning of a previous statement of a witness is unclear. Before attempting to respond to such a statement, it is best to clarify what the witness actually meant to say. Unfortunately, ambiguous statements left unclarified may sometimes be interpreted in unexpected and damaging ways in final rebuttal speeches.

As potentially damaging as unclear arguments are unexplored plan provisions. Some academic debaters make the mistake of developing plan attacks without fully understanding all of the provisions of the plan or how the plan operates. If your opponent argued against apartheid in South Africa and for increased U.S. economic sanctions against the segregationist government of South Africa, you would need to know more about the nature of the sanctions being proposed. Is a total ban on U.S. exports to South Africa being proposed? Would the sale of South African goods to the United States be banned as well? Are there exceptions? Would U.S. industries be required to divest all their investments in South Africa? What kind of time frame would operate? What specific steps would be required of the South African government before the sanctions would be removed? A few such questions of clarification can prevent misdirected plan objections and may even reveal weaknesses in the plan, which were not initially apparent.

Unnecessary questions of clarification should, of course, be avoided. Asking the opposition to repeat an argument because you were inattentive or too slow in taking notes is better than missing the argument altogether; such questions, however, do not enhance your credibility. In general, asking questions of clarification should not be the major purpose of a cross-examination period, but some questions of clarification are usually necessary and appropriate.

Commit to a Position

Just as it is important to clarify a witness's meaning early in controversies, so is it equally important to commit him or her to a particular position on undeclared issues. Ambiguity of any sort is dangerous ground on which to build arguments. The more certain you are of where a witness stands, the less possibility there will be for a strategic shift in position later in the debate. Based on the analysis presented, it may seem logical to assume that an advocate would take a particular stand. However, such assumptions can cause problems later. What to you seems like a perfectly consistent position for the opposition to take may not seem so to them. For example, a person might be opposed to the direct censorship of student newspapers and yet approve of the establishment of standards governing the use of profanity. By committing the opposition to a stand, you can avoid wasting time on inappropriate arguments. Often, you may have a choice of arguments to use depending on what position the opposition takes. When you force your opponents to commit themselves at an early point, you not only facilitate the selection of the most appropriate counterargument but also make possible a fuller debate on the issue.

Refute Previous Statements

The most important function of cross-examination is to refute, or at least to establish a basis for refuting, the arguments of the opposing side. Cross-examination is the primary means of refutation used by lawyers in court and an important means for experienced debaters. Contradictions, irrelevant judgments, overgeneralizations, inadequate evidence, incomplete analysis—all of these failures and more can be demonstrated through effective cross-examination. The cross-examination process is uniquely suited for exposing such weaknesses because a carefully designed line of questioning brings them into focus. Moreover, its confrontational nature causes listeners to remember inadequacies demonstrated through cross-examination. Admissions gained through cross-examination serve as the strongest kind of evidence and often make it unnecessary to present additional data.

Prepare for Constructive Arguments

A fourth purpose of cross-examination is to establish the basis for constructive arguments, which have not yet been presented but which will be developed later. Because witnesses tend to concentrate on their own previous testimonies, they can sometimes be led to make less guarded statements about other matters. Although these statements will seldom be damaging in themselves, they can be used to provide links to disadvantages, to establish a means for weighing the impacts of a disadvantage, or to form the basis for topicality arguments. If, for instance, an affirmative case claimed to save the government money, you might wish to use cross-examination to highlight this fact, and later use this fact as a link to a disadvantage on increased defense spending. Experienced questioners are sensitive to the potential of these kinds of questions and often have several such questions prepared.

Undermine Witness Credibility

Undermining the credibility of witnesses is a function of cross-examination that is generally limited to courts of law, although it is occasionally used when questioning is part of audience forums, especially political debates. In courts of law where so much depends on the perceived credibility of witnesses and where, in fact, some witnesses lie, major portions of cross-examination may be spent in attempting to undermine the witness's character or authority. Unlike the other purposes of cross-examination, this one does not focus directly on the substance of the controversy but rather on the personal integrity or authority of the witness. This purpose is generally inappropriate in academic debate.

PSYCHOLOGY OF CROSS-EXAMINATION

The psychological aspects of cross-examination are of great importance. In fact, legal textbooks on cross-examination devote almost as much space to discussing the psychology of cross-examination as they do to the specific techniques of questioning (see Wellman). In their effort to elicit useful answers or to avoid harmful admissions, inexperienced questioners and witnesses often ignore the psychological impressions they create. When you participate in a cross-examination session, judgments will be made about your competence, trustworthiness, and fairness on the basis of your handling of the questioning. The cross-examination periods provide a greater opportunity to compare directly the personalities and characters of the contestants than at any other time in the contest. As an advocate, therefore, you must be concerned about the image you create during the cross-examination process. Although the primary purposes of cross-examination deal with the substance of the controversy, the psychological impact of the ways in which questions are asked and answered cannot be ignored, and may even have a significant effect on the listener's decision.

Psychology of Questioning

It is important for the cross-examiner to establish early his or her control of the questioning session. Failure to assert reasonable dominance of the situation may result in an unproductive cross-examination. Particularly in situations where the witness is hostile or unfriendly, an indecisive manner of questioning makes it difficult to elicit satisfactory answers. The time limits of academic debate further magnify the importance of the questioner's control. A weak manner of questioning by a debater can encourage the witness to use up limited time with overly long answers.

Important as it is for the questioner to gain control of the cross-examination, a fine line must be walked. An overly assertive or aggressive manner can be counterproductive. Rather than simply gaining control, an overly forceful debater may actually cause the witness to become unduly defensive. When witnesses feel threatened or dominated, they respond by being evasive and uncooperative. Thus, the questioner's manner must be one of control but not dominance.

The manner of cross-examination not only affects the cooperativeness of witnesses but also influences the judge's or audience's attitude toward the advocate. It is much easier to vote for someone who is pleasant than for someone who is unpleasant. In fact, studies of juries have suggested that whichever lawyer is better liked—based on impressions created in the courtroom—is more likely to win the jury's decision.

Few people respond favorably to a browbeater. If the questioning becomes too aggressive, the cross-examiner will be perceived to be abusive and domineering. On the other hand, people respond equally unfavorably to weak, wimpish behavior. If the questioning is hesitant or mild-mannered, the cross-examiner will be seen as unsure and unworthy of belief.

An effective questioner will project a pleasant, relaxed, self-confident manner. The questioner should be fair and exhibit respect for the witness. A sense of timing allows the questioner to push a rattled witness along to gain a critical admission or to relax a tense and evasive respondent. Even a little drama can be helpful: a furrowed brow, an incredulous stare, an exasperated sigh can communicate a lot to a jury or judge about the honesty of an answer or the cooperativeness of a witness.

Thus, the personality, manner, and style of the questioner are important psychological variables in cross-examination. They are important factors that not only influence the responsiveness of the witness but also have an unconscious, but profound, effect on the ultimate decision rendered in the controversy.

Psychology of Answering

The witness, as well as the questioner, must be careful to create an appropriate psychological impression. This is especially true in courtroom situations where much depends on the perceived integrity of the witness, although respondents in all cross-examination situations will find psychological impact a crucial consideration.

So important do lawyers consider the psychological impression of witnesses that they will occasionally bring in outside consultants to help train critical witnesses in how to respond to questions more credibly and persuasively. The personal impressions created by academic debaters, of course, occur throughout the round of debate, in constructive and rebuttal speeches as well as during cross-examination. Nevertheless, the impression created in the questioning period can be a dominant one.

Witnesses, like questioners, must find the appropriate middle ground. Respondents who are too evasive in answering questions may appear to be hiding something. Thus, whatever is gained substantively in not giving direct answers to questions may be lost psychologically through reduced credibility. Moreover, a witness's perceived evasiveness may actually cause a question or series of questions to assume greater importance in the mind of the judge or audience, so if an admission is ultimately won, its impact will be even greater. On the other hand, respondents who are too cooperative and answer questions thoughtlessly may reveal more than is necessary. Such careless answers to questions not only weaken the substantive position of the advocate but also create an impression of incompetence.

Ideally, a witness should be open and honest with nothing to fear. Witnesses who understand their position will have nothing to hide and should welcome the opportunity that cross-examination provides to further explain their analyses. Questions damaging to a witness's case can be minimized by providing the answers directly, briefly, and casually. A sense of humor can also assist a witness in dealing with difficult questions or overly aggressive cross-examiners. When a witness senses that the questioner is trying to hurry a response, he or she should remain calm and try not to be rushed. Overall, the witness wants to appear calm, competent, and in control.

TECHNIQUES OF THE CROSS-EXAMINER

A thorough understanding of the subject matter of a controversy is absolutely essential for effective cross-examination. Mastery of the subject matter alone, however, cannot guarantee witnesses' responses. What kind of questions to ask, the ordering of questions, the phrasing of questions, how far to go in questioning—all of these will affect the productivity of a cross-examination. Witnesses under cross-examination do not intentionally want to aid the cause of the questioner; therefore, their answers must be carefully directed, focused, and controlled. The guidelines below are designed to help questioners develop effective cross-examination skills.

Construct Basic Questions

Cross-examination should not be unplanned fishing expeditions. Random questions should not simply be tossed out in the hope that a stray response or two might be useful. Good questioners know what they want to accomplish during cross-examination. Such a conscious awareness of the objective to be achieved gives direction to the cross-examination and aids in the generation of specific questions.

Preparing questions for the purposes of clarifying an issue or committing a witness to a particular position is usually not difficult once the objective is identified. When the purpose of the questioning is refutation, however, many beginning debaters have more difficulty in knowing where to begin. In these instances, the preparation of specific questions should begin with the methods of refutation. The methods of refutation constitute the overall approach within which the specific questions will be prepared to achieve the advocate's goal. Advocates should decide at the outset what the weaknesses in the opponent's argument are. Is there something wrong with the evidence offered to support the argument? Is there an unstated premise that needs to be identified and refuted? Has an inappropriate conclusion been drawn from the evidence? Is the problem exaggerated? Once the method of refutation is identified, then the advocate will have a clearer sense of direction and be able to construct appropriate questions.

Ask Factual Questions

The use of factual questions is the single most important technique of cross-examination. A questioner should always know the answer to the question asked in order to avoid being surprised or embarrassed by unexpected responses. The answers to factual questions are reasonably predictable, and thus, they both direct and limit witnesses' responses. Questions that ask witnesses to interpret or evaluate data or ask for opinions are more open-ended; they do not limit the witness's response, and the answers are less predictable. "How" and "Why" questions, for instance, provide latitude and allow the witness to provide more creative answers that may be beneficial to his or her cause rather than to yours.

Beginning debaters sometimes have difficulty distinguishing between factual and opinion questions. Questions, for example, that ask for a yes or no response are not necessarily factual questions. The answer to the question "Isn't it better to be employed than to be without the money and sense of purpose which a job supplies?" may seem so obvious that it is easy to think of this kind of question as factual. But since the question really asks for a judgment, it could be answered with a "No, not always." The answer to factual questions are verifiable. The verification may be possible by reference to the flow sheets kept during the debate or by reference to specific evidence. Questions such as "Did you ever deny the solvency evidence presented in the first speech?" or "Have you read any evidence or provided any analysis to deny the link to the disadvantage?" are examples of factual questions that can be verified by reference to what happened in the round. "How many U.S. soldiers died during our military intervention in Grenada?" or "What provision in the War Powers Act could have prevented the president from initially sending troops into Grenada?'' are factual questions that can be verified by reference to evidence. Even a slight change in the wording of a question can make it less verifiable and shift the question from one of fact to one of opinion. "Can you provide any evidence to deny the harmful effects of radon?'' is a different kind of question from "What evidence did you offer denying the harmful effects of radon?'' At best, the first question can only be verified in the future and is subject to considerable interpretation. The second question is more easily verified.

Use Short Series of Questions

It is usually difficult to accomplish any of the goals of cross-examination with a single question, but several questions in a short series can provide the basis for substantial counterargument. The initial question in a series is often used to identify the general area of the controversy that will be explored. After that, succeeding questions attempt to elicit individual responses that, when pulled together, will refute a conclusion of the opposition. Each individual question may be thought of as providing a building block for an overall solid attack. The following example illustrates how a series of questions helps to build an argument.

1. You have said that there is no significant relationship between the private ownership of guns and violence, is that correct?
2. Were guns involved in the assasinations of Robert Kennedy? Martin Luther King? John F. Kennedy?
3. Can you tell me, of the 121 police officers killed in the line of duty last year, how many were shot with handguns?
4. How many U.S. citizens die each year as a result of gun accidents?
5. How many robberies annually involve the use of guns?
6. In how many assault cases are guns used?
7. What is the only major nation in the world that does not control the private use of guns?
8. What nation leads the world in death by gunfire?

Use Analogies and Parallel Situations

Generally, cross-examination witnesses have carefully considered their positions on the specific case or topic under discussion. Within the specific subject matter area, therefore, respondents tend to have more thoughtful answers. When questions use analogies and parallel situations, however, the questioning is removed from the familiar subject area and from the carefully prepared analysis by the witness, and respondents are guided to desired conclusions. In responding to analogies and parallel situations, the witness is forced to rethink idea relationships and may be more easily led by the questioner. The use of parallel situations is illustrated below.

1. One of your arguments is that marijuana should be legalized because it is extremely difficult to enforce antimarijuana laws. Am I right?

2. Is the purpose of our laws against speeding to deter drivers from driving too fast?
3. In spite of these laws, don't many people sometimes speed when they drive?
4. Don't people often violate our parking ordinances?
5. In spite of our murder laws, don't more people get away with murder each year than get caught?

Do Not Draw Conclusions

One of the greatest temptations in cross-examination is to go too far with a line of questioning. After three or four questions, it generally becomes clear toward what conclusion the questioner is working. Once this occurs, witnesses begin to limit and qualify their answers. In the series of questions above, an advocate would be unlikely to get the desired response to a concluding question such as, "By your reasoning then, shouldn't we also legalize speeding and overtime parking and murder?" By pursuing the line of questioning too far, the cross-examiner provides the witness with an opportunity to qualify and explain his or her answers, and ultimately makes the cross-examination less useful. Moreover, it is often more persuasive to allow the judge or audience to reach the conclusion on its own. To guarantee that the significance of a particular line of questioning is not overlooked, references should, of course, be made to it in later speeches (the lawyer's summation or the debater's constructive or rebuttal speech).

Cut Off Witnesses

Occasionally, witnesses will attempt to qualify even the most obvious answers or will spend more time than is reasonable qualifying answers to which a direct response is difficult. Once the basis of the witness's answer is clear and the qualification becomes excessive, you must exercise your right to maintain control of the question session. The silencing of a respondent, however, must be handled tactfully and timed carefully. Once the decision is made to cut off a witness, you must not be hesitant or unsure. You should move directly to the next question while speaking slightly louder than the witness. If you attempt to cut off the resondent too early, you will be viewed as unreasonable. On the other hand, if you wait too long, you may lose control of the question session.

Drop Unproductive Questioning

It is not uncommon for a line of questioning to run into some difficulty in reaching its desired goal. In some cases, you may not fully anticipate the answers you receive and may be unable to build further questions on the answers. In other cases, the respondent may simply refuse to provide answers to obvious questions, causing your line of questioning to bog down. In such situations, it is useless to press the line of questioning further. You should simply drop that line of questioning and move on to another. If you do not appear upset or rattled by the witness's unexpected answers or uncooperative manner, no harm will have been done to your credibility.

Use Admissions

Because of the give-and-take nature of cross-examination, it is not always possible to develop ideas completely or to relate ideas systematically during cross-examination. The procedures of academic debate and of courts of law, therefore, provide for formal speeches following the cross-examinations. One of the purposes of these speeches is to build on the lines of questioning and to relate them to the total case analysis. Perhaps the most obvious weakness of academic debaters' use of cross-examination is their failure to follow up on the answers in their speeches. Statements such as "As the witness admitted under cross-examination. . ." or "As was pointed out during the question period. . ." or "The cross-examination revealed. . ." should punctuate the following speech. Your failure to refer to the cross-examination in your formal speech suggests that the cross-examination was ineffective.

Develop Stock Questions

One of the reasons why some lawyers and debaters are less successful at cross-examination is that they approach each contest as if it were unique. They fail to understand that certain questions or lines of questions are relevant to many different cases within the same subject area. Many of the articles in legal periodicals that discuss cross-examination do little more than provide stock questions for particular types of cases and situations—medical malpractice, product liability, attacking a witness's expertise, and so forth. Perceptive debaters learn that there are certain standard questions that should regularly be asked. When a counterplan is presented, you should always ask if it is intended to be conditional. If it is conditional, under what circumstances will it be dropped? If a topicality challenge is to be advanced, you should ask the affirmative for its definitions of critical terms. You should have questions ready to ask about the uniqueness of disadvantages and the threshold for the impacts. Other stock questions may be developed to deal with specific arguments that recur on a given topic. The important point to remember is that productive questions once developed should not be forgotten. In some instances, it might even be helpful to prepare a file of stock questions for use with particular kinds of cases or types of arguments (see Dawson, Marcus, and Vines).

TECHNIQUES FOR RESPONDENTS

In all situations where questioning is used, one should know the skills both of answering and asking. Knowing how questions are asked helps a witness respond more appropriately, and knowing how witnesses are likely to answer helps a cross-examiner prepare questions. Lawyers especially need to understand how to respond to questions in order to prepare their own witnesses. Debaters also need to know how to respond to questions, since they will be required to serve both as witnesses and cross-examiners. The guidelines below are designed to assist you as a respondent to contribute positively to the dialogue while maintaining your basic analysis of the question under consideration.

Think before Answering

Do not allow yourself to be rushed into an answer. Try to anticipate where the questioner is headed so that you can give an honest, but not unnecessarily damaging, answer. You should not, of course, take too long to think before answering or you may appear to be stupid or to be stalling. The point is that a second's reflection before answering any question is a good idea. A moment's thought may prevent your saying too much or carelessly overstating your response.

Qualify Your Answers

Often, you may wish to qualify an answer to prevent it from being misinterpreted later. Qualifying statements can limit the scope or context of an answer and build in the basis for rebuttal responses. Unfortunately, questioners often cut witnesses off once they have the desired answer, and the important qualification never gets communicated. In order to protect yourself from being cut off too soon by the questioner, you should state your qualifications first and then give a direct answer. The order of the answer should be "But. . .yes," not "Yes, but. . . ." An example of how to state your qualifications is illustrated in the following exchange from a debate on airline safety:

QUESTIONER: Isn't it true that the number of deaths from airplane accidents has increased in each of the last three years?

WITNESS: The number of passenger miles flown has also increased significantly and airplane travel remains the safest form of transportation. But yes, there has been some increase in deaths from air travel.

Notice how the witness provided more relevant information than was required to answer the question directly and how this information gave perspective and placed the answer in a less damaging context.

Understand the Question

In their desire to appear alert and knowledgeable, respondents sometimes attempt to answer questions they do not completely understand. A question may be poorly phrased, or insufficient context provided. A technical or unfamiliar term may make a question difficult to comprehend. Whatever the reason, seek clarification of the question before giving an answer. Your credibility will be less endangered by asking for clarification or restatement of the question than by giving a vague or inappropriate answer.

Provide Obvious Answers

Witnesses sometimes view each and every question as a threat to their analysis, but many questions call for straightforward, obvious answers. To attempt to qualify or hedge on questions with obvious answers creates a bad impression and destroys much of the value of cross-examination. The best way to answer an obvious question is to provide a short, direct answer.

Admit Ignorance

Obviously, it would be nice to be able to answer every question knowledgeably and with authority. Inevitably, however, a question will be asked for which you will not know an answer. Some witnesses, afraid of admitting ignorance, attempt to bluff their way through some sort of answer. Such bluffing, however, is easily exposed, since good questioners know the answer to a question before they ask it. Although it is uncomfortable to be asked a question for which one does not know the answer, the best possible response in this situation is to admit ignorance and make light of it.

Do Not Permit Questioner Conclusions

While the questioner has the controlling role in cross-examination, that role is limited to asking questions. When a questioner goes beyond this limit to present a speech or to draw a conclusion from answers you have provided, you should tactfully note this point. For example, you can interrupt the statement and ask, "Is that a question? I would like to respond to what you have said." In courts of law the judges and opposing lawyers help to regulate the cross-examination, but in other advocacy situations you will have to be prepared to keep the questioner in line yourself.

SUMMARY

Direct examination of the witnesses occurs when lawyers question friendly witnesses to help present their side of a case. Questions used in direct examination tend to be fairly open-ended. Cross-examination differs from direct examination in that witnesses are likely to be less friendly to the questioner's cause. Cross-examination, thus, requires the questioner to exert more control during the questioning process by asking more specific and closed-ended questions.

There are five primary purposes of cross-examination: (1) to clarify previous statements of witnesses, (2) to commit witnesses to particular positions, (3) to refute the validity of previous testimony, (4) to prepare the way for constructive arguments, and (5) to undermine the credibility of the respondent.

The psychological aspects of cross-examination are very important. The personality, manner, and style of the cross-examiner will influence the witness's responsiveness and the judge's and audience's evaluations. The questioner should seek to project a pleasant, self-confident, and relaxed manner. The way in which witnesses respond to cross-examination can strongly influence judgments regarding their credibility. A respondent should appear calm, competent, and in control.

Nine guidelines can assist the questioner in preparing for cross-examination: (1) construct questions based on the purpose of cross-examination and the methods of refutation, (2) ask factual questions, (3) use short series of questions to build responses, (4) use analogies and parallel situations to guide respondents to desired conclusions, (5) do not ask witnesses to draw conclusions, (6) cut off witnesses who overqualify answers, (7) drop unproductive lines of questioning, (8) use the admissions gained through cross-examination in the following speeches, and (9) develop a repertoire of stock questions for each topic.

Six guidelines can assist respondents in answering questions: (1) think before answering, (2) qualify answers first, (3) do not attempt to answer questions you do not fully understand, (4) be prepared to provide obvious answers, (5) admit ignorance when you do not know an answer, and (6) do not permit the questioner to draw conclusions or make short speeches.

SELECTED BIBLIOGRAPHY

COPELAND, JAMES M. *Cross-Examination in Debate.* Skokie, IL: National Textbook, 1982.
DAWSON, JOHN M. "Cross-examination of the Quantitative Expert." *Defense Law Journal* (April 1983): 258–71.
HEGLAND, KENNEY F. *Trial and Practice Skills.* St. Paul: West, 1978.
MARCUS, ERIC H. "Defending Mental Injury Claims: Cross-examining the Plaintiff's Expert Witness." *Trial Diplomacy Journal* (Spring 1988): 37–42.
SCHWARTZ, LOUIS E. *Proof, Persuasion, and Cross-Examination.* Vols. 1 and 2. Englewood Cliffs, NJ: Executive Reports, 1975.
VINES, LANNY S. "Cross-examination of an Expert." *Trial Lawyers Quarterly* (Summer/Fall 1987): 41–48.
WELLMAN, FRANCIS L. *The Art of Cross-Examination.* 4th ed. New York: Macmillan, 1966.
ZIEGELMUELLER, GEORGE. "Cross Examination Re-examined." In *Argument in Transition: Proceedings of the Third Summer Conference on Argument,* edited by David Zarefsky, Malcolm O. Sillars, and Jack Rhodes, 904–17. Annandale, VA: Speech Communication Association, 1983.

STUDY QUESTIONS

1. Why is the ability to ask a series of questions essential to the nature of cross-examination?

2. To what extent is skill in cross-examination a tool of inquiry as well as a tool of advocacy?

3. To what extent are the principles of cross-examination discussed in this chapter relevant to questioning in the job interview situation? In the counseling situation? In a legislative hearing?

EXERCISES

1. Prepare three lines of cross-examination. Use these with a witness in class. Have other class members evaluate your efforts.

2. Have one class member present an oral argument based on an unstated value premise; attempt to expose that value premise through cross-examination.

3. Listen to one of the television interview programs such as "Meet the Press." Compare the approach to questioning in this type of public inquiry forum with the approach used in public advocacy forums, such as courts of law or academic debates.
4. Discuss the questions used in one of the cross-examination periods from the debate transcripts contained in this book's appendixes. Analyze the questions in terms of appropriateness and effectiveness.

CHAPTER SIXTEEN
ADVOCACY SKILLS

The preceding chapters have attempted to provide you with a basic understanding of those concepts and methods required for critical thinking and public advocacy. Mastery of these ideas and skills is necessary, but it is not sufficient to ensure routine success in persuading others that your position is correct. Many beginning advocates—debaters, lawyers, legislators—are frustrated when they have carefully researched their cases, organized their data, and rationally responded to the specific arguments of the opposition only to lose their cases or fail to win their audiences. As the ancient rhetoricians observed, sound arguments are naturally stronger than false ones, but truth alone is not always sufficient to persuade an audience. A sound argument poorly communicated will often lose to a weaker argument effectively presented.

There are many aspects of audience analysis, style, and delivery that influence an audience's, judge's, or jury's ability to discern the ultimate validity of a position. Entire books have been written on each of these subjects. In this chapter, we will attempt to comment only on those skills that are of particular importance in formal advocacy situations, for example, in academic and public debates and courts of law. The specific advocacy skills discussed are (1) oral delivery, (2) language usage, (3) focusing of ideas, and (4) story telling.

ORAL DELIVERY

Although arguments may be presented in either oral or written form, much argumentation is completely oral. Even when the argumentation is primarily written, it is often supplemented by oral presentations—as for example, when cases are argued before the Supreme Court. These oral communication situations present special problems to the advocate. Audiences have limited attention spans; they are easily distracted; and they must comprehend the argument the first time they hear it because they cannot go back and reread what they missed initially.

Directness

Directness in manner and physical presentation helps in maintaining the attention and interest of listeners. Just as in personal conversations we like the individual with whom we are conversing to look us in the eye, so audiences want the person addressing them to look directly at them and not down at notes or across to the opposition. It is sometimes easy for debaters and other advocates to become so involved in the details of their analysis that they fail to lift their eyes from their notes to look at their judge or audience. Eye contact with the intended receiver can provide important feedback regarding the listener's understanding or acceptance of the argument being advocated. Although trained advocates are inevitably more concerned with the accurate statement of data and the careful wording of arguments than are other communicators, that attention to precision ought not become an excuse for indirectness.

Advocates can ensure greater eye contact with their listeners by carefully positioning themselves before they begin speaking. If a table or chair interferes with your ability to comfortably position yourself in front of the audience, move the interfering object. If the speaker's stand is too high or too low, then adjust it, or arrange a more convenient way of handling notes. Prepare briefs and other notes so that they are legible and can be read easily. Some debaters develop the

bad habit of placing their notes on a low table and bending down to read them. As this practice prevents eye contact with the judge, it is easily avoided by simply picking up the notes. Preparing notes or briefs on card stock or other heavy paper makes them easier to hold without bending or wrinkling.

Rate

The amount of time advocates have to present their cases is often limited. As we saw in Chapter 11, academic and public debates almost always operate within prescribed time limitations. The Supreme Court limits oral arguments to one hour, and time limits may be imposed in parliamentary forums. Even in less formal situations, the attentiveness of audiences imposes practical time constraints. The advocate who speaks too slowly will not be able to present his or her entire analysis, whereas the advocate who speaks rapidly may fail to be understood by the judge or audience.

An excessively slow rate of delivery can be a serious problem, not only because it limits the number and depth of arguments that can be presented but also because it is frequently accompanied by a less lively and varied pattern of delivery. Greater familiarity with the material to be presented, rehearsal within the time limits, and the use of feedback through recorded presentations can help to ensure better paced and more animated speeches.

Excessively rapid delivery is a particularly common problem among academic debaters. The impression of speed is partly a function of the receivers' limited knowledge on the topic and their inability to decode the message without additional explanation. Nevertheless, it must be admitted that students trained in debate tend to talk very rapidly. The problem of rapid delivery is often compounded by a series of other related practices—careless articulation, excessive loudness, and lack of variety in rate, pitch, and volume. Obviously, it does not matter how many arguments are presented or how well-documented and thorough the analysis if the intended listener cannot comprehend what is being presented.

There are a number of ways in which advocates can adjust to time limitations without resorting to excessively rapid delivery. Often, speed is necessitated by such poor practices as overemphasis, inefficient language usage, insufficient selection of arguments, or a combination of the three. The mechanics of orally emphasizing an idea require time, so by using less emphasis a debater can save time. In addition, economy of language makes it possible to express the same arguments in fewer words. Finally, careful selection of arguments limits the number of ideas to be presented and, therefore, reduces the need for excessive speed.

Studies have demonstrated that audiences can follow arguments even when they are presented at fairly rapid rates (see Voor and Miller). There is even some evidence to indicate that a lively rate of presentation may contribute to the speaker's perceived authoritativeness. Thus, speed of delivery, per se, is neither a certain liability nor an absolute virtue. The critical factor seems to be the speaker's overall ability to control his or her presentation so that other elements of delivery are not compromised. Contrast is important; speed should not be constant. Articulation needs to be especially precise when speaking at a rapid rate. Further, speed may contribute to increased tension of the vocal chords and result in an unpleasant increase in pitch; rapid delivery is acceptable only when normal pitch can be maintained. A good general rule is not to speak any more rapidly than is absolutely necessary. When speaking at a faster rate, be especially careful to maintain other good vocal practices.

LANGUAGE USAGE

Skilled advocates need to know how to use language to convey meanings precisely, concisely, and interestingly. In advocacy, language must be used precisely so that arguments convey their intended meaning. If we state conclusions carelessly, we may claim more—or less—than we can prove. Thus our ability to communicate the findings of our analysis accurately depends on our ability to phrase our conclusions carefully. Not only must our language be precise, but it should also allow us to express our ideas concisely. Because of the time limits imposed informally by audiences, and formally in certain forums, it is important to be able to explain positions in as few words as possible. Moreover, excessive wordiness clutters our message and makes it less clear and less interesting. Language choices should be interesting so that our ideas will capture and hold the attention of listeners. The words in which we dress our ideas can enhance or detract from the acceptability of the concept. Among the most common sources of inefficient and uninteresting language are jargon, clichés, and filler phrases.

Jargon

Webster's describes jargon as "technical, esoteric or secret vocabulary of a science, art, trade, sect, profession, or other special group. Language full of circumlocutions and long, high sounding words." The primary problem caused by the overuse of jargon is that it fails to communicate with the nonspecialist—lay judges in academic debate or jurors in a courtroom, for example.

Almost every debate topic has its own set of technical jargon. At the beginning of the debate season, even fairly knowledgeable judges may have difficulty understanding the jargon relevant to specialized case areas. The problem of jargon is compounded by the widespread use of acronyms such as ABM for Anti-Ballistic Missile, BMDs for Ballistic Missile Defenses, and SDI for Strategic Defense Initiative. The technical nature of jargon and acronyms should contribute to greater precision in meaning, but it frequently has the opposite effect. This occurs because the technical term moves into the nontechnical vocabulary of nonspecialists, who use it in a less exact manner. When the colleges debated our military commitments to the North Atlantic Treaty Organization, for example, considerable confusion resulted because technical terms such as "deep strike" and "maritime strategy" were used imprecisely.

In addition to the jargon that emanates from the subject matter being debated, academic debaters are also prone to use certain technical terms, which derive from the procedural rules and practices of the activity. Phrases such as "pull it through," "there is no threshold," and "it is not unique" are often used in careless meaningless ways. It may be that in using these terms debaters mean to suggest a rich complex of ideas, but the labels have been so frequently used—and abused—that without further explanation they communicate very little. They become simply circumlocutions and high-sounding phrases.

Of course, it is not always possible to avoid the use of technical terminology, nor should it be avoided altogether. Technical language, carefully used and explained, can enhance accuracy of meaning. What should be avoided is excessive reliance on jargon and the misinterpretation and misapplication of technical language. When specialized language is used, its meaning should be carefully explained and consistently applied.

Clichés

A cliché is "a trite phrase that has lost precise meaning by iteration; a hackneyed or stereotyped expression" (*Webster's*). By definition, cliches detract from the precision and interest of our language. They usually contribute to a lack of conciseness as well, since they are often used simply as "filler phrases." If intended to convey meaning, they must be further explained.

Expressions such as "costly bureaucracy" or "devastating impact" illustrate debaters' use of cliches. Both expressions are overused, imprecise, and sterotyped. "Costly bureaucracy" does not describe the nature or cause of the cost, nor does it suggest the extent or harmful result of the added cost. To say that "administrative supervision reduces welfare benefits by half" is a more precise and less hackneyed statement of the same argument. Similarly, "devastating impact" fails to reveal the exact nature or extent of the expected harm. The importance that a judge or audience will give to an argument frequently depends on the language used to express it. When an idea is expressed with cliches, the listener may be unmoved because he or she is simply hearing the "same old thing."

In an effort to be colorful, a debater recently described his opponent's argument by saying, "It sucks." Although this phrase may not suffer from excessive iteration (fortunately) in the world of academic debate, it is, nevertheless, a trite and meaningless expression on the street corners. "It sucks" attracted attention to the speaker, but it did not provide specific meaning to the listener.

Cliches are used because they are readily available and do not require extra thought or effort. They are the typical, ordinary, stock ways of expressing ideas. Unfortunately, it is this ready familiarity that makes cliches so uninteresting and uncompelling. Advocates should seek to express critical ideas in language that is both specific and fresh. In order to avoid cliches and to find fresh, less frequently used words, a thesauras is helpful.

Filler Language

Most advocacy requires the participants to engage in the extemporaneous presentation of their ideas. Except for the first affirmative speech, most of the argumentation in academic debate is presented extemporaneously. Parliamentary and courtroom debates similarly depend on the ability of the advocates to develop and respond to arguments without reliance on prepared manuscripts. The inability to plan the wording of arguments in extemporaneous situations creates special demands on the advocate. Extemporaneous presentation makes it tempting to rely on jargon and cliches and also promotes the use of filler language.

Filler language refers to unnecessary verbiage, which fills the void without adding to the substance of an argument. Such expressions as "My third argument is. . ." (instead of simply "third"), or "I'm going to contend that. . ." or "He wanted to tell us that. . ." (instead of "He said") are examples of filler language. In some cases, filler language unconsciously substitutes for vocalized pauses ("uhs" and "ers"). The extra language helps the advocate introduce an argument while at the same time provides a moment to think about what he or she wants to say. The problem with filler language is that its use quickly and unconsciously becomes habitual. Once this occurs, a debater's speech becomes weighted down with excess words, and the crispness and interest necessary for a persuasive presentation are destroyed. In addition, excess verbiage may prevent the debater from responding comprehensively to opposing arguments or, alternately, force him or her to speak too rapidly.

The most effective way to prevent filler phrases from creeping into your speech is to be aware of the problems they create and to be watchful for them. It is helpful to have someone else—your partner, coach, parent, spouse—assist in monitoring your use of language in actual oral presentations. You can also tape-record your speeches and listen for filler language as you play back the tape. Once you are aware of the problem, it is easily controlled.

FOCUSING CRITICAL ARGUMENTS

In both oral and written argument it is essential for advocates to focus the attention of listeners or readers on those parts of the analysis that they consider to be of greatest importance. A primary objective of the study of argumentation as critical thinking is to assist you in identifying those aspects of a topic that are essential to its proof. Unfortunately, in public advocacy, it is not sufficient simply to know what is essential; advocates must also be able to communicate that judgment to their audiences.

Researchers are sometimes frustrated when they present detailed, well-documented cases for government action, only to have legislators refuse to act because of a single oft-repeated argument by lobbyists. Debaters, likewise, are frustrated when their comprehensive answers to an argument are ignored by the judge in favor of fewer forcefully argued responses by the opposition. The success of the lobbyists and the opposition debaters in these cases may have had less to do with the overall adequacy of their analyses than with their ability to direct the attention of the decision-makers to those aspects of the controversies where they were strongest. Throughout a campaign or a debate, it is important to keep the controversy centered on those ideas that are most important to your cause. This ability to focus on winning issues is even more important in the final stages of a campaign or trial or in the rebuttals of an academic debate. There are four techniques that are helpful in focusing critical arguments: (1) ordering, (2) time and space allocation, (3) vocal emphasis, and (4) grouping.

Ordering

Successful lawyers give careful attention to the order in which witnesses are called, and experienced debaters likewise order their arguments for, what they hope will be, the maximum persuasive effect. It is difficult to set forth firm guidelines regarding how arguments should be ordered because a variety of factors, such as the relative strength of one argument over another and the specific strategy of the opposition, must be considered. Nevertheless, certain general principles may be identified.

First, each speech and each individual series of responses to specific issues should begin with a strong—in some cases, your strongest—argument. It is important to get the judge or audience on your side as rapidly as possible. Listeners tend to be most attentive at the beginning of a speech, so you want to present a particularly strong argument at the point of their greatest receptivity. A strong initial argument may also have the effect of conditioning listeners so that they will be more open to later, perhaps less strong, arguments. In addition, many debaters—even successful ones—tend to spend more time responding to those arguments presented first by their opponents. Given this tendency, the presentation of a strong argument first helps to ensure that the clash will occur on your strong ground.

Second, if an important argument has been ignored or insufficiently considered by the opposition, you should begin your presentation with that argument. Simply pointing out the opposition's insufficiency of response in the midst of several other arguments often does not adequately focus the listeners' attention on the significance of the opposition's failure. By selecting the ignored argument to begin your speech, you not only highlight your opponent's failure to clash but also indicate that you believe the neglected argument is of vital importance.

Third, when, in your judgment, the opposition has been particularly effective in winning over the judge or audience on a specific issue or issues, begin your speech by directly addressing that issue(s). Normally, in a debate or campaign you want to keep the controversy focused more on your ground, on your strong issues. However, if the opposition has clearly succeeded in gaining the listeners' acceptance of his or her perspective, then you must begin with the issue or issues they have identified. Once the audience has accepted the critical arguments of the opposition, those arguments must be disposed of before you can effectively move the audience or judge to consider other issues. As long as the audience is convinced by the opposition's dominant issues, it is not likely to have its mind changed by arguments peripheral to those issues.

Fourth, whenever possible, conclude a speech with a strong argument that has some emotional impact. In general, persuasion research indicates the importance of primacy and recency as ordering principles, i.e., strong arguments should be placed first and last (see Hovland, Miller and Campbell, Lana). First and last arguments tend to be remembered longer, and if the last argument also has emotional impact, it is more likely to have motivational force. The blame and cure issues tend to be more technical arguments and thus have little emotional impact. Ill and cost arguments, on the other hand, are more likely to be concerned with human factors and have greater potential for emotional responses.

Time and Space Allocations

The amount of time spent developing an argument orally or the space devoted to explaining it in writing should be roughly proportional to the importance of the argument. The greater the time or space, the greater its significance; the less the time or space, the less its significance. Culturally, we are conditioned to think of those things that are larger or occupy more time as being more important. Moreover, the more time or space given to an argument, the more opportunity there is for it to capture our attention.

In a political campaign a candidate must decide whether a particular issue deserves a paragraph, an entire speech, or several speeches. If Social Security is mentioned in only a few short paragraphs of a few speeches throughout a campaign, it is clear that the candidate does not place that program very high on his or her list of political priorities. On the other hand, if Social Security is the central focus of one or more major television addresses and receives several long paragraphs in other speeches, the candidate is communicating a more important commitment to the issue.

Academic debaters should be even more sensitive to the role of time allocation in focusing issues because of the severe time limits imposed by the activity. A political candidate who misjudges the issue focus early in a campaign can make major adjustments in time and space allocation in the closing weeks before an election, but a debater operates in a much narrower time frame. Most debaters are concerned about being able to answer all of the necessary arguments in the time allotted, but too few debaters give enough thought to how much time individual arguments deserve. In every debate, many arguments are advanced that simply are not critical; a deliberate decision should be made to ignore these so that more time can be spent on the crucial issues. Time is required not only to explain and prove issues but also to communicate your judgment regarding the argument's overall importance.

Just as arguments you want to emphasize should be given adequate time, so arguments you wish to deemphasize should be given less time. A strong argument of the opposition cannot be ignored, but it should be answered as succinctly and briefly as possible. In this way, the opposition's argument can be deemphasized, while saving time to emphasize your strongest issue.

Vocal Emphasis

In addition to the ordering of arguments and the allocation of time and space, arguments may also be focused by means of vocal emphasis. Just as important ideas can be emphasized on the printed page through the use of *italicized print* or **bold lettering**, ideas may be highlighted orally. Vocal emphasis is not simply a matter of speaking louder. Although speaking loudly may be used for emphasis, volume will not focus an idea if the loudness is consistent throughout the presentation.

Contrast is the key to effective vocal emphasis. Contrast in volume, rate, pitch, and overall intensity are required. If a speaker addresses a large audience and speaks at a louder than normal level, he or she can emphasize important ideas by momentarily reducing the volume. Even if the audience has to strain to hear, the sudden lower volume will capture their attention and give added importance to what is said.

Changes in pitch and rate can be equally effective. Many first affirmative speakers repeat the statement of their major contentions as a means of emphasizing their importance. A more artistic and effective way to achieve this result is to pause for an instant before the argument and then to state each word slowly and deliberately with a slight increase in volume. In this way, the major contention is made to stand out as if it were verbally in bold print.

As we observed earlier, many debaters often talk very rapidly. An important difference between fast speaking debaters who are successful and those who are not is that those who succeed know how to slow down to emphasize and underline important concepts.

Grouping

A final method of focusing issues is to group several individual arguments and to give a single response or single set of responses to the grouped arguments. The grouping of arguments helps advocates guard against getting involved with too many individual lines of analysis and allows them to narrow the areas of clash. Narrowing, which is possible through grouping, provides more time for explaining and supporting critical arguments.

Advocates should be careful not to misapply the grouping technique. Obviously, not all lines of analysis can be grouped together and given a single answer; many arguments are substantively different. If unrelated arguments are inappropriately grouped, necessary refutation may be overlooked, and a strategic opportunity provided to the opposition. At least three circumstances invite the use of grouping. Arguments may be grouped when the same conclusion is stated in different ways and offered as several distinct arguments, when different arguments are based on the same premise, and when different arguments are subject to the same technical weakness.

It is not unusual for advocates to present several arguments that sound different but are all essentially the same. In arguing for greater controls on the press, one advocate offered three attacks on the news media. He accused it of abusing its rights, of distorting the truth, and of selectively presenting the facts. These arguments are simply variations on a theme; the selective presentation of facts is a method of distoring the truth and an example of the abuse of a free press. These arguments could easily be grouped and answered as one.

Even when arguments are reasonably distinct, they will still be interrelated and often involve chains of reasoning. When a fundamental premise underlying a chain of reasoning or a cluster of arguments can be identified, the arguments can be grouped and refuted by denying the underlying assumption. Those who are opposed to the United States' continued restrictions on the sale of designated strategic goods to unfriendly nations inevitably respond to the alleged disadvantages of ending strategic embargoes by arguing that the disadvantages assume that embargoes are effective. The argument is that unfriendly nations are inevitably able to obtain embargoed products through sales from other suppliers, third party sales, and espionage. Thus, the opponents of strategic embargoes are able to group all of the disadvantages and focus the conflict on what they consider to be a critical issue by attacking the basic assumption of the disadvantages (that U.S. strategic embargoes are effective).

A third circumstance when arguments may be successfully grouped for refutation is when different arguments manifest the same technical flaw. Proponents of banning cigarettes usually win the health hazards of the smoking issue by reducing it to a question of the better evidence. When the studies that claim smoking is harmful are attacked and counterstudies presented, the advocates of banning cigarettes group the specific study indictments and respond that their studies use the best methodology, reflect the greatest consensus, and are the most objective. The technical weaknesses of the opposition evidence allow the grouping of many individual arguments and the focusing of the issue.

STORY TELLING

An important aspect of advocacy, which has been practiced effectively by lawyers and politicians for many years but which has only recently received much theoretical attention from communication scholars, is the narrative concept (see Fisher, McGee and Nelson, Rowland). According to this view, listeners tend to accept or reject a persuasive message or argumentative case, not primarily on the basis of individual pieces of evidence or lines of analysis, but, more wholly, on the overall credibility of the story presented. The relationship between the individual parts of a case is what is considered to be important. In an effectively presented case, the drawing of relationships should provide a kind of narrative theme to hold the story together.

Drama critics sometimes attack playwrights for failing to resolve adequately the conflicts in their plots and for leaving too many loose ends unexplained. Television reviewers criticize TV series that do not have a clear concept guiding the shows. Movie critics object when the leading actor's and actress's performances

reveal significantly different interpretations of their relationship. Academic debate judges complain when, at the end of a round, neither side has "put the debate together." The message from all these various evaluators is essentially the same: the narrative is poorly presented; the story is not told well.

The presentation of a persuasive story does not require the abandonment of evidence or of an analytical case structure. What it does require is attention to broad relationships (particularly in the opening and concluding speeches), sufficient explanation, and a concern for overall believability. Two specific ways of facilitating a narrative emphasis in your argumentation are suggested below.

Philosophical Position

One of the most important means of developing a narrative perspective is to begin with a central theme. Too often debaters construct cases by simply stringing together individual pieces of evidence. In these instances, the evidence may be grouped together under headings that become contentions, but little or no thought is given to the underlying values or philosophical perspectives of the case. The establishment of a clear value perspective, such as equality of educational opportunity, can provide a narrative theme for arguments based on the fact of regional differences in educational achievement. This value perspective interprets and gives meaning to the factual data and forces the opposition to respond on a philosophical, as well as a descriptive, level. Equality of opportunity thus becomes a unifying affirmative theme.

Negative debaters also need to have a philosophical basis from which to argue. It is possible, of course, for negative debaters to refute an affirmative analysis on an ad hoc basis, without attempting to articulate a definite negative stand. Such a stance, however, not only lends itself to inconsistencies but also precludes any clear narrative theme. Even when negatives do state and defend a specific position—such as a defense of present policies—they do not always explain, or even understand, the rationale behind their position. An individual arguing against an expansion of public welfare might express a philosophical position in the following terms:

> Our present approach to aiding our most disadvantaged citizens is well conceived and ought not to be fundamentally changed.The federal government cannot, and should not, attempt to meet all of the needs of all of our citizens. Through the combined efforts of private, state, and federal programs, our needy citizens already have available to them food, shelter, and medical care. For the federal government to try to do more would undermine individual responsibility, preclude innovative state programs, and endanger our national economy.

This statement identifies three values—individual initiative, state innovation, and a sound economy—that could provide the basis for arguments justifying present assistance programs and that could also be used as a basis for disadvantages. By maintaining a unifying theme, the negative can provide a more persuasive narrative.

Metaphors

An interesting way of establishing a narrative theme is to tell a simple story and draw parallels between the incidents or characters in the story and the analysis you will advance. If the story is appropriately selected and imaginatively presented, the metaphor can greatly enhance the impact of the overall argument.

Richard Lewis of Harvard University used a metaphor in an artistic way to begin his first affirmative speech in a final round of the National Debate Tournament.[1]

> "All the people who lined the streets began to cry, 'Just look at the Emperor's new clothes. How beautiful they are!' Then suddenly a little child piped up, 'But the Emperor has no clothes on. He has no clothes on at all!' " In 1947 the United States created the Central Intelligence Agency and donned the cloak of secrecy to pursue communism. Experience has proven the cloak we donned was nothing more than the Emperor's new clothes, hiding far less than we have long pretended and exposing America to peril.
>
> Because Joel and I believe it is time we all recognized the American Emperor's mistake, we stand resolved that executive control of the United States foreign policy should be significantly curtailed. We believe the executive should be prohibited from carrying out covert operations. (Rives, 139–40)

The story of the emperor's new clothes was a particularly appropriate metaphor for the Harvard team since its debate case argued that the discovery of CIA activities was—like the emperor's nakedness—inevitable. At the conclusion of his analysis, Lewis once again returned briefly to the metaphor to complete his narrative.

> "Still in all the people started to whisper to one another that what the child said was so. 'The Emperor doesn't have any clothes. A little child is saying it and it is true.' The Emperor began to squirm, and all at once he knew that what the people said was right." (Rives, 142)

As this example demonstrates, metaphors, in the hands of creative advocates, can be an effective means of visualizing and dramatizing the narrative theme of a speech.

SUMMARY

Mastery of the critical thinking and strategic aspects of argument is not sufficient in itself to ensure consistent success in advocacy. Advocates must also be skilled in the presentation of their analyses.

Although there are many individual skills associated with oral delivery, two of particular concern in formal advocacy situations are directness and rate. Directness in manner and physical bearing is essential to maintaining the attention and interest of audiences and to monitoring their understanding and acceptance of arguments. An extremely slow rate of delivery limits the number and depth of arguments that can be presented and results in a less lively style. Rapid delivery is an especially serious problem when accompanied by poor articulation, shouting, and lack of variety. Excessively rapid delivery can be avoided by selective use of emphasis, by efficient language usage, and by limiting the number of arguments.

Careful selection of language contributes to precise, concise, and interesting expression. Jargon, clichés, and filler language are major sources of ineffective language usage. Jargon is technical language, which is full of high sounding words. Clichés are trite, stereotyped expressions, which have lost precise meaning through overuse. Filler language is unnecessary verbiage, which adds nothing to the substance of an argument.

The techniques for focusing arguments help an advocate keep the controversy centered on those ideas that are most important. The order in which arguments are presented strongly influences which arguments will become most important. The time or space devoted to an argument also affects its importance. In general, the more time or space given to an argument, the greater significance it will assume. Vocal emphasis through obvious changes in rate, pitch, and volume can further help in highlighting critical arguments. Finally, by grouping related arguments for refutation, an advocate can narrow the area of clash and focus the controversy on fewer central ideas.

The term story telling is used to describe the importance of a strong thematic emphasis in the presentation of an argumentative analysis. A good analysis, like a well-told story, must be consistent and credible. The identification of a clear philosophical position helps in establishing a narrative theme. The use of a central metaphor is an interesting way to highlight the narrative theme.

NOTES

[1]In both passages, Lewis is quoting directly from the text of Hans Christian Andersen's *The Emperor's New Clothes*.

SELECTED BIBLIOGRAPHY

BETTINGHAUS, ERWIN P. "Structure and Argument." In *Perspective on Argumentation,* edited by Gerald R. Miller and Thomas R. Nilsen, 130–55. Chicago: Scott, Foresman, 1966.

FISHER, WALTER R. *Human Communication as Narrative: Toward a Philosophy of Reason, Value, and Action.* Columbia: University of South Carolina Press, 1987.

HOVLAND, CARL I. Pp. 23–32 in *The Order of Presentation in Persuasion:* New Haven: Yale University Press, 157.

LANA, ROBERT E. "Existing Familiarity and Order of Presentation of Persuasive Communication." *Psychological Reports* 15 (1964): 607–10.

MCGEE, MICHAEL CALVIN, and JOHN NELSON. "Narrative Reason in Public Argument." *Journal of Communication* 35 (1987): 139–55.

MILLER, NORMAN, and D. T. CAMPBELL. "Regency and Primacy in Persuasion as a Factor of the Timing of Speeches and Measurements." *Journal of Abnormal and Social Psychology* 59 (1959):1–9.

RIVES, STANLEY G., ed. "1969 National Debate Tournament Final Debate." *Journal of the American Forensic Association* 6 (1969): 139–63.

ROWLAND, ROBERT C. "Narrative: Mode of Discourse or Paradigm?" *Quarterly Journal of Speech* 73 (1987): 264–75.

VOOR, JOHN B., and JOSEPH M. MILLER. "The Effect of Practice upon the Comprehension of Time-Compressed Speech." *Speech Monographs* 32 (1965): 452–54.
Webster's New International Dictionary. 2d ed. 1958.

STUDY QUESTIONS

1. Some debate theorists contend that the story telling approach is unethical because it takes argument out of the arena of logic and rationality. Do you agree or disagree? Why?
2. How does the advocacy situation in which you are participating affect your oral delivery and language usage? Which advocacy situations justify greater use of jargon? More rapid delivery?
3. Discuss how a speaker's effectiveness may be decreased by the use of jargon, clichés, and filler language.
4. Why is a well-told story often more effective than a large quantity of statistical evidence?
5. How can the use of philosophical positions and metaphors increase a speaker's effectiveness?

EXERCISES

1. Attend or read an intercollegiate debate and identify the jargon, clichés, and filler language used by the debaters.
2. Attend or read an intercollegiate debate and identify the methods used by the debaters to focus on critical arguments.
3. Use an audio-recorder or video-recorder to tape one of your rebuttal speeches in a practice debate. View or listen to the tape in an effort to improve your oral advocacy skills. Specifically, identify (1) problems with rate, (2) problems with jargon, clichés, and filler language, and (3) the methods used to focus on critical arguments.
4. After completing Exercise 3, determine a specific plan of action to improve on each of the three areas. Rerecord your rebuttal speech. Listen to the speech. Were you able to improve?
5. Watch a political debate or read a transcript of a political debate. How did the candidates use philosophical positions and metaphors to focus their positions? Did any of the candidates use a story telling approach?

APPENDIX A

**1988 NATIONAL CEDA TOURNAMENT FINAL DEBATE:
HAS THE AMERICAN JUDICIAL SYSTEM
OVEREMPHASIZED FREEDOM OF THE PRESS?**

Edited by James R. Brey*

The Third National CEDA Debate Tournament, sponsored by the Cross-Examination Debate Association, was held at the United States Air Force Academy on April 1-5, 1988. Major Larry James of the Air Force Academy hosted the tournament. Dr. Kevin Twohy of Carroll College served as Tournament Director.

Eight preliminary rounds and six elimination rounds resulted in a final round between Southern Illinois University and William Jewell College. John Lapham and Mark West, coached by Jeff Bile represented Southern Illinois University on the affirmative. Raymond Roberts and David Israelite, coached by Gina Lane, represented William Jewell College on the negative.

The final round was judged by Walter Ulrich from Vanderbilt University, Paul Gaske from San Diego State University, Steven Hunt from Lewis and Clark College, Larry James from the U. S. Air Force Academy, Kim Wong from

*James Brey is a Doctoral student of The Florida State University. This project was partially supported by Grant number 484240504 from the Communication Research Center at Florida State University. Reprinted with permission.

Massachusetts Institute of Technology, Pam Joraanstad from North Dakota State University, and James Johnson from Colorado College. The decision was 5-2 for Southern Illinois University.

The debate was transcribed from a cassette tape recording. Except for the correction of obvious unintended errors, this is as close to a verbatim transcript as was possible to obtain from the recording. Evidence used in the debate was supplied to the editor immediately following the round. Sources of the evidence have been verified as indicated in the Works Cited. Footnotes supply the exact quotation and other information when necessary. When the source was not available to the editor or was not located after a reasonable search, the term ''source indicated'' is used in the footnote together with any additional information provided by the debaters. Quotation marks surround statements from unverified sources only when the debater has provided the editor with a photocopy of the original. Descending time signals are included in brackets.

FIRST AFFIRMATIVE CONSTRUCTIVE

JOHN LAPHAM, SOUTHERN ILLINOIS UNIVERSITY

On behalf of the SIU squad and Southern Illinois University, the Department of Communications and the Department of Speech, our department chair and our secretary, Dorris, who does an awful lot for us, I'd like to thank Larry James, the tournament host for bringing us here. I'd like to thank the competitors this weekend for a wonderful, excellent competition, and that we were fortunate enough to get here.

I'd like to thank the people who didn't get here also, because I think there are a lot of wonderful competitors out there who aren't standing here right now. I would like to thank the Saluki debate squad, uh, the seniors, Hoss [Parsons], Mike [Korcok] Bibi [Christoff] and John [McHale] models. And I would like to begin the 1AC.

I believe that our planet is now on the brink of environmental disaster. We agree with the conclusion of the 1980 International Conference on the Environmental Future. It is:

> There is now a high probability, almost a certainty, [if the world continues as at present] that within 50 years there will occur, exceeding past ecodisasters, the greatest catastrophe in the history of the world. This might be a world-wide famine or war, which could destroy civilization and nature, or it might be a combination of effects caused by unwise actions. But there is also the possibility that such a catastrophe can be averted if the right decisions about the environmental future are taken. Clearly decisions made now and during the next 30 years will determine the future of mankind and of the world. These decisions may be the most important of all time. (629)

Observation one is analysis of this semester's resolution. Initially we define the phrase freedom of the press as the right to publish facts, ideas, and opinions without interference from the government and note that this right applies both to the print and the broadcast media. The judicial system's historical understanding of this definition of the press was explained by Professor Benno C. Schmidt, former dean of the Columbia Law School, and now President of Yale, in 1976 when he wrote that the "First Amendment theory has long been the preserve of laissez-faire thinking" (29).

We delineate in two subpoints today. The (A) subpoint is the print press. For decades the American Judicial System has recognized [SEVEN] the concept of publisher autonomy at the expense of access claims. Professor Schmidt notes the historical protection from claims of access. "With one early exception, decisions concerning constitutional claims of access to private owned print media have denied claims of access for both ads and articles" (107).

Professor Steven Smith of the University of Idaho concurs in 1987:

> The Supreme Court has been largely unmoved by the argument for rights of access and indeed has ruled that the first amendment not only does not require rights of access, but in fact also precludes legislatures from granting rights in some contexts. (720)

The judicial system will apparently continue to emphasize publisher autonomy. Professor Schmidt predicts in 1976 "The doctrines of freedom of the press may increasingly center on the concept of publisher autonomy" (239).

(B) subpoint is the broadcast press. Shortly after the Supreme Court's decision in Red Lion Broadcasting Co. v. FCC to uphold the constitutionality of the Fairness Doctrine, the Court adjudicated attempts to gain access to the broadcast press. Professor of Journalism at Drake University, William Francois noted in 1973 the effects of the Court's CBS v. DNC decision

> Instead of Red Lion being applied as an access case to the print media, as Professor Barron [SIX] believed might happen, it now is beginning to look as if the tradition of print journalism is going to be applied to broadcasting. . . . Access to the media appears to have been administered a severe setback. (188)

Professor Jerome Barron noted in '81: "The years since the CBS decision have, on the whole, seen a turning away from the interpretations of the 1st Amendment which would impose affirmative obligations upon the media" (3).

Observation two, rules for the road and paradigm. Parameters and focus for debate are noted initially in (A) subpoint, ecological awareness of human extinction is criteria. Mr. Rifkin argued in '80: "The only hope for the survival of the species is for the human race to abandon its aggression against the planet and seek to accommodate itself to the natural order" (256). We look to save the earth.

The (B) subpoint is preserve the ecology. The one subpoint is that ecological systems are critical for continued human life. Professor Paul Ehrlich of Stanford University explains in 1980 that the ecological systems maintain the quality of the atmosphere, dispose of our wastes, recycle essential nutrients, control the vast majority of potential pest and disease vectors, supply us with food from the sea, generate soils and run the hydrological cycle, among other vital services.[1]

[1]Source indicated.

The second subpoint is that the status quo will destroy the present eco-system. [FIVE] Ecology professor G. Tyler Miller of St. Andrew College notes the ominous implications in 1985 that:

> [I]f present trends continue, the world is headed for economic ruin, increased political instability, and threat of global nuclear war because (1) the maximum sustained yield of many of the world's renewable resources may be exceeded and (2) there will be shortage of affordable supplies of nonrenewable fossil fuels. . . .(8)

Subpoint three gives a decision rule. That is that 1988 is pivotal year. Sue Cross argued in March of this year. ''1988 is the greatest biological crisis since evolution began three-and-a-half billion years ago'' (A11).

We offer two contentions to support the resolution. Contention one, freedom of the press entrenches the old paradigm. Explanation in two subpoints. The (A) subpoint is the autonomous press supports the old world view. The mass media currently is based on the old paradigm. Environmentalist Hazel Henderson explains in 1978 that:

> Current mass journalism is still largely based on the old, fragmented Newtonian vision—where humans were the dispassionate, objective observer of the world. Even though few people still believe that humans can ever observe the world objectively because they are an interacting part of it, there is still a widespread lag on the part of our mass media in perception of this integral nature of reality. (274) [FOUR]

The mass media diverts us from the development of an new environmental ethic. Ecologists Devall and Sessions note in 1985:

> In technocratic-industrial societies there is overwhelming propaganda and advertising which encourages false needs and destructive desires designed to foster increased production and consumption of goods. Most of this actually diverts us from facing reality in an objective way and from beginning the ''real work'' of spiritual growth and maturity. (68)

Further, the mass media exacerbates environmental problems by overwhelming the voices of those who promote the new environmental ethic. The Science Action Coalition, an environmental group, concludes in 1980: ''Those living simply are starting to speak out, but their power to publicize is minuscule compared to that of the mass media, which depend on complex living habitats for their livelihood'' (Fritch, 6).

The (B) subpoint is the transition of the new view requires access to the mass media. The transition to this new consciousness will only be achieved through media dissemination of information about our environmental needs. Dr. Capra notes in his seminal 1983 work, *The Turning Point:*

> If the new ecological awareness is to become part of our collective consciousness, it will have to be transmitted, eventually, through the mass media. These are presently [THREE] dominated by business, especially in the United States, and their contents are censored accordingly. (409)

Access rights for key environmental groups will make the journalists ecologically aware, though, as Capra explains that:

> Once we succeed in reclaiming our mass media, we can then decide what needs to be communicated and how to use the media effectively to build our future. This means that journalists, too, will change their thinking from fragmentary to holistic modes and develop a new professional ethic based on social and ecological awareness. (409)

Further, the media can change attitudes about our environment today. Communication professors McLeod, Glynn, and Griffin explain in 1987 that "At least in regard to the energy issue, audience exposure to messages specifically dwelling on the topic seems to heighten agenda-setting effects" (34).

Absence of access rights will risk disaster for you. Henderson concludes in 1978 that to address adequately the need for more democratic access to public opinion, as well as to meet its huge responsibilities as our most powerful educational system, mass journalism, both electronic and print, must face up to a greatly enlarged function in a complex, mass society. If it fails, the environmental consequences will be disastrous.[2]

Contention two, the old paradigm must be deemphasized to save the environment. [TWO] We must shift from the old Cartesian paradigm to a new holistic environmental ethic. Professor Miller argued in 1982 that:

> Our survival seems to depend on accepting this holistic world view. In other words, we must change from an agriculturalist society based on humans against nature to a sustainable earth society based on humans and nature. This means that we must cooperate with nature rather than blindly trying to control it. (27)

The (A) subpoint of contention two is holistic awareness promotes environmental understanding. Our position is summarized by philosophy professor Michael Fox in January, 1988 that:

> Truly understanding ecology demands that we see things whole, that we care for the entire biosphere, which can happen only when we abandon a human-centered value system and live in harmony with the world around us. (18)

We further note that holism is essential for solving for our environmental ills. The old Cartesian world view is terribly inadequate. Capra explained in 1983 that:

> We live in a globally interconnected world, in which biological, psychological, social, and environmental phenomena are all interdependent. To describe this world appropriately we need an ecological perspective that the Cartesian world view cannot offer. (19)

[2] "To address adequately the need for more democratic access to public opinion, as well as to meet its huge responsibilities as our most powerful educational system, mass journalism, both electronic and print, must face up to a greatly enlarged function in a complex, mass society. If it fails, the environmental consequences may be disasterous" (275).

The (B) subpoint is that ecological understanding promotes environmental quality. Hope for solutions [ONE] to current environmental ills lies in the new environmental ethic. Devall and Sessions argue in 1985 that:

> If enough citizens cultivate their own ecological consciousness and act through the political process to inform managers and government agencies of the principles of deep ecology, some significant changes in the direction of wise long-range management policies can be achieved. (158)

The Ehrlichs concur in 1987 that "[h]uman beings already have the power to preserve the Earth that everyone wants—they simply have to be willing to exercise it" (252).

Fortunately we note that a transition to a new environmental ethic of deep ecology is feasible. After decades of abusing the environment, Americans are now prepared to [HALF] make a shift in consciousness. Ecology Professor Miller finally argued in 1982. Fortunately, the United States has never been in a better position to make such a transition as long as more of its citizens are willing to become environmentally aware and politically involved.[3]

CROSS-EXAMINATION

DAVID ISRAELITE QUESTIONING LAPHAM

Israelite: You indicate on the (A) subpoint the print analysis, right? The card from Benno Schmidt, correct? Lapham: Yep. Israelite: All right, what specific court case indicating no right of access to the print media? Lapham: You see, Schmidt goes so far beyond that. Through the entire American judicial system since 1919, which 1AC indicates as a holistic type of . . . . Now, let me answer the question so you'll have a better idea what's going on. Since 1919 there has only been one exception where they haven't granted access. That's what Schmidt argues.

Israelite: OK, what's been the latest case? Lapham: The lastest case? I'm not concerned, because I argue the system and not the case. Israelite: Well, I'm concerned. Do you know the latest case? Lapham: I have no idea. Israelite: You have no idea what the latest case is? So, holistically they ruled against rights of access right? Lapham: Yeah.

Israelite: Now did the case ever come to the Supreme Court for environmental access specifically? Lapham: For environmental access specifically, no. Israelite: So the Supreme Court has never ruled specifically on allowing environmental access, right? Lapham: You see, you're missing the link to the resolution, I think which is the (A) subpoint. Israelite: I think I understand the link.

Israelite: (B) subpoint on broadcasting you indicate the Red Lion case, right? Lapham: Yes. Israelite: OK, what was the Red Lion case dealing with, what types of access? Lapham: The Red Lion case dealt with the fairness doctrine. It was more of a right to reply standard, but because that is mutated it also ended up

---

[3]Source indicated.

denying access rights to broadcasting. Israelite: OK, but when the case came before the Supreme Court they dealt with the generic right to access, right? Lapham: No they dealt with the right to reply. Access ideas have mutated since then. Israelite: But the issues put before them had nothing to do with environmental issues, correct? Lapham: The issues before that case did not talk about deep ecology. You are correct.

Israelite: Has any case come to any court talking about specifically environmental rights to access? Lapham: Yes, I mean, that's why I argue observation one for you. Israelite: What cases? Lapham: Not just to kill time but to indicate that it is the autonomy of the press that has caused— Israelite: OK. I'd like to see case titles. Lapham: You see, I don't argue specific case titles. Israelite: I understand you don't argue, that. I'm asking if there ever in history has been a case that dealt specifically with this area. Lapham: Specifically, environmental ecology? Israelite: Yes. Lapham: I don't know if there's a Supreme Court case on the deep ecology. All I know is that in order to justify the resolution you look to whether or not the American judicial system has given too much autonomy.

Israelite: OK. Let's just make this real clear with one last question. Has the court ever ruled uniquely against environmental access? Lapham: Yes. Israelite: When? Lapham: When? I don't know the date. Israelite: What's the case? Lapham: The answer to your question— The court's say there is autonomous press. They don't have to grant rights of access. Israelite: Sir, that's not the question. I'm asking if there has ever been a case— Lapham: If you don't want an answer, why do you keep asking? Israelite: You said there's been a case, and you don't know the date. Do you know the title? Lapham: Yes. [Laughter] Israelite: Could you tell us? Lapham: I mean I honestly, in 1AC, have no knowledge of the title. Israelite: No knowledge of the title? Lapham: I do not in first affirmative read you a single one case that talks about this. Israelite: Does Mark know? Lapham: I give the judicial system. You see, we are arguing the judicial system. I think William Jewell College needs to do the same thing.

Israelite: Now, solvency is dependent upon action taken after the access is used, right? Lapham: Solvency for the ethic? Israelite: Um hum. Lapham: Well, the (B) subpoint in contention two, if you want to— Israelite: Solvency, you have to prove one that the environmental groups will use the right and two that the public will respond, right? That's the burden? Lapham: The burden of solvency first of all does not impact on the resolution. Israelite: In order to prove no ecological harm you have to prove they will use the right and that the people will respond, right? Lapham: No, what you have to do is say that the overemphasis has occurred, because they have allowed the environmentalist not to have the access. When you don't have the access the Cartesian view is perpetuated.

FIRST NEGATIVE CONSTRUCTIVE

RAYMOND ROBERTS, WILLIAM JEWELL COLLEGE

On behalf of the William Jewell College forensics program, I'd like to say that I'm very glad to be here and I'd like to first of all thank our coach, Gina Lane. I'd also like to thank our squad members who put in a lot of work and time and effort and helped, not only themselves, but helped Dave and me a lot. I'd also like to thank all of our friends who have been pushing for us all day and have been helping us, and I'd like to thank David.

Off case observation number one will be in terms of whole resolution. I'll tell you in terms of (A) subpoint standards. One subpoint intent of CEDA is whole resolution. Tomlison explains in 1983: "Another hallmark of CEDA has been to ask debaters to remember the intent of the resolution. These are qualities to be retained by any CEDA round. To ignore them is to reject the basic philosophy of the organization"(2).

Two subpoint under this is the focus of CEDA is on the resolution. *CEDA Yearbook* in 1987 explains. "The debate is limited to determining the truth of the resolution whether it is one value, a fact, or pseudo-policy" (21). In other words we're talking whole-res[olution] here.

(B) subpoint, violations. I will tell you first of all that the affirmative is only talking about ecological impacts and only talking about ecological access. On that level not talking about entirety of resolution. And I think that becomes very clear in cross-examination when David stands up here and tells you "OK, we're talking about access, right? Well, yes, no." What about cases, "Well, yes, no." Again, only a very narrow part of the resolution. On that level, I would say, (C) subpoint that this violation. It's a prima facia issue and should be a voting issue this round.

Observation, the one on top of case. Definitions are fine; we'll go specifically go to the (A) [SEVEN] subpoint on printed press. The printed press is fine, but the only thing I want to go to is the Smith in '87 card. One response on this is going to be, Supreme Court says that it is unmoved on this specific situation. Two subpoint, on that level Supreme Court is not overemphasizing. Three subpoint, means Supreme Court is doing absolutely nothing, I mean affirmative evidence specifically tells you it is unmoved. Clearly would indicate to me no overemphasis.

On the (B) subpoint on broadcasting I will tell you in terms of one subpoint they give us no specific case to environmental rights of access. Two response on that, therefore, there is no condition of overemphasis by broadcasting or by any type of media because there is no specific case dealing with the right to access. I will extend, however, and make a distinction between press and broadcast.

I will tell you in terms of one response press is institutional and speech is individual. Lange explains in '75: "The role of the "autonomous" press is institutional in the sense that the press enjoys a separate constitutional status in the American society, a status quite apart from individual rights of free expression" (81).

Second response under this will be that framer's required and recognized the distinction. Stewart explained in '75:

> Between 1776 and the [SIX] drafting of our Constitution many of the state constitutions contained clauses protecting freedom of the press while at the same time recognizing no general freedom of speech. By including both guarantees in the First Amendment, the Founders quite clearly recognized the distinction between the two. (633-4)

Next response on this is that legality infers different meanings. Nimmer explains in '75:

> As nature abhors a vacuum, the law cannot abide a redundancy. The presumption is strong that language used in a legal instrument, be it a constitution, a statute, or a contract, has meaning, else it would not have been employed. (640)

Fourth response under this is speech is oral and press is written. Nimmer continues:

> It may be surmised that this duality was deemed necessary because the reference to "speech" might be construed to protect only oral expression, so that the reference to in the press was added in order explicitly to protect written expression. (640)

Five subpoint under this broadcasting is not press. One extension on this is going to be from Lewis in '80: [FIVE] "I think whatever rights inure in those clause inure to everybody because I don't think the word 'press,' for the historical reasons I gave, meant the media. I think it meant the product of the printing press" (918). On that level broadcast does not apply. When we look on case broadcast is the major impact of all of the things that they talk about. On that level, not specific.

Observation two, (A) and (B) subpoints, group, please. This is talking about ecological awareness and our need to preserve the ecology. One response here is going to be this is all based on environmental ethic which I will get to later. Two response, the thesis of environmental ethic is that people will not act until there has been some kind of disaster. Three subpoint, on that level the environmental ethic will not change until there is some type of disaster and on that level access will not solve.

Specifically off of the little two card that they talk of destroying the ecology and renewed resources and a shortage. One response, this is talking about destroying the ecology. Two response renewed resources and a shortage. Three response energy crisis in the early '70s when we were talking about running out of fuel and supposedly being the end of the world,—it didn't. On that level, I want to contend that this is the same thing here. Nothing is going to happen and there are going to be no impacts.

Specifically, on the third subpoint on decision rules. Simply an opinion here and I contend that it will not come about. [FOUR]

Contention one, on (A) subpoint talks about press being an old world view and it observes that view. One response to this is not due to the American judicial system, I mean the American judicial system is not telling the press how they should act on environmental issues. This is a press issue not a court issue.

Two subpoint. On that level the problem is not the fault of the system. Specifically, off the Sessions evidence on environmental ethics, apply the environmental ethics standard I give you above.

Specifically on the Scientific Action Group that they said was an environmental group. One, the evidence was from an environmental group. Two, on that level I would contend it is slightly biased towards saying that the environmer needs to be protected.

Specifically, on the (B) subpoint. Group these answers. One response access supposedly equals more information. Two subpoint, we already have access. Three response, access says everyone has a right to get their views across or a right to express their views. Fourth response, however, does not say that they should all have equal amounts of time or equal impacts or equal [THREE] effects. On that level simply because people who support the environment don't get out and are not as involved and the press doesn't give them as much time is not the fault of rights of access and certainly not the fault of the American judicial system.

Contention two. First of all, on the Miller card he says we have to look at the whole world view. I would contend that's probably right, but I would contend in this debate round they should also look at the whole resolution.

On the (A) subpoint, on awareness equals understanding. Group all of these cards. One response says awareness equals understanding. Two response does not say that this understanding is going to do anything for protecting ecology. Third response specifically, off the Miller in '82 card says more critical awareness and political involvement is what is necessary. Fourth response this means people must take action to solve, specifically off of that card. Fifth response is that they don't show that there is any action taken whatsoever. They simply say that they will equal more awareness and more ability. And on that level I am going to contend that there is no solvency here.

I think this should be pretty clear, I mean when they are talking about the narrow example of ecology, [TWO] can't even give us one case that talks specifically about ecology where they have ruled in areas of rights of access I would contend that clearly shows it is not the fault of the American judicial system.

Also, when we're talking about rights of access equal rights of access is not guaranteed, it simply says that each person must be able to view their points. That is fine. Does not indicate that they must have equal amount of time to view those points.

Again on the contention two. They don't say that they are going to solve anything. Indicate some type of involvement and they must prove solvency.

CROSS-EXAMINATION

JOHN LAPHAM QUESTIONING ROBERTS

Lapham: In order to make my partner happy I need to get the evidence you read on the (B) subpoint of observation one. Roberts: Sure. The cards marked and the top card on (C). Lapham: The whole resolution argument indicates that you should search the truth of the resolution, correct? Roberts: Indicates that you should search the truth of the whole resolution.

Lapham: All right. When people like Professor Bile write on whole resolution they're indicating that you must, in order to prove somebody is not whole resolution, set up some kind of standard for induction perhaps or indicate how the negative team is failing to induce their example, right? Roberts: Uh hum. Lapham: What standards for inducement or for induction do you set up in the first negative speech? Lapham: We tell you that when you are only looking at environmental

:thic its not looking at the entire area of rights of access is not— Lapham: In terms of the theoretical argument of whole resolution, what standards for induction do you set up that the affirmative team should meet? I realize that you say we are one example. What standards do you set up to indicate that say we should be six examples, we should be one big example, we should be one small example, or what? Which standards are we using? Roberts: The standards that I think should be used in this round is first of all you should at least be more than one example of the specific area you are talking about, i.e., access.

Lapham: Let me ask you this, which standard was argued in the first negative speech? Roberts: The standard is argued in the first negative speech is that the intent in this whole resolution is the focus should be on the resolution and not on the— Lapham: Which standards on induction were set up? Roberts: The standard of induction that was set up was that you only talk about an example you should be talking about the entire resolution.

Lapham: You say we talk about an example though, but you don't indicate how you prove that an example is whole-resolutional or how an example is not whole-resolutional, right? You simply indicate that an example can or cannot be. What standards do we use to indicate whether or not an example is whole-resolutional? Roberts: Whether or not an example is whole-resolutional or not is whether it encompasses the whole resolution. I mean when you're talking—

Lapham: I'm going in circles here. Let me try to change my question, all right? People at this tournament have to run cases that are whole-resolutional without standing up for eight minutes and reading eight different cases to give significance to the resolution, because there is a case that exists like ours that are the whole resolution. How would you determine through the standards you set up which cases are and which cases aren't? Roberts: Well, at the end of this round we'll find out whether or not your case is. Lapham: How in the first negative speech did we set this up? Roberts: We set it up in the first negative to say we should examine the entirety of the resolution. I contend that by only looking at environmental ethics you are not.

Lapham: OK. (B) subpoint of contention one, your second response is access now. I guess I missed the card or there wasn't one there because I don't seem to remember us having access now. That was why we read observation one on case, right? Roberts: Right. Lapham: There's not access now? Roberts: What I was getting at by that contention is the only thing that is granted under terms of access is that we are allowed to express our viewpoint. Lapham: What's— Roberts: That does not determine that we have to equal— Lapham: What's the substantiation to the second response for the (B) subpoint that says "access now"? Roberts: I didn't read any evidence on that. Lapham: Thank you.

SECOND AFFIRMATIVE CONSTRUCTIVE

MARK WEST, SOUTHERN ILLINOIS UNIVERSITY

As is John, I am very happy to be here as well representing Southern Illinois University and Jeff Bile our coach.

I think that the environmental ethic is a very important thing that we should

strive for, and I think that in a whole-resolutional analysis access prevention k
the Supreme Court and by the entire American judicial system is bad and we
should try to encourage access by certain groups.

I would like to begin with the off case observation on the whole resolution. I
would begin with the (A) subpoint. My first response is that you should have a
reasonable interpretation. If we are arguing that the entire autonomous press is
bad that is certainly examining the entire resolution.

My second argument is that access is an extremely common case and when
examining the topic and when examining general access cases that would be a
common interpretation that the whole resolution and should be allowed.

On the (B) point where they argue violations. They only say we're only talking
about ecological access and therefore we are not whole resolution. My first argument is that this is not true. We are talking about the entire system of preventing
access by the autonomous press. So the violation in and of itself is incorrect.

My second argument is that we are also arguing that free press is bad. It is
a very simple holistic interpretation of the topic and I don't understand the violation. I don't even think it's prima facially a violation because they only say we're
talking about ecological access which is not correct.

My third argument is that the Schmidt evidence we [SEVEN] give you under
observation one says that always the Supreme Court has held there is no right
to access. If that is not a whole resolutional analysis throughout history I don't
know what is.

My fourth argument is that additionally the Smith evidence that we provide
under observation one says that they even go beyond not allowing access and that
they prevent the legislature from allowing access. That is certainly an overactive
American judicial system and a broad interpretation.

The fifth argument is that the Barron evidence, that is not discussed, either
under observation one, says that there is a general trend to the future and how
access will be denied.

The final argument is that if they demand a Supreme Court case that is specific
to the environment I will provide one to determine that specifically that the environment is provided for as well. Goldstein argues in '86 the environment and
how the Supreme Court has prevented environmental access:

> The court's present posture on Freedom of Speech and advertising was defined most
> clearly in 1980 in Central Hudson . . . . The court held the government interest
> in conserving energy, while important, could not overcome the utility's right to free
> speech. (26)

I certainly don't think this should be a voting issue if we have a reasonable
interpretation of this topic under an access level. [SIX]

I would like to go to case now. Dealing with case, the definitions aren't really
responded to. Under the (A) subpoint we discussed the print press. He first argues
that the Supreme Court is unmoved and that the Supreme Court is not overemphasized.

My first argument is that the Smith evidence goes on to say, if they were to continue reading the evidence, that they've gone even beyond not allowing for access and stopped the legislature from providing access. That is quite an intrusion.

My second argument is that this guarantees autonomy of the press and that is free press being bad and that is our general position.

He argues under the (B) subpoint that it is not specific to case and it is not overemphasis. First argument, it is a systems analysis. We are saying that the system has generally prevented access. Secondly, we provide a specific example of how the environment is prevented as well when it comes to access. And finally, I would suggest that this violates the whole resolution, because they're asking us to discuss only one specific case rather than the whole resolution. Certainly they aren't consistent with their own position.

I would now like to argue the five arguments he says about how the press is special. I will argue this off case because there are a number of arguments. He first argues that press is a special case. [FIVE] My first argument is all his evidence says is that the press is being created as an autonomous press. This feeds our position. The press is autonomous, out of government control, and it can act on its own.

He next argues that the Framer's made a distinction. I don't think that Framers intent is what we should necessarily look to. The frst argument is that there was no consensus in 1750 about the meaning of the first amendment. Don Pember argued as a professor at the University of Washington (my home) in 1977:

> There was probably little consensus on the exact meaning of the concept even among the Congressmen who drafted the First Amendment. There is little consensus today on the meaning of the First Amendment. Were it not for the Supreme Court, which periodically defines the First Amendment, the law would be in a terrible state. (51)

The second subpoint is that the constitution does not even reveal how to interpret it. Richard Posner argues in '87:

> Even the decision to read the Constitution narrowly, thereby, "restrain" judicial interpretation, is not a decision that can be read directly from the test. The constitution does not say, "Read me broadly," or, "Read me narrowly."[4] We don't really know how to interpret it.

His third argument says that there is a different meaning. My first argument here is that this evidence only refers to one case and one case of interpretation. This is not necessarily whole resolutional [FOUR] as we discussed. My second argument again, this assumes framers' intent which above I argue we should not necessarily turn to.

His fourth argument says that speech is oral and press is written. My first argument, there is no free press distinction. They fall under the free speech principle. Schauer argued in '82:

---

[4]Source indicated.

We may wish to say that some forms of communication represent a constraint governmental power even greater than that established by a general Free Speec. Principle, but this powerful constraint would properly be keyed as to political content, and not to the presence or absence of a printing press or transmitter. (109)

I.e., there is no distinction when you look at it generally.

The second argument is that the Surpeme Court and the American Bar, for example, have always agreed with this. Don Gillmor and Jerome Barron argued in '74: "The Supreme Court like most of the American bar has engaged in a long standing practice of making interchangeable use of free speech cases in freedom of the press cases and vice versa" (8). Clearly this is not a distinction.

He next argues five subpoint that we're not dealing with broadcast. First argument, this is only dealing with framers' intent. My second argument, the difference is broken down. There is a trend toward making these the same. Baron Carter, Professor of Communication and Lawyer, 81: [THREE] "Once subjected to scrutiny however the attempted differentiation of print and broadcast media breaks down in a number of ways" (49). There is not really this distinction.

Continuing on with case. Contention one, observation one we discussed criteria. They say that we are only dealing with the ethic and ethic only assumes we wait 'til a disaster happens. This is blatantly false. The first argument, you do not wait until a disaster happens when we are discussing the ethic. We are advocating that you move toward a holistic interpretation saying that man is as important as nature. This is a blatant assertion that is completely unsubstantiated in holistic thought.

He argues then under the (B) subpoint that under ecology that in 1970s this did not happen, and this is only dealing with ecology. My first argument is that this 1970s assertion does not take out our position, it only shows that we are building toward an ecological problem.

Second argument, please extend the evidence. The Rifkin in 1980 evidence under the (A) subpoint indicates that the earth is at risk. The (B) one subpoint from Ehrlich 1980 says that human survival is at stake. The very beginning of our case evidence from the International Task Force says in 1980 there is the greatest threat of danger we see. Extend as well that the status quo is destroying this and the decision rule is 1988. He says it's one opinion, I think [TWO] it's a good opinion.

Contention one. He says it's not the American judicial system. Our position is simply here is that it is the American judicial system because they have created an autonomous press.

Under the (A) subpoint the media is the old paradigm. He says not the system but please extend the media encourages the Cartesian paradigm they stop the ethic and that they prevent and encourage the environmental problems. He says that this evidence is biased, I think it's good it is biased, these people are shocking us into realizing that the environment is at risk.

The (B) subpoint says that you need access. I would argue first of all, we do not necessarily advocate there is equal time for everyone. We are saying that the environmentalists should get on the air and the autonomous press prevents it.

Second subpoint is that the media denies us access presently. Please extend. The Capra evidence says that only access will solve. Access, Capra in 1983 argues, that this is the most important thing to solve. And the McLeod evidence shows you studies indicating that it would indeed solve the problem.

Contention two argues that the old paradigm is bad. He says whole resolution must be examined. I think we are examining the whole resolution. He says that it's only one case [ONE] but it certainly is an examination of the whole resolution from an access level.

He says we don't show that they actually can solve. My first argument is that the studies indicate that they do solve. He ignores the McLeod evidence on case. Second argument is that studies prove that there is an actual attitude effect. Evidence comes from Fortner and Lyon, 1985: "A comparison of test scores between the treatment group and the control group and within the treatment group indicates that people can learn from an environmental documentary on television" (18).

The next subpoint is that studies prove behavioral change occurs. Professor McLeod again in 1987: "Energy conserving role models from a local cable television programs produced some long-term [HALF] changes in energy conservation behavior among viewers participating in field experiments" (30).

The next subpoint is that the American public would adopt the ethic with this information. The Science Action Coalition again in '80:

> People want to get involved [in environmental issues] but often don't know how. However, a hidden obstacle to the lack of urgency is procedures for going out to others, sharing with them, and joining forces with socially oriented citizens. (Fritch, 218)

He next argues that it is a political necessity. No the evidence says you need to adopt the ethic. Finally, he says you need action to solve. The evidence I give you says studies show people will act. Please extend the (A) to the (B) subpoints this is the best way to preserve the environment.

CROSS-EXAMINATION

RAY ROBERTS QUESTIONING WEST

Roberts: OK. First thing I need is Central Hudson card that you read me which is your environmental ethic case. West: It's not our environmental ethic case. Roberts: Well, I mean the case that talks about the environment.

Roberts: OK, now within the context of that card, it said that they ruled on speech and advertising in this case, right? West: Right. Roberts: What does that have to do with press? West: Speech and press are the same. Roberts: OK. Speech and press are the same thing. They ruled on advertising. What does that have to do with press. West: That's speech. Roberts: That's part of speech. So you're going to contend that commercial speech is press. It's all First Amendment. West: Right, you have to understand, I don't care about this piece of evidence that I read to you. I just did it to satisfy the need to have a Supreme Court case. Roberts:

OK. West: That is not our position. Our position is that the media prevents environmental access and the Supreme Court and the American judicial system encourage an autonomous press. So I don't care about this piece of evidence.

Roberts: OK, all right. So the problem isn't actually the court system, the problem is that they've created an autonomous— West: The problem is certainly the court system. The court system has overemphasized a free press by creating an autonomous press that doesn't allow access.

Roberts: OK, so now then press is autonomous. Is it the fault of the Supreme Court that the editors in those papers will not print environmental ethic or will not run environmental PSAs or whatever the case may be? Is that the fault of the Court? West: Well, now we're getting into sort of a debate problem, and that is if you establish an initial link and then other teams require you to prove this link throughout every single level until you get to your impact the result is silly argumentation, because there are incredible burdens of proof that we cannot— Roberts: Could it also result in the fact that the link is simply not there? [Laughter] West: No, because the link— Roberts: Does that have anything to do with it? West: That has nothing to do with it. Roberts: OK. OK. West: Can I answer your question? Roberts: Yeah. I'd be glad to hear that.

West: I don't know why. We debated you guys on access cases before, and you didn't seem to have a problem with it. The argument is that the resolution must be proven true. Did the Supreme Court and the American judicial system overemphasize the free press? They did by creating an autonomous press. The result of that is that they don't allow access to environmentalists.

Roberts: OK. That's fine. Now then, let's just stop with autonomous press. What is the harm from autonomous press? Is there a harm from autonomous press? West: They don't let environmentalists on TV. Roberts: OK. So now then, the only reason there is an overemphasis is because there is a harm, i.e., that environmental ethic not being allowed, correct? West: That's kind of the way the debate has worked all this year.

OK, cool. Now who's fault is it that they're not allowing that environmental ethic? AJS? West: The judicial system. Roberts: Judical system, why? West: Because they've created this autonomous press. [Laughter] Roberts: Now just a minute ago you told me there was no problem with autonomous press except that the fact that they wouldn't allow environmental ethics on there. Now is AJS telling them that they can't have an environmental ethic on there, or are they simply saying you're autonomous, you do whatever? West: I have no idea how this is relevant to this debate.

Roberts: OK, all right, that is fine. Third subpoint off of contention two (A) says behavior will change long term, right? Correct? West: I mean are you saying we can't argue an impact to a case? That's silly. Roberts: I have a question. '88 brink, right? West: The brink is subjective. A brink just means they have to start trying now. Roberts: Oh, just start trying now, so there's really no threshold, here, right? West: No, the threshold is thirty years, and that's the evidence you drop on the top of case. Roberts: OK, cool.

SECOND NEGATIVE CONSTRUCTIVE[5]

DAVID ISRAELITE, WILLIAM JEWELL COLLEGE

Last year when Ray and I watched the final round of this tournament, it was our dream that perhaps someday we could be here, and this is a dream come true. I would also like to thank our coach Gina Lane and the members of our squad who helped us a great deal. Raymond as well and I'd like to thank my parents.

Off case observation number one. Resolutional links. (A) subpoint is standards. First subpoint is, the word "has" in the resolution equals direct action. Second subpoint is, the Supreme Court will only rule on issues presented before it. Third subpoint, typicality. For the affirmative to be typical, they must deal with all cases and aspects of access. Final subpoint, therefore, you cannot deal with effects. For example, when the Supreme Court approved abortions, they did not approve all abortions.

(B) subpoint is links to my VO. If I can prove that when the Supreme Court or any court ruled on access they ruled correctly, or that the courts have never ruled on environmental access when they ruled on general access, then the affirmative is only left with effects and that's illegitimate.

(C) subpoint is impacts. Impacts in terms of solvency. Because the courts have not dealt with environmental access, it's not their fault. This now becomes a solvency press.

Second observation, and it is in terms of Central Hudson. The sole purpose of this observation is to demonstrate that the court has not ruled on environmental access. First, this was not an access case, therefore it's not the court's responsibility. Second response, it wasn't even an environmental case. Third subpoint is Posadas v Puerto Rico updates Hudson. This is from the *Hastings Constitutional Law Quarterly* 1987: "Indeed, the Court most recently applied the Hudson analysis in Posadas De Puerto Rico Associates vs. Tourism Company of Puerto Rico" (Nienow 878). Four subpoint, this equals protection.

Final subpoint is Posadas is a trend towards full protection. *Connecticut Law Review* in '87:. "The doctrine (in Posadas) has since matured into a rule affording nearly full first amendment protection to truthful commercial speech" (Almond, 125).

Please now go to off case value objection. Public access won't do any good. First subpoint is, access rights won't increase the flow of information. Baker in 1980: "Even if greater diversity is desirable, it is doubtful that access rights would significantly increase the flow of diverse information or viewpoints" (860). Second subpoint, wouldn't help society. Baker again in '80: "Assuming that the technical facilities necessary to handle public access requests existed and anyone

---

[5]Due to technological problems, the first six minutes of the second negative constructive speech were not recorded. The information in brackets reflects the evidence, analysis and arguments offered by Mr. Israelite. The speech was reconstructed as accurately as possible based on the editor's conversations with participants and judges. The evidence was verified based on the briefs given to the editor after the final round.

who wished to print or broadcast a message could do so, society could gain litt▓ if few people listened" (860).

Next response is kills market place of ideas. Stanley Ingber, in 1984:

> In addition to being based on a naive belief of a "true" or "best" result, this reform approach also poses the danger of presenting the public with more information than it realistically can assimilate. Consequently, rather than guaranteeing all perspectives an opportunity for success, the equal access for viewpoints approach may only make the public perceive the marketplace as an arena full of nothing but "noise", and thereby decrease the public's willingness to reassess opinions it already holds. (53)

Four subpoint is too ambiguous. Ingber again in 84:

> Both forms of equal access, that which focuses on individuals as well as that which focuses on viewpoints, suffer additional infirmities. Both define ambiguously what must be equalized. For example, should a viewpoint indifferently held by a few receive access equal to that of a perspective passionately held by many? If so scarce resources may be wasted on trivial ideas, and the marketplace may reflect inaccurately the strength, and possibly the values of positions competing for adherents. (53-4)

Next subpoint and that is it actually increases marketplace of ideas bias. Ingber tells us:

> If the first amendment requires that unpopular ideas be given an opportunity to defeat established dogma, government officials should not be allowed to determine the adequacy of access. In short, adequate access proposals almost inevitably further the status quo market bias. (52-3)

Six subpoint is it's impossible to work. Ingber states:

> Regardless of equal access values in which the public have been indoctrinated or socialized will still prevail, and speakers with stature, influence, and skill will still be more persuasive than those without. Because equal access still allows variance in the opportunity to influence among differing individuals or viewpoints, equal opportunity to influence can be attained only through affirmative action such as giving that least popular or least able speaker the most access to the marketplace. (54)

My next subpoint will be seven, will not promote equal influence. Ingber in '84:

> Furthermore, guaranteeing such equal access is virtually impossible without an intricate and extensive leveling system of public subsidies and spending restrictions. Even if government officials could design and properly administer such a system, there is no guarantee that an opportunity for equal access would create an opportunity for equal influence. (54)

Next subpoint, causes government manipulation. Ingber in 84: "Second, such a process might invite manipulation by the very governmental bureaucrats apointed to insure access'' (56). Next argument will be, cannot solve for bias. Ingber tells us in '84 that:

> Thus, overcoming the marked bias in favor of the statured communicator may create an even more unfortunate result: it may require us to be confronted most by those who may, in fact, have the least of significance to say. Equal access reform proposals, therefore, either prove insufficient to correct marketplace bias, or create problems equal to those they correct. Additionally, all market reform proposals pose the danger of unacceptable governmental interference with the market. (55)

My next extension is going to be that this will actually equal a chill to the press. If you will allow access you actually get a clouding of issues and you don't get anywhere. Ingber tells us in '84 that: ''First if government requires media to bear the cost of providing access for those opposing a viewpoint that the media have presented, media managers may simply choose not to present controversial issues'' (56). I.e., they just won't talk about it at all.

Next subpoint and that is that this will actually snowball to governmental control and again this will flip everything they give you on case. Ingber tell us in 1984:

> Finally, governmental interference may escalate from access regulation to more dubious types of governmental control. For example, giving government administrators discretion in access decisions risks the use of administrative machinery to force the media to conform to official positions. (56-57)

Exactly, if you have a generic right of access that's going to mean that the government actually expresses their views more than anyone else. And to that extent you just increase the bias.

Next subpoint, and that is going to be that this will actually violate newspaper individuality and that's why the court ruled against it. There are simply too many bad things to go with it. Lockhart tells us in 1987 that:

> I would also rely on that part of Tornillo . . . holding that a forced right of reply violates a newspaper's right to be free from forced [ONE] dissemination of view it would not voluntarily disseminate, just as we held that Maynard must be free from being forced by the State to disseminate views with which he disagreed. (PG&E vs CPUC 16)

Now I know what they're going to do, and I'm going to make a little preempt on the bottom of this. They're going to do one of two things. Claim one that the problem is the monopolies, or secondly, we have a link because they actually caused it. If they're going to claim a monopoly harm, I'm going to contend the courts didn't do that, because the problem is from the monopolies, not the courts. If they're going to claim that the courts are responsible for this, I'm going to contend that if you're going to hold the Court responsible for destroying the world then the nation that ruled on those issues.

At that point, if all they rule on is what comes before them and all that comes before them is political issues and then they never rule on environmental control then it is not their fault we don't have environmental access. That's why the Court has ruled in this favor.

If a case came to the Supreme Court and said we need environmental access it might have ruled differently, if they saw the great harm. But it is not their fault that the issue of environmental access never came to them. In light of that you have no resolutional link and you will vote negative.

CROSS-EXAMINATION

MARK WEST QUESTIONING ISRAELITE

West: We can't look at the results of access, right? Israelite: Only direct results, not secondary results. West: What is the difference between a direct result and secondary result? Israelite: Direct result is if you want to talk about rights of access, you look directly at what they did; not secondary effects. West: You just repeated that. What is the difference? Israelite: The court never ruled against environmental access. What you're claiming is that they ruled against generic access if you don't have generic access then you don't have environmental access and therefore the Court is responsible.

West: The top level is American judicial system. Israelite: Yeah. West: I just want to get a little image here so we understand what we are talking about. First we have the American judicial system. It does something to access. It stops access, right? Israelite: O.K. West: So that's one to two. Three is the result of that stopping of access, right? Israelite: Not necessarily. West: Why not? Why doesn't the result— Israelite: Because when the Supreme Court when, the first step from one to two, when the Supreme Court stopped access, if you're going to hold them responsible for what they voted on or what they decided, you must look at the values and the ideas that were put before them to decide on. West: OK. You're jumping the gun. I'm not really talking about specifics, I'm just saying generally, like when humans think, you have the American judicial system which ,causes an absence of access which has results, right? I mean that's the way normal people think right? I mean is that— Israelite: Normal people? If you're going to look at the link of the rights of access—

West: Is there such a thing as a result of an absence of access? Is there a concept in the world like that? Israelite: Sure. West: OK. You discussed some of them. Your first one is there is no increase in information flow as a result of an absence of access. Israelite: Correct. West: You next argue there is not a help to society as a result of an absence of access, right? Israelite: Right. West: You next argue there is a killing of a marketplace of ideas as a result of an absence of access, right? Israelite: Yeah. You don't have to read each point. West: I would like to. Your next argument is that there is information overload as as a result of an absence of access, right? Israelite: Yes. West: Your next argument is, well, too ambiguous is a different point. Well, I think I made my point. How come we can't talk about the results of an absence of access, i.e., the environmental ethic, but you can talk about the results? Israelite: Oh, you can talk about them all you want, but they're not .going to vote for you, because there's no resolutional links. West: So, this is not. What you just make. The arguments, these twenty points you just made are not warrants against the resolution, is what you're saying? Israelite: They are warrants, all they're doing— I don't even want these weighed as VO's. That's not the purpose. West: Why do you read these? Israelite: The purpose. I read these to establish that when the Court ruled against access they did so correctly and they are not to be held responsible. West: So these are warrants then. Israelite: No. West: No? Then what are they? Just a way to make sound [Laughter] Israelite: I mean not in terms of impacts. West: I can't believe that we are not allowed to look at impacts. I guess that's what— Israelite: You are allowed to look at impacts that the American judicial system has caused. West: I only have thirty seconds. Israelite: Not impacts they didn't cause.

West: I only have thirty seconds. Final question. This is from Ingber right, I mean virtually the majority? Israelite: No. Um, first card and second card are not— West: All of that— Israelite: Um, fourteen, fifteen, sixteen card are not. West: And all of that refers to equal access, right? Israelite: Some of the cards do, some of them are theoretical access, although he talks about equal rights a lot of his theories apply to all access, equal access.

FIRST NEGATIVE REBUTTAL

RAYMOND ROBERTS, WILLIAM JEWELL COLLEGE

Off of whole res[olution] on (A) subpoint, standards. He says we have to look to the intent of the resolution and he says his access case is looking at the entirety of access. I will say that is fine but when we show you that they do not look at all access, then you can vote on whole res[olution] and that should be clear.

Specifically, his next two responses off the (B) subpoint on violation, group those. I'll tell you in terms of one subpoint, system denied equals no access. Two response, then he says that the free press is bad. Three response, on that level American judicial system is not responsible because they don't control what the free press does, they allow a free press but they don't control what they do, i.e., they don't say that you have to allow someone to print environmental ethic ideas in your content.

Specifically, off the three and four cards where he talks about Schmidt card and the Smith card. One response, still says that they are unmoved specifically on environmental issues which feeds the whole resolution argument we give.

Fifth response and sixth response [FOUR] on trend and demand. One response, gives Central Hudson case ruling for here. Two response this was not an access case. Three response, not an environmental ethic case. Four response, long after the environmental problem ever came about. I mean they give us evidence that this is an environmental problem, we deny access and this is bad and then they give us the one case that they link to Central Hudson which is after all this has ever happened which again indicates that there's no American judicial system link. Fifth response, breeds no AJS link.

Case. (A) subpoint. Extends the Smith in '87 evidence that says it goes beyond and then says that this created an autonomous press. One response, did not deal with environmental ethic, and two response, the Supreme Court has been unmoved on the environmental issues. On that level, no AJS link.

Specifically, off the third response where he says systems prevent. One response, what has happened is not bad. Two response, no access is not bad unless it is specific to environmental access, and he grants me that in cross-examination. Three response, on that level what the Supreme Court did was not bad and had no impact. Fourth response, means that there is no overemphasis by American judicial system in this round and you vote negative.

(B) subpoint on broadcasting. Specifically, I want extended my first response that says that there is no specific environmental rights to access and that has not been denied.

Specifically off his first response, says autonomous [THREE] press has acted on its own. One response, that means autonomous press is bad and that is horrible if our resolution was that the autonomous press had overemphasized the freedom of the press, but it is not, it is American judicial system. Two response, on that level not American judicial system's fault.

Specifically next two responses. Says no consensus for framers and Supreme Court not interpret. One response, two conclusions and two separate clauses we have in the Constitution not one. On that level I would contend they are separate and distinct.

Specifically off of my third response he says legislative differences. He says one, evidence is only talking about in one case and assumes framers intent. One response, all the evidence says is that its senseless for us to be redundant whether it be in a Constitution or in a contract or whatever. Two response, when we have two separate clauses, i.e., speech and press if they were meant to be the same they would have been included as one and the same and on that level there's no redundancy.

Specifically off his next response off my fourth, group those two. One response does not deny that there's a distinction between oral and written and that is all I need.

Fifth response, on broadcasting not press. He says it is only framers' intent and the difference is broken down. One response, this is not talking about framers' intent this is talking about [TWO] how another proceeds it. Two response, says the distinction is still there and three response, broadcasting is not part of the press on that level.

Observation two. Specifically, he says we don't wait until the environmental ethic has occurred or until a disaster has occurred we move on holistic. One, I will tell you in terms of first subpoint here that people simply don't believe something until they are convinced. Two, response, the oil spill on the Ohio river earlier this year was a prime example of that. I mean when that happened people became concerned, i.e., a disaster brought them to movement. It wasn't the added press coverage that brought them to movement but was the disaster itself.

Three response, on that level means that that brought attention. Fourth response, it allows environmental to have access. I mean this is a clear indication where there was an environmental problem and they got access, I mean for three days, four days, nothing on the news was there except for this environmental problem which would deny that there's no access to environmental information.

Two subpoint off of the environment [ONE] One response says this assumes that this is not taking out and we're building toward. One response, if we are building toward. Two response, that means that this happened before the case which restricted access which is, three response, means this feeds that there is no American judicial system link. I mean he tells me perfectly this is building toward. We are moving forward on this level of having the problem with environmental ethic. But then he gives me a case that's after all this has already started, which would indicate that the American judical system was not responsible. Again goes back to a time as press being responsible.

Contention one. Cross-examination. We find out that it's not bad autonomous press. Only thing is that autonomous press does is environmental ethic. On that level you have no American judical system link.

Off of Contention two. The only thing I need here is that they have to show behavior is going to change. I mean they say thrity years down the road we're going to have a problem. Let's see that that behavior will change within that thirty year period. I think it's pretty clear that there's no link to American judicial system. Fault of problem here is autonomous press. On that level you vote negative.

FIRST AFFIRMATIVE REBUTTAL

JOHN LAPHAM, SOUTHERN ILLINOIS UNIVERSITY

The (A) subpoint of observation one on case. He says it violates whole resolution. But first subpoint, we provided whole resolution by offering you a single case. The second subpoint is that we extend the (A) subpoint evidence. It gives you historical analysis, future preparation, and a guarantees of autonomy, all which is systems analysis we support the American judical system for the resolutional rquirements.

Please go to his last argument on observation one. He says doesn't mean Supreme Court is not bad and access equals environment not bad. The first subpoint is that both squads have certainly argued pejorative cases this year which require you to look to effects.

Second subpoint they have yet to justify you today why you do not look to effects. And certainly to evaluate the resolution properly in a value context you must do that as argued by Mark in the second affirmative speech. Please go to the (B) subpoint he says that no specific cases. The first subpoint is that I'm glad we offer you no specific cases. I hate to violate whole resolution as I support the authors who write this. The second subpoint is the fault of the link on observation one which clearly guarantees autonomy for you.

He next says there are two clauses of the Constitution and there are two clauses and they don't want to be redundant. The first subpoint is I'd ask you to extend the evidence in the second affirmative. It says the framers themselves had no consensus. [FOUR] Certainly clauses in a sentence don't prove this for you. The second response is that the Constitution then also does not reveal interpretation. And because they're both included under the First Amendment they are a single issue. You evaluate the single issue. Furthermore, please extend the evidence at the bottom of the (B) subpoint that says the distinction has to last, from Schauer in '84.

He combines the answers in observation one that there's no framers' intent. The first subpoint is, the evidence was specific to framer's intent. The second response is, because we are now presently evaluating the American judicial system you have to see that technology has advanced and therefore you need to look to broadcasting.

Observation two on criteria. He says people don't believe. The first subpoint is waiting is bad. That's the criteria, the decision rule in 2AC. The second response, you get the ethic from the (B) subpoint in contention one which indicates people will believe you when you go to the mass media. Third subpoint is, don't look for piecemeal solvency, instead look to the fact you can solve the right through the media.

Please go to (B) subpoint on observation two. He says build equals happened before. But, first subpoint is the system requires whole resolution. Second, subpoint, whole resolution is proven in observation one (A) and (B) subpoint and I would argue by the negative team in terms of being [THREE] the whole resolution argument.

Contention one. He says autonomous equals environment. But, first, subpoint though is the affirmative—please extend the evidence media equals status quo. You divert solvency, you exacerbate the problem. The next subpoint then is overemphasis is proven by the (A) subpoint which clearly allows the American judicial system to do this.

Please also extend that you have guaranteed autonomy.

I would ask you to go to the (B) subpoint of contention one. He doesn't argue this. It indicates you do not allocate time. Media denies presently.

Contention two. He says show change. Well, I think Mark did an excellent job of doing this. He indicates studies will solve. Attitudes are effected. Behavior will change and we could adopt the ethical information. The only obstacle now is the media.

Please go to whole resolution The first subpoint on whole resolution, he says that's fine but you need whole res[olution] But, first subpoint is, we are all access. Second subpoint, we choose one case I mean we choose one impact in order to justify why the court is forcing the system of autonomy is bad. The third subpoint is our impact is justified as it is the largest one.

Please go to where he said AJS is not responsible. First subpoint, I've argued this before on case and above. He says the court is unmoved. The first subpoint, [TWO] the Schmidt evidence indicates they always rule this way. The final subpoint indicates they go beyond and preclude legislation.

Please go to the last answer. He say there's no environmental case. The first subpoint, that's because we justify the system. The second response is, communication is a speech and the autonomous press removes it. And the final response is it's not a voting issue, argued by the second affirmative speech, and not refuted by the first negative rebuttalist.

Please go to the first observation by the second negative. I will argue first subpoint and that is they preclude affirmative obligation with the AJS overemphasis. The second response is all cases since 1919 was the evidence in the first affirmative. Third subpoint is, the environment is the greatest threat and that is not argued in 1NC. The fourth subpoint then is that you look to the effect, because the system has continuously denied this. That's the evidence given in observation one.

Please go to solvency on the 2NC observation one. My first subpoint is that you need to preclude legislation in solvency. The second subpoint is this is direct from the court. Precludes affirmative obligation. Cross-[ONE]examination also shows direct results are legitimate and you must vote for these.

Observation two. My first subpoint is it indicates access does not because of the environment. The second response is the example is ruling on the environment to prove observation one is true and to prove why the American judicial system causes harm. The third subpoint is Posadas is one case. Certainly violates whole resolution. The final subpoint is commercial speech is not protected as it perpetuates Cartesian viewpoint.

Please go to value objection. The first subpoint is that they dejustify the resolution. The second subpoint is the court is justified and then they give the overemphasis because they have this definition which clearly decreases the marketplace of ideas.

Please go to the beginning of his argument. The first subpoint is that they ignore contention one which gives the only mass media solvency. The second response is when he applies the Glenn evidence here which indicates they can change. [HALF] (C) subpoint. One, Ingber says time is all equal ideas. Second response, affirmative doesn't advocate all equal ideas. I would argue next subpoint and that is government chill will be fine because right now the press is Cartesian viewpoint. There is no snowball because we indicate private censorship is far worse, and this comes from Boyan in '74: "None of these rules requires any licensee to offer any time to anybody for any office, or to editorialize on any issue or to deal with any controversy. No one may use a licensee's facilities to reply to silence" (144).

Final subpoint is it is not a warrant against access. Jacklin in '81: "Given the preferences and power of the broadcast industry, the government has usually opted for no regulation. The fairness doctrine is rarely enforced" (279). And that is time and I would argue the value objection does not stand alone.

SECOND NEGATIVE REBUTTAL

DAVID ISRAELITE, WILLIAM JEWELL COLLEGE

1AR hands me the round when he mishandles the link off case. I'm on whole resolution. One response, he indicates that we are typical of access. At that point he grants the standard that they must be typical of access. At that point if they are typical of access throw the whole resolution out. They still have the burden of being typical access and that is exactly what off case is. That is all that I want from this. Especially down at Central Hudson. All I want to say here is that was not abandoned that is not typical.

I am now off case. This is where William Jewell is going to win this round. He mishandles this. In terms of standards please group his four responses. One response, and that is, the system does not deny. Second response, you do not look at impacts at this point because I am talking about a resolutional link, I am not talking about weighing the impacts at this point.

I am on (A) one subpoint. Has equals direct action—granted. Two subpoint, the court will only rule on the issue before it—granted. Three subpoint, to be typical therefore you have to deal with all access—granted. Four subpoint, therefore you cannot deal with effects—granted. I don't care if you like it, I don't care if you believe it he should have dealt with it and he dropped it, at that point I want no new responses.

If I can prove to you that holistically access is a bad idea I absolutely win this round because [FOUR] he does not deny that they have to be direct action. He does deny that they have to be typical, and he did not deny that the courts only rule on issues before it, if they do not have the issue of environmental ethic before them it is not their fault. He mishandles this so badly that it means we win the round.

I'm now on the off case or second observation on Hudson. My first response, is going to be this is not an access case, therefore it is not their responsibility. Second response, it's not an environmental case, it's talking about specifically just commercial speech again they're not being typical of the case. Third response indicates Posadas is a trend away and therefore we indicate trend is for full protection which turns everything. And fourth response, this is not whole res[olution] for us because we do not have to meet that burden.

I'm now on the VO. This round is won here. Because if I can prove that the court ruled correctly, they do not deal with environmental impact, or its a good idea not to have access then vote negative. In terms of the first two responses. I have one response, this does not deny theory above and that will take that out. On his second response, please group his two responses. My one response is contention one does not take this out either because it does not talk about impact in terms of environment.

On (C) subpoint please group the responses. You know, one response is *Miami Herald* and Red Lion the cases that the Court ruled on did talk about equal access and therefore the access cases talked about what [THREE] Ingber's theory talks about.

Now, I have a lot of responses that I give out telling you why I think access is bad. I think those are untouched. I would ask you to extend one, it does not increase information. Two it does not help. Third, it kills MOI. Four, it's bad. Fifth point, it increases bias. Six point, it won't work. Seven, eight, nine, extend it all because it is not touched. I want no cross applications, because 1AR doesn't do it. I want no 2AR answers on this, because it is not extended. And I will extend proving that access, generally is a bad idea.

First subpoint, public will not get information. Ingber tells us in '84:

> By equalizing access for all view points, these reformers seek to neutralize the advantages of "well-packaged" and frequently offered messages. In addition to being based on a naive belief in the existence of a "true" or "best" result, this reform approach also poses the danger of presenting the public with more information than it realistically can assimilate. (53)

Next subpoint and that is that it actually deters press freedom. Alpert tells us in '73:

The newspaper's right to print what it wishes is protected by the First Amendment. If a newspaper is required, under the threat of the sanctions of the Florida Statute, to provide free space which it does not wish to provide and print words which it does not wish to print, it may very well be deterred from printing words it does wish to print. This chilling effect clearly destroys freedom of the press in its most basic sense. (25)

Next subpoint and that is, this will harm First Amendment. Alpert tells us in '73: "Since compulsory printing inhibits freedom of the press at least as much as civil damages, clearly, freedom of the press prohibits any legislatively required right to reply, particularly so when libel is not involved" (29).

Next subpoint and that is going to be, inconsistent with freedom of the press goals. [TWO] Paul and Bealey, '73:

Though the issue in this case is not a technical one of state action. The issue is whether the government can tell the newspapers what to print. Professor Emerson has pinpointed the reason that the Florida statute is unconstitutional, it means that the government can tell the newspapers that the newspapers can be forced to print material they don't want to print. This is the very opposite of freedom of the press. (5)

You know, my extensions are not touched and I am going to contend that the Court ruled on this and they ruled correctly. He punts the above standards. That's the standard you have to use. They have to show a direct link, they have to show that they ruled on the issues, and they have to show that the resolution actually causes, and they can not do that, because I prove to you holistically access is a bad idea.

In terms of case side, you know they may be right. Environmental access may be a good idea, you might want to have it, so what. You may kill thousands of people if you don't have it, so what. It is not the fault of the American judicial system.

In terms of the (A) subpoint. [ONE] He indicates that we always talk about these kinds of harms, why change now? You know this is finals so lets just set the resolution straight here.

(B) subpoint on broadcasting. All I want to extend here is that there are no specific cases, therefore no link.

On the two subpoint on the framers' intent and that stuff. All I want to extend here is that they still continue and they don't change their position and most importantly even if it's not it should be. To that extent, even if you don't have a difference there should be a difference.

Observation two on rules. I want one response here that they do not meet the burden of balancing and down below I want to extend it here that it, that observation one (A) and (B) do not pose independent harms.

You know, contention one and contention two don't matter, you don't look to the impacts until you first look at prima facia burdens and if they can't prove a link to the resolution then you don't even go to looking at dead people on the flow. At that point what you will first go to when voting on this round is first go to my standards off case and what they have to prove. Look at the drops. Then you apply those standards on my VO and if you feel they don't show a direct link, if you feel the court has not ruled on this issue, or if you feel they are not typical of the whole resolution in terms of access, then you will vote negative and you will vote for William Jewell.

SECOND AFFIRMATIVE REBUTTAL

MARK WEST, SOUTHERN ILLINOIS UNIVERSITY

I've had a great time at this tournament, and I've had quite a few rounds, and it's been very tiring, and this one seemed kind of scary until the last speech, but I think there's an important burden of rejoinder, and John makes some good arguments that I talk about in cross-examination. This enormous dump that he makes about this value objection is not relevant in this debate. Ingber is not talking about access, he's talking about equal access. And the position is that equal access requires a response and it requires an enforced diversity of ideas. We are not advocating an enforced diversity of ideas, we are saying that you should allow environmental people access and that is the impact of our case. One group, not people responding to each other, not diverse ideas, we think that's bad, because it crowds out environment.

I will discuss specifically this value objection now. All I want to respond—He says that we do not deal with the above stuff, but I will talk about the bad effects above. He says contention one is not beat. But I would suggest that impact. You know, look at the biggest impact in the round. He says that the reason. He reads extension evidence and the results in a danger to ideas. This assumes equal access, which is Ingber, which is not responded to. That is John's third argument in 1AR, he does not meet his burden of rejoinder, please extend it. All of this evidence assumes that.

He next argues that it destroys freedom of the press, [FOUR] harms the First Amendment, and it is inconsistent with freedom of the press goals. Grant. That is our position in this debate, that the freedom of the press is bad, the American judicial system has created an autonomous freedom of the press that does not allow access to environmental groups. You should be able to look at the effects of certain things. And I will now go to whole resolution in order to justify that argument.

He only extends on whole resolution that it must be typical of access. My argument first of all, is that, again, he doesn't meet his burden of rejoinder. Please extend the third argument from 1AR that says impacts are justified. You look at the largest impact when you are discussing access.

My second argument is that there is no warrant in this debate against access. The warrant that is presented against access is not relevant as he agrees in his second negative rebuttal. It is dealing with equal access, which is not access, that is right to respond, that is fairness doctrine, which is different, as John argues. Which means that the value objection is not relevant and [FOUR] there is no warrant against our case. Our case now becomes the largest example of access and you look at our impacts, which he fluffs off in the 1NR and he fluffs off in the 2NR. You cannot do that when you are examining the third argument from 1AR on whole resolution that the impact is justified as far as the largest impact goes. I think this is very clear.

I'm now on the two resolutional arguments that he presents as far as resolutional standards. He wants to extend that the system is not justified and you do not look at effects, etc. First argument, effects are OK. Because as he's arguing, as I think I clearly indicate in cross-examination, this whole twenty point argument that he presents are all the effects of access. He justifies this contextually by arguing effects himself.

Secondly, you have to look at effects now, because the only argument presented by the negative is not relevant in this debate, because it is equal access, it is right to respond, which is not access, which is our case.

He next says that the system does not justify, I think you should look at the whole resolution, when I get back to case and discuss the top of [TWO] it.

He argues observation two, you don't look at specific cases, that's true, you shouldn't, you should look at the system and you should look at the top of case, that's where I am now.

He only wants to respond that there are no independent harms. Please extend the 1AC and the 1AR. He argues that they are violating whole resolution by requiring a look at each case. Extend the (A) subpoint that the Schmidt evidence, that they have always ruled against general access, the Smith evidence that they have stopped a legislature from ruling on general access, and the Schmidt evidence that this will increase in the future. The (B) subpoint also says that broadcast in 1AC the Barron evidence on the bottom says there is a trend toward a general movement against access. What you have is a general interpretation by the affirmative saying that general access is being ruled against by the American judicial system, and general access is good because this one group of people, the environmentalists want to get on, and they can't get on, and they should be able to get on without any kind of equal access, right to reply, fairness doctrine, [ONE] and stuff like that. They should be able to get on and have their say, and that is the first contention.

As far as these arguments on free speech and free press being the same, he basically collapses out of this and says that it should be the framers' intent. I think we read you better evidence saying framers' intent is not really true and not really, you know, relevant. This is not relevant to this debate anyway.

I am now on observation two, criteria. This is not responded to. Please extend. You argue a round, and you discuss criteria to evaluate that round. The criteria in this debate is the preservation of the ecosystem. [HALF] Who preserves the preservation of the ecosystem is the question that must be answered in order to determine who wins this debate. If any of this value objection dump impacts upon the ecosystem please vote against us. It doesn't. Please extend contention one and contention two, indicating (A) subpoint that the media is the old paradigm, it is supported by the autonomous press, and this is the greatest threat to man and the earth. That is the criteria.

William Jewell is a fine team, and I've enjoyed debating them throughout this year, but I certainly think that they have made an error in this debate. They don't make relevant arguments. Please support access. [Applause]

WORKS CITED

ADAMS, NANCY, and TIM WILKINS. "The Role of Justification in Topic Analysis." *CEDA Yearbook.* Ed. Brenda Logue, 1987.

ALMOND, LINCOLN. Posadas de Puerto Rico Association v Tourism Company of Puerto Rico: A New Weapon in the Battle to Ban Tobacco Product Advertising." *Connecticut Law Review* 20 (1987).

ALPERT, JONATHAN. "Amicus Curiae Brief." The Miami Herald Publishing Company vs Pat Tornillo [418-US 241]. Before the United States Supreme Court (October term 1973).

BAKER, C. EDWIN. "Press Rights and Government Power to Structure the Press." *University of Miami Law Review* 34 (July 1980).

BARRON, JEROME. *Public Rights and the Private Press.* Toronto, Canada: Butterworths, 1981.

BOYAN, STEPHEN. "The Ability to Communicate: The First Amendment Right." *The Mass Media and Modern Democracy.* Ed. Harry Clor. Chicago, IL: Rand McNally College Publishing Company, 1974.

CAPRA, FRITJOF. *The Turning Point.* New York: Simon and Schuster, 1982.

———. "The Turning Point: New Vision of Reality." *Futurist* Dec. 1982.

CARTER, T. BURTON. "Right of Reply Versus the Sullivan Rule." *Loyola Law Review* 29 (1981).

CROSS, SUE, "Radical Earth First Is Second to None in Speaking Out for Environment." *Salt Lake Tribune* 27 Mar. 1988.

DEVALL, BILL, and GEORGE SESSIONS. *Deep Ecology.* Salt Lake City, UT: Peregrine Books, 1985.

EHRLICH, ANNE, and PAUL EHRLICH. *Earth.* New York: Franklin Watts, 1987.

FOX, MICHAEL. "Animal Research Reconsidered." *New Age Journal* Jan.-Feb. 1988.

FRANCIOS, WILLIAM. "Media Access: Romance and Reality." *America* 129 (22 Sept. 1973).

FRITCH, ALBERT. *Environmental Ethics.* Garden City, NY: Anchor Books, 1980.

FORNTER, ROSANNE and ANNE LYON. "Effects of a Cousteu Television Special on Viewer Knowledge and Attitudes." *Journal of Environmental Education* 16 (Spring 1985).

GILLMOR, DONALD, and JEROME BARRON. *Mass Communication Law: Case and Comment* St. Paul, MN: West Publishing Co, 1977.

GOLDSTEIN, TOM. *A Two-Faced Press?* New York: Priority P., 1986.

HENDERSON, HAZEL. *Creating Alternative Futures.* New York: Burkley, 1978.

INGBER, STANLEY. "The Marketplace of Ideas: A Legitimizing Myth." *Duke Law Journal* Feb. 1984.

JACKILN, PHIL. "Access to the Media: A New Fairness Doctrine." *Mass Media Isues.* Ed. George Rodman. Chicago, IL: Science Research Associates, 1981.

LANGE, DAVID. "The Speech and Press Clause." *UCLA Law Review* 23 (1975).

LEWIS, ANTHONY. "Panel Discussion at the 5th Annual Baron de Hirsch Meyer Lecture Series." *University of Miami Law Review* 34 (July 1980).

McLEOD, JACK, CAROL GLYNN, and ROBERT GRIFFIN. "Communication and Energy Conservation." *Journal of Environmental Education* 18 (Spring 1987).

MILLER, G. TYLER. *Living in the Environment.* 3rd ed. Belmont, CA: Wadsworth Publishing Company, 1982.

———. *Living in the Environment.* 4th ed. Belmont, CA: Wadsworth Publishing.Company, 1985.

NIENOW, THOMAS. "In RE R. J. Reynolds Tobacco Co., Inc.: The "Common Sense Distinction Between Commercial and Non-commerical Speech." *Hastings Constitutional Law Quarterly* 14 (1987).

NIMMER, MELVILLE. "Introduction—Is Freedom of the Press a Reduhdancy: What Does It Add to Freedom of Speech?" *Hastings Law Journal* 26 (January 1975).

Pacific Gas and Electric vs California Public Utilities Commission [89 L.ED.2d1], 1986.

PAUL, DANIEL. "Reply Brief for Appellant." The Miami Herald Publishing Company vs Pat Tornillo [418 US 241]. Before the United States Supreme Court (October term 1973).

PEMBER, DONALD. *Mass Media Law.* Dubuque, IA: Wm. C. Brown Publishers, 1977.

POLUNIN, NICHOLAS, ed. *Growth without Ecodisasters.* New York: John Wiley and Sons, 1977.

RIFKIN, JEREMY. *Entropy.* New York: Viking, 1980.

SCHAUER, FREDRICK. *Free Speech: A Philosophical Enquiry.* Cambridge, England: Cambridge UP, 1982.

SCHMIDT, BENNO. *Freedom of the Press vs. Public Access.* New York: Parger Publishers, 1976.

SMITH, STEVEN. "Skepticism, Tolerance and Truth in the Theory of Free Expression." *Southern California Law Review* 60 (1987).

STEWART, POTTER. "Or of the Press." *Hastings Law Journal* 26 Jan. 1975.

TOMLINSON, JAMES. "The Philosophy and Development of CEDA." *CEDA Yearbook.* Ed. Don Brownlee, 1983.

APPENDIX B

1988 NATIONAL DEBATE TOURNAMENT FINAL DEBATE: SHOULD THE UNITED
STATES REDUCE SUBSTANTIALLY ITS MILITARY COMMITMENTS TO NATO
MEMBER STATES?

Edited by John K. Boaz*

The Forty-Second National Debate Tournament, sponsored by the American Forensic Association and the Ford Motor Company Fund, was held at Weber State College in Ogden, Utah, on March 25-28, 1988.[1]

The seventy-four participating teams debated the 1987-88 intercollegiate debate proposition: "Resolved: That the United States Should Reduce Substantially Its Military Commitments to NATO Member States."

Eight preliminary and five elimination rounds, all using cross-examination debate

---

*John Boaz, Associate Professor of Communication and Associate Vice President for Administrative Services at Illinois State University, is a former President of the American Forensic Association. Reprinted with permission.

[1]The tournament director was Professor David Zarefsky of Northwestern University, and the tournament host was Professor Randolph J. Scott of Weber State College.

format, resulted in this final debate between Dartmouth College and Baylor University.[2]

Representing Dartmouth College on the affirmative were Shaun Martin and Rob Wick, and representing Baylor University on the negative were J. Daniel Plants and Martin Loeber. Judges awarded the decision to the affirmative team from Dartmouth College.[3]

FIRST AFFIRMATIVE CONSTRUCTIVE

SHAUN MARTIN, DARTMOUTH COLLEGE

At the outset we'd like to thank Randy Scott, Becky Johns, Pierre Heidrich, and all the people at Weber State for a great NDT. We'd also like to thank the NDT Committee, Dean David Zarefsky, and the tournament staff.

This debate round is for our coaches, Herb [James], Ken [Strange], John [Culver], Jeff [Leon], Lennie [Gail], Erik [Jaffe], David [Rhaesa], David [Cheshire], and for all the debaters at Dartmouth. Personally, I'd also like to thank Vicki [Drinnon], Mike [Green], Mike [Body Saperstein], and my family, most especially my mom and dad who have always been proud of me. [Laughter] Not because of anything I did.

Contention (I): Nuclear proliferation is bad. We begin with (A), proliferation increases the risk of war. Representative Ed Markey argued in '82:

> As more and more nations crash the nuclear club, the risks inherent in nuclear proliferation rise geometrically; at any moment, a seemingly local crisis may suddenly escalate beyond any possibility of control. The entire earth could be in the grip, and at the mercy of, a "use it or lose it psychology" among nations with the bomb. (ix)

A number of specific scenarios follow: First of all, catalytic superpower war. Nye argued in '84: "[L]ooking further out into the future, if one imagined a rapid rate of proliferation of nuclear weapons, the number of candidates for attempts at catalytic action might increase (65)." Professor Beres concluded in '86:

> [I]n a region of many nuclear powers, it would become possible for a nuclear-armed aggressor to launch its weapons against another state without being identified. Unable

[2]The debate was held in the Promontory Ballroom of the Hilton Hotel, Ogden, Utah, on March 28, 1988. Coaches of the two teams were Erik Walker of Baylor University and Herb James, Ken Strange, John Culver, and Jeff Leon of Dartmouth College. The twenty-five teams qualifying for the elimination rounds were from Baylor University, California State University (Fullerton), Concordia College, Dartmouth College, Emory University, Georgetown University, Harvard University, University of Iowa, University of Kansas (two teams), University of Kentucky, University of Louisville, Loyola Marymount University, University of Michigan (two teams), University of Northern Iowa, Northwestern University (two teams), University of Pittsburgh, University of Redlands, University of Texas, Wake Forest University (two teams), Wayne State University, and Weber State College.

[3]Judges for the debate were Professors John Bart (Augustana College, South Dakota), Steve Ellis (University of Kansas), Sherry Hall (Harvard University), Joel Rollins (North Texas State University), Roger Solt (University of Kentucky), Fred Sternhagen (Concordia College), and Bradley Ziff (Georgetown University). The decision was 5-2 for the affirmative team from Dartmouth College.

to know for certain where the attack originated, the victim state might lash out blindly. In the resulting conflagration, a worldwide nuclear war enveloping even the superpowers might ensue. (9)

The second scenario is nuclear coups. Brian Jenkins of Rand argued in '80:

[T]here are subnational actors other than terrorists who may come into the possession of nuclear weapons. One faction of a disintegrating government that already has nuclear weapons could seize the country's nuclear arsenal, or a political faction in a nuclear nation could seize and threaten to use nuclear weapons in a coup. (8)

Spector noted in February of '87: "Thus there are historical episodes that remind us that where you have internal turmoil and the presence of nuclear weapons, you can have a very, very dangerous combination (10)."

The third scenario is unauthorized use. Professor Beres argued in '86:

[R]egional nuclear proliferation would also increase the probability of the unauthorized use of nuclear weapons. This is the case, again, not only because of the expanded number of existing risks, but because the new nuclear powers would almost certainly lack the safeguards now in place in superpower arsenals. In response to the need for a quick-reaction nuclear force which can be fielded as soon as possible, new nuclear powers will inevitably turn to automatic or nearly automatic systems of nuclear retaliation which are not encumbered by complex and costly command and control checks. (6)

Stephen Meyer of MIT argued in 1984:

[N]uclear command and control could be so lax as to give lower level military command elements the prerogative to launch nuclear attacks. A particularly enthusiastic commander might decide that ever-lasting glory could be attained through the destruction of an American force. (163-4)

The fourth scenario is terrorism. Professor Friedlander argued in '86:

Demaris concludes his well-researched study of international terrorist organizations with a dire warning: "Nuclear terrorism is the wave of the future." With the proliferation of nuclear weaponry and the incremental growth of states capable of developing a nuclear military technology, the mathematical chances of a terrorist group stealing, adapting, or constructing a nuclear device is not beyond the realm of reasonable prediction. British security agencies reluctantly concede that a potential terrorist incident is undeniably credible. In their view, the issue is no longer *if* such an event is feasible, but rather *when* an episode of mass destruction will finally occur. (156)

Professor Beres argued in '86:

The expanded number of nuclear powers would create the conditions whereby microproliferation. . .might be accelerated. [A]n anonymous terrorist detonation could be mistakenly blamed upon another state by the attack victim. In this way, microproliferation could actually spark regional or systemwide nuclear war between states. (10)

The fifth scenario is crazy leaders. Professor Beres of Purdue argued in '76:

> The greater the number of nuclear powers, the greater the probability of irrational national leaders with nuclear options. Such irrational leaders might initiate nuclear strikes against nuclear states even though enormously destructive or annihilating consequences were anticipated. (4-5)

Professor Beres continued:

> What about *rationality*? The durability of any system of nuclear deterrence is always contingent upon this assumption. . . . Should a new nuclear weapons state fall under the leadership of a person or persons suffering from madness, severe emotional stress, or major physiologic impairment, this state might initiate nuclear first-strikes against other nuclear states even though enormously destructive retaliation could be anticipated. (3)

The choice of these leaders is often beyond our control. Lewis Dunn of the Hudson Institute argued in '82:

> The significance [of these command-and-control deficiencies] is magnified by the domestic political instability of most of the countries that may acquire nuclear weapons by the early 1990s. Nearly all. . .are developing countries, while many either have experienced a successful or aborted military coup d'etat within the past decade or could in the future. (75)

In the sixth scenario is accidental nuclear war. Prolif increases the risk. Leonard Spector with the Carnegie Foundation argued in '84:

> The more nations that possess nuclear weapons, the greater the risk that such arms will be used accidentally or inadvertantly. No nuclear command and control system can be fool-proof. The greater the number of such systems, the higher the probability of failure. (4)

Proliferants won't have security systems. Nashif argued in '84:

> Any mishap arising from technical or human failure, of course, would probably bring nuclear tragedy, and the guarantees against mishaps and errors are likely to be diminished as the proliferation of nuclear arms increases because small states cannot overcome the complex technical and administrative problems involved very easily. (70)

The seventh scenario is preemptive attack. Systems vulnerability would encourage preemption. Stephen Meyer argued in '84:

> [T]he potential for crisis escalation is particularly strong. SNFs are likely to be small and vulnerable with fragile C^{3}I. Hence, there will be strong incentives for preemptive first use of nuclear weapons. (175)

Instability only adds to this risk. *Africa Today* argued in '85:

> The general instability affecting most regions of the world makes nuclear weapons in such areas a greater potential for pre-emptive conventional wars that could easily trigger nuclear exchange or pre-empt first-strike. The management and control of nuclear weapons in nations whose technological capacities are suspect can also create serious risks and dangers. (78)

Preemption, thus, becomes inevitable. Martin Goldstein argued in '80:

> For a proliferant to lose these weapons on the airstrip or the launching pad would be a catastrophe beyond the endurance of most political leaders. Hence, the compulsion to launch early would be enormous. . . . .In such a situation, escalation is likely to be terrible and swift. (26)

The eighth scenario is first-strike. Bitter rivals will use nukes. The Carnegie Endowment for International Peace argued in March of '88:

> The presence of two nuclear-armed adversaries with a history of recent wars facing each other across a common border would present a far more volatile situation than can be found today between any pair of nuclear powers. (27)

Nashif argued in '84:

> To have a stable nuclear deterrence, it is not enough to have a nuclear technical balance. There should also exist a psychological balance. . . . [D]eep hatred and enmity. . . . .increases the likelihood of a crisis developing into a nuclear war. (78)

An attack is, thus, inevitable. Professor Beres argued in '86:

> The expanded number of nuclear powers would ultimately create the conditions whereby first-strike attacks could be unleashed with impunity, whatever the condition of the intended victim's willingness to retaliate or the security of its retaliatory forces. (9)

(B) subpoint, impact. Regional wars alone would be devastating. Professor Beres argued in '86:

> Even the most limited nuclear exchange would signal unprecedented catastrophe. The immediate effects of the explosion—thermal radiation, nuclear radiation, and blast damage—would cause wide swaths of death and devastation. . . . Such a war could also have devastating climactic effects. (11-12)

There wouldn't be just one war. Professor Beres argued in '86: "If. . .the nuclear 'firebreak" were actually crossed. . .other pairs of antagonistic states would be more likely to think the unthinkable. A ripple effect would begin to be evident (9)." These wars would escalate. Senator Glenn in '87:

> What is the national security cost to the Administration's inconsistency. Fledgling nuclear weapons programs in volatile areas mean greater strategic uncertainty for

the United States. They add to the risk that terrorists will gain access to nuclear materials, either through theft, capture, revolution, or coup; they threaten U.S. military forces deployed abroad; and they increase the chances that—through a premptive strike, an unauthorized or accidental use, or a premeditated nuclear attack—the United States could be drawn into a devastating nuclear exchange. (28)

Calogero of the University of Rome in '78: "[T]he spread of nuclear weapons. . .would also provide the most likely mechanism whereby the present nuclear-weapons states, especially the two superpowers, might be drawn into a nuclear conflict. . .(19-20)."

It would cause a nuclear winter, as Dr. Caldicott argued in '84: "[T]he explosion of 200 megatons on urban centers could induce a 'nuclear winter' which could destroy most biological systems on the planet (25)."

Guess you're wondering what the plan is. The sale of nuclear powered submarines to Canada will not be allowed. This will be done through denial of technology, use of technical safeguard agreements, and appropriate diplomatic measures with emphasis on incentives under the Defense Production Sharing Agreement of 1959 and other U.S.-Canadian defense procurement pacts. Enforcement and funding through normal means. Affirmative speeches will clarify what we mean.

Contention (II): We reduce the risks of proliferation. (A) Canada wants nuclear powered submarines. In June 1987, the Canadian government released a Defense White Paper which proposed, among other things, the acquisition of a fleet of nuclear subs. Since Canada lacks the technology to design and build nuclear subs, it will have to buy the boats. As the 1987-88 edition of *Jane's Fighting Ships* reported: "The Canadian government has. . .made a somewhat startling decision to purchase ten (or a dozen?) nuclear attack submarines (119).

(B) The U.S. is committed to Canadian subs. The U.S. is committed to assisting in the development of Canada's military capability. In general this commitment is embodied in the NATO treaty. As former Assistant Secretary of State Martin Hillenbrand testified in '70:

> Under Article 3, the parties agree to maintain and develop their *individual* and *collective* capacity to resist armed attack. The article provides that this is a *separate* and *joint* obligation, to be effectuated by means of "continuous and effective *self-help* and *mutual aid*. Under this article, therefore, the United States has undertaken. . .the obligation to assist the other parties to become and remain militarily strong. (2226-7)

The commitment to Canada was reported in *NATO's Sixteen Nations* in '85:

> Indicative of his Canadian Prime Minister [Mulroney's] approach is the joint declaration on international security which he made with President Reagan at the "Shamrock Summit". . . In it the two countries *committed* themselves to "reinvigorate" their defense and security partnership" through. . .[among other things] cooperation in defense production and procurement. . . . (33)

These commitments have been carried out with Canada's purchase of subs. According to the *New York Times* in 1988: "Mr. Shultz. . .said that. . .the United States would be prepared to sell certain [nuclear submarine] technology to the

Canadian defense industry (A3)." The *Wall Street Journal* indicated in that year [1988]: "Mr. Schultz told reporters the U.S. would "fully cooperate" with Canada's plan to expand its submarine fleet (19)."

(C) Proliferation will be encouraged. Nuclear subs must use highly enriched uranium. For Canada to obtain this weapons grade material would violate existing nuclear safeguards. *Canadian Dimension* editorialized in November of '87: "Should Canada proceed to purchase 12 nuclear powered submarines which use reactors fueled with weapons grade. . .uranium, we will also have violated the 1978 Canada-Euratom agreement as well as the Non-Proliferation Treaty (28).

Such a violation would undermine the existing non-proliferation regime. William Epstein of the UN Institute wrote in August 87:

> If Canada proceeds with the bizarre plan to acquire nuclear-powered subs. . .[i]t will create difficult problems for the International Atomic Energy Agency's non-proliferation regime ("New Defense" A7).

Canadian Centre on Arms Control and Disarmament Director, John Lamb, concurred in September of '87:

> If Canada does acquire nuclear powered submarines, it will. . .be easing the way for other countries, including some regarded as proliferation risks, to acquire unsafeguarded fissile material. As a result, the IAEA's work will be made more difficult, [and] the NPT regime will be weakened. . . .(11)

At this point, we should clarify what is meant by the Non-Proliferation regime. Structurally, the regime consists of the NPT, IAEA safeguards, and other agreements. While these arrangements include technical barriers to proliferation, their more important function is to maintain an international consensus against proliferation. Mitchell Reiss of the IISS explained in '88:

> [T]he international non-proliferation arrangements. . .attested to a view shared by most of the world community that nuclear proliferation should be prevented. . . . These arrangements in effect legitimized and universalized a consensus against nuclear proliferation. (263-4).

Reiss continued in '88:

> These arrangements. . .provided mechanisms with which countries could advertise their nonnuclear intentions, both to those countries which were parties to these arrangements and those countries which were not. They specified and codified under international law a political commitment not to devolop nuclear armaments, and projected this commitment into the future. . . . To the extent that the international nonproliferation arrangements achieved this objective, they had a restraining influence on the decisions to acquire nuclear weapons taken by Sweden, South Korea, Japan, Israel, South Africa, and India. (263)

Now is not the time to allow any actions which might threaten the NPT. Dr. Lamb wrote in October of '87:

If the NPT regime collapses (as nearly happened at the 1985 treaty review conference and as could yet happen at the 1990 review) and if countries like North and South Korea, India and Pakistan, Brazil and Argentina, and Israel and Iraq begin openly acquiring nuclear weapons, the world would be a lot more dangerous and the risk of Third World crises escalating into superpower confrontations would be much greater. This is hardly the time for Canada to take steps likely to weaken the Non-Proliferation Treaty regime. (18)

(D) Solvency. Diplomatic actions will solve. The efficacy of this approach was demonstrated by VMI professor Wayne Thompson in '88: "Ties with the United States restrain and complicate the making of Canadian defense policy. Canadians must always ask themselves what their partners want them to do. . .(106)."

Technical means involve control of technology transfer. The plan would not allow Canada the means to build the subs. The ability to control technology was reported by the *Financial Post* in '87: "U.S. Navy clearance is essential for these firms [General Dynamics and Newport News Shipbuilding to assist Canada in construction of submarines], because the navy owns some of the rights to all submarines it orders (2)."

Such control would be complete, since Canadian subs would inevitably require U.S. technology. For example, the *Alberta Report* reported in June ['87:] "[A]n American-designed pressurized water reactor. . .is the most likely power source for the [Canadian submarine] fleet (15)."

Additionally, it should be noted that Canada had to seek U.S. permission to obtain nuclear technology, regardless of the source. The CSM [*Christian Science Monitor*] made this clear in [22] February of '88:

> Canada is currently negotiating with both the British and French government a "memorandum of understanding" which will permit transfer of technology needed to build the subs in Canada. . . Under a Canadian-American treaty of 1959, though, the U.S. congress must approve the sale to Canada of any "military nuclear reactors and/or parts." (11)

Thus, through diplomatic and technical means the plan avoids Canadian development and weakens the non-proliferation regime. The importance of Canada's role in the non-proliferation regime was noted by Weiss in '86:

> [E]ffective persuasion is more likely to come from non-nuclear-weapons nations (such as Canada. . .) that had the obvious capability to become military nuclear powers but elected not to do so. It is in the context of active diplomacy that Europe and the United States must collaborate in engaging such third-party persuaders in this endeavor. (24)

The Council on Foreign Relations concluded in '86:

> [I]t is. . .essential to preserve and extend the international consensus against proliferation that now exists among most states capable of acquiring nuclear weapons

or helping others to do so, and the international commitments reflecting and rei▪
forcing that consensus. (7)

CROSS EXAMINATION

MARTIN LOEBER QUESTIONING MARTIN

Loeber: It seems to me, why do the reactor sales, which is what gets sold, right? They're not armed with nuclear weapons. Martin: No, these forces are not armed with nuclear weapons. Loeber: Right, but they have nuclear reactors on them, right? Martin: That's nuclear subs. Loeber: Well, why wouldn't the sale or transfer of nuclear technology to Brazil, Argentina, West Germany, and a lot of countries in the world have the same effect of weakening the NPT as this did? Martin: Well, there are numerous answers to that question. Loeber: Why? Martin: The first of which being that Canada's the most important nation. The evidence we read— Loeber: Why? Martin: I believe on the last two cards it says, is because it would demonstrate most the— It would uphold most the NPT regime— if those nations which clearly had the technology to become military powers and used fissile material militarily— didn't exercise that option, and that would uphold the— Loeber: OK. Martin: —international consensus against proliferation. Loeber: So, why do people prolif? Out of security fears, or do they prolif just because they think it might be a good idea? Martin: I have no clue. Loeber: Can I see the whole link evidence you're reading to the proliferation rather? Martin: Yes, you may. Loeber: OK. Loeber: So when does the sale go through? Martin: When does the sale go through? Loeber: Um, hum. Martin: I believe they eventually acquire their subs, I don't know, about the year 2,000. Right? The sale is '88, but they don't— Loeber: OK. Let me ask you this. Martin: 1996, but the intention to buy makes proliferation— Loeber: Right. Right. Why is it that buying a nuclear sub creates the perception that people all of a sudden think nuclear weapons are a good thing? Martin: Well, it doesn't necessarily. Loeber: Well, why do people prolif? Just explain that. Martin: They have their own reasons. Maybe some envy— Loeber: They envy the nuclear subs. Why wouldn't they prolif with nuclear subs? Martin: Why wouldn't they prolif— Loeber: Why wouldn't they just build an SSN? Martin: Well they might very well. Our argument is the non-proliferation regime constrains that by having an international consensus against proliferation. Loeber: Why is that? Why is Canadian proliferating by achieving these? Martin: Why is Canadian? That doesn't seem to be a sentence. Loeber: Why is Canadian—or Canada, rather, proliferating? Or they're not proliferating, right? Martin: They're not proliferating. Loeber: Well, why is the atomic reactor part of the NPT that critical to the international consensus? Martin: Because it violates the Euratom-Canadian Agreement and the Non-Proliferation Treaty. It violates it. Loeber: So what if it violates it? Why is that important to the international— Martin: You are now using weapons grade material for military uses. Loeber: Oh, oh. I see. So, oh, OK. Which card says that they're weapons grade on the a— Martin: Oh. I talked to you about it. It is—the *Canadian Dimension* card. Loeber: OK. Thanks Cool. Martin: Is that it? Loeber: Yeah, that's all.

FIRST NEGATIVE CONSTRUCTIVE

J. DANIEL PLANTS, BAYLOR UNIVERSITY

Good evening. Marty and I are ecstatic to be here and to represent Baylor University. First of all, we'd like to thank Randy Scott and his staff from Weber State for a well hosted NDT. We'd also like to thank David Zarefsky and the tournament staff for an efficiently run tournament. We would not be here without the help of the country's finest coaches: Lyn Robbins, Griffin Vincent, Carrie Voss, and of course, Erik Walker. All of the Baylor debaters have worked very hard to help us prepare for this tournament. David Jardeen and Robert Wood have been invaluable. They deserve very much more to be here than we do. We are grateful for the tremendous support from all of the people at Baylor particularly Professor Glenn Capp, Dr. Bill English, and Dr. Lee Polk. Finally, my gratitude couldn't be completely expressed without telling my family how much their support has meant to me. Their faith in me has never waivered. For this I owe them.

Topicality. Overview. It's obviously an a priori voting issue. Each comparative interpretation of the topic decided [unintelligible]. Specific standards will be defended within each violation. The first violation is they're not substantial. The (A) subpoint interpretation of "substantially." Subpoint (1), substantial means "much" or "most." "Paving Plus vs. Professional Investments" says, "A building contract is 'substantially performed'. . .if all the essentials necessary to the full accomplishment of the purposes for which the thing contracted for has been constructed is performed except for some slight and unintentional defects. . . (217)." The second argument is they have to be over fifty percent. Where is this card? All right. *Words and Phrases* says in 1987: " 'Substantially consummated,' for purpose of Bankruptcy Codes provision dealing with whether a Chapter 11 plan has been 'substantially consummated,' means more than half way and more than a mere preponderance (263)." Third, comparison is required. The only way to determine if a reduction is substantial is to evaluate it in the context of our overall military commitments to NATO. You have to look at the part as it relates to the whole. The fourth argument is criteria for measurement. We will embrace any objective criteria and permit the affirmative to defend that, whether it's monetary value, number of weapons systems, force levels, etc., but they have to defend an objective, quantifiable standard.

The (B) subpoint, they don't meet this. They won't be fifty percent of anything. They're just going to argue that they're important. (C) subpoint is our interpretation is better. We preserve meaning for the term "substantially." Each word serves a unique function in the topic. Ignoring one word distorts the meaning of the entire proposition. This is especially true for "substantially." *CJS* [Corpus Juris Secundum] says, "While it [substantially] must be employed with care and discrimination, it must, nevertheless, be given effect (765)."

Second violation, not a commitment. The (A) subpoint is definition of a commitment. It means a pledge to use force. This is from Paul in 1973: "The National Commitments Resolution. . .defines a national commitment as '. . .the use of the Armed Forces of the United States on foreign territory, or a promise to assist a foreign country. . .(6).' " The (B) subpoint is the violation. This has not

anything to do with the pledge to use force. This is just a weapons system. ⸍
(C) subpoint is our interpretation is better. First, our definitions are contextua
It's from Paul who wrote a book called *Military Commitments*. The second is delimita
tion and [unintelligible] allow any single arms sales. We would indicate that it
has to be something to do with the U.S. pledge which binds us to action in the
future.

Counterplan. We offer the following conditional counterplan to be implemented
through normal alliance decision-making processes: Consultation with all NATO
allies regarding the reduction of the U.S. commitment to Canada will occur prior
to any decision to reduce these commitments is made. Allied input and concerns
will be given consideration in deciding whether commitments should be reduced.
Funding and enforcement through normal means; negative speeches clarify what
we mean.

Observation one: It is not topical. (A) It is not a reduction. There is no guarantee
of topical action. At best, an effects evaluation is required, which would mix
burdens, reduce clash, and severely usurp negative ground. (B) It's not U.S. The
counterplan involves NATO action, not United States.

Observation two: Competition. (A) Mutually exclusive. Counterplan postpones
ultimate decision until consultation occurs, whereas the affirmative mandates immediate reduction. (B) Net beneficial. Effective consultation requires that no prior
decision be made. Rose in '83:

> [N]o member should, without prior consultation, make a firm policy decision or
> pronouncement on a matter of major concern to an ally; members should take the
> views and interests of their Allies into account when developing their national
> policies. . . .(2)

Advantage: Consultation is good for NATO. Van Heuven says in '82:

> On balance, however, the argument favoring consultation within the Alliance is over-
> whelming. In defense, NATO manages common programs involving large sums of
> money. Even in those areas where members retain their national freedom of action,
> consultation is the essential element without which the Alliance defense effort would
> make little sense. (114-6)

First disad. West German prolif. The (A)subpoint here is the INF puts West
Germany on the brink. The *Economist* says in 1987:

> In the present case, a sensible attempt to cull the world's oversupply of these weapons
> has produced. . .the danger. . .that emotions may not switch the other way, so that
> in the 1990s it finds itself facing a West European army with a German finger on
> its nuclear trigger. And all this because of an agreement to remove less than a 20th
> of the world's nuclear warheads. (18)

The (B) subpoint is the link. First, Canada is on the brink of neutralism now.
Hasek says in 1987:

> This coincides with a time when Canadians who have personal memories of our na-
> tion as a vigorous, unafraid power, are fast retiring from positions of influence. War,

and rumor of war, have taken on mythical qualities for the majority of the younger generation. Canada is nearing a crisis of self confidence. (41)

Hasek says in 1987:

> Therefore, any new defence policies must reaffirm our commitment to NATO, as the first part of a massive educational campaign designed to teach the media and the public the reasons for the maintenance of Western solidarity as well as for the existence of the Canadian military per se. The magnitude of the effort needed can only be comprehended when the methods and resources that are being used to neutralise Canada are examined. (38)

The third subpoint is this causes war. Hasek says in 1987:

> If Canada were to withdraw from NATO and NORAD, the armed forces would be neutralised and Canadian sovereignty would be meaningless. While the political damage cannot be calculated, the balance between the Western democracies and the Soviet bloc would certainly become destabilised. This would immeasurably increase the risk of war. (38)

The fourth argument is decrease commitment equals West German prolif. Boston Study Group says in '82:

> It is possible that. . .West Germany. . .will require nuclear weapons if the United States reduces or withdraws military force which, in their view, support their defense. In the cases of West Germany and Japan, we have gone to some lengths to avoid providing any incentive or excuse for increased armament or acquisition of nuclear weapons. (10)

The (C) subpoint is impact. World War. Calder in 1980:

> [I]f West Germany makes the bomb it may be the end of the world, in the near-literal sense of nuclear war. As noted in the previous chapter such a move would enrage the Soviet Union and it is one of the very few imaginable events that could set the Soviet tanks rolling into Western Europe and into the nuclear war promised by NATO. (74)

Next disad, Southern discomfort. The (A) subpoint is on the brink now. Bush-Dukakis matchup will be real close. *Salt Lake Tribune* said two days ago, "In a Bush-Dukakis matchup, 46 percent of all registered voters polled said they favored Bush and 45 percent chose Dukakis (A3)." The (B) subpoint is they insure a Bush defeat. First, the plan equals Reagan soft line. Bush's fate will be tied to Reagan's. Broder says in 1988:

> Even now, as he closes in on the GOP nomination, Bush can be faulted for simplistic, sloganeering approach to the issues and for his nearly sycophantic dependence on the popularity of his silent patron, President Reagan. (30)

Second, soft line ensures defeat. Bush needs to be tough to persuade Southerners to vote for him. Nixon says in 1988:

It is fine to talk about being tough, but when your hand is called, you have to h
something to be tough with. The lesson of every postwar U.S. election, except t.
anomalous victory of Jimmy Carter in 1976, is that no one can be elected presiden
by advocating a policy of weakness abroad. (12A)

(C) subpoint, impact. Trade wars. Future protectionism will overwhelm any
candidate except for Bush. *Wall Street Journal* in 1988:

> Signing this "acceptable" bill primarily will legitimize and keep alive the ghost of
> Richard Gephardt. The protectionists will return to present the next President with
> another assault on the world's economy. We now know that it is politically possible
> to stand up to this bunch. George Bush just proved that. (24)

It equals atomic war. Harrigan says in 1985: "Protectionism will breed stag-
nation, retaliation, and world-wide depression. Remember Smoot-Hawley.
(30)" Cornish impacts in '80: "Even worse, an economic crisis could lead to a
world war, as the bitter experience of the 1930s demonstrated so powerfully.
(29)"

The next disad, Gorbachev. Glasnost at a critical stage now. *Washington Times*
said in February of '88:

> "Mr. Gorbachev has set in motion a 'political earthquake' but still faces an uphill
> struggle within his own ruling dictatorship and a government bureaucracy hostile
> to his economic and political reforms. (3)"

The (B) subpoint is they save him. Coser says in 1987:

> "Gorbachev's reform measures will be followed up only if he feels that he is not
> forced to tighten the reins because of Reaganite threats and the beating of war
> drums by American rightist diehards (194)."

The link here is that these things would—if it would free U.S. SSNs for maritime
strategy. (This one, or this one?) Sokolsky says in 1987:

> From the U.S. perspective, the Canadian decision to acquire SSNs offers some benefit
> yet also suggests future complications. The benefit would be that Canada would be
> able to assume more of the burden of North American defense, thus freeing U.S.
> Naval resources for duty elsewhere in the world.

Our argument is that if these forces will be freed up then we can put pressures
on the Soviets. That is what would stop Gorbachev, but if they act this way, it
would keep him in power.

Also, maritime strategy link puts pressure on him. Leggett in 1987:

> Other objections to the Maritime Strategy leap to mind. Just when a Soviet leader
> seems genuinely intent on a military build-down, NATO has produced a plan in-
> volving attacks on the Soviet homeland, and has even begun to rehearse them in
> peacetime. Ammunition aplenty has been provided for Kremlin hawks to argue
> against the allure of disarmament. (12)

The first impact is equals Soviet adventurism. Glasnost strengthens Soviet aggressiveness. Metcalf in '87:

> [Glasnost] could be seen as the first stirrings of a potential economic giant, bent on aggression whose weight of natural resources and sheer industrial power, no longer hobbled by the Soviet system, could—in the long run and in the geo-political sense—prove irresistible in a bid for world dominance. (12)

Whelan says in 1986:

> So-called "wars of national liberation, Soviet supported and sometimes directed. . .has contributed immensely to the sense of interminable upheaval in the Third World. All of these varieties of regional conflicts have disrupted regional peace. . .and even endangered world peace by risking superpower confrontation (6-7).

The second impact is Yugoslav corridor. First, Romanian resistence to Glasnost causes the Soviets to invade. Urban in 1987:

> Ceausescu has been openly critical of Gorbachov's analysis of "real existing socialism" and said the Soviet way was not for him. . . .
> I can forsee a number of interesting developments. The spectacle of undernourished communist Romania being "liberated" by Soviet tanks with popular Romanian approval is only one, if Gorbachov stays the course. (22)

Yugoslav-Romanian security ties equals nuclear war. Yugoslavia would have to come to Romania's assistance. That would draw the U.S. in. Winsor in 1981: "In general, then, the particular importance of Romania lies. . .in its association with Yugoslavia and in this potential for this association to detonate a major international conflict in the event of an East European crisis (207)."

The last impact is Soviet biological weapon breakout. Glasnost causes this. *Wall Street Journal* in 1987:

> We're beginning to get a fuller understanding of what a versatile concept *glasnost* is. In its constant efforts to steal Western technology, the Soviet Union has now come up with an aboveboard way to access secrets: use international organizations.
> . . .[T]he Soviet Union and its allies have shown an unusual interest in biotechnology, proposing resolutions to increase information and technology transfers between East and West. . . .(34)

The impact is a plague. Kucewicz in'84:

> Indeed, genetic engineering could carry mind-boggling military potential. An aggressor armed with such new biological weapons could, for example, vaccinate its own armed forces and population against this new disease, leaving them the only survivors of a world-wide plague. Another nation could be attacked surreptitiously. . . . (30)

Who would even know who started the epidemic?

Case. We're starting on the third contention. On the (A) subpoint. They sa̲
that Canada wants these things. That's fine. On the (B) subpoint, the U.S. commitment. First, he says it's terrible. Doesn't say anything about how this is com-
mited. It just says that we've agreed to give them to them. The second argument
here doesn't even say that we're going to give them. It just says that we will assist
them. The final argument, there's no indication that they have given these
things—is a commitment. Our definition of a commitment is a pledge, not simply giving them a weapons system. Additionally, none of this—this—evidence just
says that we're committed to their defense. Right? Which may be true, but that
doesn't change our pledge to defend them, or anything like that. They would
only change the means of doing this. Right? But that doesn't change the commitment. They're only changing a means for fulfilling that, but not an actual pledge.

On the (B) subpoint, equals prolif. The first thing here is they have to isolate
all the scenarios. Right? Some of these cards talk about different countries, but
they have to have specific impact scenarios for these countries. Right? They have
to have evidence that says if Iran prolifs and this will happen in these other countries. Just reading the evidence up above, the generic evidence on prolifs, the
plan doesn't apply.

Second argument is Canada won't have nuclear weapons on board. These
things—Sokolsky in '87:

> Arms control groups, which have regarded Canada as an important actor in efforts
> to control the proliferation of nuclear weapons and as a country in a position to pro-
> mote restraint on the growing strategic competition in the Arctic, have also voiced
> misgivings. This, even though the SSNs will not be armed with nuclear weapons. (13)

Next argument here is plan to acquire is reasonable. Sokolsky in 1987:

> While some allied governments and groups abroad may regard the SSN announce-
> ment as a radical departure for Canada, the origins of the decision are rooted in
> Canadian defense. . .Western collective security system. Viewed in this context,
> Canada's plan to acquire SSNs appears to be reasonable, not only in terms of its
> own interests, but also in terms of allied interests. It is also a decision that need
> not stand in the way of new arms control efforts—to reduce the arms— (13)[5]

Down below on the (D) subpoint, solvency. The first argument here is not
unique. They could get it in other ways. Britain and France and the U.S. already
have these kinds of submarines. It's no indication that they couldn't get them
that way. The next is nuclear power plants provide enriched plutonium. Thus,
they could get it these ways. Donnally in 1987:

---

[5]"While some allied governments and groups abroad may regard the SSN announcement as
a radical departure for Canada, the origins of the decision are rooted in Canadian defense policy and
Canada's somewhat unique place within the Western Collective Security System. Viewed in this context, Canada's plan to acquire SSNs appears reasonable, not only in terms of its own interests, but
also in terms of allied interests. It is also a decision that need not stand in the way of new arms control
efforts relating to the Arctic.''

Development of uranium enrichment capabilities continues in several countries, including some with less industrial standing. The development of laser isotope separation is also becoming more prominent. If this should succeed, and there seems little reason to expect otherwise, the ability to produce weapons-grade uranium could spread quickly. (176)

The next argument here is reactor-grade plutonium makes these weapons. Wilmshurst says in '84:

Another source of concern was the acceptance by expert opinion in 1974 that the distinction hitherto made between "weapons-grade" and "reactor-grade" plutonium, though still a valid technical distinction in terms of isotopic content, was no longer a valid distinction in terms of proliferation risk. ("Development" 26)

The next argument here is that the NPT fails us. Marin[-Bosh] in 1985: "The present state of affairs regarding the NPT can be described as a distressing example of unfulfilled promise (45)."

The next argument here is that new proliferants threaten the treaty. Goldblat says in '86: Accession to the Non-Proliferaton Treaty by the most critical threshold states is doubtful for the foreseeable future (38),'' indicating that the NPT doesn't apply to the countries that are the greatest risk.

The next argument here is threshold states are not members. This is from Wilmshurst in 1984:

If no new gestures can be devised to bring the potential weapon states into the non-proliferation system, there is not only the risk of another weapon state appearing but an equal danger that the non-proliferation community may split. ("Reforming" 153)

The next argument here is that the superpowers will thwart it in other ways. McGrew in 1984:

In 1980, the NPT Review Conference was unable to agree [on] a final communique partly as a result of assertions that the superpowers had abandoned any serious commitment to restraints on their own actions as implied in Article VI (5).

And that's the last argument there.

At the top. The first argument here is that prolif is inevitable. This is from Wilmshurst in 1984:

The most essential component of a nuclear military programme is not the nuclear material nor the nuclear technology, but the political will, supported by a minimum of scientific and industrial capacity. If the political will is there, any country will, sooner or later, succeed in producing and creating the necessary nuclear material and technologies. ("Development" 46)

Also, they can't stop for this. Right? All their evidence says that they would be able to keep them in check, but this evidence indicates that there are other factors driving people to proliferate. They can get the weapons.

Next is nuclear power plants are a mechanism. I'm reading evidence on t. below. The next argument here is no barrier. This is from Schwartz and Derb⟨…⟩ in 1986: "[T]his process has now advanced so far that it can only be a matter of time before the capacity to make or steal nuclear warheads becomes available to any nation or major organization that seeks it (43)."

Next argument here is nuclear states are increasing. This is uniqueness answer. Spector says in 1985: [V]irtually all the threshold countries appear to have taken steps, in some cases significant, toward developing or expanding nuclear weapons capabilites." (11) This is also an empirical [unintelligible] to the impact, if all their preemption evidence is true about how people would strike before the people get the weapons.

The next argument here is prolif would be slow. Gummett in 1984: "Waltz, a leading exponent of the view that 'more may be better,' objects to the term proliferation on the ground that nuclear weapons have diffused too slowly to deserve that description (77)."

All this impact evidence assumes fast. The next argument here is doesn't usual use. Waltz in '83: "Fourth, the possibility remains of one side in a civil war using a nuclear warhead at its opponent's stronghold. Such an act would produce national tragedy, not an international one (121)." This also takes out escalation. "The question then arises: Once the weapon is fired, what happens next? The domestic use of nuclear weapons is, of all the uses imaginable, least likely to lead to escalation and to threaten the stability of the central balance (Waltz 121)." On the second channel, based on nuclear coups. Won't happen. Waltz in '83:

> Although one may prefer civil control, preventing a highly destructive war does not require it. What is required is that decisions be made that keep destruction within bounds, whether these decisions are made by civilians or soldiers. Soldiers may indeed be more cautious than civilians. *Uncertainty* about the course a nuclear war might follow, along with the *certainty* that destruction can be immense, strongly inhibits the first use of nuclear weapons. (123)

The second argument here is there is no indication that this will cause more [unintelligible] to be used. They will have to win crazy leaders to get this, that these people will be more militaristic.

On unauthorized use, the first argument here is the coup argument takes this out above. The second argument here is safety measures. This evidence that says they won't use them is bad. They could have safety measures. Authorities empirically denied by the superpowers have never been authorized use, and we'll say some more about the other scenarios later.

CROSS-EXAMINATION

SHAUN MARTIN QUESTIONING PLANTS

Martin: All the links on disads are soft line, correct? Plants: Ah, no. Martin: Well, perhaps you'd like to explain which ones aren't? Plants: OK. The Canada argument isn't. Martin: The Canada argument, meaning the links to Gorbachev, the SSNs? Plants: On the West German prolif argument it is linked directly if of Canada. The evidence says that we need to be able to reaffirm our commitment to them now. We don't do that. That causes Canadian neutralism. They take trips out of Europe. They decrease their European or Continental commitments, and that causes West Germany to prolif. Martin: Robert, did you listen to this? Rob Wick: No. Martin: The link to West German prolif is Canadian neutralism, and they pull their forces out of Europe. Plants: Right. Martin: Robert, did you hear that? Wick: Yes. Why should they go neutral? Martin: Why do they go neutral? Plants: Because we don't sell them the subs. Martin: Well, the evidence says that right now is a critical time to reaffirm NATO commitments. Plants: Right. Martin: For them, and the only—the motivation for them to do that is our commitments to them. Plants: Is any evidence specific to·sub causing neutralism? Martin: Uhm, are any of the cards specific to subs? Wick: You could say, no. Plants: Or you could just say, yes. Martin: Gorbachev in here says they free up U.S. SSBNs. Plants: Right. Martin: Is that a good idea? Plants: We didn't take a position on that, but we did say that frees up U.S. SSBNs which means we could put more pressure on the Soviets. Martin: Is that good? Plants: Well, from the standpoint— Martin: Will you ever take— Plants: From the standpoint of Gorbachev—our position on Gorbachev, it's good. Martin: Will you ever take the position that's bad? Plants: Maybe. Martin: How can you do that consistently, oh conditional counterplan master? [Laughter] Plants: Well, I mean, depending on the way the matrix of arguments in the debate come down, maybe we would end up taking that. Martin: Well, my question is, once we straight flip this, can you then go the other way and say, huh huh, you've fallen into our trap. Plants: Well, ·we haven't taken a position on whether or not maritime strategy is a deterrent. Martin: Does that mean, yes, you can do that. Plants: Yes. Martin: So what's the incentive for you not to just run links to all your disads and then kinda just sit back and see what we do? Plants: Well, but this is a link to another argument which has an impact to it. Martin: In that case, should you be allowed to go the other way on the impact? Plants: Not on West German prolif. We've already taken a position on— Martin: On Gorbachev, SSBNs? Plants: We couldn't go the other way on Gorbachev, either. I mean— Martin: Well, but could you go? Plants: The impacts— Martin: Once we flip this internally, can you say, that's bad? You're reserving the right to do that? Plants: We're reserving the right to go either way on whether maritime is good or bad. From the context of how it impacts Gorbachev, our position is consistent, and we won't— Martin: So, would it be consistent for us—uh. Thank you very much.

SECOND AFFIRMATIVE CONSTRUCTIVE

ROB WICK, DARTMOUTH COLLEGE

I don't have any little introduction. That'll be it for the 2AR. Do it then. OK.

"Substantial" topicality [unintelligible] argument. First, commitments is plural which proves that it doesn't have to be a commitment to all nations. Secondly, fifty percent is an arbitrary standard. Justify, three, fifty percent. It only has to be fifty percent to Canada. One NATO member state—one or more NATO member states, and this is clearly more than fifty percent to Canada. Next, has no exact meaning, because no rule can be laid down that fixes exact meaning. Next argument, it just means important words [unintelligible]. "Substantial" means a moment of being important. Next, "substantially" modifies "reduce." Thus, it is a relevant comparison to other reductions of commitments. This one is as large as any other that has occurred. Next, small reduction can be substantial. *Words and Phrases* in '87: "[D]efendant would be found to have transacted a 'substantial quantity of business' in Vermont. . .even where percentage of defendent's gross business done. . .was .036%. . .(282)," which takes out his objective quantification standard.

Next argument I guess is that reduction in these commitments is standard. The topic doesn't say reduce the commitment or all commitments, only that some commitments should be reduced. The next argument is reasonability is sufficient. *Words and Phrases* in '87: Defendant's conduct is a "substantial factor" where it is of sufficient significance in regard to reasonability.[6] The last argument is we give them plenty of ground. This has been run by Iowa. This has been run by lots of other teams. Oh, and the last argument is that it overlimits [unintelligible]. There would only be as few cases as fifty percent, and the other fifty percent, he says, use of armed forces. Number one, this overlimits. This means promise not to defend any NATO countries is the only case 'til we decrease the commitment to defend with those subs.

Next argument is that the arms sales are military commitments. We reduce them. *Congressional Quarterly* in '69: "In recent years, members have attempted to scale down U.S. commitments by reducing the annual military aid authorization request (70)." Next argument is we reduce the commitments to Article 3 of NATO. That's the Hillenbrand evidence from 1AC. Leonard Johnson in '85: "[T]he Treaty obligates members to maintain their individual and collective ability to resist armed attack. . .(51)." The next argument is that we reduce the commitments made at The Shamrock Summit. That's the 1AC *NATO's Sixteen Nation's* evidence that says we committed ourselves to the defense and security partnership through cooperation in defense production and procurement. Certainly stopping the sub reduces the cooperation on defense procurement. Next we reduce submarine pledges to Canada. 1AC *New York Times* and *Wall Street Journal* evidence says Shultz pledged full cooperation on sub acquisition. Next we reduce our commitment to Britain and France. We eliminate the pledge to let them sell to Canada. *Financial Post* in '87: "These co-operative Canada-U.S. military procurement pacts, along with 17 similar memorandums of understanding between the U.S. Defence Department and other allies, are coming under the magnifying glass to see if they meet basic U.S. objectives (Gherson '46)." Finally, we decrease the commitment under NATO under Article 2 which says that you have to—you're pledging to help the entire alliance to protect each other and themselves.

The consultations counterplan he says is not topical. First of all, it's topical. It reduces from an unconditional commitment to a conditional commitment. For the counterplan, there's no doubt that after it there's a huge debt. Secondly, this

---

[6]"Defendant's conduct is a 'substantial factor' where it is of sufficient significance in predicting the harm as to lead reasonable persons to regard it as a cause and to attach responsibility (251)."

is the U.S. acting in terms of reducing the commitment from conditional. Third, the impact is an affirmative ballot. It justifies the resolution. Only have to do it by one example. Next argument, traditional arguments are better. Rewards them. The more we clash with them, they should just throw them out. Also, you can't allow them to just kick you out in conditional argument because that's de facto conditionality.

(A) subpoint, mutual exclusivity. You can obviously go through most of the plan expressly [unintelligible]. Secondly, it adopts through normal means which includes consultation within member states. (B) subpoint, net benefits. First, it's not unique. The status quo does not consult. Secondly, do the plan, and then consult on whether or not you should reverse the plan. The third argument is, if adopting the policy without consultation precludes benefits, then the status quo is precluded benefits. Next, he can't take the submarines back, so you have to do the plan before you do the consultation. The next argument, there's no guarantee that they would actually do the plan, and any risk of the advantage would outweigh the nothing advantage of this counterplan. Next, two, the plan is a fallback in case consultation doesn't come out the right way. Next argument, subtrafuge. Have the U.S. lead them to this conclusion in order to be sure of getting the advantage of the plan.

West German prolif. One, we saw the strong NPT regime would stop them from proliffing. They are among the specific countries mentioned in our solvency evidence. Two, this proves the case harms on a more general level. Three, it assumes that we decrease European commitments, and I will argue that the subs are directed against the U.S. Denied perceived as a hard line policy. *Washington Post* in '88: "External Affairs Minister Clark has acknowledged that the decision to spend several billion dollars for the submarines was driven more by concern over the United States than because of any fear of Soviet military activity in the Arctic (16)." Next, the subs free up lots of money for alternatives. *Electronic Times* in '87: In a recent paper he says the twelve nuclear powered submarines [unintelligible] twelve diesel-electric subs [unintelligible].[7] Next argument, there's no backlash. The solvency evidence says that Canada would accede to us. Also, they avoid competition with the U.S. Lemco in 1987:

> It must be acknowledged at the outset, however, that it is never in Canada's interests publicly to embarrass the United States. For all the tensions that exist, Canadian officials will always try to put the best face on things for fear of irritating their giant neighbor. (91)

Next argument is subs are isolationist. These subs will trade off with the forces in Europe. Charles Doran in 1987: "[T]he realities of politics are such that the drive to establish a credible submarine force for continental defence may come at the expense of the commitment to Europe (9)." Next, subs trade off with surface ships which are more visible. *Jane's Fighting Ships* in '88:

[7]Source indicated.

The effect on the destroyer frigate building programme could have an impact NATO force levels of the "Halifax" class if not followed by sufficient new constru_ tion. The overall total of such ships throughout NATO is now lamentably low an_ there is not a single fleet which is exempt from financial constraints on its building programme. (121)

Next visible systems are better. Visible systems are a better deterrent. Epstein in [Oct.] '87: "Nuclear-powered attack submarines would do little to. . .enhance deterrence in the Atlantic and Pacific. . . . Invisible submarines cannot do this nearly as well as can highly visible aircraft, icebreakers, and other surface ships (12)." The next argument, I guess, is that—nope, there is no more.

The Dukakis-Bush advantage. The first argument is it's not certain. It's far— wait. The first argument, there's no certain link. This is far from Europe which is what he talks about. His hard line link evidence talks about—ah, no. It's far from the election. That's what the "E" stood for. Secondly, we could just do the plan after the election. There's no reason you'd have to announce it now. The third argument is that it flips above; would take it out, and makes them look more [unintelligible]. Next, it's not unique. Troop decreases. Mann in '87: "U.S. troop withdrawals from Europe. This could become an issue by itself, apart from curtailments in conventional forces. . .(16)." Next, it's not unique, because of Carlucci [Frank C., Secretary of Defense]. Mann in '88: "The Reagan Administration's retreat from major increases in defense spending, began a year ago. This was accentuated by the appointment recently of Frank C. Carlucci. . .(18)." Next, the character does not fit the policies of the re-election. Mann in '88: "Thus far, the 1988 U.S. Presidential campaign has been dominated by controversies over the character and integrity of individual candidates. Issues and policy have been secondary, including national defense and the civilian space program (16)." Next, it's too early to impact. Mecham in '88:

> The lack of focus on defense does not surprise Stephen J. Wayne, a political scientist at George Washington University here, who specializes in the presidency. "It's too early in the campaign," he said. "It's not what the average person is looking forward to in the primaries (19)."

The next disadvantage is Gorbachev. First of all, the flips above would take it out. Secondly, there's no impact to Soviet adventurism if there's no prolif. Three, do the plan later on. Means Gorbachev has already consolidated his power. Four, the subs aren't going to be here until 1996, so there wouldn't be any shift in U.S. subs until then. Next argument is that the subs will just obstruct the U.S. maritime strategies. Sokolsky in '87:

> [I]t is difficult to see how Canada's abandonment of plans to acquire its own SSN fleet, capable of under-ice operations, will persuade the United States to abandon its plans. For those in Canada and elsewhere concerned about unilateral U.S. naval activity in the region, a greater Canadian presence can be seen as desirable since it would, at the very least, restrict U.S. freedom of action. (16)

Next, won't be built for years. *Christian Science Monitor* in [19 Feb.] '88: "The ırst sub is not scheduled to come out of a shipyard until 1996 (9)." Next, they trade off with AHW. No, I don't want that. The next argument is that they're too few subs to matter. Eayrs in 1987: "It is hard to see how a few additional boats—at most three in each ocean, three, in refit—would make much difference to the Soviet planners' calculation of the overall 'correlation of forces' (10)." Next, there's no big Soviet sub threat anyway. This is Donald Cox in '87: "With the development of. . .long-range ballistic missiles, there is no obvious reason for the Soviets to wish to deploy ballistic-missile-bearing submarines (SSBNs) in the Canadian Arctic (100)." I guess that's— Martin: Not unique. Wick: The next argument is it's not unique. This is the *USA Today* today [28 March 1988]: "[T]he 3,200 troops deployed to Honduras. . .would be back by Wednesday. Another 1,100 troops, a Fort Bragg engineering unit in Honduras since January, also go home this week. . .(1A)." They argue at the bottom, CBW epidemic, but we're arguing—it says, we—unless you vote for us you'll break the taboo on using weapons of mass destruction which also includes biological weapons.

The (A) subpoint, he argues topicality. The evidence isn't bad. It distinctly says we have pledged to defend all of each other. The "Shamrock" sentiments, etc. He says, commitment is not a pledge, but we're pledging to—our pledge to help them—is to help them get the means to defend themselves.

(C) subpoint, prolif. He says, specific scenarios. We're getting them. He says, Canada doesn't have weapons on board, but the weapons grade uranium could be used to make a weapon. This is a source for other countries to make a weapon. He says, they have reasonable need, but this is answered on the flips also. It doesn't kick out prolif.

(D) subpoint, he says Britain and France, but they're under the NPT Treaty. They can have 'em. He says, you can, and France will give them, but they won't do so. We're preserving an international [unintelligible] against that. He says, reactor creates uranium, but which doesn't matter, because it's not concentrated enough to be weapons grade. There's the huge difference thats— The (C) subpoint evidence makes the distinction. He says, NPT falls first. First of all, prolif is not inevitable. This is from Lewis Dunn in '83:

> There is no inexorable dynamic leading to a world of many nuclear weapons states. On the contrary, such current estimates probably will prove as unfounded as those 1950s predictions that confidently warned of twenty-five or thirty nuclear weapons states of the mid-1970s—and for similar reasons. (205)

Next argument is that it has been successful. Fischer in '87: "[T]he NPT and its regime have been an effective break on further 'horizontal' proliferation. Far from unraveling, the treaty is' more viable than in 1980 (228-9)." Next argument is it doesn't matter if the technical safeguards are broken. We're preserving the international consensus. Gets it. Which has empirically worked. That's the Council on Foreign Relations. Next, Canada is the key NPT state. That's the 1AC evidence. Next, the subs encourage prolif. Epstein in [Oct.] '87: "Canada's precedent would weaken the entire nonproliferation regime. It would create problems for the International Atomic Energy Agency's safeguards system and fc Canadian compliance with it. It would encourage other states to do likewise (11).' They argue at the bottom that the superpowers would thwart the plan. Is an example of them not doing that. It preserves the ways that cannot do so. He argues at the top of the case that it's inevitable. He argues, we don't solve which is above. He says, nuclear power plants, but they're not good enough to give weapons grade uranium. That's in the (A) subpoint or (B) subpoint of case, forget which.

On contention (II). He says, no barriers to acquisition but the IEA safeguards and the international consensus deters people from doing it whether they've signed the treaty or not. He says, it's increasing, because of Pakistan. There's no proof of this. This is only speculation. Also, we would still preserve from other countries. He says, empirically no impact which is because there hasn't been prolif in the past. They've only been [unintelligible] with standing powers. He says, empirically been slow, and the impact evidence. It seems fast, but the impact evidence doesn't assume fast or slow, and if you get rid of these safeguards there will suddenly be a lot of increased prolif. On two, no. He says, eight, they wouldn't ever use them, but we're giving specific reasons why it would. Vulnerability, insanity, the fact that you could plant one, and nobody could tell who had planted it, and choose, etc. All confused. He says, it wouldn't happen, but then Jenkins says it would. Turmoil would make it dangerous. They would use in a coup or acquire it in a coup. It's empirically happened a lot of times. There's been lots of coups. He says, caution, but these poeple are fighting desperately for the lives. Also, all the unauthorized use and other stuff, and he says, no war without crazy leaders. But we're winning crazy leaders. He grants that. All the reasons why prolif is bad are granted. We're winning massively a link to proliferation. More evidence on the solvency of the NPT Treaty if I get time. I seem to have time. That it's been successful. Flow this on the top. This is—right where he argues solvency. Louis Dunn in '87:

> [S]ince 1970 only one additional country is known to have detonated a nuclear explosive device. The treaty clearly is a success in helping check the further spread of nuclear weapons, serving the security of all its parties, indeed to all countries. (18)

Next argument is they don't show how you could get weapons grade uranium absent Canada's example in the plan. Also, the next argument—more evidence from *Non-Proliferation and Global Security* in '87: "The current non-proliferation regime, as embodied in the Treaty on the Non-Proliferation of Nuclear Weapons (NPT). . . , has been relatively successful despite growing criticism. . . (Ing 119).

CROSS-EXAMINATION

J. DANIEL PLANTS QUESTIONING WICK

Plants: The first question I have for you is, your answer on one of the disads is these things won't be built 'til the late 90s, right? Wick: Yeh. Plants: Now, how is it that these other countries prolif once we give these to Canada? Is it that they get the weapons grade uranium for them? Wick: Two reasons. The first— well—the first is all this general weakening of all the laws, rules, and internaional consensus is like international pressure not to do it. Plants: But they don't have any access to the uranium that way. Wick: That's not true; they could get it also, that's the other thing, Canada presents the (C) and (D) subpoint, the (C) subpoint evidence says that. What they do is, they follow Canada's example. They buy themselves a nuclear power— Plants: Who's going to tell it to them? Wick: The same countries that'll sell it to Canada. Plants: The U.S.? Wick: —unless we prevent them. Plants: The U.S. Wick: Yes, or Britain or France. Plants: Do we have any commitment to do that now? To sell to these other countries? Wick: No, but that's because none of the other ones have the gumption to ask us to do this. Canada couldn't get away with it. We should shut 'em down. Plants: OK. Then, when would they do this? Like who wouldn't sell these subs to Canada 'til like 1996, and they wouldn't get them, and these other countries wouldn't get them 'til at least later, right? Wick: Than what? Plants: Than '97—I mean there's no way that we would be giving them subs— Wick: Well, you've assumed that they can't—that they don't have any access to uranium which obviously isn't true. Plants: Well, now, you made this distinction about how— what—a certain kind of uranium, there's only one kind that will do it. Wick: Well, what the distinction is is how enriched it is. Plants: OK. Well, how do they get that? Wick: I mean, they could steal it. They could buy it from China, the Soviet Union, France, or Britain, etc. Plants: Now, wait a second —Wick: While we're preserving a consensus that stops them from doing that. Plants: Wait. Rob, your answer to the first argument about how Britain and France would construct them, but the plan was, they were under the NPTs so that there was no way that they would give this weapons grade uranium to these other countries. Where are they going to get it from? Wick: Well, we solve this in two ways. We're preserving the international consensus which means the individual nation won't move to acquire the weapons grade uranium. And secondly the consensus stops other countries from selling it. If you violate the consensus, Britain would say, there's no reason we shouldn't do the same thing the U..S. does and make a few bucks by selling to, you know, to Y.

Plants: On West German prolif, does any of your evidence that says it frees up resources, any of it talk about the Canadian commitments and how they view their role in Europe or NATO? I mean, your card says that there is a monetary trade off. Wick: Yes, it's all from like the Canadian Defense Center and the Canadian Cabinet sources basically. Plants: Well, the cards say that like there would be less surface ships, but there's no evidence about like continental defense, is there? Land troops? Wicks: This says, um, we the Canadian Parliament—I mean Cabinet have decided that this would trade off with our other purchase plans to increase our commitments.

SECOND NEGATIVE CONSTRUCTIVE

MARTIN LOEBER, BAYLOR UNIVERSITY

You know, if you run a new case, you should at least listen to the link arguments that we make in the first negative. Our link answer, our link arguments that we're making in the first negative on defense consensus in Canada, there is no answer to this which means even if I grant all their evidence on how it trades off with conventional forces, big deal. If you have a defense cut, then it destroys the co. sensus. In addition, we'll read evidence below that says, the only way to get Canada to spend money on defense is to make them mad, and we make them mad by violating their straits, so they buy subs from us, so that's the only way to get a defense consensus. I think we'll clearly win the debate. In addition, if we win West German prolif, we'll link flip the case.

First argument, he says, we solve. NPT. First argument is that there's no evidence that says West Germany makes their decisions on this. They don't give a dang about the NPT. They only care about security considerations. Second argument is strong NATO stops. This is Kosminsky in '86:

> Rather than resulting from a calculated decision to reinforce deterrence within an Alliance or European framework, a German move to acquire nuclear weapons would be more likely to occur under political and military conditions marked by a radical loss of confidence in its allies. (26–7)

Third argument is he concedes the brink evidence. More evidence on this from the *Economist* in January [1988]:

> The first has emerged on West Germany's right wing, where mutterings can be heard that if West Germany's allies will not defend it adequately (French and British nuclear weapons are seen as no substitute for American ones), then West Germany must have its own finger on a nuclear trigger. (11)

The last argument here is West German prolif equals world prolif. In addition I would point out that this is a faster time for him, because they're claiming on the case that they get 1996, right? But our argument here will be that as soon as you do the law Canada neutralizes. That causes West German prolif which out-flips and out-time-frames the case. Dunn says in '82:

> Should West Germany acquire nuclear weapons, at least some other European countries will be pressured to do the same. . . . And by acquiring nuclear weapons, those two countries would fundamentally undermine any remaining nonproliferation efforts. . . . [T]hose countries that had not "gone nuclear" before for fear of sanctions would have less reason to hold back and the position of opponents to the acquisition of nuclear weapons will be weakened. (67).

And I'd like to point out also that this evidence gives a much better rationale than the case, because it doesn't deal with reactor technology but more with the actual weapons themselves.

He says, second, case harms. We're flipping that. Third argument, assumes decrease European commitment. They're out of it. First argument, extend the evidence that says they're on the brink of neutralism. There's no answer to this which means Canada is on the brink which means they don't get any new answers. Also, Hasek says in '87:

> The campaign to disarm the West psychologically dates back more than half a century. Now, when the new Soviet leader has made it apparent that the Politburo is

placing an unequalled emphasis on the whole programme of indirect attack the danger is greater than ever. (40-1)

Hasek says in '87:

> We are now witnessing the last phase of neutralisation. This is a concerted propaganda campaign which is designed to "Finlandise" Canada and to sever the links with NATO and NORAD. The psychological preparation for this campaign has been evident for the past several years, but the overt mass appeal could be said to have started with the television showing. . . . Tina Viljoen cast doubt on the value of Canada's sacrifice in the past wars by arguing that the wars had nothing to do with Canada. In any case, from a long-term historical viewpoint, nothing was solved by them even in Europe. Therefore, according to the films, the only sensible option is for Canada to be concerned solely with its own sovereignty to leave NATO and NORAD. (37)

And I'd also like to point out that this link evidence says that they don't have an inherent commitment which means the only way to secure that is to make them mad by violating their sovereignty and giving them subs.

Third argument is you have to reaffirm NATO commitment in order to keep them in NATO. The Hasek evidence says that new defense policies must reaffirm our commitment to NATO, i.e., something like a sub in order to educate the public and keep them involved in NATO. Hasek says in '87:

> The roots of the armed forces have to be firmly anchored in society at large by revitalizing the reserves and reforming the officer training corps and high school cadet units: The exposure of a greater proportion of young Canadians to military training will not only restore confidence in our ability to defence ourselves. . . .(41)

Fourth argument is he concedes the impact evidence that says if Canada neutralizes that that would destroy NATO because our defenses would be weakened. Also, Hasek says in '87:

> Exploited by forces hostile to democracy, the continued crisis in Canadian defence can be fatal to Canadian sovereignty, cause irreparable damage to the Western Alliance and seriously destabilise the nuclear balance. It is time to enact policies which will permit a secure Canada to play a stronger part in maintaining peace. (36)

Next argument is C^3 [Command, control, communications] vulnerability equals West German fears. You'll note that all the link talks about NORAD and if we abandon NORAD that that would equal vulnerability of first strike. That scares the Germans. Williams in '86:

> [I]f the Soviets know that they cannot decapitate the American command structure, U.S. retaliation being then imminent, the value of deterrence is increased. This knowledge must increase European confidence in the American extended deterrent system upon which their own security continues to rest. (8)

Next argument is perceptions of superiority equal West German prolif which would be likely if we lost NORAD. Drum says in '82:

> But there are certain possible shocks that might cause West Germany to rethink or question its reliance on the security framework provided by NATO. West German perceptions of increasing Soviet strategic superiority, for example, could lead to more vigorous questioning of the alliance's effectiveness and of the American guarantee. (66)

He says, number four, subs are directed versus the United States which is the reason they're asking for them in order to protect their sovereignty which proves the only way that you can get them to build their subs is to make them mad by violating their sovereignty. The second argument is that they wouldn't build anything else otherwise. The only reason they're doing this is to protect their sovereignty. Shallhorn in '87:

> At about the same time senior Department of National Defense officials began telling the parliamentary defense committee that nuclear-powered submarines were "affordable" and were being considered to replace Canada's three British-built Oberon diesel-electric submarines, Canada seemed prepared to spend billions on under-ice-capable nuclear-powered submarines just to keep tabs on the U.S. Navy. (16–7)

Aviation Week in '87: "A primary objective of the expanded maritime role is to deter, rather than simply monitor U.S. and Soviet intrusions into Arctic waters that the Canadian government considers to be violations of national sovereignty. (57)" Sokolsky in '87:

> It is these nuclear-powered submarines that will give the fleet a more balanced ASW capability. They will allow the navy to operate in all three oceans. . . . The passive fixed system will still be crucial for surveillance and sovereignty protection, since most of the time the SSNs will be in the Atlantic and Pacific. But the government regards it as important to Canada's sovereignty, as well as to its ability to contribute to North American defense, that the navy have an active under-ice capability similar to the active air defense forces that back up ground-based radar. (14–5)

Which proves that the reason they do it is in order to protect their sovereignty, but it is also useful in defending NATO. He says, number five, sub prevents dollars for alternatives. First argument is they can build the subs. There's no cost problem. *Aviation Week* in '87: in 10 Canada's long-delayed defense white paper, scheduled for release in June, will decree a more active military role for the 21st century, with a three-ocean maritime strategy reliant on 10 new nuclear-powered attach submarines. . . . (56)

Next argument is that they enhance security. Sokolsky says in '87:

> Nor is the decision inconsistent with Canada's support for arms control measures. In the long run, Western collective security and the cause of arms control can be furthered by a greater Canadian maritime capability in all three of its oceans. (16)

Next argument is independently, they won't send any troops. Their troop level is low. Our link is no longer troops out rather NORAD and the collective defense of the Arctic. This is *McLean's* says in '87: "Canada could not live up to its 19-year-old NATO commitment to help defend Norway in wartime (14)." *McLean's* says in 87: ". . .Ottawa is preparing to surrender its commitments in Norway (14)." Also, Canada is second to the bottom in spending which means they don't spend money, and the only way to motivate them to spend money is to make them mad by violating their sovereignty. Simpson says in '87: "The raw numbers told it all: Canada was spending the second-lowest per capita amount on defense of all the NATO countries. Thank God, ran the joke, for Luxembourg (9).

Hamilton says in '87:

> Canada has been reluctant to do so, though it has recently reviewed its overall defense policy. Indications are that a greater emphasis on conventional defenses of Canada will result. In addition, Canada, whose defense spending as a percentage of GNP is the second lowest among NATO allies, needs to do more for common western security. (E1758)

Sokolsky says in '87:

> The total personnel level is about 85,000 and the defense budget is roughly $10 billion in Canadian dollars ($7.5 billion U.S.), which translates into just above two percent of gross domestic product, placing Canada next to last in NATO, just above Luxembourg. (13)

All this evidence proves that Canada doesn't spend that much which means that they have no inherent reason to do it. The only way you could do it is to force them to sovereignty, and the only thing they'll do when you violate their sovereignty is buy nuclear subs.

He says, six, there's no backlash, and they avoid embarrasment. That's not our link. Our argument is they have to reaffirm their commitment to NATO. Otherwise they'll become neutral which causes C³ vulnerability. In addition it would also cause neutralism which could tip the balance to the West. Our Hasek evidence is better.

He says, seven, subs trade off with forces in Europe. All this evidence says is that if they spend more money on subs they might not be able to put forces in Europe. First argument is counterplan. We'll give Canada money. We will take the money from conventional forces in the United States that are not deployed anywhere. This will take out the flip, right? Which means they get money which gives them enough money to keep their forces in Europe. Second argument is there's no evidence that says that if you get the money—no, no—if they get more money by banning subs that they would build more conventional forces. Our above evidence says that they're unlikely to spend more money. They have an inherent reason not to.

He says, eight, trade off with surface ships and visibles are a better deterrent. First argument is even if it does we're still winning the NORAD and neutralization links. Second argument is there's no evidence that says that abandoning subs would result in an increase in funding for surface ships. All it says is that if you spend money on subs you can't spend it on surface ships which means we're still

winning on link. Third argument is the fact that it is visible and a better de[...]
rent is not our link to West German prolif. We're still winning the Canadi[...]
neutralism debate.

Now we can concede all these arguments about trading off with surface ASW.
There is no answer in the 2AC trading off with surface ASW. There is no answer
in the 2AC to the Canadian defense consensus, and for them to reach an answer
to this in the 1AR, I suggest, would be new which means we win the debate there.·

Southern discomfort. He says, it's far from Europe—no, no—far from the election, but our evidence says the polls are close. In addition, there's every reason
to consider that this would be translating concern especially since the plan is done
over the near term. He says, second, they could do the plan after election. First
of all, this contradicts their conditionality bad arguments. They're changing the
plan. If anything, it should be a reverse voting issue on them. I'm not going
to claim that, but if they go for conditionality, make them eat this as well. Second
argument is the plan doesn't do that, right? It does it immediately. In addition
if you want to vote for them after the election, I suggest you do so. You should
vote, for us in this debate.

He says, third, the flips above. I'm sure the South perceives that. They're more
likely to perceive as hosing over Canada. Perceptions of credibility are critical
to Bush. This is *Wall Street Journal* in March [1988].

> If a genuine liability was exposed Tuesday it is the belief that a candidate can
> build his agenda around polls or press clippings. . . .
> The successful candidate for high office must have some credible, discernible core
> of beliefs. . . .
> George Bush, after a long career, has achieved credibility with a large constituen-
> cy. (24)

Next argument is the plan kills that, right? The plan ensures that Reagan looks
bad. He reverses himself on this decision. That translates into Bush which means
independently of whether or not—independently of whether or not they increase
deterrence, they still make Reagan both bad by making them think that we're
hosing over the Canadians.

He says, troop decrease and Carlucci. There's no evidence on why that's our
link. In addition the Canadian link on how we're hosing them over would take
this out.

He says, five—or six, that character doesn't affect the election. Our evidence
says that they destroy Bush's character. In addition our evidence says that empirically that's the way to get himself elected.

He says, seven, it's too early to know whether defense has an impact. That's
no longer our link. Our link is credibility of Bush being consistent with our allies.

And extend the impact. Trade users. There's no answer.

Gorbachev. He says, flipped above, but if I grant out the uniqueness answers,
it'll take it out. He says, there's no impact to Red spread. That's true. He says,
they do it later in 1996 which all takes this out. Oh, also the subs are not built
'til 1996 which takes out any kind of links in this, but it wouldn't play into West
German prolif nor Southern discomfort, since they'd be perceived. He says, subs

struct maritime strategy, but our evidence says—that—our evidence on the other ~de says, enhance security. He says, for years, that's fine.

CROSS-EXAMINATION

ROB WICK QUESTIONING LOEBER

Wick: Marty, your argument is that rather than trading off with other naval forces—rather than trading off they would just put it into solve their deficit, right? Loeber: Who? Wick: Canada. Loeber: Ah, yeh. They might have a couple of AFDC programs, or something. I don't know. Wick: If that's true, then why wouldn't your counterplan to give Canada money just put money back into their deficit? Loeber: Oh, because it's stipulated on them keeping the troops in Europe. Wick: Where do you—OK—Why doesn't this take out the link to your disadvantage? It proves that Canada is not going neutralist, because the U.S. is sitting there guaranteeing that— Loeber: That has nothing to do with Canadian—Wick: —Canada's forces stay in Europe. Loeber: No, no, no, no, no, no, no, no. That has nothing to do with Canadian neutralism. Our link to Canadian neutralism— Wick: Wait a minute, how can Canada be neutral if it's stationing forces in NATO European countries? Loeber: Our link to Canadian neutralism is that Canada no longer perceives a need to defend the West. All right? Wick: Yeh, so, Canada has forces in Europe. Why isn't that defending the West? Are they going to put them in Eastern Europe? Loeber: No, they're going to pull the troops out. Wick: Your counterplan makes sure that they cannot do that, so where's the link? Loeber: No, we don't. The counterplan just gives them money to do so. We don't, we don't like hold a gun to Canadian troops and make them stay in Europe. Wick: OK. So the counterplan gives them money and doesn't tie their hands at all? Loeber: No, the counterplan says, if you plan to put troops in Europe, we'll give you money for it. Wick: But otherwise, eh—Loeber: We won't. Wick: OK. Well, why wouldn't Canada just accept free money to to like pay for all their people to stay in Europe? Loeber: Well, because they might not like the risk. Wick: If they wouldn't like the risk, then the counterplan can't solve, correct? Loeber: Right. All this does is counterplan out your turns. Wick: Tell me word for word, what does the counterplan do? What are the stipulations? Loeber: The counterplan says, if Canada wants to maintain forces in Europe, we will help them do so.

Wick: If they want to maintain forces in Europe, we will help them. Loeber: Um, hum. Wick: OK. So we will make it like free for them to maintain forces in Europe. Loeber: No. We'll just help them pay the—keep the money. Wick: Pay them how much? Loeber: As much as they—as we think is necessary. Wick: Well, how the hell are Shaun and I supposed to figure how much that is? Loeber: Current levels. To maintain current levels, we will pay them. Wick: OK. So now where's the link to your disad, and how can they be neutral if they're keeping Western European troops in Europe? Loeber: See, you're making a wrong assumption. If they become neutralist by collapse of the Canadian consensus, then they no longer would desire to keep troops in Europe. Wick: OK. Now, em, why if Canada had troops in Europe would West Germany prolif? Loeber: What? Wick: Western—even if Canada was neutral, but they had troops in Europe defending Germany— Loeber: For one thing, NORAD would collapse and they'd perceive

C³ vulnerability. They'd also perceive— Wick: What's the risk to NORA[vulnerability? Loeber: What? Wick: Isn't NORAD on land? How do you pro tect NORAD better? Loeber: What? NORAD is our defense command in the north, a part of the DEW line in Canada. Wick: On land, so how do subs defend it better? Loeber: We're not arguing that. That's the point. You missed the whole link in the first negative. Wick: You said NORAD vulnerability. Loeber: Right, because you erode the defense consensus.

FIRST NEGATIVE REBUTTAL

J. DANIEL PLANTS, BAYLOR UNIVERSITY

This bio weapons turn is silly. There's no way they get that. Extend the evidence. It says, Glasnost caused them to break up. They'll get our technology.

On the counterplan, non-topicality. He says. topical. Unconditional versus con- ditional. First, this does not explain. Second, they shouldn't get to explain it in 1AR. Second, it wouldn't be a substantial reduction. It would only be a small decrease in our pledge. Their argument, this is wrong. This commitment would remain until the reduction was actually implemented. There wouldn't be any reduction in commitment until we voted to do away with something. The fourth argument here is it will be a political not a military commitment. Kennedy in '84: "Consequently, NATO consultation is a *political* rather than a legal imperative (12)."

[Unintelligible] he says will be the U.S. action, but it wouldn't be. We'd only be going into these things. Also, it would be a NATO decision. The [unintelligi- ble]. He says impact. Affirmative justifies ballot. But, first, that's not true. The competition arguments are granted away. We can kick it out on that. Second, there wouldn't be any advantage to that. Even if they could seize it, even if they consist, there would not be an advantage to [unintelligible] for the topic. He's pimping the advantage on the counterplan when he's saying it doesn't mean anything. Wouldn't be a reason to vote.

Off conditionality, he argues, first, there's no impact to that. It's not a voting issue. Second, there's no impact as well. It's the counterplan advantage does not flip the [unintelligible] warning away from these things. Even if we were stuck with it, it wouldn't hurt us. The third argument here is no different from other things. We can grant out link arguments on these things. The fourth argument here is there is no impact to clash on any of these kinds of things as well.

I just want to go off the mutual exclusivity on the competition. He says the plan equals. That's fine. There's no value that they can give to the advantage. He says it's not worth anything. Also, the Rose evidence says you can do it at the same time. Then there isn't any value from this, from our claim of the counterplan any more. But, they're not getting any value off doing this.

Topicality. Voting issue. No [unintelligible] from the first violation. We're short enough on prep time as it is. The argument on commitment. He says, first, that would be overlimit. But it would not be over limitation. There would be lots of pledges. There would be U.S. troops, U.S. tacticals in there. Also, our first use pledge. We would indicate that our weapons would still be part of it. As long as our weapons are [unintelligible] a force to the future. But selling arms to somene else for them to have the arms independently, to be sovereign weapons, and that's not a pledge, because we're not bound to action. If those subs are sunk as whatever, then we're not necessarily bound to fill in.

Off the second argument, he says they meet that. But they don't or they don't decrease the pledge. All they do is change the means to fulfill that pledge. Right? This is the whole point of the argument. The pledge remains definitive. All they do is change the means to that. In order to be topical they have to do away with the pledge itself.

Off the third argument, he says that arms sales are military commitment. First, that's not true. [Unintelligible]. The (C1) subpoint is [unintelligible]. On limitation. Also the second argument here is this would legitimize all kinds of other cases. Anything dealing with arms also. The Paul definition supersedes this. He says, first, it won't decrease the commitment to NATO. Reading the Johnson evidence, or according to the Johnson evidence, defense pledge, they change the means to fulfill the pledge. It has not reduced itself. I explained that above. Second subpoint is their interpretation requires effects. That would require you to look at the effect of taking away with this and the effect it had on our overall capability to do the pledge. He says, at this point reduce the commitment to defense. Stop the subs. But the pledge to defend subs only proves we have a broader pledge to defense. It proves that they don't stop that pledge. They don't change the commitment.

Off six subpoint, he says decrease subs a commitment. The 1AC Schultz evidence. First this is not a commitment. We have only agreed to help them. Second, it is not a definition. He has casually discussing this in the literature. The Paul evidence is conjectural. He's trying to [unintelligible].

Off number seven, he says decrease [unintelligible]. First, no commitment to do this. Only a memorandum of understanding. Second, that's not a commitment. The Paul definition answers. He says the last thing is they decrease Article 3, the pledge to help them. That's only proving my argument that the pledge is in effect. It changes the way we would do this.

Off the second contention, on the case, off the (B) subpoint, not U.S. commitment. He says, pledge to defend. Pledge to help. This evidence is terrible. You can read it at the end of the debate. None of these cards say that this is a military commitment. The cards talk about how we have an overall pledge to them. That just proves that they don't do away with this commitment. All they do is change the way that we would implement that.

Off the (B) subpoint, the prolif argument. He says, actually, first of all, they have to isolate scenarios. He says they do. That's not true. None of the evidence is country specific. Make them read evidence that says that Brazil prolifs or that Argentina will do this, or whatever, like that.

Off the second argument, Canada won't have the uranium. The uranium would be used. First they won't have the uranium. There won't be nuclear arms. He's conceding the evidence that says they won't put nuclear warheads on there. There will be no reason to have the uranium. Second it takes out the prolif link. There's no way that these other countries could get the uranium. So Canada wouldn't have it. Even if the subs are nuclear capable, it wouldn't be given to them. T[unintelligible] wouldn't need it.

Off the third argument, the plan to acquire, to [unintelligible]. Oh, the las[unintelligible] argument above, there's no evidence about future sales. Canada is a unique country. There's no way that we would sell these kinds of things to Chile or anyone like that. There's no reason that could do this. Down below, off the next group of arguments on solvency on the (D) subpoint, first of all, not unique. They can get it in other ways. He says these people are under the NPT. First, that takes out prolif. If that's true that these other countries are, then his argument about future sales to these people wouldn't happen. That proves that they wouldn't be giving it to them. Takes out all the prolif. Second, it's an absolute meaning to the case. International consensus will be eroded. They can say this through rebuttals all they want, because last word about international consensus, but if we're not selling things to these people and these people can't get access to this and the fact that barriers to prolif have gone down won't matter, because they can't get the stuff to prolif.

Off the second, nukes of the plan, he says France already has, but there is no indication that France would give these away.

Off the third argument, reactor. He says, not weapons grade proving that the countries couldn't get it.

Off number four, NPT fails. He says, inevitable. First, post dated. Second, the Fischer evidence concludes negative. It said that support is decreasing. The third subpoint, the international consensus argument is answered above. The fourth, subs don't lead to others. There's no indication why that's true. U.S., Great Britain, and France will already have these things which is unique. The fifth argument is not give to these other countries. There is no propensity for these sales to happen in the future. They're not indicating that these things should be done. The sixth argument that [unintelligible] states are not member states. That proves that support for the NPT is irrelevant. The countries that might prolif are on the fringe anyway. They're not within the NPT, so strengthening it doesn't help.

Off number seven, the superpower's [unintelligible]. He says, plan preserves, but he drops the Soviet Union. That's at least a part of what we need. Extend the evidence that says these things won't be armed with nuclear arms, et cetera. All that's granted away. He's not answering that.

Top of the case. All prolif is bad. The inevitability argument, he says, answered above. That's answered above. He says, can't solve. He says, above. That's fine. Our third subpoint, nuclear power plants. He says, not good enough. It's either meet need, or it proves that they won't be able to get these things in anyway. Off fourth subpoint, no barriers. He says, IEA. An international consensus for our program up above that would [unintelligible] nuclear states is increasing. Extend that. Number six, prolif would be slow. I don't have an answer to this. It takes out all the transitional stuff. Extend the evidence that they would do it slow. It solves for the impact as well. Off the stuff—now he reads more cards about how the NPT solve. It says the treaty helps, but he's dropping that these people nt membership, so it doesn't matter. Off nuclear coups, extend my arguments ᴴere that says, assumes a past war. Also, there's no propensity for a coup to happen. He's not reading any evidence on general military instability. Off the [unintelligible] on unauthorized use, just extend that it's empirically denied by the superpowers, and he doesn't extend the other scenarios. Right? He doesn't even mention them. It's the same thing as putting pressure on him, and any other way of forcing him to drop things. He doesn't even mention them in the 2AC. He shouldn't be able to claim them in the 1AR now.

FIRST AFFIRMATIVE REBUTTAL

SHAUN MARTIN, DARTMOUTH COLLEGE

Topicality. We say went over limits. He says, it's like a first use pledge. But if first use is topical, then we're topical as well. We decrease this commitment [unintelligible]. On our second subpoint, decrease commitment, he says, you won't achieve your means. That's the same as their first use. You would overlimit. You would only make that—not responding—topical. Our third subpoint, emphasis on commitment, group his answers. First of all, doesn't legitimize all kinds of show. There's still little [unintelligible] for you debating. You can debate all the weapons systems. Second of all, you certainly get an [unintelligible] in this debate. Third of all, we reading contextual evidence. That's best. It's certainly in the literature. Fourth subpoint, decrease Article 3. Says, you only change the means. First of all, it's directly in the Treaty. That certainly a limitation enough. Second of all, it's not effects. It's under the specific arms control treaty. I see no answer to the fifth subpoint, reduces "Shamrock." Sixth subpoint we have a pledge to NATO. He says, not broader interpretation. However, release to decreasing that promise sets enough ground. Seventh subpoint, decrease commitment to Britain and France. He says, this is only political. We say, that's not true. It's contextual evidence. I think it's best. The eighth subpoint is show up above as well.

West German prolif, please. We say, first of all, we solve. Please group his answers. First of all, you can still constrain somewhat. At least we get somewhat of a flip. Second of all, NATO strong. It's flip to our tradeoff. That'll be argued below. Second of all, it's perceived as increase for NATO. He says, the link is ridiculous. Our argument is that it is perceived as isolationist, which is direct flip off the internal link. *Financial Post* in '87: "A nuclear fleet amounts to a declaration of independence from NATO doctrine (Bagnell 55)." Fourth of all, West German prolif doesn't necessarily equal war prolif. They could still be constrained by U.S. factors, etc.

Off our third subpoint, decrease— Oh, off the second subpoint, group all his extend the link answers. First of all, they don't do it against the United States. If anything, if they do do foreign ships against the United States, that means we specifically increase the U.S. directed commitment. The Canadian commitment to NATO isn't what's important. We're increasing U.S. commitment. Give that as a defended against us. Second of all, they're perceived isolationist. That's above. Third of all, allies oppose subs because of trade offs. They at least perceive this. Sokolsky in '87: "Canada's allies are understandably concerned that the SSN project will draw resources away from other Canadian contributions. . .(15)."

Fourth of all, Europe fears this. Sokolsky in '87: "NATO allies are concern
that expenditures on a fleet of SSNs will reduce resources available for Canada
land and air forces, as well as for other parts of its navy, especially surface ship
(13)," which means the counterplan wouldn't solve. Fifth of all, Canadian forces
are an important symbol. We uniquely increase them. Honderich in '87: "[T]here
is a tremendous political utility in having a symbolic Canadian presence on the
continent of Europe (19)." Sixth of all the Canadian cuts sets precedents for U.S.
cuts which takes out the counterplan as well. Sokolsky in '86: "There is
pressure. . .to reduce the size of the U.S. forces unless the Europeans spend more
on defense, and some in Congress might seize upon a Canadian decision to pull
out of Germany to support this call (102)." Next subpoint, the subs tradeoff with
forces in Europe which is our specific flip. [Leyton-Brown][8] in '87: "[E]xpen-
ditures on nuclear powered submarines will inevitably to distort priorities in
Canada's defense budget (5)." They could decrease the Canadian troops in
Europe. The next subpoint, his evidence isn't specific to Canada. Next of all,
we don't stop [unintelligible]. That'll be on the fifth subpoint that there is no
backlash. The last subpoint, we stop Soviet strategic superiority. Right? He's dropping all flips on FPMS. We're directly delivering that link.

Off the third subpoint, he says, wanting to do this is no reason to do it. First
of all, it still flips the direct link. We're increasing the U.S. presence which increase U.S. superiority. Given these subs, they will [unintelligible] against us.
Second of all, the evidence below will take out. This evidence says you can still
use the subs. They would attack against the United States. And third of all, there's
no link to the sovereignty link. He's just making up. Please read our cards.

Fourth subpoint says, free elsewhere. He says, there are no subs now. Group
his answers. First of all, you might be able to build the subs, but they still turn
off better things [unintelligible] disad. Second of all, we're flipping his troop
evidence—his troop argument. His evidence contradicts the 1NC position, so it
shouldn't be allowed. It only talks about Norway; it doesn't talk about Canada.
Third of all, we will make them mad, so they'd increase spending to defend their
own straits which would flip this. Fourth of all, they're still modernizing forces.
Blackburn in '87: "Nuclear submarines would require a huge expenditure that
would use up scarce resources and force cancellation of other essential equipment
purchases (17)."

He says, fifth subpoint, they backlash. He says, there's no link; you must reaffirm the commitment. Our argument is that there isn't a backlash. His argument
requires them to get upset at us. Our fifth subpoint says, they won't get upset
at us. Extend from Knelman in '87: "Canada is subservient to the U.S. interests
in all senses, including the geopolitical, economic, and geostrategic (32)." [Mahant
and] Mount in '84: "Economic integration with the United States has reached

---

[8]"A second group is less supportive, because of the fear that expenditures on nuclear-powered submarines will inevitably distort priorities in Canada's defence budget. There is concern that other needed
modernizations could be delayed or eliminated, and some even fear that Canada will ultimately be
faced with a choice between the submarine program and the continuation of Canada's troops in Europe,
because it could not afford to do both."

.evel where Canada simply cannot afford to confront the United States on just .ny issue where Canada's interests may be at stake (260)."

He says, sixth subpoint, subs increase commitment to Europe. He counterplans it out. First of all, that directly increases the commitment. Takes out the disad. Second of all, they shifted to deficit, and he doesn't have any evidence on this. Third of all, it would cause a deficit disad. *Boston Globe* in.'87: "[T]he goal of the deficit reduction through spending reduction must be paramount (1)." *Business Today* in '86 [1988]: If we don't resolve the budget deficit dilemma, the market told us that we would have a depression,[9] and he reads the [unintelligible] evidence.

He only counterplans out troops. We have an independent advantage, plus his counterplan is conditional.

Disad two, on Bush. We say, third subpoint flips above. Our evidence is specific. It says, they perceive isolationist. Fourth subpoint said, now you achieve troop decrease. He says, why is this a link? It's at least topical on link. He drops the fifth subpoint, not unique. Carlucci. He says, character is irrelevant. Our argument is character is talking about Iran-contra, not this.

Gorbachev, please. We say, flips above. He says, takes out uniqueness. However, it still pulls the disad somewhat. He says, across (B) subpoint, it's structural, maritime [unintelligible] which flips the other disad. The seventh subpoint, too few [unintelligible] where also takes out the other disads. And the ninth subpoint, not unique. This evidence is from today. West German prolif would be happening now.

Contention (II). (B) subpoint is topicality. He says, our evidence is bad. Please read our evidence. It's only conjectural evidence. (C) subpoint is on the links. Please group his one, two, and three. First of all, there's no counter evidence on our scenarios. Second of all, it doesn't take out prolif. You won't grant out the fissionable material link, however, you still have the nonproliferation regime, and that stops their will to get this. (D) subpoint, solvency. He says, one, two, three. Britain and France. Group it. First of all, Britain and France are not unique. Canada is key. Second of all, his evidence up over the (A) subpoint says, they can't get this type of material which we uniquely solve. Four, five, and six. Group his big doubt. First of all, the NPT [unintelligible] empirical [unintelligible] taking out his argument. Second of all, this is relevant to will. We decrease their will. Third of all, Canada is key. Fourth of all, we're reading better evidence than his here.

Off the top of the case, please. He says—group all of the stuff on the top of the case. First of all, we have a lot of scenarios. We'll certainly get that. Second of all, his third subpoint evidence says, no barrier to doing it. We independently decrease their will. Third of all, this takes out his arguments on the U.S. The Soviet Union could stop them, because this evidence says they could have these materials in the future which we would deem to uniquely stop that. All we're saying is, if you hold a nonproliferation regime, that individuals won't want to get nuclear weapons.

[9]"Richad Menschel, managing partner of Goldman Sachs, says that concern over the deficits will continue to worry investors. 'If we don't resolve the budget deficit dilemma, the market told us through the October 19th experience that they would resolve it for us. . .(37).' "

SECOND NEGATIVE REBUTTAL

MARTIN LOEBER, BAYLOR UNIVERSITY

There are two considerations as to why we should win this debate on West German prolif. First of all, all these answers he makes in the 1NR are new. Rob didn't make any of these answers. For him to get up here and read isolationism evidence and perceives isolationism and allies perceive evidence, all this evidence is new. You shouldn't allow it. Secondly, is we out time-frame them. They're claiming on the case that they have 1996 time-frame, but if you West German prolifs equals would prolif that happens a lot faster than the case.

First argument, he says, off West German prolif that they're still constrained by the NPT. That's ridiculous. He doesn't answers my arguments that they don't care about it. All they care about is NATO commitments.

He says, second, NATO is strong. That's beside the point. If we win the Canadian demilitarization impact, then we would win the debate, because it says that it destroys Western Security independently. The C^3 links are dropped as well.

He says, third it's perceived as isolationism. First of all, is the counterplan would solve for that. If we counterplan by giving Canada enough money to solve for their defense budget, then it would solve for that. Second is the counterplan wouldn't take out the link. If we win our argument as to why they have to have more and more defense programs in order to educate the public for the need for them. In addition we're reading evidence that says that they build SSNs for both sovereignty and NATO security reasons. Also, the subs would inevitably be coupled. This is *Aviation Week* says in '87:

> They believe surveillance of the Arctic could be conducted less provocatively with sonar technologies and that aggressive maritime operations with attack submarines might, in the event of war, embroil Canada in the U.S. maritime strategy of blockading the Soviet Northern fleet in the Barents sea, near Murmansk and the Kola Peninsula. (56)

He says, four. West German prolif doesn't equal world prolif reading us evidence.

Second argument, case harms. He says, first, they don't do it against—Oh, that they increase Canadian defense, etc. But, first argument, extend our argument that says if you do any defense cuts that it equals a perception of neutralism, and they begin to question their commitment to NATO. Second, this is especially true in this case, because they've promised to build these subs. People say that they're to defend themselves and NATO, and then all of a sudden they're reversing on that.

Third, it's counterplan takes out any turns. He says, second, isolation. That's above. He says, third. [unintelligible]. The counterplan solves. He says, four, Europe fears. First of all, is they fear C^3 vulnerability works. Second argument is Canada wouldn't increase absent solve external motivation. I am making those link answers. He doesn't answer it. In other words, the only reason they're building the subs is because we're violating their sovereignty. They wouldn't build anything in return. They wouldn't build a stubby frigate. They wouldn't build anything, because the only way to get political capital is to violate their sovereignty.

He says, five Canadian forces are key, but there are not very many troops. The key thing is their commitments to NORAD, etc., which means even if they win this force trade off, it's irrelevant.

He says, six, Canadian cuts equals U.S. cuts. Counterplan solves. He says, seventh, it doesn't trade off, or it does trade off with Europe, but that's beside the point, because they don't have very many troops here. In addition, our evidence says that they're more concerned about NORAD. The Hasek evidence says, if Canada becomes neutral, it's more of an impact. He says, not Canada. Yes, it is. He says, nine, doesn't stop Canada with [unintelligible] which isn't true. Our link evidence says that if you have any decrease in commitments, it decreases the educational value to the public, and this is especially true, since they have committed themselves to building these subs.

Off the arguments on subs prevent alternatives. He says, they increase U.S. precedents. Well, we're flipping that, because we counterplan this out. He says below, use diesel subs, but my evidence is specific. It says they don't think diesel subs are sufficient. In addition, they're committed to nuclear subs which means any reversal at this point would destroy the defense consensus. He says, third, no link. That's above.

Off the arguments on no backlash. He says, they build the subs, and they flip troops. The counterplan will solve. He says, they don't make them mad, etc., or they do, but there's no reason for that. They only say that—to insure their sovereignty is to build subs. He says, modernizing forces equals a tradeoff which is answered above. He says that there's no backlash, no upset, no defense consensus, which isn't true. I'm extending the evidence that says that if you do something that cuts back on defenses that it makes them mad. In addition, our evidence says that the only way that you can motivate them to build up forces is to violate their sovereignty and the only thing that they'll build in response to that is nuclear subs.

He says, counterplan gets the disads, because it increases commitments which equals no disads, but the plan and the counterplan together gets the Canadian neutralism disad, because Canada withdraws on its subs which means the counterplan would solve for that. He says, no evidence. I don't need any. He says, four, deficits, and he counterplans out the troops. AC's not answering the argument that I make in the 2NC. That will just draw down U.S. forces that are based in the United States that are not committed to NATO in order to fund them. There's no answer to this. I don't have to answer this deficit stuff which means if you compare the plan and the counterplan, we get more of a link to West German prolif, because we avoid Canadian neutralization.

Southern discomfort. He can have the links. Gorbachev. There's no flip. It's long term. In addition, I granted out uniqueness answers. I don't have to answer this.

Top of the case. I'll concede all these scenarios, but I'd like to extend number three, the nuclear power plants are a meet need to the case. Also, extend the sixth, prolif is slow. Also, nuclear states are increasing now which takes out his arguments which means there's inevitability to this which means that you would want to vote negative in order to avoid this.

Contention (II). We say—oh, he can have the T[opicality] arguments. Off the (C) subpoint, he says, there's no counter evidence. Doesn't take out prolif. Talking about the international regime, but he's not answering our evidence that says, they don't have nukes. There's no reason why nuclear reactors would cause this. In addition, we won't sell 'em. All he's winning now is the regime link.

Off the (D) subpoint, solvency. Extend that Britain and France makes this not unique. He just makes some answer to this, but he doesn't answer this. Also extend that the NPT fails. He says, it's empirical, but it's not. Also, extend that threshold states are not members which means they're not winning any link, and the seventh argument is superpowers thwarts as well. We explain that West German prolif link flips the case and faster time-frame, because the subs don't cause prolif at least until 1997.

Confronted with the daunting task of researching this topic this year, I asked myself several times, is it worth it? After a 4-4, losing in octas on a 3-0 (could have been a 3,000-0) at West Georgia this year, I was really skeptical of the point of the activity. No longer. I would like to thank several people for support and encouragement: Erik [Walker], Danny [Plants], Cary [Voss], John Lombard, Robert [Wood] and David [Giardini], Melisa Minton, Steve Mancuso, Dallas [Perkins], and the rest of our squad. And even though they're on the other side, John Culver, Ken Strange, and Lenny Gail have given Danny and me inestimable self respect. We value their opinions highly.

SECOND AFFIRMATIVE REBUTTAL

ROB WICK, DARTMOUTH COLLEGE

I think we'll win a lot on case, but I also hope to persuade you that we're flipping only disadvantage in the round. The fourth argument, troop decreases makes the West German prolif disadvantage happen. Right? They want their allies to defend them. The United States, its strongest ally, is not defending them any more. The fifth subpoint, Carlucci has promised that he would pull United States forces out of Europe. He doesn't counterplan out that its only cause of West German prolif. He said they care about the U.S. much more than Canada. Obviously the U.S. is the mainstay of the NATO alliance. The Gorbachev argument. We're arguing the fifth subpoint, obstructs the U.S. maritime strategy which means that isolationism is not new. We argued in the 2AC that this would be used to enforce Canadian sovereignty, that it would not be directed toward Europe, that it would be directed against the United States, so it—these isolationism arguments aren't new. Also, it decreases the maritime strategy, so it flips the link, it flips security, it flips protection of NORAD, etc. Also, the perception of Canadian neutralism would be flipped, because they're not isolationist any more. The seventh argument, there's too few to matter. He doesn't answer this. There's no perception by Germany that this is important, that this will cause Canadian neutralism or any decrease in security versus the Soviets. The ninth argument is an independent uniqueness argument. We decrease forces today which means it takes out the West German prolif disadvantage. At the top of the West German prolif disadvantage he says, it's the new one in our answers. I've already explained that we argued that it would be used against the U.S. It would be isolationist, that it would be used to protect sovereignty. More evidence that it will be used to [unintelligible] subs to U.S. David Cox in '87:

> Theoretically, Canadian nuclear submarines might take responsibility for patrol of the Canadian Arctic and denial of passage to the Soviets, but this will hardly please the U.S. Navy if their primary purpose is transit of the Arctic basin to achieve access to Soviet sanctuaries. (104)

The second argument is all these perceptions distinctions don't come out until the 2NC. Does the 1NC argue perception distinctions? No. So, we just argued that Europe does perceive the terms that we already argued. He says, secondly, the time frame is 1996. No. The incentive to acquire is immediate. Secondly, decreased security does not happen 'til West Germany 'til then. Right? So there would be no Canadian neutralism, or anything, 'til then. Also, there's no evidence that West Germany would perceive that they would suddenly need these subs in 1996.

The third argument is that the surface forces are much more visible which means that it will reassure Germany more. Off of the first answer in the 1AR, contain somewhat, the West German prolif. He says, they don't care about it. They only care about the NATO commitment. They care about the international consensus. Right? The international consensus deters them. They don't want to alienate their security partners which are part of that international consensus. He says, two subpoint. Canadian demilitarization is bad, but the subs cut more visible programs which means it looks like they're demilitarizing even more. Off of the three subpoint in the 1AR, isolationist flip, he says, the counterplan solves this. The subs themselves are isolationist. Right? They're used to keep the United States away. *Aviation Week* in '87: "On a larger scale, the concentration on national maritime strategy will proceed hand in hand with a somewhat diminished international role (56)." The whole point of this is to protect the Soviets. The Calogero evidence in the 1AC. The second argument is the 2AC evidence or Gorbachev says that this constrains the United States and defends Canada alone. Next, his perception argument isn't in 'til 2NC. It's justified now in 1AR. Next, the counterplan only solves troops. That's what he says in the 2NC, so it doesn't solve the trade off the surface frigates and all these other things. He says, doesn't take out the link on defense programs, but these are more visible defense programs. They're surface ships. We're reading evidence on this in the 2AC. This educates them, because these are more vulnerable. If they're more visible, he says, the subs are inevitably coupled, but they're more visible, he says, the subs are inevitably coupled, but they're used against the United States. We have the only on point evidence. He says, next the neutralism is perceived if cuts, but there's no backlash. The evidence is Russia. The United States can persuade them. They don't want to anger the U.S. That's all the evidence Shaun reads on the five subpoint. He says defend against. He says, defend selves, and NATO, etc. but the visible programs would do that better. Also, he says, the counterplan solves, but it's independently isolationist to have the subs at all. Off of the three and four subpoints, he says C^3 vulnerability, etc. is bad. The maritime strategy flips C^3 vulnerability. Also, Europe perceives and fears this trade off with European forces. The counterplan wouldn't solve the perceptions of that. He said next, NORAD is keeping—we increase the maritime strategy which defends NORAD. Also, it defends it more visibly. The rest of his arguments are repeats. The fourth argument, dollar trade off, he says, counterplan out, but he—this takes out the link to the disad. The U.S. is still maintaining the commitments to West Germany, and so is Canada. Also, he only counterplans out troops. We would cut other existing naval programs if we sold the subs. He says, up to five subpoint that the counterplan solves this which isn't true. The argument here—the argument on they need the subs to guarantee their sovereignty is a huge lie. We will continue to intrude on their sovereignty. Unless there is a tradeoff with other programs they would have to massively build up other programs if they didn't have the subs in order to try to get rid U.S. sovereignty programs. In terms of the sixth subpoint, counterplan, he says, no disadvantages which isn't true. We're still winning flips. Absent the counterplan, he says, the plan flips the counterplan. He says, neutralism. No, because we get tradeoffs with other more visible programs. [Unintelligible] can leave the counterplan directly, yet it insures that there will never be neutralism. Also, it doesn't solve the fact that the subs themselves are perceived as isolationism. Up the deficit disad, he says, decrease other forces. This is the link. It decreases U.S. forces somewhere. Secondly, it was new. It was not the 2NC. Shifting in the 2NR is illegitimate. The third argument that it still links, this is from Owens in 1985: "[N]o shifting of resources among subcommittees under a single committee is permitted (F. 4575)." Loeffler in '85: "Congress needs some good tough budget rules that can't be bent, broken, or simply ignored as they are now (H 8504)." Also, the impact of this is war. It doesn't solve the submarines themselves.

The case. Group all his solvency arguments together. First, we're getting something off of international consensus. Second argument is it is not inevitable. It's empirically worked. The third argument is nuclear power. It doesn't take out, because it's not high enough for weapons grade. Doesn't violate any sanctions. Next, France and Britain don't take out, because the prolif treaty explicitly allowed them to do this.

We're winning a hell of a lot of scenarios, at least some degree of solvency of them, and I think we're flipping West German prolif if anything.

I would like to at this time say that I did the best I could with the strategy, Ken. I know I didn't do it justice, but I still think it's enough to win. I also at this point want to thank all the Dartmouth coaches that have meant a lot to me and taught me so much. My particular debate mentors have been Mike Morris, Bill Pucket, David Cheshire, and then Ken [Strange], Lenny [Gail], and Erik [Jaffe]. And I especially want to thank Shaun who has put up with me, taught me from a terrible freshman to hopefully a not so terrible senior now, and I'm going to miss this activity. [Applause]

AGYEMAN-DUAH, BAFFOUR. "Nuclear Weapons Free Zones and Disarmament." *Africa Today* 10 Dec. 1985.

BAGNALL, JAMES. "Nuclear Subs Give Navy New Strategic Option." *Financial Post* 16 Nov. 1987.
_____. "U.S. Could Sail into Fray for Canada's Sub Contract." *Financial Post* 28 Sept. 4-Oct, 1987.

BART, JOHN. "1986 National Debate Tournament Final Debate, Judge Critique." In *1986 Championship Debates and Speeches*. Ed. John K. Boaz. Normal, IL.: Printing Services, Illinois State U, 1986.

BERES, LOUIS RENE. "Introduction." *Security or Armageddon: Israel's Nuclear Strategy*. Ed. Louis Rene Beres. Lexington, MA: D.C. Heath, 1986.

BLACKBURN, DEREK. "Canadian Sovereignty, Security and Defence: A New Democratic Response to the Defence White Paper." The New Democrats, Les Neo-democrates: 1987.

THE BOSTON STUDY GROUP. *The Price of Defense: A New Strategy for Military Spending*. New York: Boston Study Group, 1979.

BRODER, DAVID S. "Bush, Dukakis Know-How is Winning Votes." *Houston Chronicle* 10 Mar. 1988.

BRYANT, MICHAEL. "1986 National Debate Tournament Final Debate, Judge Critique." *1986 Championship Debates and Speeches*. Ed. John K. Boaz. Normal, IL: Printing Services, Illinois State U, 1986.

CALDER, NIGEL. *Nuclear Nightmares: An Investigation into Possible Wars*. New York: Viking, 1979.

CALDICOTT, HELEN. *Missile Envy: The Arms Race and Nuclear War*. New York: William Morrow, 1984.

CALOGERO, FRANCESCO. "Steps to Halt Nuclear Proliferation." *Opportunities for Disarmament*. Ed. Jane M. O. Sharp. New York: Carneigie Endowment for International Peace, 1978.

Carnegie Endowment for International Peace Task Force Study quoted in Joseph A. Jiampietro. "Report Released on Nuclear Proliferation in South Asia." *Arms Control Today* Mar. 1988.

COLBERT, KENT R. "The Effects of CEDA and NDT Debate Training on Critical Thinking Ability." *Journal of the American Forensic Association* Spring 1987: 194–201.

"Congressional Concern: Discontent in Congress Over Direction of U.S. Foreign Policy Accelerates." *Global Defense: U.S. Military Commitments Abroad*. Washington: *Congressional Quarterly Service* Sept. 1969.

CORNISH, EDWARD. "The Great Depression of the 1980s; How It Might Begin." *Futurist* June 1980.

COSER, LEWIS. "Comments." In Seweryn Bailer. "How Far Can Gorbachev Go?" *Dissent* Spring 1987.

Council on Foreign Relations. *Blocking the Spread of Nuclear Weapons: America and European Perspectives*. New York: Council on Foreign Relations, 1986.

COX, DAVID. "Living Along the Flight Path: Canada's Defense Debate," *Washington Quarterly* Autumn 1987.

DENTON, HERBERT H. "U.S. to Consult Canada on Use of Northwest Passage." *Washington Post* 12 Jan. 1988.

"Deputy at CIA Warns of Soviets." *Washington Times* 2 Feb. 1988.

DONNELLY, WARREN H. "Nonproliferation Policy of the United States in the 1980s." *SAIS Review* Fall 1987.

DORAN, CHARLES F. "Sovereignty Does Not Equal Security." *Peace and Security* Autumn 1987.

DUNN, LEWIS A. *Controlling the Bomb: Nuclear Proliferation in the 1980s*. New Haven, CT: Yale U P, 1982.
_____. "The NPT and Future Global Security." *Nuclear Non-Proliferation and Global Security*. Ed. David B. Dewitt. New York: St. Martin's P, 1987.
_____. "Nuclear Nonproliferation: A View from the Potomac." *Strategies for Managing Nuclear Proliferation: Economic and Political Issues*. Eds. Dagobert L. Brito, Michael D. Intriligator, and Adele E. Wick. Lexington, MA: D.C. Heath, 1983.

EAYRS, JAMES. "Assessing the Ice-Pack Rationale." *Peace and Security*, Autumn 1987.

EPSTEIN, WILLIAM. "New Defense Plan May Suck Canada into Star Wars." [Toronto] *Globe and Mail* 24 Aug. 1987.
_____. "New Stance Tarnishes Canada's Reputation." *Bulletin of the Atomic Scientists* Oct. 1987.

FISCHER, DAVID A. V. "The Third NPT Review Conference, Geneva, 27 August to 21 September 1985: A Retrospective." *Nuclear Non-Proliferation and Global Security*. Ed. David B. Dewitt. New York: St. Martin's P, 1987.

FRANCIS, DAVID R. "Canada Gives Cautious Reception to Soviet Arctic Proposals." *Christian Science Monitor* 19 Feb. 1988.
_____. "Canada Takes Nuclear-Sub Plunge." *Christian Science Monitor* 22 Feb. 1988.

FRIEDLANDER, ROBERT A. "The Armageddon Factor: Terrorism and Israel's Nuclear Option." *Security or Armageddon: Israel's Nuclear Strategy.* Ed. Louis Rene Beres, Lexington, MA: D.C. Heath, 1986.

GHERSON, GILES. "Pentagon Review Worries Canada's Defense Firms." *Financial Post* 16 Nov. 1987.

GLENN, SEN JOHN. "Nuclear Non-Proliferation and U.S. National Security." Hearings before the Committee on Governmental Affairs, United States Senate. One Hundredth Congress, First Session, 25 Feb. 1987. Washington: USGPO, 1987.

GOLDBLAT, JOZEF. "Will the NPT Survive?" *Bulletin of the Atomic Scientists* Jan. 1986.

GOLDSTEIN, MARTIN E. *Nuclear Proliferation: International Politics in a Multinuclear World* Latham, MD: U P of America, 1980.

GUMMETT, P. "Academic Perspectives on the Non-Proliferation Problem." *The International Nuclear Non-Proliferation System: Challenges and Choices.* New York: St. Martin's P, 1984.

HALSTEAD, JOHN. "Canada's Role in the Defense of North America." *NATO's Sixteen Nations* 5 Sept. 1985.

HAMILTON, HON. LEE H. "Current Issues in United States-Canadian Relations." *Congressional Record* 6 May 1987.

HARRIGAN, ANTHONY. "Free Trade's Costs." *American Spectator* Feb. 1985.

HARRIS, SCOTT. "1985 National Debate Tournament Final Debate, Judge Critique," *Journal of the American Forensic Association* Summer 1985: 56–8.

HASEK, JOHN. "The Disarming of Canada." *Army Quarterly and Defence Journal* Jan. 1987.

HILLENBRAND, HON. MARTIN J. "United States Security Agreements and Commitments Abroad: United States Forces in Europe." Hearings before the Subcommittee on U.S. Security Agreements and Commitments Abroad of the Committee on Foreign Relations, United States Senate, Ninety-first Congress, Second Session. 24 June 1970. Washington: USGPO, 1970.

HOLLIHAN, THOMAS A., KEVIN T. BAASKE, and PATRICIA RILEY. "Debaters as Storytellers: The Narrative Perspective in Academic Debate." *Journal of the American Forensic Association,* Spring 1987: 184–93.

HONDERICH, JOHN. "The Arctic Option: NATO and the Canadian North." *Canadian Forum* Oct.

ING, STANLEY. "Emergent Suppliers, the Non-Proliferation Regime and Regional Security." *Nuclear Non-Proliferation and Global Security.* Ed. David B. Dewitt. New York: St. Martin's P, 1987.

Jane's Fighting Ships, 1987–88/90th Edition. New York: Jane's, 1987.

JENKINS, BRIAN MICHAEL. "Nuclear Terrorism and Its Consequences." *Society* July/Aug. 1980.

JOCKEL, T., and JOEL J. SOKOLSKY. *Canada and Collective Security: Odd Man Out.* New York: Praeger, 1986.

JOHNSON, LEONARD V. "Canada and NATO: What Price Symbolism?" *Defending Europe: Options for Security.* Ed. Derek Paul. Philadelphia: Taylor and Francis, 1985.

KENNEDY, EDWARD M. "Forward." In Edward J. Markey. *Nuclear Peril: The Politics of Proliferation.* Cambridge, MA: Ballinger, 1982.

KENNEDY, THOMAS J. *NATO Politico-Military Consultation.* Washington: Fort Lesley J. McNair, 1984.

KIRK, DON. "U.S. Troops in Honduras Leave Today." *USA TODAY* 28 Mar. 1988.

KNELMAN, F. H. "Canadian Defense Policy: The Branch Plant Model." *Canadian Dimension* Nov./Dec. 1987.

KNELMAN, FRED. "Holding Hands with the Nuclear Monsters: Canadian Complicty with Reagan's Strategy." *Canadian Dimension* July 1987.

KOSMINSKY, JAY. "European Nuclear Security: Beyond Current Dilemmas." *Securing Europe's Future.* Eds. Stephen J. Flanagan and Fen Osler Hampson. Dover, MA: Auburn House, 1986.

KUCEWICZ, WILLIAM. "Soviets Search for Eerie New Weapons." *Wall Street Journal* 23 Apr. 1984.

KURKJIAN, STEPHEN. "Reagan Submits Budget; Figures Show Major Shift." *Boston Globe* 19 Feb. 1988.

KURTZ, BILL. "What's Next?" *Business Today* Winter 1988.

LAMB, JOHN. Quoted in "Challenge and Commitment: Comments on the Defence White Paper." *Behind the Headlines* Sept. 1987.

LAMB, JOHN M. "Roiling the Arms Control Waters." *Bulletin of the Atomic Scientists* Oct. 1987.

LEGGETT, JEREMY. "The Next (Nuclear) War Happens at Sea." *New Statesman* 6 Nov. 1987.

LEMCO, JONATHAN. "The Myth of Canadian-American Harmony." *Atlantic Community Quarterly* Spring 1987.

LEYTON-BROWN, DAVID. "U.S. Reaction to the Defence White Paper." *International Perspectives* July/Aug. 1987.

LOEFFLER, HON. TOM. "The Federal Deficit." *Congressional Record* 8 Oct. 1985.

MACKENZIE, HILARY. "Retreating from Norway." *Maclean's* 23 Feb. 1987.

MAHANT, EDELGARD E., and GRAEME S. MOUNT. *An Introduction to Canadian-American Relations.* New York: Methuen, 1984.

MANN, PAUL. "Canadian Defense White Paper Will Call for Nuclear Subs, More Patrol Craft." *Aviation Week & Space Technology* 11 May 1987.

———. "Domestic Issues Apt to Prevail Over Defense in 1988 Race." *Aviation Week & Space Technology* 4 Jan. 1988.

MARIN-BOSH, MIGUEL. "The Non-Proliferation Treaty: Fifteen Years of Frustration." *Disarmament* Spring 1985.

MCGREW, ANTHONY G. "Introduction: Nuclear Non-Proliferation at the Crossroads?" *The International Nuclear Non-Proliferation System: Challenges and Choices.* New York: St. Martin's P, 1984.

MECHAM, MICHAEL. "Defense Downplayed As Issue in Early Presidential Race." *Aviation Week & Space Technology* 4 Jan. 1988.

METCALF, A.G.B. "The Issue of Our Times." *Strategic Review* Spring 1987.

MEYER, STEPHEN M. "Small Nuclear Forces and U.S. Military Operations in the Theatre." *Small Nuclear Forces and U.S. Security Policy: Threats and Potential Conflicts in the Middle East and South Asia.* Ed. Rodney W. Jones. Lexington, MA: D.C. Heath, 1984.

NASHIF, TAYSIR N. *Nuclear Warfare in the Middle East: Dimensions and Responsibilities.* Princeton, NJ: Kingston P, 1984.

"The Next German Question." *Economist* 23 Jan. 1988.

NIXON, RICHARD. "Nixon: Demos Shifting Gears." Express-News [San Antonio, TX] 7 Mar. 1988.

NYE, JOSEPH S. JR. "Arms Control and Prevention of War." *Washington Quarterly* Fall 1984.

"Other Items on the Agenda" from the newsmagazine "The Economist" of London. *World P Review* Nov. 1987.

OWENS, HON. MAJOR R. "Deficit Reduction Fiasco." *Congressional Record* 10 Oct. 1985.

PAUL, ROLAND A. *American Military Commitments Abroad.* New Brunswick, NJ: Rutgers U P, 1973.

"Poll Shows Bush, Dukakis Running Even." *Salt Lake Tribune* 25 Mar. 1988.

REISS, MITCHELL. *Without the Bomb: The Politics of Nuclear Nonproliferation.* New York: Columbia U P, 1988.

"Review and Outlook: Safeguarding Biotechnology." *Wall Street Journal* 4 Aug. 1987.

"Review and Outlook: Super Politics" *Wall Street Journal* 10 Mar. 1988.

ROSE, SIR CLIVE. "Political Consultation in the Alliance." *NATO Review* Apr. 1983.

SCHWARTZ, WILLIAM A., and CHARLES DERBER. "Arms Control: Misplaced Focus." *Bulletin of the Atomic Scientists* Mar. 1986.

SHALLHORN, STEVE. "Standing up to the United States." *Bulletin of the Atomic Scientists* Oct. 1987.

SHIPLER, DAVID K. "U.S. and Canada Close Extradition Gap." *New York Times* 12 Jan. 1988.

SIMPSON, JEFFREY. "Canada Roused by Military Plan." *Bulletin of the Atomic Scientists* Oct. 1987.

SMITH, R. "Judging philosophy statement." In *National Debate Tournament Booklet of Judges.* Ed. Walter Ulrich. American Forensic Association: 1988.

SOKOLSKY, JOEL J. "The Case for the New Policy." *Bulletin of the Atomic Scientists* Oct. 1987.

SOUTHWORTH, WILLIAM. "1984 National Debate Tournament Final Debate, Judge Critique." *Journal of the American Forensic Association* Summer 1984: 53–6.

SPECTOR, LEONARD S. "Nuclear Non-Proliferation and U.S. National Security." Hearings before the Committee on Governmental Affairs, United States Senate, One Hundredth Congress, First Session, 24 Feb. 1987. Washington: USGPO, 1987.

———. "Nuclear Proliferation: The Pace Quickens." *Bulletin of the Atomic Scientists* Jan. 1985.

———. *Nuclear Proliferation Today.* New York: Vintage, 1984.

"Substantial Factor." *Words and Phrases, Permanent Edition, Volume 40, 1987, 1987 Cumulative Annual Pocket Part.* St. Paul, MN: West, 1987.

"Substantial Quantity of Business." *Words and Phrases, Permanent Edition, Volume 40, 1987 Cumulative Annual Pocket Part.* St. Paul, MN: West, 1987.

"Substantially." *Corpus Juris Secundum, Volume LXXXIII.* Brooklyn: American New Book, 1953.

"Substantially Consumated." *Words and Phrases, Permanent Edition, Volume 40, 1987 Cumulative Annual Pocket Part.* St. Paul, MN: West, 1987.

"Substantially Performed." *Words and Phrases, Permanent Editor, Volume 40, 1987 Cumulative Annual Pocket Part.* St. Paul, MN: West, 1987.

THOMPSON, WAYNE C. "Canadian Defense Policy." *Current History* Mar. 1988.

URBAN, GEORGE. "Language & Power in Soviet Society (II): Can Gorbachev Change This System? A Conversation between Alain Besancon and George Urban." *Encounter* [London] June 1987.

URQUHART, JOHN. "U.S., Canada Sign Navigation Pact for Arctic Waters." *Wall Street Journal* 12 Jan. 1988

"U.S. Navy." *Financial Post* 28 Sept. 1987.

VAN HEUVEN, MARTEN. "U.S. Policy, the P, and the Atlantic Alliance." *The Future of European Alliance Systems.* Ed. Arlene Idol Broadhurst. Boulder, CO: Westview P, 1982.

WALTZ, KENNETH N. "Toward Nuclear Peace." *Strategies for Managing Nuclear Proliferation: Economic and Political Issues.* Eds. Dagobert L. Brito, Michael D. Intriligator, and Adele E. Wick. Lexington, MA: D.C. Heath, 1983.

WEISS, LEONARD. "Blocking the Spread of Nuclear Weapons." *Bulletin of the Atomic Scientists* June/July 1986.

WHELAN, JOSEPH G., and MICHAEL J. DIXON. *The Soviet Union in the Third World: Threat to World Peace?* Washington: Pergamon-Brassey's, 1986.

WHYTE, KENNETH. "Beatty's Direct Art." *Alberta Report* 22 June 1987.

WILLIAMS, GEOFFREY LEE, and ALAN LEE WILLIAMS. *The European Defense Initiative: Europe's Bid for Equality.* New York: St. Martin's P, 1986.

WILMSHURST, M.J. "The Development of Current Non-Proliferation Policies." *The International Nuclear Non-Proliferation System: Challenges and Choices.* Eds. John Simpson and Anthony G. McGrew. New York: St. Martin's P, 1984.

_____. "Reforming the Non-Proliferation System in the 1980s." *The International Nuclear Non-Proliferation System: Challenges and Choices.* New York: St. Martin's P, 1984.

WINDSOR, PHILIP. "Stability and Instability in Eastern Europe and Their Implications for Western Policy." *Soviet-East European Dilemmas: Coercion, Competition, and Consent.* New York: Holmes & Meier, 1981.

Index

recording, 82–84
researching for, 72–84
sample evidence card, 83
specific tests, 96–101
Example, argument by, 106–109
characteristics, 106–107
tests, 107–109
negative instances, 108
sufficient examples, 109
typical examples, 107–8
Existence of fact, frame of, 32–33
Expert opinion evidence, 59
Exposing fallacies of composition and division, 210–11
Exposing inconsistencies, 206–207
External consistency, test of, 90–91

Factual evidence, 58–59
descriptive historical statements, 58–59
statistics, 58
verbal examples, 58
Fact/value controversies, strategies for advocacy, 171–81
affirmative case strategies, 173–77
nature of strategy, 171–73
negative case strategies, 178–80
difference from affirmative, 177
Fallacy of composition, 210
Fallacy of division, 211
Field, 149
Fields of argument, 149–153
Field context standard, 26
Filing evidence, 84
Fisher, Walter R., 239
Flow-sheeting, 204–5
Focusing critical arguments, 235–39
grouping, 238–39
ordering, 235–36
time and space allocations, 236–37
vocal emphasis, 237–38
Format, 149, 156–167
Forum, 149, 153–56

General issues research, 73–74
Goal/Criteria case, 188–89
Goals of a system, 49
Gottschalk, Louis, 91
Grammatical syntax standard, 26

Hypothesis-testing, 159, 168
Hypothetical syllogisms, 129–30

Identifying fallacious appeals, 211–12
ad hominum, 211–12
ad misericordiam, 211
as populum, 211
ad verecundiam, 211
Identifying irrelevancies, 209
Ill issue, 40–41
Immediate cause for discussion, 27–28
Independent corroboration, 91
Indexes, 74–80
bibliographies, 78–79

books, 75
card catalog, 75
essays, 77–78
government documents, 77
newspapers, 76
periodicals, 75–76
searching manually, 74–79
searching with a computer, 79–80
search terms, 74–75
Inductive arguments, 105–118
argument by analogy, 109–112
argument by correlation, 112–16
argument by example, 106–109
Inductive reasoning, 60
Information-seeking advocacy forums, 155–56
audience controlled forums, 155
public debate, 156
Inherency, 41–43
attitudinal, 42, 198
philosophical, 42
related to ill issue, 43
structural, 42
Inherency, denial of, as a method of refutation, 208–209
Inquiry
defined, 3
Internal consistency, test of, 90
Issues, 20–22
defined, 21
real and potential, 22
relation to arguments, 21
relation to presumption and burden of proof, 22

Jurisdiction
frame of, 29–31
in fact/value controversies, 29–31
in policy controversies, 39–40

Klumpp, James, F., 47–58, 51
Knowledge, limitations on, 6

Language usage, 232–235
cliches, 233–34
filler language, 234–35
jargon, 233
Legal advocacy forums, 154
Limits standard, 27
Lincoln-Douglas debate format, 164–65
philosophical and educational underpinnings, 164
speaker duties, 164–65
type of proposition, 164

Maximizing, 208
McGee, Michael C., 239
Meaningful standard, 26–27
Mill, John Stuart (Mill's canons), 113–115
Minimizing, 207–8
Mock trial formats, 166–67
sample format, 167
Mutual exclusivity, as a counterplan burden, 196